D1598360

Rhythmic Gesture in Mozart

Rhythmic Gesture in

MOZART

LE NOZZE DI FIGARO

&

DON GIOVANNI

Wye Jamison Allanbrook

University of Chicago Press

CHICAGO AND LONDON

Wye Jamison Allanbrook teaches at
St. John's College in Annapolis,
Maryland.

The University of Chicago Press, Chicago 60637
The University of Chicago Press, Ltd., London

© 1983 by The University of Chicago
All rights reserved. Published 1983
Printed in the United States of America

90 89 88 87 86 85 84 83   12345

Parts of this book first appeared in the following
publications and are reprinted here with permission:
Musical Quarterly 47 (January 1981); *Music and Letters*
63 (1982); *Studies in the History of Music*, vol. 2, Ronald
Broude, editor (© 1983 by Broude Brothers, Ltd.);
and *The St. John's Review* 26 (April 1974), 31 (July
1979), and 33 (Winter 1982).

Library of Congress Cataloging in Publication Data

Allanbrook, Wye Jamison.
    Rhythmic gesture in Mozart.

    Includes index.
    1. Mozart, Wolfgang Amadeus, 1756–1791. Nozze di
Figaro.   2. Mozart, Wolfgang Amadeus, 1756–1791. Don
Giovanni.   3. Rhythm.   4. Dance music — History and
criticism.   5. Ballroom dancing — History — 18th century.
I. Title.
ML410.M9A73   1983   782.1'092'4   83-9184
ISBN 0-226-01403-7

To my mother and father

CONTENTS

LIST OF FIGURES

PREFACE

Some notes on the procedures I have used in preparing this book may be helpful to the reader. Translations of texts from Italian, German, French, and Greek are my own unless otherwise specified. Lack of space has prevented me, in quoting from treatises and other secondary sources in foreign languages, from including the original texts. I have, however, given the quotations from da Ponte's libretti and from the works of Beaumarchais and Molière in their original language in the text, with my translations in footnotes, because I wanted the reader always to have the lively original before him. I have followed the Ricordi libretto for da Ponte's texts rather than the Neue Mozart-Ausgabe because I found the original versification of the texts often to be of significance in my consideration of particular movements.

In studying the operas, and in preparing the musical examples, I have consulted both the Neue Mozart-Ausgabe and the Eulenburg miniature orchestral scores. The Eulenburg system of numbering measures — continuously from one aria or ensemble to the next, through any intervening recitatives — I have found to be the most precise means of locating references in the recitatives, and so I have adopted it rather than that used in the Neue Mozart-Ausgabe. For the form of my references I have used either act, aria or ensemble number, and measure number (I, 2, 11), or act, scene number, and measure number (I, ii, ll), depending on which version more conveniently locates the passage in question.

For describing the quality of various rhythmic gestures I have adopted a system of notation which may at first seem confusing; I have spelled out its eccentricities in note 2 to chapter 7.

Finally, I follow Leonard G. Ratner in viewing Classic "form" as essentially a compositional procedure, which follows a basic harmonic plan; I have adopted his terminology to describe it. I discuss the matter at greater length in note 3 to chapter 5.

There are two people to whom I owe more than mere thanks, without whom this book would not exist. One is Leonard Ratner, whose brilliant work in the syntax and style of Classic music is the point of departure for any good thoughts I have had about the subject. The other is my husband, Douglas Allanbrook, whose intelligence and impeccable taste have influenced this book at every stage of its preparation, and whose constant and generous support made it possible to do what at times seemed impossible. Further, I would like to thank Virgil Thomson, whose enthusiasm for my work and trenchant comments on it spurred me on at a critical moment, and Janet M. Levy, Beate Ruhm von Oppen, and Elliott Zuckerman, who were unfailingly generous with editorial advice and encouragement. Kathryn Kinzer of the St. John's College Library was indefatigable in bringing the contents of other libraries to me in Annapolis. In preparing the book for publication I was extremely fortunate to have the services of Christina Davidson, who is responsible for the elegant calligraphy and autography in the book, and Hunter Davidson, who engineered the complex process of entering the manuscript in a word processor. They brought regularity and system to an eccentric manuscript, and were extraordinarily inventive in handling the special problems it presented. Finally, thanks are due to the Corporation of Yaddo, for the chance of two summers' tranquil and productive work, and to St. John's College, where for the past fourteen years I have been, among other things, learning to think more intelligently about the elements of music.

Wye Jamison Allanbrook

INTRODUCTION

Expression, Imitation, and the

Musical Topos

One of the most exalted moments of music in Mozart's operas occurs midway through the second-act finale of *Le nozze di Figaro*. The Countess, Susanna, and Figaro have just managed to outwit the most recent of Count Almaviva's strategems and, united in their precarious triumph, are asking the Count to cease his attempts to sabotage Susanna's and Figaro's coming wedding (while the Count under his breath mutters imprecations on the head of the tardy Marcellina). The music of the ensemble is extraordinarily beautiful, and lifts the brief moment up out of the temporal bustle of the comedy (ex. i–1).[1] In all its transcendent beauty this passage can at the same time be classified as a specific musical type: it is an example of a musette-gavotte, a dance gesture which is associated with the genre of the pastoral.[2] Four other pieces in the last two acts of *Le nozze di Figaro* have as close a connection with the pastoral, and the poetry of da Ponte abounds in pastoral images. The opera in fact turns out to be a special vision of the refuge offered by the pastoral world to true lovers, and has as its business to explicate those adjectives "pastoral" and "true." This musette-gavotte in the second-act finale is doing its work as part of the complex of associations which confirms and defines the role of the pastoral image in the opera.

That the pastoral plays any role at all in *Le nozze di Figaro* has not previously been much noticed. It has instead become a commonplace to describe the opera as a drawing-room comedy with strong undertones of revolutionary protest.[3] Yet the claim that the opera has a pastoral ambience draws its support not from private intuitions, but from a study of Mozart's musical imagery — a study the mere possibility of which has

1

Example i-1

been too long ignored by most writers on his operas. For Mozart was in possession of something we can call an expressive vocabulary, a collection in music of what in the theory of rhetoric are called *topoi*,[4] or topics for formal discourse. He held it in common with his audience, and used it in his operas with the skill of a master craftsman. This vocabulary, when captured and categorized, provides a tool for analysis which can mediate between the operas and our individual responses to them, supplying independent information about the expressive content of the arias and ensembles. For in it music and words about music are united; each musical *topos* has associations both natural and historical, which can be expressed in words, and which were tacitly shared by the eighteenth-century audience. Because of their connections with certain universal habits of human behavior, these *topoi* are also largely in the possession of the opera-going audience today, although modern listeners may not be aware of the source of their particular perceptions. An acquaintance with these *topoi* frees the writer from the dilemma he would otherwise face when trying to explicate a given passage: that he can at the one extreme do no more than detail the mere facts and figures of its tonal architecture,[5] or at the other merely anatomize his private reactions to a work. By recognizing a characteristic style, he can identify a configuration of notes and rhythms as having a particular expressive stance, modified and clarified, of course, by its role in its movement and by the uses made of it earlier in the piece. In short, he can articulate within certain limits the shared response a particular passage will evoke.

Current notions of the term "topic" or "characteristic style" seem often to include under that head all which is musically eccentric or exotic, or belonging to that rather questionable bag of tricks, the imitation of natural phenomena. Membership in the class is considered to mark a figure, a rhythm, or a style as necessarily of limited utility to the composer; it will be much in demand on certain special occasions, but only on special occasions. In the meantime the rest of music moves serenely on down purer and more respectable paths. Only one exception is universally granted — in the high Baroque the *Affektenlehre*, or "doctrine of the affections," with its thoroughgoing attempts to codify the connections between figure and affect.[6]

Yet the music of the Classic style is pervasively mimetic, not of Nature itself but of our natures — of the world of men, their habits and actions. The doctrine of art as imitation, as a "mirror to the world," is often today regarded as a puzzling or distasteful teaching. Although it was for centuries the center of the canon of aesthetic theory, it suffered a devaluation in the nineteenth century, when poets and composers began to consider the end of artistic endeavor to be instead the transmission into a poem or composition of the artist's own interior state of being.[7] Romantic formulations like the following by Franz Liszt, taking for granted the origin of the creative impulse as "the impressions of [one's own] soul," crowned music as the highest of the arts because it alone was capable of expressing inner feeling untrammelled:

> Music embodies *feeling* without forcing it — as it is forced in its other manifestations, in most arts, and especially in the art of words — to contend and combine with *thought*. If music has one advantage over the other means through which man can reproduce the impressions of his soul, it owes this to its supreme capacity to make each inner impulse audible without the assistance of reason.[8]

In the word "expression" the preposition *ex-* now drew to itself all the emphasis. The source of the work of art was the soul of the artist; his task was to "press *out*" the stirrings within himself, to give them expression in words or notes.[9] In previous centuries, on the other hand, it had been the art of making the imprint which alone mattered — the *Druck* of the German word for expression, *Ausdruck* — for as sources of the imprint were intended not the private and personal, no matter how transcendent, but the beings outside of us which impinge on us, the "things that are."

The accumulation of a collection of *topoi* for expressive discourse is the natural concomitant of an aesthetic which sets as its goal the mirroring of aspects of the universe. Each branch of the arts will develop a storehouse of devices appropriate to its own medium whereby those universals can be represented — or imitated. The argument for music as an imitative art runs in the most general terms as follows: objects in the external world make an impression on our souls; music can, by imitating those impressions, move our souls in a similar fashion, placing us "in tune" with certain substantial entities. The entities to be imitated are various: the higher orders of being, perhaps, or the passions of our fellow men — different ages esteemed different objects. In the theologically ordered cosmos of the Middle Ages and Renaissance the soul vibrated in tune with the natural numbers, seeking to know its kinship with God through the mediation of physics. But Aristotle, who was for all who came after him the prime exponent of the doctrine that the arts should be imitators of real objects, held an alternative view of the kind of objects which it is proper for makers of imitation to catch in their mirrors. "The objects of imitation are men in action," he stated flatly in the *Poetics*.[10] And since a man's bearing will help to reveal his character, as the *Nichomachean Ethics* states,[11] any imitation of a man in act will show us how he performs those actions — with dignity, basely, with joy — and will thus uncover his true nature. Only by witnessing a man in the motion of action can we judge him in an ethical frame. Aristotle considered music to be an art particularly apt for transmitting the qualities which men exhibit in action:

> Rhythms and melodies especially contain likenesses to the true natures of anger and gentleness, and further of courage and temperance and of all their opposites, and of the other moral qualities (and this is clear from its effects, for when we hear these things we are changed in our soul).[12]

The eighteenth-century doctrine of imitation followed not the Renaissance but the Aristotelian view of the proper objects of imitation: "Not to portray ideas of inanimate things, but passions and feelings of the heart, is its [music's] particular and final goal," said the late eighteenth-century theorist Heinrich Christoph Koch, author of a music lexicon and a treatise on composition.[13] Koch's formulation resembles those of the *Affektenlehre* theorists earlier in the century (it lacks only their detailed attempts to correlate figures with affects). The passions to be portrayed are those emotions in the throes of which men act. They are not the private emotions of the composer, except indirectly as he experiences those passions in common with all men. Each passion is considered to be distinguished by a certain kind of motion, which differentiates it from all the other passions. For that reason, says Koch, we sometimes call the passions *Gemüthsbewegungen* ("soul-movements").[14] Music can successfully imitate the motions of the passions, stirring up a similar motion "slumbering in the spectators."[15] The process is kinaesthetic, and might appear to be merely a pseudoscientific elaboration on the notion of sympathetic vibrations, but for one important addition: it identifies the kinaesthetic and ethical spheres. The "vibrations" set up by a certain configuration of tones and rhythms stir our souls infallibly to a particular perception of the nature of each action; sensing them, as Aristotle put it, "we are changed in our soul." It is the duty of the composer to make the study of the passions his life's work.[16]

The importance to early eighteenth-century music of the doctrine of the affections is relatively well understood. But, in operatic music at least, this kind of mimesis could not fulfill its highest potential until later in the century, with the advent of the new freedoms of comic opera. The rigidly structured conventions of the serious opera of the period put strict limits on the situations in which the passions could be imitated: a character singing an aria could only assume a static posture of reaction to an action previously rendered in recitative. Thus the formal music of *opera seria*, with all its lofty aspirations, nevertheless fulfilled only half of Aristotle's dictum: it could imitate men, but never their actions. The often crude and simple *opera buffa*, because it admitted dramatic action to the arena of the set piece, was far more Aristotelian in character. Only when action became musically respectable and music was allowed to range beyond the limits of the soliloquy, could opera become a full-blown example of the imitative art. Music could then make its contribution to the opera's structure of metaphor through the imitation of the affective configurations of an action.[17] And, as is often pointed out, Mozart was the particular benefactor of *buffa's* innovation.

Before we can turn to the operas themselves there remains one further question to be dealt with, that of the means by which Classic music effected its imitations of "men in action": the particular content of Mozart's thesaurus of *topoi* must be spelled out. As every period differs in the set of objects it chooses to reflect in its surfaces, so the natural limits of each of the arts help to dictate both the proper subject matter of each art and the means of its mimesis. A misunderstanding of music's

proper means of imitation may be one reason for the modern reluctance
to apply the doctrine of imitation to music. The ubiquity of that mislead-
ing catch phrase, the "imitation of nature," suggests the more trivial
types of program music, where music's unnatural efforts to represent
natural phenomena in tones imitate not nature but the powers proper to
another art—that of painting—and only serve to render music laugh-
able. But music's proper limits were defined very simply by one eighteenth-century French writer on music (and composer of libretti),
Michel Paul Gui de Chabanon:

> Imitation in music is not truly sensed unless its object is music. In
> songs one can successfully imitate warlike fanfares, hunting airs, rustic
> melodies, etc. It is only a question of giving one song the character of
> another. Art, in that case, does not suffer violence. When one moves
> away from this, however, imitation grows weaker, actually because of
> the insufficiency of means which music can employ.[18]

Chabanon's formulation allows "tone-painting" to remain strictly a metaphor. He was plainly offended by musical gimmickry, an excess to
which every era is given in some fashion, from the naive pictorialism
of a few Italian and English madrigalists down to the carefully codi-
fied pictorialism often attributed to J. S. Bach himself. Composers,
Chabanon felt, should never attempt the vain task of forging a direct
link between music and the thing it imitates. Instead, art music should
represent the passions through the mediation of the simpler music
which men use to accompany their daily activities and amusements.
Music could then retain a dignified autonomy without thereby denying
the human subject matter of the art.

Chabanon was only legitimizing in words the common practice of
composers of his time, a practice observed even in the domain of instrumental music, where it would seem one could most easily make a case
for music as an abstract or private art. One example from the piano
sonatas of Mozart will suffice to illustrate the point, introducing at the
same time some of the topics in his expressive vocabulary. The first
movement of the Sonata in F Major, K. 332, is a miniature theater of
human gestures and actions, which is crafted by imitating the kinds
of music written to accompany these gestures. It begins with four measures in a simple singing style, answered by a four-measure parody of
learned counterpoint (ex. i–2). The double opening statement of the
sonata is balanced by ten measures of hunt calls (mm. 13–22), which
fall to a strong cadence in F major (ex. i–3). A passage of *Sturm und
Drang* music (mm. 23ff.) dramatizes the move to the dominant, its minor
tonalities and arpeggiated sixteenth notes imitating the self-consciously
"tragic" style often affected by C. P. E. Bach, and by Mozart and
Haydn after him (ex. i–4). Moving into C minor, the *Sturm und Drang*

Example i-2

Example i-3

Example i-4

Example i-5

culminates in an augmented sixth and a dramatic cadence on the dominant. Arrival in C major is "nailed down" by a bright and symmetrical minuet tune (ex. i–5). The minuet is interrupted momentarily by a *Sturm und Drang* parenthesis (m. 56), but reasserts itself in measure 71 (beginning on the subdominant as a reminder that its neat periods have been interrupted), and brings the exposition to a close.

The exposition of this *Allegro* is theater, although it has no aspirations to actual narrative. Mozart makes palpable the harmonic drama of the section — the modulation from the tonic to the dominant — by imitating various human gestures along its arch. This imitation is effected through the mediation of the kinds of music which characteristically accompany these gestures. In instrumental music the reigning affects did not need to be spelled out in words; sonatas were subliminally referential, and required no "program." Each musical motive,[19] because it had an implicit connection with an ordinary human posture, appealed directly to the listener's experience.

All the words I have used to describe the *topoi* of the *Allegro* — posture, stance, gesture — concern movement of the body, and hence rhythm. Supporting the successful projection of each posture in the sonata is a characteristic rhythm. In the "singing allegro" the slow-moving, long-breathed legato of the singer is set off by the perpetual and even motion of the "Alberti" bass figure.[20] The contrapuntal gesture is fundamentally a rhythmic one as well, for it is the overlapping repetitions of a single motive which conceal the regular punctuations implicit in normal period structure. Rhythm is the essence of the minuet gesture, with its six beats of nearly equal weight evenly distributed across two measures of moderate tempo. The dignified and noble affect which the horn calls project is derived from the minuet rhythms which animate the evocative harmonies, voice leading, and "orchestration" constituting the horn sound.

It is not at all surprising that rhythm — the number, order, and weight of accents and, consequently, tempo — is a primary agent in the projecting of human postures and thereby of human character. The German term *Gemüthsbewegung* itself suggests the primacy of rhythm in the anatomy of feeling: each passion is termed a *movement* of the soul. Indeed the German word for tempo, *Bewegung* (French *mouvement*), emphasizes not rate of speed but quality of motion. The rhythmic *topos* or characteristic rhythmic gesture lies at the base of almost all of Mozart's affective vocabulary, and in opera especially. There the subject is explicitly the actions of human beings, and rhythmic gestures choreograph the movements of each character in the drama. In the eighteenth century it was still possible to agree with Aristotle that bearing is character. As one dancing master of the period put it:

> A man's gestures and postures provide a considerable demonstration
> of his dispositions and habits, which sometimes are manifested in the
> most trivial actions. . . . From outside appearances, from his gestures,
> words, movements, and the least externals, one can get to know the
> most important internal matters. That is where the saying comes from:
> to know someone from his face. Every man should attend to two things

in himself: a modest walk and gestures suitable to an intelligent and well-bred man.[21]

The motions of the singer on the stage will be directly revelatory of the character he portrays, which is as much as to say that the music written for that character is in itself a demonstration of his nature. Koch approvingly quotes Rousseau as remarking of the performer in opera:

> It is not enough for [him] to be an excellent singer, if he is not also at the same time an excellent mime. . . . The orchestra ought not to execute any thoughts which do not appear to come from his soul. His steps, his bearing, his movement, all must constantly match the music, without it seeming to have been planned that way.[22]

The music of Classic opera was no longer bound in an ancillary relation to the text. Using its own vocabulary of rhythmic *topoi* it assumed the primary responsibility for the motivation, literal and figurative, of its characters. The librettist was freed from the necessity of writing pallid *sententiae* in rhyming couplets in order to render the protagonist's commentary on his psychic state, for a character in the motion of action would reveal himself more naturally than could any number of explanatory soliloquies. He need never step out of the frame of the drama, and his actions could belie his words. Dramatic music could bear any number of relations to the text: it could contradict, question, interpolate, or reinterpret. It had become the prime mover, and Mozart a choreographer of the passions.

PART ONE

MOZART'S RHYTHMIC TOPOI

— There is, continued my father, a certain mien and motion of the body and all its parts, both in acting and speaking, which argues a man *well within*; and I am not at all surprised that Gregory of Nazianzum, upon observing the hasty and untoward gestures of Julian, should foretell he would one day become an apostate; — or that St. Ambrose should turn his *Amanuensis* out of doors, because of an indecent motion of his head, which went backwards and forwards like a flail; — or that Democritus should conceive Protagoras to be a scholar, from seeing him bind up a faggot, and thrusting, as he did it, the small twigs inwards. — There are a thousand unnoticed openings, continued my father, which let a penetrating eye at once into a man's soul; and I maintain it, added he, that a man of sense does not lay down his hat in coming into a room, — or take it up in going out of it, but something escapes, which discovers him.

— Lawrence Sterne, *Tristram Shandy*, vol. 6, chap. 5.

CHAPTER ONE

The Shapes of Rhythms

Meter, Dance, and Expression

It should not come as a surprise, in light of what has been said, that meters can in themselves possess affects. Although meter is an element of music which in general we consider as merely a handy temporal measure (beneath the threshold of expressive values), a meter is usually the first choice a composer makes, and all signs indicate that in the late eighteenth century that choice amounted to the demarcation of an expressive limit. One finds in glancing through the writings of late eighteenth-century theorists that a description of the expressive qualities of meters is regularly included in discussions of how to "paint the passions":

> Tempo in music is either fast or slow, and the division of the measure is either duple or triple. Both kinds are distinguished from each other by their nature and by their effect, and their use is anything but indifferent as far as the various passions are concerned. . . .
>
> Composers rarely offend in this matter [the affects of various tempos], but more often against the special nature and quality of various meters; since they often set in 4/4 what by its nature is an *alla breve* or 2/4 meter. With 6/8 meter the same confusions occur often enough, even with well-known composers, and in cases where they cannot use as an excuse the constraint occasionally placed upon them by the poet. Generally many composers appear to have studied the tenets of meter even less than those of period structure, since the former is cloaked in far less darkness than the latter.[1]

> Music is based on the possibility of making a row of notes which are indifferent in themselves, of which not one expresses anything autonomously, into a speech of the passions. . . .

13

[Meter's role in the "speech of the passions":] The advantages of
subdividing triple and duple meter into various meters with longer or
shorter notes for the main beats are understandable; for from this each
meter obtains its own special tempo, its own special weight in performance, and consequently its own special character also.[2]

But it is clear from the little I have said here about the different
characters of meters that this variety of meters is very suitable for the
expression of the shadings of the passions.

That is, each passion has its degrees of strength and, if I may thus
express it, its deeper or shallower impression. . . . The composer must
before all things make clear to himself the particular impression of the
passion he is to portray, and then choose a heavier or lighter meter
according to the affect in its particular shading, which requires one or
the other.[3]

It makes sense that meter — the classification of the number, order, and
weight of accents — should take on an important role in an aesthetic
which connects emotion with motion. Since meter is the prime orderer
of the *Bewegung* or movement, its numbers are by no means neutral and
lifeless markers of time, but a set of signs designating a corresponding
order of passions, and meant in execution to stir their hearers directly
by their palpable emanations in sound. The composer can study the
shapes of meters to learn their potential for expression, he can manipu-
late them, but he did not invent them.

Yet it is frequently assumed that this notion, although a signal principle of the *Affektenlehre* theories of the early part of the century, had
dropped out of fashion by the late 1700s, at the same time as the number
of time signatures in use had declined and qualifying adjectives were
being more frequently employed at the head of a movement to indicate
the proper tempo — and character — of the work.[4] In the face of this
opinion it is striking that late eighteenth-century theorists' discussions
of rhythm and meter remained as detailed as those of their counterparts
earlier in the century;[5] accounts of the subject in lexicons, manuals, and
treatises spelled out carefully the individual configurations of each time
signature in current use and of many which had fallen into disuse.[6] J. P.
Kirnberger's classification ran to twenty-eight meters,[7] and Carlo Gervasoni, writing around the turn of the century, still treated under separate headings as many as sixteen.[8]

Kirnberger sketches out the form he considers the discussion of any
given meter should take, listing three main heads, the first two of which
are especially relevant here (the third concerns the special case of the
setting of texts):

1) That all kinds of meters discovered and in use up to now be described to [the composer], each according to its true quality and exact
execution.

2) That the spirit or character of each meter be specified as precisely as possible.[9]

Most theorists' discussions tend to follow this sketch, with the result that the meters examined settle into a sort of affective spectrum, or gamut. Consider first the lower number of the time signature — the designator of the beat. From the beginnings of Western polyphony a particular note value has usually been tacitly considered to embody what I shall call the *tempo giusto*, the normal moderate pace against which are measured "faster" and "slower."[10] By the eighteenth century the *valore giusto* had become the quarter note and, insofar as there is a modern notion of *tempo giusto*, it remains so today. In eighteenth-century French music, for example, 3/4 was often expressed by the single symbol 3, presumably in recognition of its status as the normal or *tempo giusto* among triple meters.[11] A spectrum of meters is readily organized around the lower number of the time signature, radiating in each direction from the central number 4; both tempo and degree of accentuation are established by the relative duration of the note receiving the beat:

> As far as meter is concerned, those of longer note values, such as *alla breve*, 3/2, and 6/4, have a heavier and slower movement than those of shorter note values, such as 2/4, 3/4, and 6/8, and these are less lively than 3/8 and 6/16. Thus for example a *Loure* in 3/2 is slower than a Minuet in 3/4, and this dance is again slower than a Passepied in 3/8.[12]

> The meters written on the staff all indicate a particular performance. In meters, for example, with notes of long duration, execution must always be slow and sedate, in conformance with the large note values; but in meters with notes of only short duration a lighter execution is required, since these notes by their nature must be passed over quickly. Thus, independently of the degree of tempo, meters are regulated also by the various values of the notes.[13]

The quarter note, measuring the motion of a normal human stride, occupies the center of the spectrum. Meters in half notes (2) or whole notes (1, although rare, is mentioned in some treatises) fall to the left of center, requiring a slower tempo and a more solemn style of execution. To the right fall 8 and 16 (and, at the beginning of the century, 32) in ascending degrees of rapidity, lightness, and gaiety. Thus a geometric series of numbers from one to thirty-two corresponds to an ordered range of human strides from the slowest (and gravest) to the fastest (and gayest):

1 2 4 8 16 32
←——— mean ———→

The affect projected by the meter is a direct consequence of the union of tempo and degree of accentuation:

> Sorrow, humility, and reverence, require a slow movement, with gentle, easy inflections of the voice; but joy, thanksgiving, and triumph, ought to be distinguished by a quicker movement, with bolder inflexions, and more distant leaps, from one sound to another.[14]

And so the number exemplified by meter is viewed as a "passionate" number, capable of embodying the emotions and feelings of human beings in all their range and variety.

This ordering of affects by musical numbers was by no means an arbitrary or mystical numerology, for it corresponded to a like ordering of human motions or gestures. Music had turned away from its Renaissance preoccupation with the cosmic harmony of the sonorous numbers toward a new desire to move an audience through representations of its own humanity. Priority in music was claimed for the imaging of human affairs as over against the serene encompassment of a divinely numbered cosmos. Because of this change in music's role in the world from a theological to a sensory reflector, the metrical hierarchy was now based on physical movement, the province of the dance. Dance unites bearing and character in a measured and artful expression:

> Clearly almost everything in the moral character of men can be expressed intelligibly and in a lively manner by the position and movement of the body. Dance in its way is as capable as music and speech of being modelled on the language of the soul and of the passions.[15]

In the dancer movement and affect become one. The repertory of conventional music for social dance — sarabandes, gavottes, and minuets, for example — naturally became one of the most important sources of *topoi* in the affective language of both Baroque and Classic music.

In fact it is the characteristic metrical usages of the social dance repertory that finally organize the upper number of the time signature into the metrical spectrum. The function of the upper number is of course to specify a triple or duple ordering of the beat which is represented by the lower number. Although, in the late Renaissance, dances were cast as much in duple as in triple meter, by the seventeenth century triple had become the meter most identified with dancing. At first tempi associated with triple meter were generally faster than those in duple. By the high Baroque, however, the noble and considered gestures of the folia and sarabande, although triple in structure, were set over the number 2 (the meter 3/2) at the slower end of the spectrum. Thus in the early eighteenth century, although the numerical series 2 4 8 16 32 had significance for tempi and execution, the duple and triple indications constituting the upper number of each time signature had no particular attachment to either end of the spectrum: music was written in 3/2 as well as 3/8, or 2/8 and 4/16 as well as 6/8 and 9/16.

By the latter half of the century, however, Classic composers had made a final clarification of the attachments born by the numbers on the top — the triple and duple beat groupings. Writers of the period frequently returned to the early Baroque distinction between a slower duple and a quicker, more lively triple meter:

> The different sorts of time have, in some degree, each their peculiar character. Common time is naturally more grave and solemn; triple time, more chearful [*sic*] and airy. And for this reason, it is generally agreed, that every mood of triple time ought to be performed something quicker, than the correspondent mood of common time; for instance, the measure in the slow triple of minims [3/2], ought to be made shorter than the measure in the slow common time [4/4], marked with a plain C; and the measure, in the triple of crotchets [3/4], should be shorter than the measure in the mood of the barred C [*alla breve*]; and so on.[16]

> Meter also takes its place in expression. If it is a question of expressing great, solemn, and majestic matters, Common Time is the most suitable; Triple is best for expressing familiar things and ordinary ones. 2/4 has a character which is still lighter, and more humble. 6/8 serves only for expressions of the comic and the humorous, for pastorales, dances, and the like.[17]

In classifying meters writers often identified particular dances as the "natural movement" of a triple meter,[18] and at the same time considered the "natural seat" of duple meters, especially *alla breve*, to be in the church (or, concomitantly, in fugues and choruses).[19]

This classification of duple as an "ecclesiastical" meter can be explained by certain historical associations. Sacred music was by the late eighteenth century synonymous with certain musical practices which had come to be considered antique. Fuxian species counterpoint,[20] with its long-note *cantus firmi*, heavily accented and slow of tempo, was by virtue of its venerability judged most appropriate for the expressive requirements of music for worship. It was epitomized by copy-book exercises in duple measures of half and whole notes — "white-note"[21] or *alla breve* counterpoint. At the same time, in the sphere of dance music, dances with a markedly slow triple movement were less in evidence in both the dance hall and chamber and symphonic music: composers turned away from the courante with its 3/2 or 6/4 meter and complex rhythmic patterning, and began to take the sarabande at a tempo only slightly slower than the minuet, usually adopting a 3/4 meter in place of the 3/2 signature prevalent earlier in the century.[22] These changes pushed triple groupings over toward the quicker beats at the right of the spectrum. The result was a polarization of duple and triple meters — a topical confrontation between the two metrical types which could be characterized as an opposition of divine and mundane subject matters. Not only did meter bear the stamp of human character: the various affects themselves were classified by two special types of human activity — the ecclesiastical and the choreographic.

The Classic style itself gravitated around these two poles, which took on a variety of names in their various manifestations: the learned (from its associations with "school" counterpoint), ecclesiastical, strict, or "bound" (*gebundener Stil, stile legato*, from its precise rules for dissonance treatment) at one extreme, and on the other, the *galant*, or free. The strict style had its ancestor in Renaissance and Baroque *alla breve* counterpoint, while the free style stemmed metrically and rhythmically to a great extent from the dance. The vehicle of Classic music most closely connected with the *style galant*, the "sonata allegro" or key-area plan,[23] had its origins in the simple symmetrical dance form. That highest of contrapuntal forms, the fugue, was associated principally with sacred music, and had the air of an importation when encountered in a sonata movement.[24] In the classification of affects inhering in meters, the duple rhythms of the learned style were reserved for expressions which were intended to have some connection with the ecclesiastical (an affect which was by no means banned from the "secular" sonata allegro, which reflected every facet of contemporary life in its imitations), while dance rhythms were regarded as the most direct and measurable means of portraying human passions in time. Many other types of gestures came in for their share of imitation in the *galant* vocabulary: the singing style, for example, horn calls, and the very habits of orchestral music themselves. Still the dance remained a central symbol of the human half of the eighteenth-century cosmos.

In fact, this simplifying and sharpening of contrasts in the metrical spectrum in the late eighteenth century may well have been a correlative of the emerging procedures of key-area or sonata-form composition. Composers of the high Baroque customarily explored one gesture in a movement, favoring a mono-affective style. Classic composers, on the other hand, preferred to bring into the frame of a single movement the bustle and contrast of a world in small, in a harmonic and affective "dialectic" set out in antecedent and consequent symmetries (or in the intentional breach thereof). One requirement for fulfilling this disposition to dialectic would be that the nature of the topical materials in question be clearly defined, and their relations to one another sharply and dramatically demarcated: for the listener to embrace the fact of the contrast, identification of the members involved in it must be swift and near-automatic.

But the subjects of Mozart's operas are not on the whole ecclesiastical; even the spectral Stone Guest, heaven's emissary in *Don Giovanni*, is vested in human form and arrives on foot. In secular music the left side of the spectrum served to choreograph those human passions which most resemble the divine. Danceable meters, although they are capable of expressing a broad range of passions, must stop short of the most exalted ones. When noble characters voice tragic or moral sentiments in the lofty couplets of *opera seria*, Mozart has them affect the ecclesiastical style in a gesture which still remains choreographic in an extended sense: let us admit it to the roster of *topoi* under the designation "exalted march," for it figures importantly in this catalogue of expressive devices.

To explain how the exalted march is an operatic extension of that style of music called learned or ecclesiastical, a comparison of a sample of each will suffice: for example, the last movement of Mozart's Quartet in G Major, K. 387, and Donna Anna's "Or sai chi l'onore" (*Don Giovanni*, I, 10).[25] The quartet movement opens with sixteen measures of an academic "fugue" in fifth-species counterpoint, which are answered by a contrasting *galant* cadential flourish (actually a contredanse, which would properly be scanned in 2/4). Although the movement is designated *Molto allegro*, the "white notes" of the counterpoint project one strong beat per measure, choreographing a slow, marked, and solemn stride, the tread of Aristotle's great-souled man;[26] *Molto allegro* is more appropriate to the misbarred contredanse (ex. 1–1). The text of Donna Anna's aria — her challenge to her fiancé Don Ottavio to punish Don Giovanni, her would-be seducer and the murderer of her father — is plainly material for the exalted style. Donna Anna, the one woman in *Don Giovanni* who is unquestionably of noble rank, adopts the white-note *alla breve* gesture for an aria in a grand, rather old-fashioned idiom. Unlike the quartet movement, "Or sai chi l'onore" is marked *Andante*, but each of its measures contains two beats or steps, while the quartet's *Molto allegro* measures, during the contrapuntal opening, each contain one (ex. 1–2). "Or sai chi l'onore," while not contrapuntal, imitates the same gesture as the more obviously learned and venerable species counterpoint of the quartet — music with two strong slow beats per measure and all other rhythmic action subordinated. Strides choreographed to the quartet's counterpoint and to Donna Anna's exalted march would be approximately coincident. The quartet movement is a scholium on the style of the aria, explicating in its textbook fugue the archaic and ultimately ecclesiastical sources of the *alla breve*.[27]

Modern designations for *alla breve* such as "cut time" and *doppio movimento*, and the attendant modern notions of *alla breve* as "faster than," appear to contradict the eighteenth-century account of 2/2 as the most *maestoso* of all meters,[28] "only useful for serious, heartfelt passions,"[29]

Example 1-1

"suitable for sacred song on account of its weighty slow tempo."[30] Some eighteenth-century writers shared the confusion, for instance Scheibe, who complained about the recent habit of using *alla breve* in quicker tempi for secular pieces:

> Its proper seat is in truth the church, where it was meant to be used in choruses, fugues, and polyphonic pieces; but since the meter is now also used for other pieces, one must get used to it. But this makes it all the more necessary that in every case the tempo required by the piece, whether an aria, symphony, allegro, or concerto allegro, and so on, be indicated. Nevertheless, since the operas and symphonies have taken

Example 1-2

over this meter, and it is often used for the fastest and most fiery pieces where its old dignity and seriousness have no place, it has almost taken on another character. For it is now as preeminently cherished in the galant style as it was previously venerated in the church style.[31]

Both eighteenth-century and modern confusions about the meter arise from a failure to attend to the quality of the beat rather than to the tempo marking, or to the notes which subdivide the beat.[32] The *alla breve* can appear in many notational guises and still retain its essential choreographic gesture. Neither the *Molto allegro* whole notes of the quartet nor the aria's busy-looking trappings of heavily decorated upbeats and string tremolos detract in performance from the measured yet stirring pace of the exalted march. In "Or sai chi l'onore" the gesture and affect of the *alla breve* have simply been transferred from their ecclesiastical sources into the domain of the *galant*, bearing their original associations with them; Donna Anna is a celestial heroine militant.

With the extremes of the spectrum of meters determined, we can make a rough sketch of its components. Triple meters represent the danceable passions, duple the passions closest to the divine:

Ecclesiastical (exalted passions) ←——————————→ Galant (terrestrial passions)

$$\left[\tfrac{3}{2}\right] \quad \mathbf{C}\!\!\!| \quad \tfrac{2}{4} \quad \tfrac{4}{4} \quad \tfrac{3}{4} \quad \tfrac{6}{8} \quad \tfrac{3}{8} \quad \left[\tfrac{9}{16}\right] \quad \left[\tfrac{9}{32}\right]$$

march .... dance

The meters at the outermost extremes of the spectrum, those using whole-note and thirty-second-note beats, had dropped out of use, and are included here because they were mentioned as theoretical possibilities. Pulses of the practical extremes — half notes and sixteenth notes — were seldom made into measures which would be antithetical to their habitual affects: notes of long duration were rarely any more used in triple groupings (3/2), and sixteenth and eighth notes almost never in duple (4/16 and 4/8). Toward the middle of the spectrum usage grows more ambiguous, and one term may partake of the gestures of both extremes upon occasion: certainly some dances were written in duple meters, and in turn the generally frivolous 3/8[33] was sometimes used in an *affettuoso* style. In the middle of the spectrum stand 4/4 and 3/4, as the duple and triple meters of the *tempo giusto*. Both admit of slightly slower or faster tempi and more serious or more lighthearted affects, but they never shade into the radical solemnity of *alla breve* on the one hand, or the frivolity of 3/8 on the other.

The paradigmatic gestures of 4/4 are the humbler, "terrestrial" marches, and of 3/4, the minuet. The foot march provides a transition

from the exalted to the danceable passions. Dances are artful inventions
requiring a meter susceptible to ornament; in triple meter the dis-
proportion in the times allotted to upbeat and downbeat allows the
dancer more room for an expansive step or gesture before the upbeat
drives him on to the next measure, and the next step. Characteristic of
the march and of duple meter, on the other hand, are the intensity and
inevitability of the drive to the next step; the pedestrian alternation of
right and left leaves no room for an expansive gesture, for the invented
fantasy of the dancer. Most of the more complex rhythms which are
habitually associated with the march — dotted rhythms, for example, at
their most exaggerated in the French overture — are only elaborations
of the upbeat impetus preparing for the next tread. In its intensity and
singlemindedness the march is often anything but pedestrian, as "Or sai
chi l'onore" demonstrates. Yet it can also be comically literal — a flat-
footed imitation of the movements of the poor human body at its most
unexalted. The few dances written in duple meter require a more distinctive rhythmic pattern than that of the march, a pattern which must
be achieved by some manner of tinkering with the ordinary striding
shape of the march's duple measure in order to make room for the unfolding of the dancer's movements.[34] The minuet, the danced counterpart of the march in the center of the spectrum, represents the most
artful treatment of the normal human stride. In sum, the danceable
takes its proper position to the right of the spectrum, in the company of
the more modest, worldly passions, while exalted grief and anger soar
from the left, in the tradition of the otherworldly.

Metrical Notation and the Contrast of Affects

The rather dramatic reduction, by the latter half of the eighteenth
century, in the number of meters which were actually in frequent use,
may seem to have necessitated an attendant blunting of refinement in
the expression of the various passions. Indeed, this reduction is often
taken as proof of a severed connection between meter and expression
which is assumed to be part of the "new aesthetics" of the Classic
period. Kirnberger himself was certain that such was the case:

> That these meters [2/8 and 6/16] and others . . . are considered today
> unnecessary and superfluous shows either that good and correct execu-
> tion has been forgotten, or that a part of the expression which is easy to
> maintain only in these meters is completely unknown to us. Both do
> little credit to the art, which should in our time have ascended to its
> highest summit.[35]

In fact the reduction in meters had nothing to do with a weakening capacity for refined expression. It was rather the consequence of one of

the few true "revolutions" in habits of expression in the latter part of the century[36] — the enlistment of contrast as a compositional procedure. To abandon a particular notational sign does not of necessity mean to abandon the gesture it projects. Since Baroque composers generally allowed one spun-out affect to dominate an entire movement, they could choose a time signature which would notate that affect with precision. Classic composers began to shape each movement around several affects in order to dramatize the clarity of structure resulting from the newly emphasized polarity of tonic and dominant. The practice necessitated the choice of a flexible, chameleonlike time signature, harmonious not just with one affect but with a particular handful of them. Precision of notation was partially sacrificed in exchange for the freedom to play over a wide range of expressive gestures in one piece. The choice, for time signature, of a meter at one of the extremes of the spectrum (Kirnberger's "light gigue" in 9/16, for example, or the 9/4 which he considered an appropriate choice for church fugues[37]) would prohibit the inflection of a contrasting rhythmic gesture in the movement. Composers preferred to choose a metrical "lowest common denominator" for a time signature, avoiding the radical metrical extremes.

The contrasting gestures of the last movement of Mozart's G Major Quartet quoted earlier[38] would take on a different aspect if notated separately. The fugal section beginning the movement could be set more comfortably in an *Andante* 4/2 than in 4/4 *Molto allegro* (ex. 1–3). A time signature of 4/2 was not outside the bounds of Baroque practice,[39] and the four-beat measure fits the rhythmic shape of the fugue subject better than does 4/4, a meter which fractioned the subject into four whole-note measures. (The new notation does, however, make the syncopations of the countersubject slightly more difficult to read than they were in the original.) Mozart probably adopted the expedient of whole-note measures in order to avoid notating the quick contredanse which answers the fugue in sixteenth notes, where it would be difficult to distinguish from rapid and purely ornamental concerto-style passage work. The whole-note measure, almost a parody of the notation of Bach's motet-style fugue subjects, also lends the fugue an exaggerated vener-

Example 1-3

Example 1-4

Example 1-5

ability. Still the contredanse itself has to be improperly barred in order to dovetail with the fugue; it would ordinarily appear in 2/4 (ex. 1–4).

Toward the end of the exposition of the movement (m. 92), a third and cadential gesture appears, working on a rhythmic level midway between the fugue and the contredanse: it moves in quarter and half notes as opposed to the half and whole notes of the fugue and the eighth notes of the contredanse. A quasi-bourrée, with expanded upbeat, it helps to stabilize the rhythms of the movement, striking a *tempo giusto* between the *maestoso* fugue and the breakneck contredanse. In ordinary circumstances it would more likely be written with note values halved, two measures of the original compressed into one, and the barline shifted. The first violinist must ignore a few barlines if he is to superimpose the broad arch of the bourrée on the choppy succession of *alla breve* measures (ex. 1–5). The actual time signature of this movement is of little help to a performer who is ignorant of the individual configurations of each gesture: 4/4 suits all three topics at once by not quite suiting any of them. Although 4/4 is probably the best choice as a time signature for a movement with gestures on three rhythmic levels, it cannot in itself reflect the rhythmic richness of the movement. Its virtue is the purely negative one of noninterference.

The following example from a Classic *opera buffa* may help to illustrate the ways in which the neutral time signature can be manipulated in order to reflect various characters in an unfolding dramatic situation, and also, incidentally, to show how easy it can be to miss the point.

Example 1-6

Edward Dent, in his study of Mozart's operas (a book which, although often sketchy or off the mark in its analyses, provides more helpful background to the operas than any work in English which has appeared since Dent's second edition of 1946), analyzes an aria by Florian Gassmann as an example of mature *opera buffa* at the time when Mozart was beginning to compose operas. The aria occurs in the middle of a typical *buffa* intrigue: a master (Leandro) is instructing his servant (Carlotto) to carry messages to his beloved through her servant (Marinetta) when he discovers to his surprise that Carlotto has disappeared (ex. 1–6[40]). The aria is Leandro's, but Carlotto is lurking in the orchestra. While Leandro, intent on his own concerns, describes his amorous torments in a courtly bourrée style (mm. 2–9 in the vocal line), the orchestra is simultaneously choreographing Carlotto's motions, subdividing each quarter-note beat into a triplet, for a simple peasant gigue.[41] The skirling "scotch snaps" of the inattentive Carlotto's gigue melody mock the stock histrionics of Leandro's chromatic appoggiaturas on the words *tormento* and *provo* (mm. 5–6). When Leandro comes to himself and discovers Carlotto's disappearance, the gigue also vanishes, and Leandro assumes a martial bearing in his anger (mm. 9–14 — a military march with horns and oboes added to the strings).

Even at its simplest, the *buffa* style has a genial wit and finesse, and is not without its subtleties. The "schizophrenic" dances which open this aria are not merely a description of the dramatic circumstances; they also manage to inject into the scene in subliminal fashion a suggestion of the conventional psychology of crafty servant and pompous master. Furthermore, as always in good *buffa* writing, the action confirms the harmonic arch of the key-area plan: [42] Leandro's angry march occurs at the arrival on the dominant — a harmonic move which requires both new musical energy and a consolidation of topical resources if it is to be made fully dramatic. And, reflexively, the move up a fifth mimes Leandro's coming to consciousness. If a director is aware of the topical variety in this apparently one-dimensional aria, he can exploit it cleverly on the stage. But to someone ignorant of the interplay of topics (as indeed is Dent himself in his analysis), there would seem to be little reason to prize the aria. It has no melody to speak of, nor is its harmony or orchestration particularly inventive. All Gassmann's skills as a *buffa* craftsman are engaged in making of this text a comic *scena* for three participants: singer, orchestra, and mime (the silent Carlotto).

Practical Musicians and the Vocabulary of Expression

Late eighteenth-century musicians differed in another way from their counterparts earlier in the century: they had learned to distrust attempts to concoct "cookbooks" of metrical gestures containing recipes for the expression of the passions. J. A. Hiller in his singing treatise published in 1774 expressed this distrust in a satirical paragraph about the obsession of his predecessors with classification:

> If anyone wants more divisions of style, or modes of writing, he can gain rich gleanings from *Walther's* musical *Lexikon* in the article *Stylus*. *Rousseau* himself dipped into this little work. Our dear forefathers never lacked for classifications, and if they sometimes strayed into another compartment, still there was no end to the classifying. Thus they fared with style. Everything we comprehend under the expression and character of a piece, they would include under style. They had a merry, a sharp, an expressive, an honest, a tender, a moving, even a base and cringing style. It was not enough for them to assume a special *Stylus Choraicus* for dance pieces; these still had to be *subdivided* into as many special styles as there were kinds of dances. They had the sarabande-minuet-passepied-gavotte-rigaudon-gaillard-courante-style. Other classifications of style, into the noble, middle, and low, into the serious and the comic, into the artificial and the natural, into the swollen and the flowing, appear to have somewhat more in them, and would deserve a closer examination if I did not fear it would be too detailed, and if the singer had to be as well-grounded in them as the composer.[43]

For this reason it is vain to search in Classic manuals of composition for prescriptions of the *Affektenlehre* sort. Most writers preferred to discuss a few universal principles pertaining to the passions and their proper mode of expression, and then to leave all decisions about particulars to the composer's good taste. Breaches of taste, however, did not go unobserved, especially in opera, where the text provided a standard of criticism. So, for example, Thomas Busby, studying the music of Handel, could fault the composer for the misuse of a dance topic in *Alexander's Feast*,[44] and a French writer could be sharply critical of Jommelli's application of the same dance.[45] But composers were expected to avoid the pitfalls of bad taste armed merely with such negative examples.

The Classic distaste for codification and the concurrent simplifications of metrical notation held real dangers for the musical illiterate. Good taste was still considered to be not a matter of individual caprice, but a faculty opposed to whimsy; it could be accounted for, and must be educated. As Quantz put it,

> Music, then, is an art that must be judged not by personal whims, but by certain rules, like the other fine arts, and by good taste acquired and refined through extensive experience and practice.[46]

Practical musicians were seriously concerned lest with the new movement away from prescription they raise a generation of young composers and performers ignorant of the expressive values of rhythmic shapes. "The retention or realization of a *Charakter*," warned Koch, "is one of the most important requirements of all musical compositions."[47] The practice of appending a qualifying adjective to a movement became widespread in the period probably as a means of suggesting at least approximate sets of tempo limits for performers who lacked training in the art of reading a movement's rhythmic gestures. Reluctant, however, to rely on these ambiguous directions, teachers chose to instruct their pupils in the recognition of the various expressive gestures, and used the social dances, the *danses caractéristiques*, as a primer for their study. There young musicians could examine the gestures in their natural habitat; Mozart spent his early training as a composer writing sample minuets, gigues, and marches. As Kirnberger put it:

> Every beginner who wants to be well grounded in composition is well advised to make himself familiar with the organization of all forms of the dance, because in them all kinds of character and of rhythm appear and are most precisely executed. If he has no fluency in these characteristic pieces, it is not at all possible for him to give to a piece a particular character.[48]

Pupils beginning the study of music with characterless pieces would flounder hopelessly, as an amusing piece of dialogue makes clear:

Disciple. Come, Sir, let us play a tune.
Master. A tune! There is one: play it.
Dis. How do you call it?
Ma. I do not know.
Dis. Nor I neither.
Friend. Bravo! again: let me look at it — It is a Gavot: Your Gavots have been condemned, from time immemorial, to be crucified by beginners.
Ma. And was it with a Gavot your ward began?
Friend. Exactly; a March, and then a Gavot, and then a Vauxhall Song, and then a bit from *Felton*'s Lessons, and then Adagios, Andantes, Allegros, and various other things.
Ma. . . . Strange foundations for lessons for the harpsichord!
Friend. Better begin with those than with a tune of which we cannot tell the name.
Ma. And who is the ignoramus that does that?
Friend. Yourself.
Ma. I! who told you so?
Friend. Why I saw it, heard it this instant.[49]

Classic musicians' aversion to overliteral codification must not be taken as evidence of an aesthetic of the "abstract" and "nonreferential" nature of music. Their music was indissolubly wedded to the human pulse beat, breath, and stride, shaped into an artful measure by meter. A

consciousness of the proper articulations of the rhythmic gestures in
Mozart's music makes the difference between lifelessness and liveliness
in performance. Furthermore, knowledge of the affective limits of each
gesture ensures a clearer notion of what Mozart was about when he
employed them in the operas. Since the social dances constitute a considerable portion of Mozart's expressive vocabulary, the next chapter is
devoted to their consideration.

CHAPTER TWO

The Gestures of Social Dance

Habits in the Dance Hall

Most of the dances whose characteristic patterns form part of Mozart's vocabulary of rhythmic gestures were already old-fashioned in his own time. New tastes prevailed among the bourgeoisie who frequented the new and modish dance halls; except for the minuet, the French court dances were rarely performed in public. Most of the dancing manuals written in the latter half of the century contained instructions only for the minuet and contredanse, and this pair of contrasting dances, the one reserved and the other exuberant, constituted the evening's exercises. The reason for the selection, as one dancing master explained it, was the preference of the new class of amateur dancers for dances requiring little skill and involving the greatest pleasure for the greatest number:

> In earlier times, before taste in the true beauties of dancing was refined, because of an excessive emulation of the French, no man was considered a skilled dancer who could not dance an *aimable Vainqueur, charmant Vainqueur, Passepied, dance d'Anjou, Princesse bourée* [*sic*], *Courante, Rigaudon, Cavotte* [*sic*], *Sarabande*, or *Gique* [*sic*]. People realized later that such dances were too theatrical for society, and hindered the common pleasure. Therefore they danced *Menuets* and English dances, which gave the kind of pleasure in which an entire group could participate.[1]

In fact, Classic composers of symphonies and chamber music were faithfully reflecting the activities of the dance hall when they coupled in the last two movements of their works the rhythms of the minuet and

31

contredanse, dignified *Tanz* and gay *Nachtanz*; thus also had an earlier
counterpart, the Baroque dance suite, flowered from contemporary
tastes in social dance. This trend toward choreographic simplicity was
to continue: by the end of the century the waltz, in its unfettered movements the polar opposite of the refined sarabande and courante, had
gained the ascendancy in German dance halls and was on its way to
France and England.

Mozart did not shun the new habits; he loved to dance. If we are to
believe Michael Kelly, an Irish tenor whose memoirs are a chronicle of
his acquaintance with important musical and theatrical figures of the
late eighteenth and early nineteenth centuries, Kelly had been told by
Constanza Mozart that "great as his [Mozart's] genius was, he was an
enthusiast in dancing, and often said that his taste lay in that art, rather
than in music."[2] Mozart wrote many sets of minuets and contredanses
for the dance halls, and they were at the least good moneymakers. His
knowledge of dance patterns was not, however, circumscribed by the
new narrowness of taste. Educated by his father in the true *Kapell-
meister* tradition, he knew the repertoire of French court dances thoroughly; he could write a chaconne with the best of them, as the ballet
music for *Idomeneo* testifies. He was, on the other hand, more selective
than composers in the earlier part of the century in choosing dances to
use as musical raw material, and the principle which governed his selection seems to have been in harmony with the new tastes in the dance
halls, albeit more refined in its operation: only the simplest and most
natural rhythms should prevail. The dance rhythms Mozart used most
frequently as *topoi* in his operas are the following:

Triple Meter		*Duple Meter*	*Either Triple or Duple*
minuet	gigue	march	musette
sarabande	siciliano	bourrée	contredanse (waltz)
passepied	pastorale	gavotte	

A brief account of the essential rhythmic configurations and affective
connections of each dance type follows.

It is my aim here to describe the aggregate effect which the allusion
in a Classic sonata or aria to the rhythmic pattern of a particular social
dance might have had on a late eighteenth-century audience. I have
tried to take into account the conventional associations each dance type
might have — historical, social, and emotional — and to consider the
kind of motion each dance pattern naturally projects, given the type of
measure in question and the distribution of accents across that measure.
It must be stressed that most of the examples I will be concerned with
are stylized, abstracted from the ballroom, and were thus not written
with an actual choreography in mind. Of the dances listed above, only

the minuet and contredanse were actually danced at social gatherings at the end of the century, and so their traditional French court choreographies had not the immediate relevance they would have had for earlier audiences. There is, however, an obvious connection between these artful, historical choreographies and what could be called the "natural" choreography suggested by each rhythmic pattern — that which, when caught in words, might be termed its "affect" — and so I will make allusion to the historical choreographies whenever they seem helpful.

Dances in Simple Triple Meter

The Minuet

> The dance is universally well known, and deserves preference over the other social dances on account of its noble and charming nature. . . . It appears to have been invented by the Graces themselves, and is more suited than any other dance for assemblages of persons who distinguish themselves by a fine manner of living.[3]

> It is well known over half the world, and in all classes, and although the greater part of men still considers it the easiest part of dancing, yet in the judgment of connoisseurs it takes the prize from all the others. And who can deny the minuet this honor? No one except the man who finds good taste only in the dancing of a boisterous peasant, and blindly admires the impetuous over the decorous in all movements of the body. *The minuet is the queen of all dances*; the test of every dancer who wants to acquire a reputation; . . . and . . . the best occasion for displaying everything beautiful and charming in nature which a body is capable of employing.[4]

The minuet alone of all the social dances won such encomiums; for the late eighteenth century it was the epitome of choreographic elegance and refinement. To support its reputation it had had to gain somewhat in gravity. Earlier in the century the minuet had been a rather quick dance, moving predominantly in quarter notes. By 1770 it had split into two distinguishable types, both used by Mozart. The first retained the look and tempo of the original; the second had slowed down considerably, admitting eighth notes to its figuration in a prominent role. A prototypical quick minuet is "Se vuol ballare" from *Le nozze di Figaro* (ex. 2–1).[5] The famous minuet from *Don Giovanni* (I, 13, 220ff.) is an example of the slower type (ex. 2–2). The versions share many characteristics: they both use a time signature of 3/4 (sometimes 3/8), and habitually begin on the downbeat. A moderate tempo with a regular movement, a bass moving in quarter notes to support the dancers, and a modest execution with few ornaments are among their other salient features. In either version the dance has an affect of a "noble and

Example 2-1

Example 2-2

pleasing propriety, but joined with simplicity."[6] Its restrained elegance arises from the even rhythmic attack given the three beats of its measure: /-♪♪/-♪♪/ [7] The actual dance step, the *pas de menuet*, in most of its forms acts as a counterpoint to the barline; it is two measures long, and rarely stresses the first beat of the second measure.[8] This check administered to a prominent downbeat probably contributes to the control and level contours which characterize the minuet measure. While discussing the training of singers, one English writer likened the firm and even delivery of a vocal line to the evenhanded progress of the minuet:

> The singer, having learnt as it were to walk with the voice *in plano et firmo cantu* ascending, descending, and striking the distances neatly, like the steps of the foot in the movement of the minuet, is next to be taught the ornaments and graces.[9]

Even the name of the dance, sometimes taken to derive from the French word *menu* ("small"), at others assumed to originate in the Latin *minuere* ("to slacken or diminish"),[10] suggests the climate of restraint and refinement projected by the dance in both of its versions.

Confusion shrouds the provenance and associations of the second type of minuet. Its differences from the quick quarter-note minuet type result from an exaggeration of the dance's steady, even pulse: the introduction of a motto rhythm consisting of a quarter note and four eighths, ♩ ♫♫ (often on a repeated note or chord), slows the tempo somewhat. The motto seems to be a deliberate attempt to signal "minuet." Its percussive repeated notes in thick chordal texture intensify the dance's traditional even movement and restraint, in addition to protecting the dance against the distortion of a rapid and light execution. The motto found a widespread use. For example, a collection of popular minuets published in Edinburgh in 1770 used the motive in approximately sixty percent of its pieces, in varying guises (ex. 2–3),[11] and many people today wholly identify the minuet with it, perhaps because of the fame of the *Don Giovanni* version (ex. 2–2). The new figure probably emerged as a consequence of the minuet's recently assumed role as primary representative of the *ancien régime*. It was a dramatization of the essential gesture of the dance, and may have originated on the stage. In 1770 Mozart wrote to his sister about the tempo of a stage minuet which he had seen performed in Milan:

> I shall soon send you a minuet which Mr. Pick danced in the theatre and which everyone danced to afterwards at the *festa di ballo* in Milan, solely in order that you may see how slowly people dance here. The minuet itself is very beautiful. It comes, of course, from Vienna. . . . It has plenty of notes. Why? Because it is a stage minuet which is danced slowly.[12]

The quick French court version of the minuet needed no distinctive rhythmic mottoes for protection or identification, having evolved in a milieu where professionals carefully cherished every dance gesture. On the stage, however, it is often necessary to intensify the outlines of a given gesture in order to make it project beyond the proscenium arch.

The minuet can admit of almost any figuration which does not disguise its essential movement. Mozart's minuets for orchestra, pieces written to be danced, contain triplets, groups of running sixteenth notes, thirty-second-note flourishes, Scotch snaps and other skipped rhythms, and syncopations. The fundamental minuet can also tolerate the overlay of another style or topical reference. Favorites are horn calls of the court (the fanfares of ex. 2–3a), military (ex. 2–4a), and the hunt (ex. 2–4b),[13] essays in learned style (the imitative passage from the first movement of K. 332, ex. i–2, p. 7, is set *à la menuet*), and pas-

Example 2-3

Example 2-4

a) Hessian Minuet

b) Hunter's Minuet

toral with drone bass. Mozart gives some of his orchestral minuets affective titles: a *Menuetto galante* (K. 250, the "Haffner" Serenade) moves in quarter notes with clipped dotted rhythms, and in a *Menuetto cantabile* (K. 463), running eighth notes and occasional measures of Alberti bass soften the crispness of the usual quarter-note beats.

The quick even three of the first minuet type, distinctive without being excessively *caractéristique*, won a special place in Classic symphonies and chamber pieces as a "laboratory movement," a ground for the play of permutation and combination. In Mozart's and Haydn's calculated and often mechanistic experiments with rhythm and topic, which have won the dance its greatest renown in the twentieth century, it was joyfully least itself. Numerous examples of Mozart's playful ways with the minuet gesture could be cited: in the string quartets, the minuet of K. 387 in G major, reminiscent, in its clockwork hemiola, of the minuet experiments of Haydn, or of K. 421 in D minor, a minuet with motetlike polyrhythms and a chaconne bass, or of K. 499 in D Major, a minuet become a German dance played on the hurdy-gurdy, notable for its wheezy charm. The actual nature of the minuet might be said to be the subject of the central movements of the C Major Quintet, K. 515. Mozart reverses the usual order of slow movement and minuet, putting the minuet movement first. It begins with a tuneless and sinuous version of the quarter-note minuet (ex. 2–5). For a cadential gesture in the trio, it breaks out into an exuberant waltzlike tune, the movement's only expansive gesture (ex. 2–6). Then, as though to apologize for the arch disguise of the minuet in its proper movement, Mozart makes the third movement an "Urminuet," an example of the slow stage version, for a moving tribute to the "queen of dances" (ex. 2–7).

Example 2-5

Example 2-6

Example 2-7

The Sarabande

The sarabande is perhaps best known today from Bach's stylized instrumental versions of the dance, stirring and passionate, often in a minor key, with heavily dotted rhythms and lavish ornamentation; for example, the sarabande of the Partita in E Minor. The actual dance was one of the most elevated of the French court dances, although its affect was hardly as lofty as many of these stylized versions might seem to suggest.[14] Its supposed Spanish origins were kept in mind, and at times dancers probably performed it with castanets.[15] Mattheson characterized the sarabande as a dance of "ambition . . . a haughty disposition . . . *grandezza*."[16]

By the latter half of the century, as the sarabande began to appear more frequently in 3/4 than in 3/2, it lost some of this special quality of expression. It drew closer to the minuet, and was often characterized as a slow minuet.[17] It still enjoyed the reputation of a noble and haughty dance — the castanets are frequently mentioned in sources — but its stylizations were rarely as grand and full-blown as they had been in the earlier part of the century. The sarabande was distinguished from the minuet by its slower tempo and by the characteristic rhythmic pattern

which it might use in any but the ultimate measure of a phrase: ♩ ♩ ♪
Now that the dance was no longer performed, this rhythmic motto became all the more necessary as an identifying characteristic. The profile
of the characteristic sarabande pattern, /-ʾʊ/ , is considerably more
complex than that of the minuet measure. The whole measure hangs on
the lengthened second beat: the first beat is preparation for, the shortened third release from, a moment of controlled tension. Duration
counterpoints stress here; the tension would not exist if the first and
strong beat were coincident with the dotted note: ♩ ♪♩ This accent of a
weak beat by means of duration prevents the dance from being taken at
too rapid a tempo,[18] but it also cannot slow down past a certain limit, for
"only a bent knee must sometimes support the whole body."[19] The degree of physical control which the sarabande requires of the dancer is
characteristic of a noble and dignified posture.

The sarabande became a favorite style for a slow movement in triple
meter. The slow movement of Mozart's "Dissonant" Quartet, K. 465, is
a stylized sarabande with an ornamented repeat (ex. 2–8). In moments
where the dotted pattern is not evident, Mozart still retains the emphasis on the second beat in a free and elegant play on the sarabande pattern.[20] He sometimes carries the sarabande rhythm into the minuet: in
K. 585, no. 5, a minuet for orchestra, the sarabandelike dottings slow
the tempo somewhat, since they cannot be executed both gracefully and
rapidly at the same time (ex. 2–9). This sarabande-minuet bears witness to the taming of the haughty dance, in part eventuated by the process whereby the differing habits of duple and triple meters were sharp-
ened into polarity.

Example 2-8

Example 2-9

Example 2-10

The Passepied

The passepied is universally described as a very fast or very gay minuet; its steps are the various *pas de menuet* taken at a quicker tempo. The dance is notated in 3/8, with or without an upbeat, and usually moves in a mixture of eighth and sixteenth notes, requiring a quick tempo and light execution. The passepied measure has a rhythmic profile midway between the minuet's even three beats and the waltz's strong first beat:

minuet passepied waltz

In this passepied from Mozart's ballet music for *Idomeneo*, K. 367, the quick tempo indicated by the time signature is reinforced by the smoothness of the rhythmic action and the slow harmonic rhythm (one change per measure, except in the penultimate measure of each phrase); measures are regularly grouped in twos, reflecting the two-measure minuet step (ex. 2–10).

The affect of the passepied is naturally more sprightly than that of a minuet, and is, according to Koch, one of "charming and noble gaiety."[21] Because of the quick tempo of the dance, it is no longer the individual steps with their balance and restraint which are at the forefront, but the floor patterns that the dancers describe in their course about the room. In fact the passepied, usually a dance for one couple like the elegant minuet, was sometimes performed by several couples as a contredanse, a quick dance in which attention to individual steps is all but overwhelmed by a preoccupation with the geometry of the intertwining pairs of dancers.[22] This shift in attention from the well-crafted step to

Example 2-11

1st reprise — F major   2nd - d minor

Example 2-12

the intricate floor pattern is a general tendency among the quicker dances to the right of the spectrum, and one which recommended them highly to the new amateur class of dancers.[23]

Actual passepied dance tunes have two frequent rhythmic habits worthy of note, both of which tend to retard rhythmic action near a cadence. The first is a cadence figure which produces a ritard by throwing the stress onto the second beat of the penultimate measure of the phrase (ex. 2–11[24]). The *Idomeneo* passepied (ex. 2–10) achieves the same effect by the change of harmonic rhythm in the penultimate measure. The other rhythmic peculiarity of the dance is the frequent hemiola, which also serves as a cadence announcer, but on the level of the phrase. This hemiola is sometimes specially notated, using a 3/4 measure in place of two 3/8 measure units (ex. 2–12[25]). The hemiola occurs just prior to a cadence.

Dances in Compound Duple Meters

A Note on the Term "Compound Duple"

In modern metrical terminology it is generally assumed that the division of the primary beat will be a duple one; for instance, although 3/4 is certainly susceptible of a triple division of the quarter note — ♫♫ ♫♫ ♫♫ — we assume a duple division unless otherwise advised, and usually require a special sign, ♪♪♪, for the advisement. A special category is reserved for meters in which the primary beat ordinarily has a triple division instead of a duple one, for this is thought to be the more remarkable case. Thus although the word "triple" is not found in the label of 6/8 meter, "tripleness" is central to the definition of 6/8 and of the other compound duple meters, and makes a decisive contribution to its movement and affect. Marches are occasionally written in 6/8, but they are the only gestures in which steps taken regularly coincide only with the duple level of the beat — in 6/8 the dotted quarter. Otherwise steps are usually distributed over the measure on beats 1, 3, 4, and 6,[26] marking the inequality of strong and weak parts of the pulse which is central to the nature of a triple unit. In music written for the dance, this binding of two relatively quick triple units together to form a duple unit on a higher level gives 6/8 dances a buoyancy and lightness which is appreciable even at the moderate tempo of the siciliano. For this reason the dances written in 6/8 meter — the gigue, pastorale, and siciliano — are classed with the meters in triple time at the right of the metrical spectrum.

The Gigue

By the late eighteenth century the French court gigue was no longer a social dance of any account; its 6/8 meter had been subsumed into the music of the contredanse. But the dance type was a tremendously popular one for sonata and symphony movements, especially in finales, where its buoyant rhythms projected the "mirth and cheerfulness"[27] which were thought to be appropriate to the closing movement of such a work.

In its earlier history the dance had had many variants; Mattheson lists four:

> The ordinary one, the *Loure*, the *Canarie*, and the *Giga*. The ordinary or English *gigues* have as their particular affect a *fiery* and *volatile ardor*, a *rage* which quickly evanesces. The *loures*, slow and dotted, exhibit a *proud* and *inflated* nature, on account of which they are very popular with the Spanish. *Canaries* must possess great *eagerness* and *swiftness*, or else they are a little *plain*. Finally the Italian *gigas*, which are not used for dancing but for fiddling (from which their name may have arisen [suggested by the German *Geigen*]), are constrained to the utmost *speed* or *volatility*, but usually in a flowing and not violent manner.[28]

In practice the "ordinary" gigue tended to an irregular phrase structure[29] and frequently to a contrapuntal treatment. Kirnberger quotes a danceable gigue in thoroughgoing imitative style in his *Recueil d'airs de*

Example 2-13

danse caractéristiques[30] (ex. 2–13) and the type reached its ultimate development in the elaborate and exuberant contrapuntal gigues of J. S. Bach.[31] The Italian *giga* was quicker and lighter, with rapid passagework: Prelude 11, book 1, of *The Well-Tempered Clavier* is cast in *giga* style. Later the loure ceased to be a recognizable type, and the other three variants were conflated into the one described at the head of this section.

In tempo and execution the late eighteenth-century stereotype of the gigue follows the example of the imitative type, but in its regular phrase structure it resembles rather the *giga*, or, that is, the usual two-plus-two phrases of most simple dance music. A survival of the contrapuntal type might be discerned in the gigue with imitation of Mozart's B-flat Major Quartet, K. 589, last movement, or of the canarie motif in the G Minor Quintet, K. 516, last movement (the music for the canarie, more rapid in tempo than the gigue, frequently began on the half-bar), but there is no firm guarantee that knowledge of the earlier refinements in gigue classification shaped these particular pieces; this "canarie" may in fact borrow its liveliness from the type of the 6/8 contredanse.

The movement of the gigue is moderate enough for it to tolerate changes of harmony on beats 3 and 6; Kirnberger lists this characteristic as one of the things which distinguishes the music of a gigue from mere triplets in 2/4, since four harmonic changes per measure would be too clumsy to negotiate in a quick and light style of execution.[32] The resulting rhythmic scheme for the gigue is ♪♪♪-♪♪/ Other characteristic features of the dance are frequent dotted eighth notes on the first and fourth beats and large melodic leaps (resulting in the expression *in saltarella*, from *saltare*, "to leap," for the movement of the gigue[33]). The first movement of Mozart's B-flat Major Quartet, K. 458, is a good example of a stylized gigue in an instrumental work (ex. 2–14).

The gigue was originally a folk dance, of rather vulgar origin, and when refined into a *danse noble* it still retained those country associations. It was often combined with the characteristic harmonies of hunting horns to become a *chasse*, or *Jagdstück* ("hunting piece"); the gigue just quoted is an example of this *galant* character piece, with its orna-

Example 2-14

Example 2-15

Example 2-16

mented horn fifths in measures 2 and 4 (from which it earned the sobri-quet *Die Jagd*). Two other Mozartian examples of *chasse* style are the first movements of the Quintet in E-flat Major, K. 614, and of the Piano Sonata in D Major, K. 576. As a result of its bucolic associations, the gigue is frequently used in operas to set the rustic scene. Rousseau in his opera *Le Devin du Village*, a work enshrining the simple virtues of country living, has his village peasants dance a gigue (or perhaps, more precisely, a canarie) (ex. 2–15). The conventional association is also a natural one: the gigue, with the lilt of its double-leveled meter, is a happy projection of simple rustic revels.

The Pastorale

The pastorale may well never have been a dance, although it is usu-ally classed as one in the lexicons and method books of the late eigh-teenth century. A few writers, Koch among them, explain that it is rather a song meant to express the idealized world of shepherds.[34] Questions of medium aside, it is persistently recognized as a musical *topos* distinct from the gigue and siciliano — in fact, as a mean between these two pastoral dances.

The pastorale is characterized by a moderately slow tempo, frequent slurs, and the absence of the dotted figures of the gigue and siciliano. Its affect is "natural, sweet . . . , tender,"[35] expressing "rural innocence."[36] An example of the pastorale at its simplest comes from a collection by Pleyel at the turn of the century (ex. 2–16).[37] The telling catchword *innocente* and the musette-style tonic pedal[38] catch the idealization of the shepherd world which is the hallmark of the dance called pastorale, and of the pastoral genre itself. The last movement of Mozart's F Major

Example 2-17

242

Piano Sonata, K. 332 — a quicksilver mixture of 6/8 topics including virtuoso tarantella style and brilliant gigues — ends coyly *calando* with four measures in pastoral style (ex. 2–17).

The Siciliano

Little is known about how the siciliano was actually danced, but it remained an identifiable and important *topos* nonetheless. The siciliano is the slowest of the three dance types in compound duple meter. Koch describes it at length:

> A piece of rustic, simple, but charming character which imitates the melodies customarily danced by the people of Sicily. It is set in a slow 6/8 meter, and differs from the pastorale generally in its slower tempo, and in particular because (1) usually the first of the three first eighth notes in the first half of the measure is lengthened by a dot and the following shortened note is slurred with the longer, and (2) in the second half of the measure there rarely appear eighth notes, but more often quarter notes with two following sixteenths. Through this ordering the siciliano receives a special character and meter which markedly distinguish it from all other kinds of pieces.[39]

Quantz suggests for the dance a simple ornamentation, with "no shakes or graces, but a few slurred semiquavers and appoggiaturas."[40] It is often set in a minor key.

The siciliano is closely identified with the pastoral genre; Sicily is, after all, the Italian Arcadia. On this account it was often used to set scenes of the Nativity, for instance in Handel's *Messiah* and Corelli's *Christmas Concerto*. In another vein it often bears an affect of nostalgia and resignation, passions naturally attendant on memories of a better world. A piece quoted by Busby, composed by the English church musician Battishill, combines the two in a hymn *alla siciliana* (in 12/8 meter) sung by the Christian *in extremis* (ex. 2–18).[41] This hymn, it must be said, also demonstrates the tendency to a dragging and tedious melancholy which Koch warned that the dance could display in the hands of a less gifted composer.[42]

Mozart wrote lovely sicilianos, for instance the second movement of the Piano Sonata K. 280. The dance has received no more haunting

Example 2-18

Example 2-19

treatment than in the slow movement of the Piano Concerto in A Major, K. 488 (ex. 2–19).

Dances in Duple Meter

The March

A *march* is certainly not a special dance; and when it appears in plays, the characters just stride along very slowly and nobly to the beat, without dancing, skipping, or leaping; but together they cut a figure which is pleasant to look at, especially with armed men or the military.[43]

Under a narrow definition of the term "dance," the march should properly be excluded from the category "dances in duple meter." In previous pages I have put marching in opposition to dancing, distinguishing between the artful motion of dance and the simple marching stride: the bourrée and gavotte move in successive degrees away from the stride toward the dance to the extent that their manipulations of the paradigmatic march measure, /-̲ᴜ-ᴜ/ , make possible some choreographic variation in the march's relentless "two-step."[44] But if the term "choreographic" is extended to include any activity conducted to the accompaniment of music, the march asserts a prior claim: it is the original *Gebrauchsmusik* (music written for a practical purpose, or "occasional music"). Writers in the latter half of the eighteenth century would often in discussions of the march include a pseudoanthropological excursus on the potency of the relation between music and human movement. Consider, for example, Sulzer's words on the subject:

> It was noticed probably before the invention of music that tones put together even just to make noise have great power to support the capabilities of the body in difficult work and to end fatigue. We find frequently in all histories that great tasks men wanted to accomplish quickly were accomplished to the sound of trumpets and other instruments. . . . Chardin says in his *Trip to Persia* that Eastern peoples could not lift a heavy load unless a noise was made for it. . . . Today we can still watch sailors pulling heavily laden barges against the current of the river lighten their tiring work by singing, so that the steps coincide with the measure. . . . We can see from these considerations why almost all peoples accompany the processions of soldiers and other more difficult undertakings with music.[45]

This preoccupation with music's power to control and direct the human body is clearly the product of a music aesthetic which interpreted musical numbers as a rational hierarchy of signs ordering bodily movement (regarding this movement in turn as the measurable manifestation of human passions). The march, the bare reshaping of ordinary human locomotion into artful measured movement, stands on the threshold of dance, and thus is an example of the bond between gesture and expression in its most rudimentary form. Eighteenth-century aestheticians examined the march because they desired to demonstrate that that bond existed by nature: in the march they found a primitive specimen from which to trace the evolution of comparative artifices like the social dances.

The figures admitted to the march must satisfy one requirement: they must support the activity of the marchers.

> [The march] should serve to ease the fatigue of war and to excite the spirit, or, in other solemn processions, to incline the feelings to a certain higher, more noble joy. . . . To begin with an upbeat is at all events not advisable in a true march, since the unmusical soldiers are induced by it to raise their foot immediately with the first note and thus to disturb the measure.[46]

The march must have a meter with a duple beat, preferably a slow two or a quick four (2/4, 4/4, or *alla breve*; a 6/8 meter with steps on beats 1 and 4 is permissible, but less usual). Phrases must be organized in two-measure units. Dotted rhythms, called by Charles Burney the "old-fashioned 'dot-and-go-one,'"[47] are the most felicitous impetus for stepping in time, since a short, snappy upbeat emphasizes the note which follows it. Winds and brass are characteristic military instruments, and should be employed in major tonalities — B-flat, C, D, or E-flat when trumpets are used.[48] Marches should be ceremonial in affect, "serious, but at the same time rousing."[49]

Marches of the period often imitate the characteristic sound of instruments associated with the military: dotted rhythms, parallel thirds and sixths suggesting wind-instrument figuration, drum tattoos, trumpet calls, and fanfares. In his late eighteenth-century keyboard-method book, D. G. Türk includes a prototypical march, *Maestoso*, with dotted rhythms, horn fifths, and a fanfare motive in the opening notes of the bass (ex. 2–20a). Introducing in the eleventh measure a sixteenth-note triplet (for the first and only time), he appends a playful footnote: "for connoisseurs of the trumpet" (ex. 2–20b).[50] The march suitable for the ceremonial procession of a solemn, nonmilitary occasion is slower in tempo and *alla breve*, but uses many of the figures characteristic of the military march. Mozart's march of the priests from *Ido-*

Example 2-20

Example 2-21

meneo is a good example of the type (ex. 2–21). The "exalted march"[51] is a more fiery and passionate version of this ecclesiastical *entrée*.

The Bourrée

The bourrée, like the minuet, sarabande, and passepied part of the heritage of the French court dance, is a danceable shading of the march. Written in duple meter, 4/4 or *alla breve*, with a moderate and lively tempo, it has two prominent rhythmic peculiarities: it begins with a quarter-note upbeat, ♩ | ♩ ♩ ♩,♩ | ♩ ♩ ♩,, and often uses the syncopated figure: ♩ ♩ ♩ The dance melody has the rhythmic profile

$$\cup/-\cup-,\cup/-\cup-,$$
$$4\ \ 1\,2\,3\ 4\ \ 1\,2\,3$$

or, when syncopated

$$\cup/--\ \ \cup/--$$
$$4\ \ 1\,2\undergroup{3},4\ \ 1\,2\undergroup{3},$$

The rhythmic pattern of the march measure falls into two nearly equal halves, while that of the bourrée is more of a piece, with a quick rhythmic crest and slower fall. The *pas de bourrée* is a unit consisting of a rise followed by two plain steps, the three performed to the first three beats of the measure (and preceded by a *plié* on the upbeat).[52] Phrasing with an upbeat strengthens the first and strong beat considerably in relation to beat 3, the "weak strong beat" of the march, both because the upbeat specially prepares beat 1 and because the breath articulating the next upbeat must cut beat 3 short. The syncopated pattern sharpens the differences between bourrée and march, eliding the "weak strong beat" altogether (ex. 2–22[53]).

Example 2-22

Example 2-23

With its more or less ornamented "gliding stride,"[54] the bourrée belongs to a class of gestures which might be termed *di mezzo carattere* ("of the middle rank").[55] Its affect is usually expressed as a "moderate joy,"[56] and a light execution is specified. According to Sulzer, it was used in ballets "for serious as well as playful and humble affects."[57] Haydn, in the finale of the String Quartet opus 76, no. 4, shades the bourrée scansion into a more antic contredanse style, introducing eccentric accents on weak beats (ex. 2–23). To Mattheson the particular property of the bourrée was "*contentment* and a *pleasing manner*, . . . a *nonchalance*";[58] refined but not distinctive to the extreme, it survived the vicissitudes of fashion in social dance almost as successfully as did that ultimate survivor, the minuet.

The Gavotte

In rhythmic pattern the gavotte is one step further removed from the march than is the bourrée: one more slight alteration in the 4/4 paradigm achieves in the gavotte measure the most radical manipulation of duple meter possible. The bourrée worked its changes on the march pattern by disturbing the symmetry of the two halves of the measure. The gavotte retains the symmetry of the 4/4 measure, only to turn it inside out: beat 3, the "weak strong beat" of the march, becomes the first beat of the gavotte pattern without, however, usurping the proper position and accentuation of the "true" beat 1. This transposition creates a situation which is anomalous in duple meter: it leaves only one actual weak beat among the four:

$$- - / \underline{\acute{-}} \cup , - - / \underline{\acute{-}} \cup$$
$$3 \ 4 \quad 1 \ 2 , 3 \ 4 \quad 1 \ 2 ,$$

The downbeat and the pattern-beginning, two elements of the measure which are usually united in a single entity, are split apart in the gavotte, and act as counterweights to one another. A delicate rhythmic equilibrium results: each of the three strong beats is held in suspension, neatly "beaten" as a distinct entity, until the curve of the measure peaks on the third and strongest beat of the three. With this transposition of the two halves of the least dancelike of meters, the gavotte becomes one of the most distinctive of all the *danses caractéristiques*.[59]

Late eighteenth-century descriptions of the music of the gavotte re-

flect its measured beating in their frequent use of the words "precise,"
or "distinctly accented."[60] Like the bourrée, the gavotte is a dance *di
mezzo carattere*. While not open to extremes of tempo, its moderately
quick pace can be varied somewhat in either direction, and its affect
will vary to the same degree:

> The measure can be formed in various ways, with quarter or eighth
> notes predominant, or mixed. Here and there one can make use of the
> dot and other variations, the choice of them . . . depending on the
> tempo and character one desires to give to the gavotte. For the gavotte
> can be used for various types of expression, happy and sad in various
> degrees, and can thus be performed in tempos which are more or less
> quick and more or less slow.[61]

Charles Compan in his *Dictionnaire de danse* speaks of the gavotte as
"often gay, and also sometimes tender and slow,"[62] and these two affective types are represented in two dances taken from a French violin
treatise — a *gavotte tendre* (ex. 2–24a) with its dotted slurs, and a *gavotte
vive* (ex. 2–24b) with a simpler melody and running eighth-note accompaniment.[63] Alberti basses like the one in example 2–24b are a frequent
accompaniment to the dance because their regular tick-tock rhythms
help to accentuate the separate strokes of the three strong beats.

The gavotte displays neither the simple gravity of the minuet nor the
exuberance of the gigue, but has instead, by way of the almost artificial
control of its special rhythmic ticking, an air of teasing primness, which
suggests the pastoral pastels of French *bergeries*. It was historically a
courtship dance, and also had from its origin persistent associations

Example 2-24

a) Gavotte tendre

b) Gavotte vive

Example 2-25

Filles qui en - seig-nez le dom- mag- e que les a -mants peu-vent cau- ser

Example 2-26

with the pastoral,[64] which were still very much alive in the late eighteenth century. One collection of characteristic national songs includes as the typically French example a tune barred as a gavotte, with a daintily amorous text (ex. 2–25):

> Young girls, you who teach the trouble
> Lovers can cause,
> Resist the first speeches
> With which they wish to divert you.
> If you are slow, your danger redoubles.
> Love dazzles you with its torch.
> When the eye is dimmed, all is lost.[65]

The figure opening this *bergerie* is a characteristic one in the gavotte — a stepwise descent from one note of the tonic chord to another. Mozart uses it as the opening of the gavotte in the ballet music for *Idomeneo* (ex. 2–26). This melodic fall to the downbeat matches the shape of the pattern's rhythmic arch, and when dotted, as Mozart's opening is, the figure adds a flirtatious note, its rubatolike effect momentarily retarding the expected climax of the gavotte measure. It is a frequent and effective opening figure for gavotte melodies.

The association of gavotte with pastoral was not merely a Parisian habit, but universally part of the dance's affective gamut. Antonio Salieri, in his opera *La grotta di Trofonio* (Vienna, 1785), also connects the

Example 2-27

Ah, tro— var fra ques— te pian-te po-tess'_io   qual_che ga - lan-te   A -ma-dria-de

gavotte with the classico-pastoral world. To a young man wandering in the woods and musing on the possibilities of amorous conquest of a nymph or dryad, Salieri gives an aria cast as a gavotte tune in 2/4 (ex. 2–27).[66] The text of the French gavotte tune cited above (ex. 2–25) is a coyly mock-moral warning about the gentle dangers of love — an oxymoron about the pleasures of peril. The affect of the gavotte is itself an oxymoron — a coy reserve, a teasing primness. This captured contradiction is plainly what made the gavotte a successful gesture for another world of oxymoron — the artificially natural garden of courtly shepherds and rustic nobles.

Dances Admitting of Duple or Triple Meter

The Musette

The musette is first off an instrument — the French version of the bagpipe — and second a *pièce caractéristique* which imitates the instrument's characteristic turns — the drone and skirl, or pedal point bass and melodic treble. The instrument was highly popular in the French court, a real country instrument "pastoralized" along with the real country. Elegant versions of the instrument were manufactured, and performing manuals were written for it, one by as distinguished a composer as Jacques Hotteterre (*Méthode pour la musette*, Paris, 1737). A dance called musette also appeared in the French ballet, as an accompaniment for music written for the instrument. It could be composed in any meter, duple or triple, and had a "languid, fragile character."[67]

The musette is an important musical *topos* in Classic music: it is the most directly suggestive expression of the rustic scene, for its evocative part-writing — drone and skirl — transports the listener immediately into a country context. Compan, in his *Dictionnaire de danse*, after describing the pastoral festivals of ancient times in which shepherds danced the musette, gives a nostalgic sigh for the mythical simple life of old: "One regrets not living in a country where people knew no other ambition than to please, and no other occupation than that of loving and being happy."[68] The affect of the musette is usually described in words like Sulzer's — "naive simplicity, with a gentle, coaxing song."[69]

Generally in Classic uses of the *topos*, the characteristic musette sound is combined with the rhythmic pattern of a particular dance, either duple or triple. As Sulzer explains, the musette "can be used for noble shepherd characters as well as for low peasant types; but in both cases music must conform precisely with character."[70] The musette can, for example, take on contredanse figures (ex. 2–28[71]). The most common musette meters are 6/8 and *alla breve*. The 6/8 frequently characterizes "low peasant types"; since it is already a peasant meter, the addition of a pedal bass to a gigue only compounds the rustic affect. Mozart in his pastoral opera *Bastien und Bastienne* (its libretto based on Rousseau's *Le Devin du village*) announces the approach of the village sorcerer with a musette in 6/8 in the rhythms of the gigue, (or, speaking rigorously, the canarie). He adds to the drone and skirl the inflection of the raised fourth degree, a characteristic bagpipe sound (ex. 2–29). To express a "noble shepherd character," the musette requires more sophisticated rhythms: the pastorale often has a musette-type pedal bass (see exs. 2–16 and 2–17, pp. 43, 44), and indeed any distinction between the two types is almost superfluous.

The musette-gavotte is the most common combination of a musette with dance rhythms; it is perhaps the most distinctive of all musettes. It can be traced through early French opera, and is found in the English Suites of Bach (nos. 3 and 6). Mozart's gavotte from the ballet music for

Example 2-28

Example 2-29

Idomeneo (ex. 2–26, p. 51) is another notable example of the type.
Gavotte rhythms are an appropriate gesture for a courtly pastoral musette because they themselves evoke the Arcadian world. Hiller published an example of the musette-gavotte which deserves quotation with
text in full, because it catches the naive idealization of an artificial coun-
tryside which the musette-gavotte was considered to reflect:

> A. In love we must take our lessons
>   From the village.
>   The shepherd is never fickle;
>   He loves in all seasons.
>   When, at the feet of his shepherdess,
>   Coridon describes his torment,
>   Lisa, never severe,
>   Responds to him only with love.
>
> B. Simple art paints nature
>   With a seductive luster.
>   Its mirror is the clear billow,
>   Its ornament a flower.
>   If we're in love we should say so.
>   Everything in these peaceful places
>   Speaks the language of the heart,
>   And is figured in two lovely eyes.
>
> C. I who live in the village
>   Have all its candor.
>   My habit and my speech
>   Are the image of my heart.
>   If by chance my eyes
>   Have power over yours,
>   I owe it to nature,
>   And I please without knowing it.

The poet-sophisticate-lover of these lines stands at a double remove
from nature: admiring the artless simplicity of life in the village, he fancies that it confers on him qualities possessed by the noble shepherd
Coridon, who is in turn a literary image of the real thing. The poem is
set to the tune of a gavotte, with the characteristic dotted descending
figure at the opening.[72] For the third couplet of each stanza there is
added a musette, with drone and skirl (ex. 2–30).[73] This combination of
the prim, beating rhythms of the gavotte with the musette's characteristic "country" sound constitutes a complex *topos*, many-layered in reference, which is fully the musical equivalent of that nostalgic world of
amour and artifice, the literary pastoral.

Example 2-30

The Contredanse (Allemande, Waltz)

The contredanse is also "ambimetric," but for different reasons than is the musette. The musette simply joins its country sound to the characteristic rhythms of a particular dance tune, while the music of the contredanse, on the other hand, has no fixed rhythmic pattern, tolerating any meter, duple or triple, which admits of being scanned in two light beats (6/8, two measures of 3/8, 2/4, or *alla breve*). The contredanse subverted the established choreographic habits of the late seventeenth and early eighteenth centuries, causing an irreversible revolution in social dance — the conquest of the French court choreographies by a phenomenon I shall call the "danceless dance." Its indifference to the characteristic shapes of meters is rhythmic evidence of the contredanse's revolutionary nature.

Originally native to England, the contredanse was first imported to the continent just before the end of the seventeenth century. There it split into two versions, the "contredanse angloise" and the "contredanse française," distinguished from one another more by the number of dancers and their positions than by the music which accompanied them. The English preferred a columnar figure called a "longways," similar to our Virginia reel, in which a large number of people could participate, while the French adopted a "square set" for eight, resembling the usual figure of our modern square dance.[74] By the 1760s an import called "allemande," a slightly cruder and more energetic dance, had joined the contredanse in France. Although some writers attribute other dif-

Example 2-31

Contre-danse Angloise

Example 2-32

ferences than those of figure to the françaises and angloises,[75] most opinions and musical examples link them together, opposing them to the allemande.[76] The more moderate, "aristocratic" contredanse is "less serious than the Minuet, and than most of the old figured Dances,"[77] but it does not approach the wanton or licentious. Its affect is gay, skipping, graceful, and "moderately comic."[78] It appears in 6/8, *alla breve*, and 2/4, and often begins with an upbeat. No matter what its time signature, it is beat in two—dotted quarter notes, half notes, or quarter notes. The *alla breve* contredanse is frequently barred like a gavotte (ex. 2–31[79]). But its rhythmic profile is less complex than the gavotte's because of its quicker tempo and its insistence on the *alla breve* beat:

$$
\begin{array}{c|cc|c}
\text{\musDouble} & \text{\musDouble} & \text{\musDouble} & \text{\musDouble} \\
\cup & \text{—}' & \cup & \text{—}' \\
2 & 1 & , & 2 & 1
\end{array}
$$

In these simple iambs the subtlety of the gavotte's rhythmic arch disappears. A 6/8 contredanse also can be either trochaic or iambic, as in this contredanse française quoted by Guilcher (ex. 2–32).[80] But any greater subtleties of rhythmic pattern are generally barred from the contredanse on account of the speed and lightness of its execution.

The second type of contredanse, the allemande, is quicker, more energetic, and, according to some of its critics, all too undignified. Its country of origin is of course Germany. It appears in both duple and triple meters—2/4 and 3/8. As a class the allemandes differ from françaises and angloises in their quicker tempo and customary downbeat opening. Comparing the choreographies of the dances, Chabanon characterizes the German versions as "fiery and passionate," with "those rhythmic concussions which make the dance leap," contrasting this energetic German style to the gliding of the angloise "with its thousand little steps accumulated in one measure."[81]

The contredanse comes down to us principally in its 2/4 version; Mozart and Haydn must have considered it prototypical. Of Mozart's twenty-eight contredanses for orchestra, only four are in meters other than 2/4.[82] In practice it is often difficult to distinguish precisely between the 2/4 française and the 2/4 allemande, for they are alike in essence, with differences only at the extremes. The 2/4 françaises at their most elaborate may contain some complex figurations which slow the tempo and demand more attention from the dancers.[83] The simplest 2/4 allemandes lack an upbeat and any complicated rhythms, asserting the duple beat as clearly and quickly as possible. In both the allemande and the française the smallest note values are usually sixteenths; rows of dotted notes are the exception, and they occur principally in the French character dances.[84] The rhythmic ideal in both versions is a smooth and continuous rhythmic action with no jerky or eccentric figuration. Almost every beat is marked by one of these combinations: ♩, ♫, ♫ or ♬. Slower-moving figures like ♩. ♪, or figures which work against the rhythm's natural flow — ♪♩ ♪, ♫., and ♫ ("scotch snaps"), ♫ , and ♫ — occur less frequently, often in order to match a characterizing title with a special effect.[85] It makes little difference to what degree one subdivides the beat (down to the level of the thirty-second note), if rhythmic smoothness is preserved in the division. This fluidity of figure lends a "doodling" quality to the contredanse; the figuration is meant to mark time, not to impose upon it. Many treatises prescribe feminine cadences for all but the final close of the 2/4 contredanse (ex. 2-33[86]). This practice also serves the cause of rhythmic fluency, by keeping the rhythm moving at intermediate cadence points where a masculine cadence, or full stop at the downbeat, would disturb the rhythmic flow. A selection of opening phrases from eighteenth- and early nineteenth-century collections of popular dance tunes and from the works of Mozart and Haydn will illustrate the range of contredanse and allemande figurations (ex. 2-34).[87] These examples make manifest the strict limitations of figuration which are imposed on the 2/4 contredanse: its tunes are "stripped down for action." As a result, it is the fastest and gayest of all the dances, and can also take on a comic expres-

Example 2-33

Example 2-34

Example 2-35

sion, uniting "diversion and civility" in a "pleasant joke."[88] Mozart and Haydn exploit the dance's air of civilized comedy frequently in their spirited and witty contredanse finales.

The allemande in triple meter (3/4, 3/8) is even more simplified and streamlined than is its 2/4 version. Sometimes called the "true German allemande" (if one considers the 2/4 version as a transformation worked by the French on a borrowing from the German),[89] the dance appears under a profusion of labels, all signifying essentially the same dance: allemande, boiteuse, Schwäbische Tanz (Souabe), Deutsche Tanz (Teitsch), Schleifer, ländler, waltz (Walzer). The last two titles, ländler and waltz, are modern generic terms for these quick triple dances, more commonly in use today than they were in the eighteenth century. The 3/4 allemandes are, however, the immediate ancestors of the waltz, and the dances most distant from the French court tradition; Bacquoy-Guédon's manual includes some good examples (ex. 2–35).[90] They share with the 2/4 allemande an exceedingly simple and repetitious figuration and a strong emphasis on the downbeat: /♩♩♩/ They also feature a very simple harmony, which clings close to the tonic (often moving over a tonic pedal), and usually changes harmony only once per measure.

The proliferation of names for the triple allemande can be easily explained; they are all either geographic, choreographic, or rhythmic in origin. "Boiteuse" means "limping," and refers to the triple meter of the "true German allemande": the German from Bacquoy-Guédon's manual (ex. 2–35 above) is entitled "Contre-danse Allemande ou boiteuse." "Schwäbische" simply names a German province, and "Deutsche Tanz" is the name given by Mozart to the orchestral allemandes he wrote for the dance halls in 1787 and after,[91] for example the opening measures of K. 509, no. 1 (ex. 2–36). He calls the crude peasant dance in the famous three-orchestra ballroom scene of *Don Giovanni* (I, 13, 454ff.) a

Example 2-36

Example 2-37

"Teitsch" (ex. 2–37).[92] Both "Deutsche Tanz" and "Teitsch" are clearly originals of the French translation "allemande," and of the English translation "german" in use even today. "Schleifer," "slider," describes the motion of the allemande, and "ländler" is the equivalent of "country-dance." All these titles describe a German dance in a quick triple meter with a rhythmic pattern which resembles that of the modern waltz.

The Revolution of the "Danceless Dance"

The contredanse in its several versions was the leading dance of the late eighteenth century, and it entered the repertoire while a new democratization of social life was taking place in Europe. Dance was no longer the hierarchic display it had been in the French courts. Dance halls were springing up in all European capitals, centers of social life where members of the bourgeoisie and aristocracy might meet one another and perhaps even dance a figure together. Dance, once considered a craft, and a character-building discipline, was turning into a purely amateur amusement, and the amateurs were impatient of the long training periods which the older dances required if one were to acquit oneself properly in their performance. Turning away from rigorous training in the expression of the passions to the luxury of self-expression, they also turned from the principle of variety to that of efficiency:

> These dances . . . are of many types, and can be danced by four, six, eight, and still more persons at once. Therefore usually at balls, after minuets have been danced for a while, most of the remaining time is passed with contredanses, because they can occupy more people at once and because they can be varied endlessly; for there are many contredanses.[93]

The contredanse was welcomed with such enthusiasm because of its infinite expandability: it facilitated the happy social exercise of as many dancers as the ballroom could accommodate. In the face of this versatility the older dances all fell by the wayside, except for the minuet, which was retained, one supposes, as a nod to older habits of restraint and decorum. Assemblies moved on to the contredanse as soon as decently possible, after perfunctorily performing a few minuets as a solemn prelude to the evening's more enthusiastic exercises.

The contredanse's democracy of meters is a sign of its democracy of spirit. Like the march, it admits of duple or triple meter, because it is essentially a walk or alternation of steps, and not a true dance, at least in the tradition of the French court dances. Their essence could never be simple alternation; for a dance to catch a particular passion it had to cleave to one meter or another. Explanations of the contredanse's variety of meters reveal an opposing, and "progressive," notion of dance:

> In the Music of the Contredanse one can use duple or triple time. In the first case the meter is 2/4, and serves for the greater part of the Contredanses; in the second the meter is 3/8, which in some circumstances is more suitable for the movement of this Dance, whose action can be rather varied.[94]

It is not meter which determines the choreographic action of the contredanse, but rather the reverse, and its expressive content is not limited to one particular affect. For the first time we meet with a democratic attitude toward the relation between meter and expression, and, consequently, the term "meter" moves closer toward the modern concept of it as a mere organizer of pulses.

The choreography of the contredanse was made to order for the new generation of amateur dancers. In the minuet a step takes two measures, and every motion to every beat, each attitude of the body and limbs, is part of the expressive content of the dance. The contredanse, on the other hand, since it is a group dance, emphasizes not steps and gestures — that is, the delineation of a particular affect — but figures, the aim of which is to uncouple pairs of partners, regroup them, and through a series of cleverly mapped manipulations to bring them back to the original ordering. All the interest in the contredanse is concentrated on the level of the measure-group rather than on that of the measure. One figure takes eight to sixteen measures to perform,[95] and the dancers take steps only in the aid of forming a figure. A. B. Marx describes the figure, writing early in the nineteenth century:

> In the anglaise . . . one pair after the other moves up and down the row of the remaining dancers *with a dancelike movement* and, having reached a specified place, performs some dance figure along with another couple.[96]

The notion of a "dancelike movement" would be incomprehensible in the older court dances; one never aped "dancing" while in fact merely walking or running in order to traverse a given space. The figures of the contredanse are just complicated paths for the dancers to walk, devoid of expressive content. The *noms caractéristiques* often affixed to the French contredanses[97] bear only superficial connections to the pieces; they may at the most refer to some atypical turn of the tune in question, and were probably added for novelty's sake, as a means of impressing some of the innumerable tunes on the memory.[98] The audience in the court of Louis XIV watched individual performers each straining to the utmost to perform the correct expressive gestures of their dance. The audience in a dance hall (most not in actuality spectators, but participants restively waiting their turn) witnessed a mass of gay but obedient dancers following the leader about the room, points in an abstract human geometry.[99] The contredanse is, so to speak, a "danceless" dance.

An interesting contrast in attitudes toward the relation of dance and expression is reflected in comments made on the contredanse by two writers separated by a period of twenty years. Sulzer, in his article on the 3/4 allemande, describes watching peasants at their dancing:

> Very often . . . one sees untutored dancers who dance their allemandes with a charm containing something very captivating; they give the spectator great pleasure. The allemande is a true dance of happiness.[100]

In 1791 Framéry, commenting in the *Encyclopédie Méthodique* on J. J. Rousseau's simple definition of the contredanse,[101] sees the same experience from a different point of view. His words demonstrate a growing indifference to the commonality of human experience, accompanied by a new consciousness of the self:

> There are *contre-danses* for sixteen people, and even for indeterminate numbers. The word seems to come from the English *country-dance*, dance of the country; indeed it is in the village above all that people love to gather, and prefer shared pleasures. The slow minuet, which employs only two people and does not allow the spectators any occupation except admiring the dancers, could only be born in the cities, where people dance for the sake of *amour-propre*. In the village people dance for the sole pleasure of dancing, to move limbs accustomed to violent exercise; they dance to breathe out a feeling of joy which grows constantly in proportion to the number of dancers, and has no need for spectators.[102]

In the first quotation the experience of watching country dancers, although perhaps idealized, is still viewed from a remove: country people dance in a certain manner, expressive of the way in which they live their lives. Unstated but implied is the other half of the comparison: city people dance in some other fashion, manifesting their own particular customs and habits. Implicit in Sulzer's account is the assumption that studying both sets of habits is part of the study of the nature of men. To Framéry, country and city are no longer of equal interest to a reporter; a certain disdain for city ways creeps into his tone. In the country the impulse to dance is primarily a social one, he claims in praising it; its source is the individual's desire to "express himself" in a gathering of his fellows.

The distance between expressing oneself and expressing passions common to all men is a considerable one. The French court dances could not be danced by a mob; they demanded instruction, skill, control, and refinement. The solo character of the minuet may have satisfied one's *amour-propre*, but first it required the opposite — the willingness to submit to an arduous discipline, external to oneself, in order to move other men by one's fluency in a universal expressive language. Even the most rustic court dances, the gigue and the pastorale, are only secondhand rustic; they have been refined from mere rustic dances into vehicles for expressing qualities of character which are considered to accompany the rustic way of life. The dancer does not dance them to express himself, but to catch the naively frank and free manners of country people. If this first attitude appears condescending, the position of the second writer toward the country is no less so, and at the same time he chooses to abandon his status as an observer of human character to join the communal melee and express himself along with everyone else. In idealizing self-expression and locating it in the country, he has "invented" the waltz and turned the corner into the nineteenth century.

The waltz is both an emblem and a natural end of the tumultuous social changes which took place at the turn of the century; a child of the 3/4 allemande or Deutsche Tanz, it follows in the general spirit of the contredanse explosion. Dance melodies with lighthearted affects provide less rhythmic differentiation on the level of the measure than do the more noble, serious gestures: rhythmic action in the minuet and sarabande moves from beat to beat, while in the passepied the focus of the action is on the first beat of every measure. The affect of the contredanse is the most lighthearted of all, especially in its 3/4 German version; a common phrase used to express the triple allemande's distinctive gaiety is "skipping joy," or *hüpfende Freude* (*gajezza saltellante* in the Italian).[103] The beat tends to be perceived on the measure level, and supporting harmonies rarely change more than once a measure, producing the cliché of the "oom-pah-pah" accompaniment, a salient feature both of the Deutsche Tanz and of the modern waltz. A gesture with a phrase consisting actually of four beats rather than four measures is much more open and exuberant than, for example, the gesture of the minuet, with its close and careful small steps and restrained gestures. As the affects of the eighteenth-century dances grow gayer and more rustic, the gestures involved in them become broader, more expansive, and less refined, their rhythmic patterns less complex and more sweeping. Next to the fulsome exuberance of the waltz, the tense control and delicate affective portraiture of the eighteenth-century court dances may seem less subtle than effete; the big gesture, on the other hand, allows for few nuances of expressive content. Dances called "waltz" or "Walzer" in the late eighteenth century carry the "doodling" quality of contredanse figuration to extremes; they often resemble accompaniments without melodies (ex. 2–38[104]). A. B. Marx's explanation of the relation of conventional waltz figuration to the waltz "step" is helpful and revealing:

> The waltz has two movements: first each pair of dancers turns itself in a circle around its own center; second the pair progresses with these continuous turns in a greater circumference until it reaches its starting place and the circle is closed. Each little circle is performed in two-times-three steps and is, as it were, the motif of the dance. It corresponds . . . to the single measure, which must conform to the three steps. . . . But since two such measures belong together, within them the three-part dance motif is performed twice and the little circle is complete.
>
> At the very least the waltz must bring into prominence this basic motif of movement. Each measure, or, better, each phrase of two measures, must answer to the dance motif, marking the first step firmly, and also the swinging turn of the dance. Where the measures do not point it out they must still favor it, by a melody which spiritedly turns away from the first note. This well-known waltz from Weber's *Freischütz* [ex. 2–39] . . . shows us a genuine waltz motif. . . . But this rustic

Example 2-38

Example 2-39

dance satisfies itself with the first, still "raw material," the motif of three steps, without forming clearer phrases for the completed movement of twice three steps which befits a more complete and nobler conception of the dance. . . . We see in the above piece auxiliary tones placed before the pure chord tones in the melody in order to set the first step in relief; every other melodic, harmonic, and rhythmic sharpening . . . serves the same purpose. To this fundamental content is joined as simple an accompaniment as possible, which marks the beat.[105]

Marx's phrases "the swinging turn of the dance" and "a melody which spiritedly turns away from the first note" describe the essential waltz movement; the word *walz* in German means "swinging" or "turning." These words characterize both the original waltz and more sophisticated versions of it. Von Weber's waltz resembles the simple eighteenth-century waltz quoted above (ex. 2–38, p. 64); its repetitive and unmelodic figures string out one after another with no attention to period structure, to a sculptured arch for the phrase. Although Marx was plainly used to more tuneful waltzes with some hint of periodicity, he praises von Weber's exploitation of the affective potential of the cruder waltz:

> The division into antecedent and consequent phrases does not seem essential [in the waltz in general], and thus may be less prominent, although a slight hint of this order of progress generally adorns and ennobles the music. Certainly because it is not perceptible in the haste of the waltz from *Der Freischütz*, the piece appears common, as was the composer's intent. For he wanted to portray an uncultivated group giving itself to *pure pleasure in waltzing*, recklessly; thus he had nothing sound out except the pure waltz figure.[106]

Marx's expression "die blosse Walzlust" (ineffectively rendered above as "pure pleasure in waltzing")[107] conjures up images of couples eternally turning in dizzying circles along a wider circumferential path, self-contained and oblivious planets. The intoxicating and exuberant "self-expression" of the waltz brought it to extraordinary popularity by the end of the century, obliterating all the fine distinctions of the social dances which had choreographed human passions. Instead the activity of dancing became at the least a healthy social exercise, and at its highest an ecstatic circling through a blurred landscape toward the sublime.

Thus the 2/4 contredanse and the waltz are both anomalies in the metrical spectrum. The contredanse is a dance which is not properly danced, or a quick walk notated in an improperly slow meter; its duple time signature and quarter-note beat class it with the slow march, while as a quick dance it should belong, according to long-standing metrical proprieties, with 3/8 meter. The contredanse explosion began the subversion of the metrical and affective spectrum. The waltz is an anomaly to the spectrum because as it becomes the principal dance movement in triple meter, it also begins to appear more frequently in an "improper" meter — in 3/4 rather than in the quicker and more lighthearted 3/8. It was possible to notate two quick-tempoed gay dances in quarter notes only because those dances, having eclipsed all other choreographic gestures, no longer needed to be distinguished from companion dances in an expressive hierarchy. Notation was gradually becoming a matter of convenience rather than an indicator of expressive values; the quarter note turned from *tempo giusto* into *scrittura giusta*.

The contredanse and waltz fail to register properly on the metrical spectrum because they are infiltrators engaged in subverting it. Yet the metrical hierarchy and two nonhierarchical rhythmic gestures could and did exist side by side in Mozart's music; he neither shunned the old nor exalted the new, looking on them both dispassionately as material for composition. He treated the waltz as just another dance, capable of expressing a peasant, rustic affect in the most direct, "unprocessed" manner (unlike the pastorale and gavotte, for example, where the rustic is viewed from the remove of the aristocrat). In the second movement of the C Major Quintet the waltz's exuberance serves as a foil for the serpentine minuet,[108] and its peasant associations characterize Leporello's flat-footed Teitsch with Masetto in the ballroom scene of *Don Giovanni*.[109] By setting the undisciplined verve of the contredanse against the rigor of the earlier dances Mozart caught a picture of his world in transition; *Don Giovanni* is the locus of that confrontation.[110] Both duple and triple "danceless dances" were working radical changes on contemporary mores, but at the same time they did not yet fail to take a subordinate place in Mozart's lexicon of expressive references.

The Metrical Spectrum Reviewed

The social dances and marches fall into an order according to the way accents are distributed across a typical measure of each gesture; I have sketched out this order roughly in figure 1. The stronger the downbeat section of the measure, the more apt is the gesture to make two levels of

Figure 1   The Metrical Spectrum

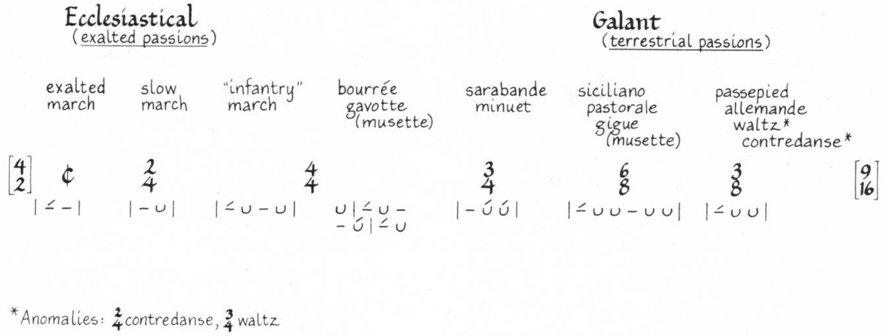

Ecclesiastical
(exalted passions)

Galant
(terrestrial passions)

exalted march	slow march	"infantry" march	bourrée gavotte (musette)	sarabande minuet	siciliano pastorale gigue (musette)	passepied allemande waltz* contredanse*

$\left[\frac{4}{2}\right]$ $\mathbb{C}$ $\frac{2}{4}$ $\frac{4}{4}$ $\frac{3}{4}$ $\frac{6}{8}$ $\frac{3}{8}$ $\left[\frac{9}{16}\right]$

| ⌣ – | | – ∪ | | ⌣ ∪ – ∪ | ∪ | ⌣ ∪ –
 – ∪ | ⌣ ∪ | | – ∪́ ∪́ | | ⌣ ∪ ∪ – ∪ ∪ | | ⌣ ∪ ∪ |

*Anomalies: $\frac{2}{4}$ contredanse, $\frac{3}{4}$ waltz

organization palpable — groupings of beats and groupings of measures. In the waltz the dancer's feet move to the pulse of three which is perceptible on its lower level, but the four-beat "phrase" shaped of measures is the more insistent line of action; sometimes in quick waltzes it operates as a "measure," and the terms "phrase" and "measure" begin to merge. In the case of compound meters, groupings of the duple beat, the higher level of action (the dotted quarter note in 6/8, for example), substitute for groupings of measures. Toward the left of the spectrum double levels begin to open up again, although less apparently, since both levels are always duple. In a duple measure one may perceive as the beat all four pulses, only pulses 1 and 3, or only pulse 1 (in an extremely fast tempo). In the humbler marches the beat may easily pass from one level to the other: in a simple 4/4 measure either quarter-note or half-note action can establish the predominant line. The *alla breve* gesture of the exalted march, however, is to the duple side of the spectrum what the passepied and waltz are to the triple: its upper level (half-note) asserts the definitive metrical contour, while action on the lower (quarter-note) level is strictly subordinated. Thus the most passionately serious and the most lighthearted gestures share the same patterns of accentuation — a firm, simple line with a secondary and more rapid action underneath — the only difference being that the secondary action is duple in the one case and triple in the other. In dances closer to the middle of the spectrum the upper level drops into the background, to be sensed distinctly as the level of the phrase. For example, the slow-tempoed sarabande's emphasis on beat 2 diminishes the usual force of the downbeat, directing one's primary attention to the unit of the measure and the patterns formed by its three pulses. The beat patterns are then grouped together to take their place in an organization of a higher power — the phrase. Since perception of the sarabande's phrase structure comes through beat patterns and not above them, no ambiguity arises about the terms "measure" and "phrase."

The metrical hierarchy clearly corresponds to an affective one; accentuation, style of execution, and tempo taken together prescribe types of movement ranging from the most stately to the most spirited. The sarabande and minuet are the most dignified dance gestures, *alla breve* the most imposing march posture. The gavotte and bourrée, both danceable compromises of the march, manifest the duple patterns which are closest in the spectrum to those of the stately triple dances, but since their compromise nature — they are altered marches or dances made up out of strides — prevents them from approaching the dignity of either the exalted march or the minuet, they should be classed as gestures *di mezzo carattere*.

Alongside the affective hierarchy there runs another means of ordering, which has been suggested in earlier pages but not fully articulated — a class or social hierarchy. The words "noble" and "base" do not carry double meanings by accident: "noble" can be used to characterize both good birth and good actions, and "base" connotes both "low" and "lower-class."[111] The rhythmic gestures of Mozart's affective vocabulary all have historical or physical connections with idealized conceptions of particular classes. The triple dances with double metrical levels have essentially peasant associations, and their combination of quick steps with the lilt and lyricism of the upper level's long-breathed phrases projects a gesture appropriate to the bucolic stereotype of happiness in simplicity. The minuet was persistently a courtly dance, and its evenly accented, moderately tempoed motion suggests the refinement and dignity at least expected of the wellborn. We have seen how *alla breve* with its ecclesiastical associations and manly tread choreographs the kind of fierce human nobility which is often characterized as "daemonic" — deriving its majestic intensity seemingly from powers beyond the human.[112]

Sulzer uses this threefold distinction of motion, affect, and class, to categorize types of theatrical dance:

> The first or lowest class is called *grotesque*; its character is riotousness or the fantastic. The dances essentially portray nothing but unusual leaps and strange, crazy gestures, amusements and adventures of the lowest class of men. Good taste gets little consideration, and there is little care to make the cadences of the dancer agree precisely with those of the music. Above all, these dances require strength.
>
> The second class consists of the *comic dances*. Their content is a little less unrestrained; they portray customs, amusements, and love intrigues of the common people. Movements and leaps are a little less abandoned, but still lively, rather mischievous, and very striking. They must always be amusing and merry. The main thing in them is agility, a quick, artful movement, and a mischievous affect.

The third class includes *the dances called in technical language "halbe Charaktere" (demicaractères)*. Their content is an everyday action in the character of the comic stage — a love affair, or any intrigue in which people from a not completely ordinary kind of life are involved. The dances require elegance, pleasant manners, and fine taste.

The fourth class includes *the dances of serious, noble character*, the requirement of the tragic stage. They consist either of solo dances which depict only noble and serious characters or of whole actions with specific content. Here all the gestures and movements which the art can provide for the expression of the nobler passions must be united.[113]

The clumsiest foot-thumping Deutsche Tänze would support a choreography of the grotesque, although usually the allemande, gigue, and passepied would fall into the class of comic dances ("comic" in Sulzer's extended sense). *Halber Charakter (mezzo carattere)*, the class of the elegant-ordinary and a mean between utter gestural restraint and utter abandon, is best portrayed musically by the compromise patterns of gavotte and bourrée, by a tone of the refined bucolic. (The middle class as we think of it today, the bourgeoisie, does not have its own expression until the advent of the contredanse, and then ultimately at the expense of the entire social hierarchy, since the careless freedom of the dance swallows up all social and affective distinctions.) To the fourth class belong the noblest triple and duple gestures — the minuet, sarabande, and exalted march.

This union of the affective with the social hierarchy may be offensive to liberal sentiments, but in a world where knowledge of a man's class was the indispensable ground for one's apprehension of him, it seemed only natural. Bearing reflected class, and thus, by extension, character. An interesting indirect testimony to this statement was the role dancing was thought to play in the moral education of the young. Dancing school was considered an ethical training ground, and the noble dances better teachers than their plebeian counterparts:

I would only wish that we would not permit young people to indulge themselves in it [the contredanse] until long practice in the minuet has developed all the graces with which they can be provided. Perhaps it would also be desirable that our wish to imitate foreigners did not carry us solely toward German and English contredanses, which are only composed of skippings and stampings suited for making the body take up bad habits; that in them we would preserve the bows and all decorum; that at least for the young, whose souls we wish to form, we would not let there be included situations of an excessive lewdness, which we would never suffer at another time.[114]

Comportment was for the eighteenth century as well as for the ancients[115] no thin veneer of society manners, but an expression of character and the key to a man's worth. Mozart's use of dance in his operas serves a different purpose from that of the dancing masters', one which befits a maker of imitations rather than a trainer of men: he uses the rhythms of social dance to reveal to the audience the virtues and vices of the characters he has set in motion on the stage. Once the social orders have lent their clarity to the more ambiguous subject of the nature of human character, the resultant words or gestures may be detached from class and used freely to pertain to all men. In an aesthetic which exalts neither the celestial nor the subterranean, taking as its point of departure instead the humble human givens of gesture and breath-length, terms of ethical praise and disapprobation naturally have their roots in another given human circumstance — the nature of the soil from which each man has sprung.

PART TWO

LE NOZZE DI FIGARO

— There is in all women a peculiar circle of inward interests, which remain always the same, and from which nothing in the world can divorce them. In outward social intercourse, on the other hand, they will gladly and easily allow themselves to take their tone from the person with whom at the moment they are occupied; and thus by a mixture of impassiveness and susceptibility, by persisting and by yielding, they continue to keep the government to themselves, and no man in the cultivated world can ever take it from them.
Johann Wolfgang von Goethe, *Elective Affinities*, part 2, chapter 7.

CHAPTER THREE

Act I

The Subjects of the Opera

One of the subjects of Mozart's *Le nozze de Figaro* — and of Beaumarchais's play *Le mariage de Figaro* from which Lorenzo da Ponte drew his libretto for the opera — is class distinctions and just what they amount to. Both the play and opera seem at first to concern characters cut from the familiar stuff of comedy — a noble couple and their two resourceful servant-confidants. One expects the usual comic imbroglio and happy resolution, that neat untangling of a delightful snarl which provides so much of comedy's pleasure. The plot of the opera is all imbroglio, as anyone trying to sort out the intricacies of the fourth-act finale will testify. But in both play and opera something more significant emerges from the melee of *la folle journée*.[1] The central theme of the play could be summed up by a passage from Figaro's famous diatribe against social inequities, a speech in which Napoleon is said to have found contained "all the revolution":

> Non, Monsieur le Comte, vous ne l'aurez pas . . . vous ne l'aurez pas.
> Parce que vous êtes un grand Seigneur, vous vous croyez un grand
> génie! . . . noblesse, fortune, un rang, des places; tout cela rend si fier!
> Qu'avez-vous fait pour tant de biens? vous vous êtes donné la peine de
> naître, et rien de plus. Du reste, homme assez ordinaire![2]

The sardonic and clever servant Figaro assumes the center in a political satire considered subversive enough to have been forbidden production for seven years after its composition.

These words of Figaro's are not, however, to be found in the libretto for Mozart's opera. Lorenzo da Ponte did follow the sequence of events in Beaumarchais's play studiously, and he borrowed much of its language. Yet the nature of his cuts and changes, the matter added by Mozart's music, and the sheer difference in nature between an opera and a stage play made the tale of Figaro's marriage into a new vehicle entirely — a radiant romantic comedy. Susanna and the Countess are the characters at the opera's center; they step out from behind the masks of comic convention, and in doing so enable some of the other characters, touched by the humanity of the two women, to undergo a similar metamorphosis. The opera concerns the two women's friendship, one based on mutual trust and affection, which has begun before the opera opens. The warmth radiating from this friendship generates in us a real concern for the various couples in their couplings and uncouplings, and raises the plot above the level of mere farce. It moves us to be genuinely happy for Marcellina's transformation, in act IV, from bluestocking harridan to beaming mother, when ordinarily we would have felt mere relief at the fortuitous resolution of a serious complication. And it makes us momentarily disappointed in Figaro, late in the day, when he fails to put his trust in the two women's grace. The opera is about this grace.

There is no good reason to expect adaptors to use the material they have appropriated for the same purpose as did its originator, nor is it reasonable to judge that they have failed in proper attention to their model when differences appear. Yet it is a commonplace today to discover that Beaumarchais's sharp social criticism is present in Mozart's opera, but closely veiled because of the authors' political timidity. (Less popular, and far less defensible, is the counterview that the adaptors removed all of Beaumarchais's satire, producing a lamer, blander version of his spirited original.) An adaptor may well view his chosen subject in a very different light from that of the originator; if in the opera more general ethical concerns supplanted Beaumarchais's political satire, it may have been because da Ponte and Mozart did not consider a friendship across the classes as a subject for easy treatment, nor conceive of class barriers as readily giving way to an access of strong sentiment. Each man's habitual world must to a great extent define him, limiting his freedom to act, and decency is not sufficient qualification for overriding those limits; even the affectionate Countess at times "remembers her place."[3] The opera takes as its task not to attack the existing orders, but to expand and irradiate them. It must first establish both women in their proper worlds, and demonstrate that each of them merits the respect of her companion. It has then to find a place for their friendship to inhabit without violating either character's delicate sense of propriety. This meeting ground must be beyond class, and with its own sense of time; it may not be permanent, or even of more than one mad day's duration.

It is my intent in the following pages to show how da Ponte's alterations in the text of *Le mariage de Figaro*, and the web of musical metaphors which Mozart painstakingly constructed around da Ponte's text, collaborated to produce a new original — *Le nozze di Figaro* — a work which sheds its own singular light on the way we live. Since the events and revelations of the opera are plotted in a carefully periodic fashion, unlike, for example, the episodic improvisations of *Don Giovanni*, the analysis will proceed step by step through the most significant of the opera's arias and ensembles.

Susanna and Figaro: The Opening Duets

After the overture — a skillful mélange in D major of bustling but neutral string figurations answered by courtly horn fanfares — a drop to the subdominant (G major) introduces a more relaxed and leisurely scene. Figaro is pacing off the bridal chamber, measuring its spaces to a bourrée rhythm marked by a dotted upbeat and the characteristic ♩ ♩ 𝄾 ♩ bourrée pattern (ex. 3–1).[4] The bourrée cadences on the dominant both in its condensed orchestral introduction and in the slightly expanded repetition of the first period which accompanies Figaro's first words. A curious internal organization gives the bourrée phrase a flat-footed quality: its antecedent member is six measures long, its consequent only two (when four-plus-four would be the norm). The long antecedent builds up tension in the arch to the dominant, but necessitates extra repetitions of the tag end of the opening figure to fill it out. The comic lack of invention in the arch becomes even more marked in the repetition of the first period, where the antecedent phrase lasts eight measures and the entire opening figure is repeated four times. An off-beat counterpoint over the barline in the basses and bassoons enlivens the dance in both its occurrences, tugging against the beat for a "stumble-foot" effect.

In its indeterminacy Figaro's bourrée phrase is good opening music and good counting music, but it cannot bring the period to a close. Instead it dovetails with a neat gavotte, Susanna's music in the repetition, which provides the rhythmic and harmonic definition necessary for a

Example 3-1

Example 3-2

cadence on the tonic (mm. 9–18, 30–36; ex. 3–2). The gavotte is typical in both rhythm and accompaniment; it has the habitual dotted
upbeat figure, and is supported by an Alberti bass in the bassoons to
accentuate the "beating" quality of the dance. Its line is decorated with
appoggiaturas on almost every beat, an ornamentation which emphasizes the yielding, feminine aspect of the gavotte. Full orchestra accompanies the bourrée, but only winds and horns the gavotte, with an occasional string flourish at cadences.

This opening duet satisfies our expectations of the comic Susanna
and Figaro: the swaggering, cocksure bridegroom and his pert bride-
to-be celebrate their coming marriage right in character, the one sur-
veying for the nuptial bed, the other in innocent vanity admiring her
new hat. They seem a perfect pair. The very leisureliness of the opening — eight measures of bourrée answered by eight of gavotte, the
whole repeated with the lovers singing the melodies of their respective
dance phrases — confirms the conventionality of the comedy, and nothing in the rest of the duet alters this impression. Susanna breaks into
buffa patter as she urges Figaro to look at her new hat, and a change in
harmony moves the piece to the second key area (mm. 42–49).[5] Susanna prevails in their game of "talking past each other," and Figaro
obligingly disengages himself from his counting to join her in her
gavotte for the rest of the duet. The neat gavotte phrase also provides
the critical profile for the second key area and the consolidation necessary at the return to the tonic. Taken next by Figaro solo, with the Alberti figure in the cellos and basses, it becomes the "second theme" on
the dominant (mm. 49–55), and it is the sole substantive material for
the return (m. 67). There it occurs in full orchestra, expanded by two
measures to a full four-measure period, and harmonized by the pair in
parallel thirds — the customary expression of connubial bliss. The gay
triplet fanfares at the three important cadences (mm. 34–35, 53–54,
73–80) seem intended to confirm this assessment.

Both the bourrée and the gavotte, as dances of *mezzo carattere*, are
meant to accompany "an action from ordinary life, in the character of
the comic[6] stage, a love affair, or any intrigue in which people from a
not completely ordinary kind of life are involved"; they require "elegance, pleasant manners, and fine taste."[7] Thus the dance gestures
which animate the first appearances of Susanna and Figaro on the stage

are fully in keeping with the social status of the couple: as servants of a Spanish count they would naturally, when alone, aspire to imitate the manners of their betters. The triplets at cadences round out the picture, supplying in the background a rustic lilt and exuberance, an echo of the rhythms conventionally appropriate for comic servants. But the *mezzo carattere* nature of these dance gestures also leaves open the possibility that the pair possesses a real, and not adopted, distinction, that they are by no means "ordinary people."

The duet also makes references forward to significant events later in the opera. Susanna's gavotte style, for example, becomes an important element in the second-act finale.[8] And the critical role which the gavotte rhythm plays in shaping this movement makes Susanna stand out a little from her mate. Although Figaro's obliging assumption of her music after her sharp "Guarda un po'" ("Look here a moment" — mm. 36–49) appears to be a bridegroom's tactful attention to his demanding fiancée, the next duet suggests that Figaro is only right to follow her lead; her native wit sometimes enables her to see things more clearly than he does, and he knows it.

Figaro starts the second duet with a typical contredanse figure, its four-measure phrases repeated three times with no variation. He is describing an event for which the couple's new bed-chamber is felicitously placed — the summons of the Countess's bell:

> Se a caso Madama
> La notte ti chiama:
> Din din, in due passi
> Da quella puoi gir.[9]

When Figaro mimes Susanna's response to the bell (m. 17), Mozart transforms the lilting contredanse with its strong downbeat into a march. He inflects the new gesture (♩ ♪ must become ♩ ♩) by adding a marked and steady bass line and quickening the harmonic rhythm (ex. 3–3). The quickened pace of the harmony and the truncation of normal phrase length — the march contracts to an abrupt three measures after the steady fours of the contredanse — comically suggest the convenience of the proximity: Susanna can get to her mistress in *due passi*, the "two-step" of the march. The march phrase also accomplishes the move to the second key area (F major; the duet is in B-flat). Once the dominant is attained, Figaro with painful literalness praises the advantages which the room's situation holds for him. Three times again the contredanse phrase is repeated (in inversion), again the bell rings, and Figaro mimes *his* march into the *Count's* chamber (back to the tonic, mm. 21–39).

Susanna takes up the contredanse strain and mimics Figaro, but with heavy irony. What if the Count should send you away, with the purpose

Example 3-3

Example 3-4

of securing me alone, she asks. Like Figaro she repeats the contredanse phrase three times, but with a radical change of color—a turn to G minor, which lends the requisite air of menacing import to her question (ex. 3–4a). Then, avoiding the clowning march cadence, she substitutes a recitativelike phrase back in B-flat, which moves from vi to the dominant (mm. 55–58) over the bass's sustained G (ex. 3–4b). Her omission of the march gesture underlines the seriousness of Susanna's point. And her spirit further manifests itself in the first phrase of the return,[10] with her angry octave leap on "Ed ecco in tre salti. . . ."[11] She brings Figaro to his senses.

The first duet typed the pair of comic servants, differentiating them only as male and female. This second duet distinguishes them in a more penetrating fashion. Figaro loves to playact; he is a natural mime who can summon up vividly any imaginary situation. He will resort to mimicry frequently during the opera, often to save both their skins. Here, however, his clowning only points up Susanna's deeper sensibilities. In his repetitive contredanse he slips from the elegant *mezzo carattere* bourrée of the opening into a more vulgar idiom, and adds in the tactlessly graphic march of his cadences a further thoughtless touch; his playacting verges on irresponsible buffoonery. The march betrays his sense of importance at being the Count's favored servant, betrothed to the Countess's favorite; he delivers himself and Susanna to their service with a pompously ceremonial flourish.

Susanna's imitation of the contredanse in minor exhibits the grace of thoughtfulness. She displays her dismay with a gentle irony, leaving the impression that she is open to a wider range of feelings than is Figaro. Although she may be proud to serve the Countess, she is disturbed to find Figaro, blinded by his pride in service, blithely serving her up to the Count as a ceremonial victim; no pride would make her serve Figaro-style. When, clearly finding the low comic march distasteful, she substitutes her pointed recitativelike phrase, all sympathies cannot help but be with her. Now the situation demands from Figaro a response which will measure up to her intelligence and wit.

"Se vuol ballare": Figaro's Dancing School

Figaro does not disappoint. His conversation with Susanna after the second duet has deflated his self-esteem, and has left him very angry with the Count. When he solicitously says to Susanna, "Corragio, mio tesoro," she leaves him with a pointed "E tu, cervello,"[12] pricking him with a further reminder of his fatuity. He pulls himself together to launch a venomous blast at the Count, treating the Count's proper music with an irony well matched to Susanna's dark parody of Figaro's musical invention in the second duet. He is indeed finally using his head.

The cavatina opens as a minuet — not the stately theatrical type, but the muscular and spare, slightly faster quarter-note pattern more likely to have been danced on social occasions. Figaro invites the Count to dance, with himself as accompanist:

> Se vuol ballare,
> Signor Contino,
> Il chitarrino
> Le suonerò.[13]

Pizzicato strings simulate the guitar accompaniment while horn dou-
blings underline the noble, ceremonial nature of the dance. It is a tribute to Figaro's wit and control that after his bitter recitative he sings not
in unbridled anger, but ironically, cloaking his insolence in the noble
politesse of the minuet. His manner of address is highly insulting — "Signor Contino," or "my pretty little Count" — but to the unsuspecting it
might appear at first to be the unctuous invitation of a sycophant.[14]

As the piece moves toward the dominant,[15] Figaro becomes the dancing master, the situation his dancing school: with the prey lured into the
trap, the trapper can turn teacher. His anger finds expression in the
orchestra now, in the menacing string tremolos and repeated notes in
the horns, but Figaro himself still preserves all decorum and goes on
with the dance. He offers to teach the Count the *capriola*, a theatrical
leaping-step:

> Se vuol venire
> Nella mia scuola,
> La capriola
> Le insegnerò.[16]

There may indeed be an actual choreographical cue for the *capriola* in
the music of "Se vuol ballare," in the dramatic weak-beat melodic
leaps[17] of a third and a sixth occurring in the four-measure extension of
the cadence of the first period (mm. 16, 18), and again, to accompany
Figaro's second rendering of the *capriola* stanza, at the first cadences on
the dominant (mm. 38, 40; ex. 3–5). In any event, the implication of
Figaro's words is obvious: "If you intend to come poaching on my
ground, I'll make you jump." His threat is reinforced by both a musical
and a verbal pun: the insistent horn calls become a leer at the hopeful
cuckolder,[18] and the nature of the capers Figaro promises to put the
Count through insultingly suggests his adversary's undignified ruttish-
ness (*capriola*, "goat-leap," is derived from the Italian *capra*, "goat").

Figaro has fashioned his caress-turned-insult entirely within the
rhythmic framework of the minuet. Although the dance has grown
beyond the eight-plus-eight-measure phrases of the usual dance tune,
still the two-measure rhythmic units of the *pas de menuet* have been retained; all the extensions are danceable. Now for a brief moment — the
X-section — Figaro steps outside the dance in order to meditate his re-

Example 3-5

Example 3-6

FIGARO

L'ar-te scher-men-do, L'ar-te ado-pran-do, di qua pu-gnen-do, di là scher-zan-do

venge. Pausing for a moment on V of vi, the point of furthest remove
from the tonic, he snaps back to the tonic with a *Presto* 2/4 contredanse,
in which he lists the Count's various devious talents and his own plans
to overturn them (ex. 3–6). The contredanse is a bold and clever invention here, working in both its affect and its conventional social usage to
complete the picture of Figaro's revenge. The scene Figaro has been en-
acting — that of the dancing master dragging his recalcitrant pupil
through the paces of social dance — would naturally end with a contredanse, the dance which regularly followed the minuet in the middle-
class society of the dance halls. In the salons of the Count's *ancien
régime*, however, the minuet stood alone, a dignified couple-dance performed by practiced dancers; the Count would be unlikely to join the
throng dancing the relatively rowdy contredanse. Figaro in his vivid
imaginings of revenge has transported the Count into an alien social
setting, with rules of behavior appropriate to the more "democratized"
city life Figaro must have led before coming to the aristocratic seclusion
of Count Almaviva's castle; he has lured his victim onto his own turf.

Figaro then uses the contredanse to move in for the attack. The simple rhythms, strong downbeat, and rapid steps of the dance suggest intoxication or dizziness: the contredanse of Don Giovanni's famous
"Champagne" aria ("Fin ch'han dal vino," *Don Giovanni*, I, 11) is often
taken as a musical evocation of inebriation. In Figaro's contredanse the
singer, unintoxicated himself, is attempting to induce the state in another. He stuns his hapless victim with a relentless litany of his own
malignant tricks:

> L'arte schermendo,
> L'arte adoprando,
> Di qua pungendo,
> Di là scherzando,
> Tutte le macchine
> Rovescerò.[19]

When in measure 80 he repeats the list again, the dancing master has
become choreographer. The tricks become couples separating from the
throng of dancers to solo now from the left, now from the right (a choreography suggested by the directions "di qua . . . di là"). The music
supports Figaro's choreography skillfully. His vocal line employs a

Example 3-7

quasi-*Brechung*[20] figuration which suggests two voices alternating in the list, now from here, now from there; the same division obtains in the accompaniment, which alternates between full orchestra, *forte*, and *piano* winds and brass (ex. 3–7):[21] The entire section lasts only eight measures, but it shows Figaro at the height of his fantasy. A good Figaro on stage must be both dancer and mime: having performed the minuet and *capriola*, he now becomes a diabolical ringmaster, cracking his whip to summon up the evidence first from this side, then from that. He exits triumphantly after a coda which recapitulates the sequence of minuet and contredanse (m. 104). After the dazzling flourishes of the contredanse, the sarcasm in the tight control of the minuet is all the more menacing.

The first two scenes of *Figaro* combine for an opening which is as throughcomposed and galvanizing in its own way as is the brilliant opening scene of *Don Giovanni*. Focusing on a contretemps in their relationship, Mozart reveals all that needs to be known about Figaro and Susanna, shaping the scenes with the simple device of pairing dances — bourrée and gavotte, contredanse and march, minuet and contredanse. Although their natures differ, the couple has a real harmony. Susanna is a little wiser than Figaro, and her judgment and taste provide a center for his powers without which he would lose all perspective. But Figaro will follow Susanna and learn from her. Having once seen the ramifications of a situation, he faces it with a wit and boldness of imagination which are as attractive in their own way as are Susanna's gentler virtues. Susanna's greater sensitivity must not diminish Figaro too much in stature; it is their union, after all, which is the concern here.

Bartolo and Marcellina

The conspirators Dr. Bartolo and his (in his own words) *serva antica* Marcellina are introduced next, as they plot to thwart the planned marriage. Bartolo announces his motive in an aside — to get even with Figaro for having helped Almaviva marry his ward Rosina.[22] These two bourgeois enemies of the servant couple just introduced are pointedly, one by one, compared with Susanna and Figaro, to their own detriment. First Bartolo's set-piece revenge aria "La vendetta" (I, 4) throws Figaro's particular virtues into sharp relief. In a white-note march the good doctor rather ponderously delivers himself of his "exalted passion," his conventional fist-shaking no match for the inventive wrath of "Se vuol ballare."[23]

Marcellina's motive is, of course, to marry Figaro. She and Susanna engage in a duel of *politesse* after Marcellina blocks Susanna's exit, wishing to provoke her. In their duet two rhythmic motives from the opening number of the opera — the bourrée and the peasant triplets — project at once surface civility and the honest feminine venom seething underneath. The *mezzo carattere* bourrée, all "elegance and fine manners," is layered over a rhythmic background of constant triplets: (ex. 3–8). Both rhythms occur almost exclusively in the orchestra; neither woman sings the bourrée motive, and only Susanna takes up the triplets, as a cadential figure in measures 59 and 63. The bourrée rhythm, abstracted from its usual dance phrase structure, is open-ended, not foursquare; cadences occur at the pleasure of the insults, not of four-measure phrases. At the outset the fourth measure of each bourrée phrase is suppressed, resulting in an overlap in the rhythmic scansion:

1 2 3 (4)   1 2 3 4
   1 2 3 (4)   Open-ended and riding on the dominant, these phrases resemble the vaudeville "vamp-till-ready" music which accompanies a stand-up comic, making cadences coincident with punch lines. Such music accompanies with equal efficiency the hissed insults of two women jockeying for precedence. As the insults reach fever pitch and the piece turns back toward the tonic, any sense of a suppressed dance structure disappears altogether. Eight times the bourrée motive is repeated (mm. 21–28), each time reaching one step higher. As it achieves and outlines the V^7 of A major, the original tonic (m. 28), Susanna delivers the vicious "Di Spagna l'amore,"[24] coming too close to home even for the jaded Marcellina. The women drop all pretext to *politesse*, the

Example 3-8

bourrée motive disappearing along with their frozen smiles. The orchestral triplets rise to the surface, and the ladies trade open insults until the final cadence.[25]

The text suggests Susanna as victor in the struggle. Her trump card
is the single phrase *L'età*, the time-honored "age-before-beauty" riposte.
Hearing it, Marcellina mutters under her breath, knowing she is fast
losing the little composure left to her.[26] Susanna, mocking Marcellina's
age and her pretensions to book-learning, crows "Sibilla decrepita!/Da
rider mi fa."[27] Her triplet flourish to the mythological insult (added the
second and third time around) is a triumphant gesture. Marcellina
weakly clings to the remnants of her tarnished refinement, letting Susanna finish with an ungenteel but victorious toss of the head. According to the stage directions, Marcellina "parte infuriata."[28]

"Non so più": Cherubino's Poetry

Cherubino makes his first entrance as Susanna is angrily reflecting
on Marcellina's pretensions:

> Va' là, vecchia pedante,
> Dottoressa arrogante!
> Perchè hai letto due libri,
> E seccato Madama in gioventù. . . .[29]

Cherubino brings with him a literary aura of a gentler sort: while Marcellina clings to pedantry as the emblem of her superiority, love-struck
Cherubino is not learned, but a natural poet. He hands Susanna a love
song he has written, either to one woman or to them all (he does not
say, nor does it seem to matter). When she asks him what to do with it,
he gives her leave, with "transports of joy" as the stage directions have
it, to read it to every woman in the palace.[30] When she chides him for
his impetuousness,[31] he answers her in song. Unlike "Voi che sapete,"
Cherubino's rendition (in act II) of his own composition, accompanied
by Susanna on the Countess's guitar, the lovely "Non so più" is not intended as a real performance. Yet it has much in common with the later
aria-staged-as-love-song. Obvious similarities are their closely related
key signatures ("Non so più" in E-flat major, "Voi che sapete" in B-flat),
their duple meters, and the prominence in them both of winds and
horns. But more significantly, in an opera whose arias are dominated by
dance rhythms, both pieces are clearly meant to be apprehended as
sung poems; measured words, rather than measured gestures, seem to
be the motive power of Cherubino's song.

Much remains to be said about Cherubino; he does not display his
full nature in this aria. A page in Almaviva's castle, and probably the

Countess's godchild,[32] he seems at first to be only a minor character, a member of a detachable subplot. Yet he gradually acquires transcendent importance as a touchstone for all the other characters in the opera. His romp with Figaro at the end of this act and his performance of his own *canzona* in act II reveal his changeling nature more fully. But "Non so più," the aria which introduces Cherubino, contains hints of it, all bound up in the literary quality of his idiom.

"Non so più" is divided into two sections. The text of the first half of the aria consists of two stanzas each containing three ten-syllable lines or *decasillabi*, and a fourth with nine syllables:

> Non so più cosa son, cosa faccio . . .
> Or di fuoco, ora sono di ghiaccio . . .
> Ogni donna cangiar di colore,
> Ogni donna mi fa palpitar.
>
> Solo ai nomi d'amor, di diletto
> Mi si turba, mi s'altera il petto,
> E a parlare mi sforza d'amore
> Un desio ch'io non posso spiegar![33]

In rhyme scheme the two stanzas are united by end rhyme — aa*bc*, dd*bc*. The first three lines of each stanza have feminine rhymes, but the c rhyme (palpi*tar*, spie*gar*) is masculine. Mozart sets the poem in a quick *alla breve* with a single bass note "plucked" on every beat while the other strings "strum" an accompaniment; the orchestra is a stand-in for the performer's guitar.

Traditionally in popular musical settings of Italian poetry the metrical foot (anapests here) established the basic rhythm of each member, setting up a "rhythmic mode" to be repeated through the line; meanwhile the number of syllables dictated the primary and secondary stresses and the cadence.[34] The same principle seems to be in operation here. A rhythmic germ with an anapestic shape, ♫ | ♩, is repeated three times in each line, with a secondary stress on the third syllable and a primary stress and cadence on the ninth. Each of the first three lines closes with a feminine ending, ♫ ♩ ♫♩ ♫| ♩ —a typical *deca-sillabo* —but the anapest is preserved in the fourth for a masculine ending and thus a full stop. In order to direct attention to its integrity as a unit line of a poem, each line is carefully set off from the next by a quarter-note rest (ex. 3–9).[35] Furthermore, all repetitions are of whole lines, and not of single words or phrases abstracted from the rhythm of their lines, as would occur in most arias.

All these elements work together to effect our apprehension of regular poetic rhythms in the aria. But there is a musical problem with the

Example 3-9

straightforward setting of a series of lines or of stanzas: "one thing after another" militates against the dramatic curve of a piece which is necessary to give it a conviction of beginning, middle, and end. In a poem read aloud, meaning, and, to a lesser extent, rhythmic variations in the prosody, provide a sense of crisis and resolution where it is wanted (as it isn't always in a lyric poem). But in an operatic aria, particularly in Classic music, where climax always has to do with the dramatization of a departure from and return to a certain harmonic place, a series of lines does not make a period, nor a series of stanzas a fully shaped whole; Mozart always has to alter the line and verse forms slightly to provide some contraction in the material, some critical imbalance which creates the demand for balance — regularity — to return. To shape the first stanza into a period, Mozart works an augmentation, with syncopation, on the anapestic line:

This transmutation of the regular anapests (mm. 9–15) permits a sense of closure at stanza's end while still carrying a suggestion of the poetic meter of the verse.

The second stanza raises the problem of the shaping of the larger-scale formal elements of the aria. Mozart decides to locate the rhythmic crisis of "Non so più" early, in the move to the dominant, and creates it by first exaggerating regularity, then breaching it. He sets the first two lines of the new stanza carefully as lines of poetry, but in a somewhat different manner than before: the short syllables of the head anapest are lengthened to occupy an entire measure, a metrical adjustment which doubles the breathing space between unit lines (two beats instead of one), and results in leisurely — musically uncompelling — phrases of three plus three,

These relaxed phrases, however, create a launching pad for the motion to the second key area, a motion paralleled by a transformation of the poetic diction, which is charming and dramatically apt. His words about the movements of his own passion move Cherubino out of the measured artifice of his verse to sing in a more direct and passionate style. The three-measure phrases quicken to urgent and breathless two-measure units,[36] the harmony, also quickening, darkens to a diminished-seventh chord on the word *òesio* ("desire"),[37] and *òesio* is itself repeated a fourth higher as the E-natural slips down to an E-flat and the beginning of a strong B-flat cadential formula (ex. 3–10). The repetition of the word *òesio* is governed by an exclusively musical necessity; for the first time in the aria a single word is repeated, lifted from its unit length of poetry, and it weakens the illusion that the singer is performing a *canzona*. But it brings a passionate intensity to this important cadence which would be lacking if the strumming metrical regularity were retained. Thus in retrospect the introduction of the leisurely three-measure line length at the beginning of this period serves to intensify the effect of the contractions of desire at its final cadence. The great wit in this manipulation lies in Mozart's realization that after the lulling regularity of the poetic lines, phrases measured purely musically — "aria-style" — would appear as the accents of true passion, rendering the final cadence on the dominant "heartfelt" and thus structurally strong.[38]

"Non so più" has no formal X-section, moving immediately back to E-flat and a repetition of the opening period. The fifty-one measures ending with the repetition of the opening material represent the main body of the aria, a strophic song adapted by clever modifications to the exigencies of the key-area process. The forty-nine measures which remain, an extended coda, introduce the poet Cherubino's special subject matter — the pastoral. His text moves love out into the country:

> Parlo d'amor vegliando,
> Parlo d'amor sognando:
> All'acque, all'ombre, ai monti,

Example 3-10

Example 3-11

Ai fiori, all'erbe, ai fonti,
All'eco, all'aria, ai venti
Che il suon de' vani accenti
Portano via con sè.[39]

The second time through the text is set to a musette with tonic pedal point, Cherubino and the violins taking the skirl (mm. 72–80; ex. 3–11). The pastoral affect, which comes to dominate the opera in its last two acts, makes a modest entrance here. Cherubino, the young court page, would surely have read or heard some pastoral poetry. Here he mimics his models, naively imitating Tasso perhaps, or another Italian poet of the pastoral mode. Yet the literary reference, and its support in Mozart's *canzona*-like setting of the text, are not merely for the sake of a convincing characterization of the adolescent poet. In "Voi che sapete" the literary frame broadens to include Dante, and Cherubino's *donne*, by then no longer the vague generality "women" but clearly Susanna and the Countess, will receive from him homage of a profounder sort. In "Non so più" the tremulous youth who, if no one else will listen, tells his love to himself,[40] becomes a creature in his own pastoral landscape; the poet is rightly not quite at home in the daylight world of Almaviva's castle.

Trio: "Così fan tutte"

The recitative following Cherubino's aria breaks its beguiling, otherworldly mood; the atmosphere turns suddenly malignant, bristling with suspicions and raw nerves. At the sudden entrance of the Count, Cherubino hides behind an armchair, leaving the Count to make leering love to Susanna until the entrance of Basilio the pander forces him to Cherubino's place (Cherubino having leapt adroitly to the protection of the seat of the same chair, and having been covered with miscellaneous articles of clothing by Susanna). Basilio as go-between continues the grotesque courtship until the Count, outraged by Basilio's invidious insinuations about Cherubino and the Countess, reveals himself in anger with the cry "Scacciate il seduttor!"[41] With Cherubino left to be discovered (the natural climax of the piece), the trio begins.

It is an open question whether the Count has a bad character or is merely insensitive and bullheaded. But Basilio leaves no doubt about himself: he is slippery, malicious, and a little feline. The knowing cynicism of his trilling "Così fan tutte le belle!/Non c'è alcuna novità"[42] (mm. 155ff, especially mm. 161–67) is banal; hardly a disinterested observer, he is a catalyst of viciousness, a gadfly of misfortune. Cherubino's *donne* he contemptuously styles *le belle*, distinguishing them for their habits of deviousness and betrayal rather than for their power to move.

Again it is an open question whether Basilio teaches the Count, or if low characters merely seek like company. The Count does appear in this trio to pick up a particular rhythmic mannerism from Basilio — an oily and sanctimonious *alla breve* which he will find to be an effective weapon later in the opera. At the beginning of the trio the Count displays only agitation and anger, and the first fifteen measures of the piece are jagged and disjunct, beginning on the dominant with no strong tonic until measure 15. The strings play a suspenseful broken scale (probably to choreograph the Count's slow but menacing advance toward Basilio), and the Count adds angry interjections in dotted rhythms. Basilio provides the first material with any shape to it. In measure 16 he intrudes a mincing *alla breve* — again a broken scale, but in smooth half-note motion and downward, proclaiming with a false fastidiousness his dismay about witnessing the embarrassing scene. Characters who use the dignified *alla breve* usually put the brakes on more restless rhythms, moving serene and sedate through the most snarled of imbroglios; a paradigm of *alla breve* movement is the music of the Commendatore, the "Stone Guest" of the last act of *Don Giovanni*, with its naturally weighty dignity. Basilio is on the contrary a spiteful lightweight, with his high tenor voice and his habit of giving every second measure of the *alla breve* a mincing feminine ending; his assumed dignity is a mock of dignity itself (ex. 3–12). But even parodistic *alla breve* effectively claps a lid of forced *politesse* on troubled situations, driving persons of naturally dignified manners to accede to a surface judiciousness and restraint. The Count learns the technique from Basilio, if he did not know it already, and uses it often later in the opera to oppress the Countess when forthrightness and straight-speaking threaten to overwhelm him.

Example 3-12

Here we get a comically menacing foretaste of the rhythm: Basilio's version occurs three more times, each one in a different dramatic context and marking a different moment in the harmonic process. The first repetition occurs just after Susanna's fainting spell has brought out a churlish solicitude in the Count and Basilio. The sycophant pander, hoping to pacify Susanna's anger so as not to lose any ground gained by the Count in his pursuit of her, uses the *alla breve* to make a false disclaimer about the activities of the page — "Ah, del paggio quel ch'ho detto/Era solo un mio sospetto!"[43] His music (beginning in E-flat major) closes the X-section, and in the next phrase Susanna turns the piece back to the tonic (mm. 92–100). The second repeat of the *alla breve* music is given to the Count in the middle of the return. Telling the tale of his discovery of Cherubino in Barbarina's cottage, he uses the mincing rhythms to mimic his own stealthy tiptoeing toward Cherubino's pretended hiding place (mm. 129–38). The page of course just happens to be hiding there again — a nice sight gag, which crystallizes the Count's already considerable anger. Basilio is delighted; although concerned to protect negotiations between the Count and Susanna, in his natural maliciousness he prefers situations of maximum discomfort for all concerned. "Ah, meglio ancora"[44] he gloats, and repeats his disclaimer about the page "con malignità," as the stage directions have it. The now obvious untruth of the declaration provides the ultimate occasion for the hypocrite's *alla breve* (mm. 175–82, after the return to the tonic). The trio ends with the three characters frozen in their respective postures of anger, fear, and spiteful delight.

As always in Mozart's great comic ensembles, harmonic and dynamic necessities merge admirably with dramatic portraiture. The inchoate material of the Count's opening is prodded into neat periodic shapes at the return (m. 101): his eleven-measure opening phrase is condensed into a trim four.[45] Material which was originally interjections in dotted rhythms floating over broken string flourishes has now become a powerful *alla breve*, with those same flourishes harnessed as accompaniment. This consolidation is a requirement for demarcating a crucial event in the harmonic process, and it also makes a good dramatic point: it shows the Count collecting his diffuse and nervous anger into a far more powerful and directed instrument, perhaps implying in the process his need of Basilio's malignity to shore him up, if not to educate him in malice. Almaviva has hit his stride, and despite the surprise in store for him (Cherubino in the chair), he manages to dominate the rest of the trio.

But, in keeping with his pander's role, it is Basilio who provides the essential material for the trio. He introduces not only the controlled *alla breve* style, but also a fifteen-measure *alla breve* phrase with pseudo-

Example 3-13

imitative beginning and detachable chromatic cadence (mm. 43–57),
which becomes important cadential material for the movement. The
progression of the cadence is simply a series of secondary dominants
preceded by an augmented sixth, but it introduces a delicious chromatic
raised fifth and fourth (C-sharp and B-natural in the F-major version of
the phrase, mm. 51–52; ex. 3–13). It is first — as a consolidating cadence for the second key area — the music of titillated solicitude with
which Basilio and the Count face the spectacle of the unconscious Susanna.[46] The staggered rests of the middle four-measure unit (mm.
47–50) are directly mimetic of her beating heart, a pulse the two
bounders are all too anxious to feel: "Come, oddio, le batte il cor!" they
exclaim.[47] This progression turns up next in the X-section after Susanna
comes to, where it is depressed a whole step from F to E-flat major by
its introduction as a deceptive cadence to her angry augmented sixth
and dominant of G minor.[48] The depression of the phrase suggests the
men's phony gravity, while the swoony chromatic cadence is now the
leer with which Basilio, that defamer of female *onor*, promises Susanna
that hers is intact.[49] The cadence is finally detached from the rest of
the phrase near the end of the return, in order to provide the node
around which the B-flat cadential action crystallizes. Repeated in two
places, the second time twice (mm. 172–75, 195–201), its chromaticism
now serves to suggest Susanna's apprehension ("Giusti Dei! che mai
sarà!"[50]), and she takes the progression's leading voice. At the same
time, the addition of the third singer of the trio to this cadential phrase,
especially since it is a feminine voice, in a high register, gives it a completion which proclaims it as the cadence of final closure for the key-
area form.

Susanna, in the trio victim and pursued, is given little other material
of any substance. Instead her music provides the transition from one
harmonic place to another: her fear begins a move from B-flat major to
F minor (m. 24), her faint clears it to F major, the second key (m. 43),
when she comes to, her gambit of outraged honor[51] starts the X-section
(m. 65), and her E-flat (m. 96) turns the F major into a dominant again.
In fact the trio is devised to obtain maximum contrast between the
men's solidly constructed phrases and Susanna's inchoate and harmonically insecure interjections. Continually the men bear down on her;

sourcefulness she barely struggles out of their grasp.
n no way "developmental," but presents two full and
changed; once Susanna has destroyed the dominant,
easure phrase and Basilio's mincing *alla breve* return
or, and the depressed E-flat becomes in retrospect a
area before the B-flat return. Anger, solicitude, and
one another in the men's music as they pursue her,
having her always at their advantage no matter who is culpable. After
Cherubino's bewitching song about the delights of being moved by
women, Basilio's sardonic epigram about *le belle* and the Count's cutting
"Onestissima signore"[52] obtrude the darker comic reality.

Two Celebrations

The next important use of a dance gesture is a public one — a feint
organized by Figaro to trap the Count unaware. He intends to force
from the Count a public pledge for the wedding of his two servants, a
wedding free from the feudal *droit de seigneur* which the Count has of-
ficially abolished, but longs to reassert. Figaro brings with him a chorus
of *contadini* and *contadine* scattering flowers in their path and singing
grandiloquent praise of the Count: in his magnanimity he has preserved
for them "D'un più bel fiore/L'alma candor."[53] The chorus sings a pastorale, the simple 6/8 shepherd's song which expresses "rural or pastoral
innocence." It moves simply, with some suggestion of the skirl of the
musette. There is one brief chromatic turn, on the word *fiore*: a C-sharp
slipped into a G major scale descending from E to G is harmonized as
V^7 of V^7. Rhythmically the most elaborate passage, it sets the most
florid part of the text (ex. 3–14). Musically the moment is breath-
takingly lovely, although the pious circumspection with which the peasants deliver up this piece of doggerel about the *virgo intacta* to the libertine Count must bring poorly suppressed smiles to their faces. The rest
of the chorus is a setting for this bright jewel of a phrase. Diatonic and
rhythmically foursquare, it moves to a final cadence cleverly truncated
by overlappings:

measures	26	27	28	29	30	31	32
	4			1	2	3	4
	1	2	3	4			

A lengthy repetition of the symmetries of the opening phrase might try
the Count's patience excessively; enough is enough.

Figaro well understands the value of a ceremony — that no one par-
ticipating in a formal observance will dare to sink below the level of its
formality. The stylized gestures and symmetrical cuts of time shaped by

Example 3-14

dance provide the ideal backdrop for such a public enactment. The innocence of the participants, at least for the moment,[54] makes the situation all the more difficult for the Count to withstand. Although he has not yet encountered Figaro the dancing master, Almaviva immediately appreciates Figaro's talents as stage manager. He testily exclaims "Cos'è questa commedia?" and later "Diabolica astuzia!"[55] The situation has trapped him successfully; he makes no other unguarded statements, except for a whispered prayer for Marcellina's speedy arrival. His forced role as benevolent master requires him to deliver to the assembled multitude a speech compounded of sugarcoated evasions and lying promises. But after the exit of the peasants, who formally frame the ceremony by repeating the whole chorus, the Count abandons this public face and parries Figaro's attack. His counterthrust, while it does not damage Figaro and Susanna directly, strikes at their affections; it spells exile from the castle for Cherubino.

The end of the first act is all Figaro's. Following the Count's announcement that Cherubino must leave the castle, Figaro, fond of the page and amused at — some would say jealous of — his adolescent love pangs, wants to sweeten the bitterness of his banishment from his amorous playground. He sings for Cherubino an aria which contains consolation, paternal advice, and encouragement, interlarded with affectionate jibes at the boy's youth and cynical comment on the nature of that glorious endeavor, war. Since Figaro is always actor and illusionist, Cherubino can't simply walk off to war; he must march off triumphantly, accompanied by an entire military band which Figaro has summoned up from nowhere for the occasion. "Non più andrai" (I, 9) is an exuberant romp for the trio (Susanna is on stage, although she does not sing), and a coming-of-age for a dreamy adolescent engineered by his affectionate but realistic "older brother."

Nothing about this picture is mistaken, as far as it goes, nor does Mozart's music belie it. The aria, in C major, is cast in rondo form. In its main section and first episode Figaro describes Cherubino as he is now, and in the other sections as he will be on the field of battle, both in a comically exaggerated style. Of Cherubino now, Figaro says:

Non più andrai, farfallone amoroso,
Notte e giorno d'intorno girando,
Delle belle turbando il riposo,
Narcisetto, Adoncino d'amor.

Non più avrai questi bei pennacchini,
Quel cappello leggero e galante,
Quella chioma, quell'aria brillante,
Quel vermiglio, donnesco color.[56]

The music which sets the first stanza is a march in 4/4 time with a dot-ted upbeat (see ex. 2–34j, p. xx, for the opening motive of "Non più andrai" set by Mozart as a 2/4 contredanse). It consists almost exclu-sively of C-major triads, with a rousing military fanfare to the words "disturbing the beauties' beauty sleep," a musical mixed metaphor which becomes a substantive trope both in the aria and in the opera (the appellation *belle* loses its cynical edge in Figaro's affectionate ban-ter). Here (mm. 6–9) the mixture is one of amorous language with mili-tary music, whereas in the first episode of the rondo (mm. 14ff) two musical styles mingle, and amorous music insinuates itself into the mar-tial ambience: describing Cherubino's appearance in a gently mocking idiom, Figaro alternates a gavotte rhythm with the orchestra's march (ex. 3–15). A "Narcisetto, Adoncino d'amor" about to enter the lists deserves a mixture of erotic and military gestures; the march and the coy gavotte with its pastoral and amorous connotations are a wholly ap-propriate conjunction here, and Figaro revels in them.

The gavotte quickly dissolves into a dominant pedal, which calls back the original march theme (m. 31). Figaro's fancy is afire: after repeat-ing the march he launches an enormously expanded episode (mm. 43ff)—the description of Cherubino at the front—returning to the same dominant pedal and bedroom march (m. 78) and adding a coda.[57] Originally the march gesture, found principally in the strings, was merely the orchestral accompaniment; now it becomes a presence on stage, brought to life as a real military march. Mozart calls on the full

Example 3-15

Example 3-16

colors of the orchestra: strings alternate with winds and brass, including trumpets, and the tympani sound for the first time. Figaro no longer
sings a human vocal line, but instead imitates a trumpet voicing battle
calls (ex. 3–16). In measure 61 the strings drop out entirely and a full
military band plays a new march, suitable for the field and not at all
singable. In the coda this field march returns, and the stage directions
read "Partono tutti alla militare"; [58] in this playful aria about playing, the
imaginative has drawn playfully near to the real, with the help of the
"realistic" rhythms and colors of occasional music.

   "Non più andrai" is an utterly enjoyable *divertissement*, a happy interlude amid the harsher realities of life under the watchful eye of Count
Almaviva. Yet it is often suggested that more goes on in the aria than
appears at first glance. Some have interpreted it as an attack on Cherubino — teasing banter meant to rub salt in the wounds — which is moti-
vated by Figaro's jealousy of the boy's appeal for the ladies or by a
plebeian's resentment of the aristocratic page. [59] In the latter case an
aside which Figaro makes to Cherubino just before the aria — "Io vo'
parlati/Pria che tu parta" [60] — is taken as a bullying invitation to a later
showdown, whispered so that Susanna can't hear. That aside, however,
has a further audience — the Count and Basilio. Although many edi-
tions have them leave the stage just before the aside, after the Count's
gloating "Inaspettato è il colpo," [61] in the 1786 libretto (and in the corresponding scene from *Le mariage de Figaro*) they do not leave, and indeed
witness the whole of Figaro's performance; the scene is rarely played
this way, and loses most of its significance as a result. A scrap of dialogue from the beginning of act II clarifies the intent of the aside
immediately. Figaro is expounding to the Countess the plan for the
Count's humiliation, which involves dressing Cherubino as Susanna
and sending him to the rendezvous with the Count. (Although later this
particular arrangement is abandoned, it anticipates the events in the
garden at the end of act IV.) Referring to the conversation he suggested
to Cherubino just before "Non più andrai," Figaro says to the Countess
"Il picciol Cherubino,/*Per mio consiglio* non ancor partito. . . ." [62] He
plainly wanted words with the boy here in act I not in order to vent his
jealousy or class resentment, but to keep Cherubino from leaving the
castle so that they could lay plans about the plot he mentions in act II.
Thus all through "Non più andrai" Figaro is sworn to keep Cherubino

back from battle; he has no intention of letting the Count disturb the ornamental life of the "amorous butterfly, flitting around night and day." In the course of the plot the lad will have to be disguised as a maiden, but the task takes almost no effort; already his cheeks have "that blushing, womanly color." By celebrating the imminent departure as if in rueful assent to it, Figaro's affectionate romp with Cherubino is meant to keep the watching Count off the scent.

Yet the artful dodge has even deeper overtones, which a few words about Cherubino may illuminate. Cherubino is indeed a strange invention; some spectators find him repellent, others merely silly. Certainly da Ponte and Mozart went out of their way to underline his mixed nature. Early adolescence is a peculiarly amorphous time of life, when youth is androgynous and undelimited — unsure of what it is or what to expect from the people around it. Cherubino knows of himself only that he does not know himself, and he is strikingly undiscriminating in his relationships. "I no longer know what I am, what I do," he confesses; "every woman makes me blush, makes me tremble." The decision to compose the role for a young woman did more than simply ensure a convincing portrait of adolescence, however. It kept Cherubino from being particularized and "embodied," located in a real place and time like the other characters in the opera. He is the only character who is "placeless," not generated and defined by the manners of a particular social world (which is one reason for his failure, when left to himself, to dance, although twice he sings; for to affect a particular social dance gesture would mark him as a member of a particular class). More precisely, he is "out of place," for he is not in his proper home, and his genealogy is left unclear.

Figaro's description of Cherubino in his "battle song" goes a long way toward explaining some of the paradoxes which surround him. There is much about the "little cherub" which evokes another moonstruck child, an antique deity — the figure of Eros-Cupid. The imagery of the libretto of *Le nozze di Figaro* is peculiarly classical, the sarcastic references to Bacchus and the Sibyl in the *politesse* duet being one very minor example. Much of this language centers around Cherubino himself; even Basilio calls him "Cherubino, Cherubin d'amore" (I, vii, 158–59), hinting at the connection with Eros, and to Figaro in this aria he is a "little Narcissus, little Adonis of love." The classical and pastoral were for the eighteenth century two genres inextricably mixed. The shepherd-lovers of late eighteenth-century pastoral pieces (usually, of course, musettes, gavottes, and musette-gavottes) are inevitably given classical-sounding names, often drawn directly from the pastoral poetry of Theocritus and Virgil; they are distant descendants of that tradition. At the end of the opera Figaro is moved to draw the connection himself: after hearing

Susanna sing her beautiful pastorale, "Deh, vieni" (IV, 27), musings on the theme of the correspondence between the twilit night and the state of a lover's soul (and meant to tease Figaro for the absurdity of his distrust of her), he is prompted, having come to interrupt her purported rendezvous, ironically to style himself as Vulcan, and Susanna and the unknown lover as Venus and Mars. The pastoral diction and musette of "Non so più" place Cherubino squarely in the Arcadian tradition; as Eros he presides over the couples in the opera — the indigenous deity of pastoral love.

The pastoral Eros of *Le nozze di Figaro* is very different from whatever Eros presides, for example, in *Don Giovanni*. There Eros wounds, and often disastrously; he strikes Donna Elvira just as Virgil's Cupid cunningly pierced the breast of Dido with a fatal love for Aeneas. In *Figaro*, on the other hand, Eros is love through his very vulnerability. In his openness to all love and love for all, he touches Susanna, Figaro, and the Countess, and makes the Count suspicious and edgy, although Almaviva is plainly never quite sure why he should distrust the young page. The Count ought to worry less about the possibility of Cherubino seducing the Countess and more about the efficacy of Cherubino's selfless brand of love, which he is unfortunately incapable of comprehending. In the dogma of Cherubino's eros, being moved by someone is equally as important as one's own success in moving the other toward oneself. Cherubino celebrates passion in the strict sense of the word — the joys and pains of suffering the object of one's affections to move one. When in the finale of the second act the Count gasps out "Rosina" (II, 15, 229–30), he is beginning to learn about this "being affected."

Cherubino's relationships with Susanna, the Countess, and Figaro reveal the many facets of his special "affection." One erotic thread runs through them all: an aliveness to the physical qualities of the beloved — his walk, his gestures, the sound of his voice — which causes a mere glimpse of him to give one an involuntary start. Cherubino presides over many relationships which are not explicitly erotic. He is fond of Susanna, and calls her *sorella* ("sister"), she dresses him up like a doll, and they banter and plot like brother and sister. When in act II they are caught in danger together they behave like two frightened children. Yet Susanna affectionately appreciates Cherubino's beauty; his physical presence moves her. "Che vezzo, che figura!/Mirate il bricconcello,/Mirate quanto è bello!"[63] she cries. Cherubino's affection for the Countess is more explicitly erotic; he steals her ribbon for a magic talisman, and she is obviously fluttered by his presence. When Susanna admires him the Countess turns away abruptly, snapping "Quante buffonerie!"[64] as though to remind herself to keep her distance from the charming boy. Rosina is not a middle-aged matron, but a young girl recently married, and suffering from the inattention of a philandering husband. But Mozart and da Ponte treat the erotic side of their affection more delicately than did Beaumarchais,[65] combining it with Cherubino's hero worship of his handsome and benevolent godmother; if anything, Cherubino's stammering when he speaks to the Countess makes her seem more matronly than she actually is.

The affection between Susanna and the Countess also patterns itself on Cherubino's eros: awakened by each other's admirable qualities, they move toward each other and to friendship. All the characters in the opera find themselves moved in some way by the absurd child. The Count's exasperation at Cherubino's ubiquity goes deeper than he realizes. When he cries "E mi farà il destino/Ritrovar questo paggio in ogni loco!"[66] the Count is only admitting to the child's disturbing influence on all the loves and friendships in the opera. Despite his awkwardness and naiveté, his constant facility for annoying, he moves them all strangely. In the character of Cherubino Mozart celebrates the way of true human attachment — an eros of many facets, binding people to one another by their mutual recognition of each other's unique and special qualities.

We return in a roundabout way to Figaro and "Non più andrai." If Cherubino is the presiding genius of the opera, offering a paradigm of the right way to love, the moment of romping joy must be more than a sugarcoated pill for a charming young rascal (and a dodge to deceive the Count). "Non più andrai" establishes an important relationship between Figaro and Cherubino. Least of all is Figaro teaching Cherubino; he is describing Cherubino, celebrating Cherubino, and enlisting Cherubino.

In the first case, Cherubino's comportment on the stage will not in itself spell out his role in the opera. Another observer is required, to single out details which will consolidate the scattered impressions generated by "Non so più." We hear Cherubino called "Narcisetto, Adoncino d'amor," have our attention drawn to his "pennacchini," his "aria brillante," his "vermiglio, donnesco color,"[67] and our impressions are confirmed; rightfully the youth reminds us of that other love child, the pagan cherub Eros.

Second, Figaro celebrates Cherubino. Susanna and the Countess need not be embarrassed about being moved by Cherubino, even in his guise as a page; for women to amuse themselves decorously with the castle mascot is perfectly proper. Figaro must also be touched by the power of the strange youth, but to show it is for him a more delicate matter. Both Figaro and Cherubino are male, and while they are near the same age, Figaro has attained his manhood. On the other hand, Figaro may be a little jealous of Cherubino's luscious youth. These circumstances prevent them from sharing the innocent playmate-friendship of Susanna and Cherubino. Later, at the end of the opera, Figaro turns away momentarily from the graces of the two women, giving in to the darker passions of jealousy and distrust. It is important that he show here that his primary attachment is to the court of Cherubino, and not to the selfish brotherhood of the Count and his satellites. Figaro will rarely reveal how Cherubino moves him; a fraternal romp in which all three join is one of the few occasions where it is possible. Figaro shows his affection for Cherubino by exercising for the boy his imaginative talents; "Non più andrai" is a moment of "loveplay" between Cherubino and Figaro.

Finally, Figaro enlists Cherubino. Figaro in his tribute to the page admits the power of Cherubino's kind of passion. Only this eros will unite all the conspirators, later on even moving an unlikely ally like Marcellina over to their side (when she sees Figaro as if for the first time, and is genuinely moved by the person of her son). To arm Eros-Cupid with arrows and shield was an ancient conceit. Here in "Non più andrai" Figaro is arming Cherubino, girding him for the struggle to come. In fact the figure of the "bedroom soldier," usually the matter of vulgar jokes, becomes in *Figaro* an emblem for the righteous of the opera, and for the right kind of passion.[68] The gesture of the military march, taking off from Cherubino's imminent field commission, becomes a testimony to trust in the powers of human affection when they are matched against the assailing brutishness of men.

CHAPTER FOUR

Act II

The Introduction of the Countess

The Countess is different from most of Mozart's other noble heroines; she lacks the usual trappings of an *opera seria* figure. Unlike
Donna Anna or Donna Elvira she does not enter at full tilt, early in the
first act, to hurl herself directly into the action. Nor does she sing music
like theirs — the "white-note" exalted style which usually characterizes
opera seria heroes and heroines. She enters relatively late in the opera
for a major character, her creators probably having desired to protect
her from the low intrigues of act I.[1] Furthermore, "entrance" is perhaps
too strong a word for her appearance: in effect we discover her, musing
in her chamber, when the curtain rises on act II. Even then we do not
immediately hear her, but first observe her silent during a long orchestral prelude. When she does sing, she shuns the exalted style almost entirely; her music is slow and contemplative, *di mezzo carattere*.
And finally there is the most pointed variance with the usual *opera seria
prima donna*: although the Countess is kept carefully separate until act II
and is introduced in a special manner, her music does not lack topical
connection with the music of the other characters in the opera. Donna
Anna, from the first sound she utters in act I of *Don Giovanni*, commands a plane far above the low *buffa* style of Leporello; their differing
gestures preserve class differences rigidly. The Countess's gestures are,
on the contrary, a noble version of movements which are already familiar. Although the music of *Figaro* does draw some distinction between
the noble-born and the base-born, we are made aware at the same time
of their common humanity.

100

Mozart effects the connections of gesture subtly. Although the beauty
of the slow lyric vein of the cavatina strikes the listener at first hearing,
he is probably not aware that fragments of two disparate topics alternate in the mosaic of this lovely introduction, or that only one of the two
topics has a direct association with the lyric mode. The first six measures announce the topical dialogue: four measures of *piano* singing
style, with solo first violin set against steady sixteenth-note pulses in the
accompanying strings, follow the three tonic, *forte coups d'archet*. In the
next phrase (mm. 7–10), single measures of a slow *forte* march with
dotted rhythms, itself an extension of the *coups d'archet*, alternate with
measures of the *piano* singing style (ex. 4–1). The measures of singing
style retain the instruments of the martial wind band (clarinets, bassoons, and horns in parallel thirds), maintaining the divertimento sound
of the courtly march while at the same time giving it an *amoroso* tinge.[2]
After two and a half lyric measures on the subdominant (mm. 11–13),
another alternation brings the introduction of the aria to a final cadence: the march breaks out again in the last half of measure 13, with
winds and dotted rhythms, only to subside in measures 15 and 16 into a
soft and singing dialogue between clarinet and bassoon.

The smooth balance of the two disparate topics in this introduction is
aided by the fact that the march and *amoroso* styles have instruments in
common. The winds have different functions in the two styles: for the
military topic they evoke the proper instrumentation for a march—the
winds and brass of music performed out of doors—while to the *amoroso*
they contribute a sweet and intimate sound. But their shared sonorities
bind the two affects together, rationalizing their appearance in the same
lyric piece. When the Countess begins to sing (m. 18), her line smoothes
over the martial topic and the singing, *amoroso* style prevails. Two ex-
ceptions are a momentary hint of the march (horns and dotted rhythms)
at the close of the first period (m. 25, giving way rapidly to the *amoroso*
clarinets) and a passionate quasi-improvisatory outburst in measures
34–37, a brief "cadenza" before the return of the tonic.[3]

Example 4-1

March and *amoroso* are an appropriate combination of topics for the Countess. The slow march — an effective curtainraiser — establishes her noble birth, while the singing style, in contrast to the march's grave formality, is intimate and contemplative. The Countess is the only character we will truly "see into" in the opera; the other characters are more at home in action, the Countess when she is thoughtful and in repose. Love also is central to the Countess's nature: her grief is about love denied her, and the text of her cavatina is a petition to Amor for release from her sorrowful bondage to him. The halo of *amoroso* winds is fit accompaniment for a lover, and will remain her hallmark through the opera. In a delicate psychological touch, Mozart does not allow the Countess to sing the march. One is never separated from the motions of one's character, and the march "motivates" her on stage in a characteristic posture. When she speaks, however, she reveals only her immediate concerns; the *amoroso* topic prevails, and the slow march remains a rhythmic echo in the distance.

This combination of military and amorous topics is not new to the opera: it also gives shape to the aria immediately preceding the Countess's — Figaro's "Non più andrai." The theme of conquest binds the two topics together in an association which would ordinarily be invoked in a comic vein. In its lowest guise it merits a leer: witness Leporello's snicker about the easy availability for the cavalier of wars and women.[4] In *Figaro*, however, the joke is more delicate. Figaro's military fanfare on the words "Delle belle turbando il riposo" begs indulgence not for the casual venery of a cavalier, but for the beguiling fantasies of a dreamy adolescent. In "Non più andrai" the joke, once made, is made substantive; in identifying Cherubino as Eros militant, Figaro enthrones him as the guardian of all true lovers. The juxtaposition of the same topical combination in the next aria is not an accident: it functions as both an expansion and an application of the original mixed metaphor. The new context, and the metaphor's new proponent, the Countess, raise to a higher power the complex of associations grounded in the figure of Eros militant, confirming it as the center of the opera; when it is removed from the lighthearted romp of "Non più andrai" we are forced to take the imagery more seriously. At the same time the Countess, by using Cherubino's vocabulary, places herself firmly under his gentle protection. She shows herself a member of the young boy's court like Figaro and Susanna, experiencing their same passions. Her prayer is addressed to Cherubino-Amor.

Thus it would ill befit the Countess to enter as Donna Anna might, or Konstanze. Their radically noble style — the direct descendant of the ecclesiastical — asserts their differences from the base-born characters in the opera, necessarily destroying the possibility of a common ground between them and Zerlina or Pedrillo. But only buffoons and villains affect the exalted style in *Figaro*: Bartolo in his vengeance aria (I, 4) and the Count in most of his appearances. The posturings of the exalted march satirize the excessive and intemperate passions of its proponents, and render inaccessible to them the special place where human beings who are properly lovers can find shelter. The slow march and *amoroso* of the Countess's aria, because they are *di mezzo carattere* and not exalted, stress the human side of her nobility rather than the divine. To be noble may ultimately mean to be closest of humans to divinity, as the Classic hierarchy of movement implies by linking the grandest passions with the ecclesiastical style. In *Figaro*, however, the music of "divine inspiration" seems at best empty posturing, and at worst the perversion of true passion, while the truer nobility resides in the humane and reflective gestures of the lyric mode.

A Quiet Interlude

After the introduction of the Countess, the high point of act II is its great finale. But before the trio and duet which prepare the grand imbroglio's first crisis, several of the protagonists spend some quiet moments together. The two recitatives and arias following "Porgi, amor" (scenes ii and iii) show the Countess, Susanna, and Cherubino plotting and playing happily together, after Figaro enters to set them to work.

Figaro again displays a certain thoughtlessness and lack of tact, and here, more unforgiveably, before the gentle Countess. His spirited but self-indulgent anger remains a foil for Susanna's greater sensitivity, now viewed in light of her affection for the Countess and Cherubino. Furious at the Count, Figaro speaks with cruel banter to the Countess about the Count's attempts to seduce Susanna. When Susanna counters "Ed hai coraggio di trattar scherzando/Un negozio sì serio?" Figaro answers "Non vi basta/Che scherzando io ci pensi?"[5] His quick retort hardly softens the pain inflicted by his thoughtless remarks. Crisis flushes Figaro; he dotes on the cleverness of his planned revenge and of the cavatina ("Se vuol ballare"), his invention to announce it. He leaves after having enjoined the two women to help him in his plot to humiliate the Count, a scheme which may in fact involve new humiliations for the Countess, for to set it in motion the Count will receive an anonymous note about an assignation which the Countess has supposedly made with a lover. In high spirits, Figaro quotes the cavatina exuberantly at exit, a cocky touch which only wounds the Countess more.[6] Her temptation to applaud a servant's insolent address to her husband — that ringing "Signor Contino" again — sharply contrasts the moment for her with happier days. Expressing only obliquely her pain at the Count's cruel philandering (and at its effects on the people closest to her), she exclaims at the inappropriateness of Cherubino's overhearing the Count's *stravaganze*. Her gentle restraint is far more poignant than would be an angry outburst. Touched, Susanna only wants to comfort the Countess, along with the woebegone Cherubino. With quick affection,[7] she draws their attention away from the unhappy turn of erotic events back to Eros himself. Her diversion is welcome, for Cherubino wants to pay court to the Countess, and the Countess to put her unfaithful husband out of her mind. Susanna indulges them both in a moment of loveplay, her indulgence in itself an act of love.

The loveplay must be merely an innocent tableau, however; it is crucial to their conception of the story that da Ponte and Mozart treat the relationship between Cherubino and the Countess less suggestively than did Beaumarchais. They took pains to eliminate certain passages from *Le mariage de Figaro* which imply more than a delicate flirtation between the two. Whereas in *Le mariage* the Countess often seems to be hesitating between two lovers, in the opera Cherubino is a pet, and never a real source of temptation. In act II, scene iii of the play the Countess excitedly prepares herself for Cherubino's arrival as one would for a lover. Da Ponte in the corresponding scene (the recitative before this aria) has her instead sadly lament the improprietous conversations Cherubino overheard when he hid in the chair in act I. He also omits a scene from the Beaumarchais (IV, viii) between the Countess and the Count in which the Countess expresses surprising anguish over the departure of Cherubino from the castle.

The text of the following aria, "Voi che sapete," is another of da Ponte's interpolations. Susanna prompts Cherubino to sing for the Countess, and in *Le mariage* he performs to the tune "Malbroug s'en va't'en guerre," a balladlike poem about a particular lad's intense devotion to his godmother. Here in the opera, on the other hand, he sings his own *canzonetta*, and da Ponte provides a text which is conventional and impersonal, addressed not to one *donna*, but to the collective *donne*:

> Voi che sapete
> Che cosa è amor,
> Donne, vedete
> S'io l'ho nel cor.[8]

The change is a material one: it is important to Mozart's conception of Cherubino's role in the opera that he be more "in love with love" than with any particular object of his desires.

Again, as in "Non so più," the text is plainly a poem, consisting of seven four-line stanzas with rhyme schemes of abab. Its sentiments are pure Cherubino:

2. Quello ch'io provo
   Vi ridirò;
   È per me nuovo,
   Capir nol so.

3. Sento un affetto
   Pien di desir
   Ch'ora è diletto,
   Ch'ora è martir.

4. Gelo, e poi sento
   L'alma avvampar,
   E in un momento
   Torno a gelar.

5. Ricerco un bene
   Fuori di me,
   Non so chi'l tiene,
   Non so cos'è.

6. Sospiro e gemo
   Senza voler,
   Palpito e tremo
   Senza saper.

7. Non trovo pace
   Notte nè dì:
   Ma pur mi piace
   Languir così.[9]

Again, as in "Non so più," Mozart must set the poem as a convincing song, underlining its literary origin. Furthermore, since in "Voi che sapete" opera's great artifice and the reality are one — Cherubino is actually meant to be singing — the stanzaic nature of the piece must be more than a mere suggestion. Yet a straight strophic construction with the same music repeated seven times would be monotonous, while the usual key-area plan is too dramatic, obscuring by its spirited curve the necessary poetic element of formal repetition. Mozart solves the problem in much the same way as he does in "Non so più," combining the key-area plan with outlines of stanzas asserted by attention to the configurations of Italian metrics. In "Voi che sapete," however, the solution is even more of a triumph. Neither element is submerged at the appearance of the other, and Mozart's attention to the detail of the text is exquisite.

In 2/4 meter, *Andante*,[10] "Voi che sapete" opens with a gesture which could in theory be a slow contredanse:

But the stately harmonic rhythm of the opening, underlined by the plucking of Susanna's guitar (*pizzicati* in all the strings), militates against the usual rhythmic excitement and compression of a key-area dance form. Cherubino's music is ingenuous and leisurely, lacking the urgency of dance. Clearly, at the outset, the principles of syllable count and of the integrity of a unit line of poetry set the limits. "Voi che sapete" uses the five-syllable line or *quinario* (the second and fourth lines of each stanza are *versi tronci*, *quinario*s with the fifth syllable mute — it is sounded only in the orchestral introduction). *Quinario* has a characteristic stress on the fourth syllable, and was often set as a galliard: ♩ ♩ ♩ | ♩ ♩ " Mozart's musical line reflects the same stress, although not the galliard's triple rhythms:

Voi che sa - pe - te

These two measures constitute a unit length, corresponding to one line of poetry, which will be deployed in various multiples as the aria progresses.

The first verbal stanza — and first period — consists of four of these lengths (eight measures), brought to closure by a four-measure cadential phrase (mm. 17–20). The first two measures of this phrase are poetically anomalous, smoothing over the *quinario* rhythms to provide a rhythmic and melodic climax which drives home the cadence; its second two measures are a rhythmic rhyme with the second of the unit lengths:

In the truncated orchestral introduction this cadential phrase serves as a neat consequent member for two unit lengths (ex. 4-2). Once one

Example 4-2

knows the aria, however, the consequent there sounds tacked on: it is clear that the introduction is a compression, and that the proper mode of the aria is the expansive spinning-out of poetic stanzas rather than the antecedent-consequent symmetries of dance. After the first period the consequent will be withheld until the two crucial moments of closure which remain — the end of the "exposition" and the final cadence of the aria. All the other stanzas will be left open-ended, "poetically" rather than "musically" conceived.

The second poetic stanza (mm. 21–28) moves to the dominant of the dominant, F major, preserving the rhythm of the preceding stanza's first eight measures except for a few small variations in the division of the beat:

This modulation introduces the first dark harmony of the piece, a D-minor triad, aptly on the word *nuovo* ("new") for a nice poetic touch. The third poetic stanza (mm. 29–36) opens in F major, the proper key of the second key area. Once the dominant has been achieved, all that is lacking is the characteristic confirmation of the new harmonic place. But this stanza, like the second consisting of eight measures modeled on measures 9–16, only postpones confirmation. Each four-measure member ends on the dominant of F major, and the interest of the stanza is in a madrigalistic touch — a pretty painting of the contrast between *diletto* and *martir* ("pleasure" and "torment"): *diletto* receives an ornamental division, while Cherubino's warblings turn dark on the word *martir* (an F-minor chord and an augmented sixth), as the pretty youth sings prettily of the pangs of love (ex. 4–3). The conventional pathos of the turn is delicately comic.

The next stanza constitutes a critical moment in the juggling of musical and poetic priorities, the problem being how to bring the second key area to an emphatic close while preserving a sense of the repetition nat-

Example 4-3

Example 4-4

ural to a strophic song. At this moment in "Non so più" Mozart breaches poetic regularities, having first rather exaggerated them. Here he takes the opposite tack, preserving the individual, closed stanza shapes while violating a firmly established principle of the key-area plan to close the exposition in an alien key. At the outset of the new stanza (m. 37) the bottom of the C-major triad (V of F) drops out (ex. 4–4). The entire stanza is set in A-flat major, a key with a remote and cool relation to the tonality of the aria. This strange modulation is suited to the text — Cherubino's description of the fire and ice of infatuation — and is rationalized by the repetition of the four-measure consequent which closed the first period (in mm. 41–44): the consequent makes a solid rhythmic rhyme back to that cadence in order to counterbalance the harmonic aberration (fig. 2, p. 110, charts the interlocking shapes which the two compositional procedures create). Thus by a clever manipulation of the elements which he set up as "musical" and "poetic" premises at the beginning of the aria, Mozart has managed a convincing close to the second key area without at all abandoning metrics. The strange key (a sideslipping modulation instead of the usual drama of the move up to the dominant) and the eight-measure rhythmic rhyme — yet another stanza — are unconventionally undramatic. (Literal end rhyme between the first and second key areas is unusual, since the dramatic point of the new key area is the movement to the new harmonic place.) Yet the four-measure consequent, marked as having a "musical" function because it diverges just enough from the regular strophic rhythms to act as a closing gesture, can still signal forcefully the end of a major formal section. Thus the second key area of the *canzona* is dramatic in asserting an essentially undramatic gesture — the rhythmic repetitions of verse.

The X-section begins with a harmonic move to G minor and a new stanza — the fifth one — in rhythm essentially resembling the second and third (mm. 45–52). Again the text is delightfully apt for the harmonic motion, speaking of Cherubino's search for a good which is outside himself, the nature and whereabouts of which he does not know. G minor is conventionally "outside" the place just abandoned, and the modulation to it is open-ended, "searching" (it passes through G as V of C and then backs up to a G tonic through an augmented sixth to D). But the firm authentic cadence at the end of the stanza (stanzas 2 and 3 both closed on a dominant, not a tonic) gives the lie to the charmingly melodramatic words of Cherubino's quest, settling gently back in a harmonic place and reasserting by its singsong rhythmic rhyme the frame of the poem.

In "Non so più" Mozart disturbs the regular poetic rhythm during the move to the dominant, balancing that gesture against the return and expansive pastoral coda. The balance is different in "Voi che sapete": the rhythmic crisis occurs in the X-section, in order to weight the eighteen brief measures of the return against the forty-four measures of "exposition." Now for the first time the repetitive trochees — ♩ ♫|♩ ♩ — and the constant four-measure units lose their hold. Urgent and breathless sixteenth notes with an iambic stress —

[musical notation]

begin a long-arched nine-measure phrase which culminates on the dominant (m. 61). Five of these iambic phrases ornament a rising chromatic scale in the bass, which overshoots the dominant by one note. A four-measure trochaic unit length emerges from the iambs and the phrase backs down to F, the dominant of B-flat, ending in a harmonic and rhythmic rhyme with stanzas 2 and 3. The text is appropriately breathless; for the first time two stanzas constitute one sentence, and the antitheses pile up to a climax: "I sigh and moan without wanting to, I quiver and tremble without knowing it, I find no peace night or day, and yet it pleases me to languish this way." These two stanzas of text are crammed into the nine measures of music. The rhyme, which provides a mimetic pause on *languir* (vii^7 of V, m. 60) restrains their breathy passion. Cherubino seems for a moment to step outside his formal song, overwhelmed with emotion. Yet his outburst does not violate the studied effects of a charming Italian ballad, since the end rhyme once again asserts the frame of the poem. The piece plays itself out in a return to the tonic and to the first stanza of text — a final rhyme both of key area and of *canzona*. The four-measure consequent makes its third and fourth appearances (mm. 70 to the end) to provide the rhetoric of cadence.

The picture da Ponte and Mozart have created, of a lovestruck youth's Dantesque poeticizing, is thoroughly realistic, and at the same time cannot be taken only at face value. The fragmented poetic and musical contents of the song demand attention, requiring us to connect the mixed nature of the piece with the mixed nature of the character singing it. A young and blushing girl, dressed as a boy, tremulously singing the clichés of passion with a cool and vibrato-free voice — the creature before us must be very special. We expect him to dance — the established idiom of the opera — and his dance turns to song. His conventionally melodramatic gestures — the chromatic turn on the word *mar-*

Figure 2 The Harmonic and Rhythmic Structure of "Voi che sapete"

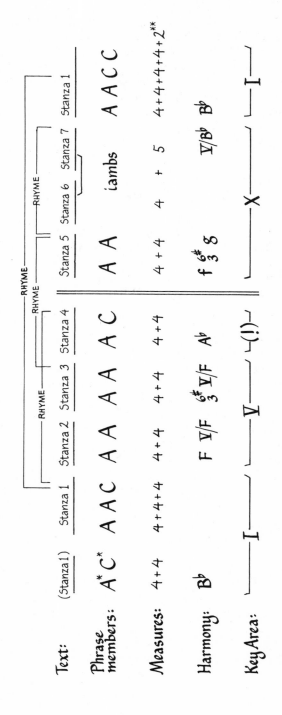

A - Antecedent, *C* - Consequent
** Orchestra only

tir, for instance — suggest a moonstruck adolescent, yet suddenly his song turns to a cool and subtle A-flat major, a strange and otherworldly place which is laid out but never explored. "Voi che sapete" confirms the presence in the opera of the androgynous Eros-Cupid, neither young or old, male or female, human or divine, of this world or alien. His song celebrates the passions which Susanna experiences gladly, and the Countess perforce sadly, which the Countess is too dignified, Susanna too matter-of-fact, to express outright. Now it can be seen more clearly why Mozart took such pains to make Cherubino a troubadour rather than a dancer. His utterly conventional poem from its first line suggests another, less conventional poet and a more serious intent: "Donne ch'avete intelletto d'amore"[12] is the first line of Dante's sonnet sequence about the fine discipline of love, and the abstract quality of its language[13] is a reflection of the tradition in which erotic love sets the soul on the path to higher things. Cherubino is celebrating the two women themselves; the opening words of his song sweep them into his court. He identifies them as "donne che sanno che cosa è amor, che hanno intelletto d'amore."[14] He dubs them secular Beatrices, mediums for the workings of Eros. A special aura surrounds them; comprehending "che cosa è amor," they are gifted with a surpassing vision of the way things are. (The Countess, it should be pointed out, returns the compliment in "Porgi, amor," directing her petition there to the god of love, Cherubino-Eros.) By addressing the two women indiscriminately as *donne*, Cherubino also reveals the special bond between servant and mistress; initiates, at least, can address them on equal terms. This relation fittingly comes to light as reflected in the eyes of its catalyst, Cherubino d'amore.

"Voi che sapete" is artifice of the highest order. The mixed conventions of the young poet's love song catch us by their verisimilitude, but at the same time point beyond themselves, suggesting a hierarchy of secular love which has the gently passionate as its priests and priestesses. "Amor vincit omnia": the lyrics of Cherubino the poet celebrate this maxim in all its delicate — and moral — compulsion.

The next aria dispels the beguiling daydream atmosphere of "Voi che sapete," as Susanna gets down to the business of disguising Cherubino for his new role as a girl. "Venite . . . inginocchiatevi . . .," Susanna's first solo aria in the opera, is superficially an "action aria," or a song which usurps for variety's sake the function of recitative. But the love-play produced by the daydream spills over into the aria, becoming startlingly explicit. The aria — or properly the duet or *pas de deux* between Susanna and a silent Cherubino — turns into a companion piece for "Voi che sapete," Susanna's return compliment to Cherubino d'amore. Her appreciation of Eros is not grandiloquent, classical, and rowdy, like Figaro's, but intimate and ironic. She treats him like a puppy, the castle mascot, but the power of the "serpentello"[15] comes through in her gently mocking words. Turning the passive Cherubino about like a dressmaker's dummy, she too points out the boy's beauty — "Mirate il bricconcello, mirate quanto è bello!" — and admires his amorous craftiness — "Che furba guardatura."[16] Their physical contact makes the situation all the more electric. Her concluding tribute to Cherubino, set aphoristically, like a moral *sententia* at the end of an *opera seria* set piece, is in obvious response to his salute to *le donne*: "Se l'amano le femmine,/ Han certo il lor perchè."[17]

The construction of an "action aria" presents a particular problem. When a character engages in solitary meditation, or gives a performance like Cherubino's, his music can employ the usual devices of instrumental music to shape a sound musical structure with clear beginning, middle, and end. Tradition allows soliloquies a formal shape, and a performance, to be believable, must explicitly mimic familiar forms; in both situations formal melodic recall at the return does not distract. Two problems arise, however, for a text which rehearses the initiation and completion of an action. The symmetries of a squared-off dance piece do not always successfully choreograph configurations in the particular action's progress; it may demand a more flexible macrorhythm for its projection. Further, at the end of an action, the actor and the acted-upon will have been altered in some way, but an obligatory recall of opening material would bar the musical portrayal of change within the confines of one piece. To solve both problems here, Mozart separates the characteristic dance patterns from their usual symmetrical phrase structure, piecing them out instead like fragments in a mosaic. When it takes its place as one of several kinds of units in a structure with broader limits, a particular dance rhythm will not define those limits, but work within them as a part to a whole.[18]

The formality of a complete melodic recall provides problems even for Mozart's more meditative and solitary arias. The *da capo* form so popular in the Baroque could be excessively rigid and artificial. Caught in its iron A-B-A symmetries, even an independent-minded character could not always in his final analysis move from his first position, whatever the emotional vicissitudes he had experienced midway through his meditations. Except for special effect, Mozart always avoided the *da capo* in his later operas. Even the key-area form, which requires in instrumental music some measure of emphatic end rhyme, eases that requirement to an extent in music with a good dramatic text. Mozart found the "double-aria" form worked better for soliloquies. The Count-

ess's "Dove sono" (III, 19), for example, has a harmonic return underlined not by recall but by innovation; changed in meter, tempo, affect,
and motive, it provides a new musical gesture and a new stance for the
singer. When Mozart runs a character through the paces of a "real
dance" — in "Se vuol ballare," for example — he reserves the right to extend, to surprise by a change of affect, to step out of the mask of the
dance for a momentary, more "true-to-life" melodic, harmonic, or
rhythmic digression.

The mosaiclike treatment of dance rhythms, however, differs from
these other procedures applied to solving the same problem. The limits
of Susanna's aria are not necessarily shaped by dance, although the repeated G-major flourish of the opening (mm. 1–2, 5–6) is perhaps, in
retrospect, a *riverenza*. In between flourishes Susanna sings a pleasant
eight-measure bourrée phrase with two measures (9–10 or 11–12? —
the scansion is delightfully ambiguous) of extension (ex. 4–5). Bourrée
1 never recurs. The orchestra carries on while Susanna, immersed in
her task, abstractedly murmurs *buffa* patter to its accompaniment. At
first the violins play delicate ornamental flourishes along an ordinary
G-major progression. As the piece moves on toward the dominant, the
winds (oboes, later joined by bassoons) break out into bourrée 2 (mm.
23–30; ex. 4–6). This simple four-measure bourrée tune, its melodic
figures arranged a-b-b-c, but abstracted from any formal dance mac-
rostructure, is an ideal "vamp-till-ready" motive; it appears only in the
orchestra. Repeated twice, it gives way to a patter climax on V of D
major, and D major, the dominant and second key, is confirmed with a
new figure, bourrée 3 (mm. 37–40; ex. 4–7). Sharing with the other

Example 4-5

Example 4-6

Example 4-7

two fragments only the prominent sonority of the bassoon, the new tune is constructed for cadencing.

   Susanna joins the orchestra for bourrée 3. Calling Cherubino to attention, she sings "Madama qui non è."[19] Measures 52–80 comprise the X-section, beginning, like the transition from the first key area, with string flourishes and bourrée 2 (m. 61), a most successful X-section motive. The X-section moves through three keys (A minor, G major, C major) in three four-measure segments of bourrée. Susanna gives a new set of instructions — a seamstress's absorbed "turn on please" — to each new tonality, Cherubino, no doubt, obliging. She breaks the sequence with the words "Vedremo poscia il passo,/Quando sarete in piè."[20] A measure (73) of military gesture[21] for Cherubino's standing posture (ironically, for *il bel soldato* has metamorphosed into a blushing girl) moves the X-section to a dominant pedal where it dissolves again into patter (m. 77). A rhythmic and motivic camouflage hides the return to the tonic. The low strings hit a G major triad off the beat and Susanna joins them a measure later in patter. Bourrées 1 and 2 are completely absent from the return. Instead, Susanna murmurs the asides to the Countess about Cherubino's fine appearance and rascality, the Countess responding with nods and a quiet smile, and their whispered patter conversation builds up to a final end rhyme: the only formed material of the return is the cadential figure, bourrée 3 (mm. 95ff), which forms a rhyme with the same figure at the end of the "exposition." To it Susanna sings her comment about Cherubino's powerful attractions: "If women love him, they certainly have a good reason."

   Susanna is one character in the orchestra's *scena*, the silent Countess and Cherubino the other two. The orchestra provides the only continuous line through the piece, choreographing the byplay of the trio to keep the action moving. The glints of the three bourrée fragments nail down important moments in the continuum; imbedded in more neutral figuration and standing out against it, they plot the shape of the aria. The absence of bourrées 1 and 2 from the return underplays the first phrases in the tonic in order to stress Susanna's final words, which also gain emphasis from the end rhyme provided by bourrée 3, the only tune in the return. One is reminded of the relentless repetitions of Leporello's aphoristic words to Donna Elvira in the "Catalogue" aria: "Purchè porti la gonnella,/Voi sapete quel che fa."[22] Words which are as cruel about the inevitability of sexual attraction as Susanna's are tender and perceptive, they receive much the same kind of musical treatment.

The heavy stress on the end rhyme suggests a reinterpretation of the "action" of the aria. To dress Cherubino is its obvious objective, but to demonstrate the proper way to deal with the powers of Eros is a no less significant intent. Susanna's gingerly erotic play with Cherubino implies that love is really a serious flirtation, requiring all one's wits and some planned defenses. But one must candidly admit the power love has over him, and never bar its encroachments completely. At the end of the first half of the aria, bourrée 3 highlights Susanna's flirtatious mock-lie to Cherubino, uttered to make him stand still: "Stop fussing; *Madame is not here*." The words for bourrée 3 in the return state the contrary: Madame is indeed here, amused and moved by the charming figure before her. "*If women love him, they certainly have good reason*" (there is a poetic, as well as a musical, rhyme between the two statements — *non è* with *perchè*). The shape of the aria facilitates a comparison of these rhymes, and they don't entirely add up. Susanna uses their lack of congruency to demonstrate the technique of facing out Eros — defend yourself from hurt and ruin, but not from submission. Her "demonstration" can reassure the Countess about two things: her love for the Count is not an unworthy passion, and to employ subterfuges to deal with it is neither dishonorable nor unwomanly. The aria is a brief course in a feminine *Scuola degli Amanti*, and both women take the advice to heart.

The events which lead from Figaro's "Non più andrai" to Susanna's finishing touches on Cherubino's disguise form a peculiar parenthesis. They are part of an elaborate plot which has no issue, for it is blasted immediately after Susanna's aria by the entrance of the infuriated Count. This plot is not entirely without influence on future events, but the real justification for the four arias concerned with it lies elsewhere. The pieces conjure up around the protagonists a charmed and magic[23] circle, whose protection provides some relief from the sordid problems exposed earlier. The flat-key tonalities and *amoroso* winds which support the Countess and Cherubino belong to a cool, distant, and mysterious place in a different plane. The arias of Susanna and Figaro, while in the tonal colors of the "real world" (C and G major), make some affective connections with "Porgi, amor" and "Voi che sapete" which place them at the intersection of the two planes. Figaro's cavalier but joyous mélange of love and war connects with the Countess's more reflective mingling of the same topics. Cherubino praises a special feminine insight into the arcana of Eros, and Susanna gives an amused and practical but nonetheless gracious acknowledgment of the compliment. She pays her compliment appropriately while in action; she shuns a grandiloquent performance Figaro-style, and she is not contemplative like the Countess. The style of her performance effects a change in the atmosphere — from flats to sharps, from clarinets to bassoons, from song back to dance, from reflection to action. Her resilience acts as a bridge back to harsh realities; without her aria as a buffer, the following trio would be difficult to bear.

II, 13: A Trio en Menuet

With the Count's appearance the idyll is over. Figaro's letter about the Countess's purported assignation has inflamed the Count with jealousy. For once the occasion informs against the Countess; circumstantial evidence convicts her, making the Count's anger on the surface of it just. Yet had the Count's attentions not been before as vigorously directed elsewhere as they are now to discovering the Countess *in flagrante delicto*, she would not have been brought to the present pass. She has the greater claim to sympathy, and the Count's bullying bluster hardly weakens her case. Nevertheless Almaviva retains the upper hand throughout the trio.

The Count's arrival increases the Countess's apparent complicity. Susanna has left the room to get a ribbon for her, leaving her alone with Cherubino. Hearing the Count approaching, Cherubino hastily slips into the dressing room, and the Countess takes the key so that the door can only be opened by the person inside. The Count, suspicious upon arrival because the Countess's outer door was locked and because she appeared disturbed, hears Cherubino knock over a chair in the dressing room and presses her harder. She stammers out the falsehood that Susanna is in the dressing room and the Count, still suspicious, demands that Susanna show herself. Thus the trio begins, setting into motion a wave of complications which will reach only a temporary resolution at the end of the act, as the plot mechanism is wound ever tighter.

Set in 3/4 meter, *Allegro spirituoso*, the trio opens with a ceremonial flourish of two four-measure phrases, the second ending in an elision:

phrase groupings:	1	2	1	2	1	2	1	(2)
harmony:	I	V	V	I	I	V	V	(I)
measure number:	1	2	3	4	5	6	7	8

The two phrases have the absolute formal symmetry of a pair of *riverenze* in a minuet; the Count's clarion challenge to Susanna imitates a trumpet call. Minuets usually choreograph a formal, controlled situation, with emotions held within reasonable bounds. Yet the Count manages to make the opening *riverenze* sound like the squaring-off of two prize fighters before a bout — the arrogance of a formal challenge rather than the amenity of a formal bow.

The women are unable to answer in kind. Their perturbation breaches the formal structure of the *riverenze*, obliterating it by a turmoil of panicked denials. A tonic pedal introduced in the orchestra breaks the minuet. The Count struggles to reassert it in G major, the dominant; measures 14–21 might be a convincing close to a simple first reprise of a action. The increase of momentum caused by the sudden prevalence of eighth notes, and by an extended six-measure phrase ending with dramatic suddenness on the dominant, aids in the destruction of the minuet. The Count struggles to reassert it in G major, the dominant; measures 10–21 might be a convincing close to a simple first reprise of a minuet. But the pedal reasserts itself at the moment of cadence and the piece finally explodes. The affect of panic and turmoil persists for almost forty measures (21–60), until the end of the second key area, while the harmony makes repeated passes at the elusive G-major cadence. The minuet rhythm does not return clearly and unambiguously until the return of the tonic (m. 71).

The broadest cadential gesture of the second key area, coming just after a deceptive cadence in measures 44 to 45, is a grand downward sequence in learned counterpoint—a chain of descending parallel $^6_3$ chords with suspensions (ex. 4–8). The counterpoint is itself adorned with *galant* flourishes in the strings and patter from Susanna. Mozart revels in lean and tightly controlled moments of complete confusion, where a seething surface conceals the firm skeleton underneath. This passage counterbalances the formal material of the first key area, the minuet; its sideslipping sequences and harmonic indirection are the antithesis of the polar symmetries and harmonic clarity of the dance. The text of the imbroglio begins appropriately with the Countess's despairing "Bruttissima è la cosa!" and the Count's sarcastic "Chiarissima è la cosa!"[24] In the "recapitulation" the imbroglio passage is repeated twice and has for key words *scandalo* and—the reigning affect—*disordine*.

Unlike many pieces in the opera, this trio is peculiarly suited to a full-blown sonata-allegro version of the key-area form.[25] After the first challenge and elusive answer all three characters pause to reflect on the next step, bringing us to the end of the "development" (a ten-measure buildup to the dominant of C major, mm. 61–70). The Count squares

Example 4-8

Example 4-9

off again, demanding at least to hear, if not to see, Susanna (who, returning with the Countess's ribbon, has quietly slipped into an alcove to
size up the situation); his action coincides with the beginning of a full
melodic recall. The Countess, regaining her equilibrium and interrupting the Count, gives a counterorder to the closet where Susanna is not.
A desperate tactic, demanding the full dignity of indignation for success, it corresponds cunningly to an ellipsis in the return, in the material
of the first key area — the omission of the first pedal (and the ladies'
panic). The Countess sings instead with great dignity the Count's original reassertion of the minuet with a one-measure extension (mm. 14–16
in the exposition, 80–83 in the recapitulation). Her phrase performs
the harmonic function of "remodulation" — reversing the harmonic
course of the original move to the dominant.

After the tonic is secured in the recapitulation, a symphonic movement will often explore a key belonging to the subdominant realm, and
this trio is no exception. The Count must go the Countess one better.
He treats the Countess's last G as a leading-tone to A-flat major — a surprising slip in key of a major third, rationalized by the use of G as a
pivot note. Caressing with oily menace the words "Consorte mia," he
snaps off "giudizio." He repeats the odd three-measure phrase in F
minor, having rationalized the minor by the move through A-flat major.
The truncation of phrases, the simple repeated notes of the Count's line,
and the emphasis of bass and strings on the first beat of each 3/4 measure combine for a momentary sensation of *alla breve*, suggesting two
9/4 measures instead of two three-measure phrases (ex. 4–9). The
Count will fall into this hypocritical idiom (which Basilio introduced in
the first-act trio) frequently, affecting the voice of reason to urge constraint and common sense. Calling upon the forces of order and decorum to justify what is essentially thoughtless and inhumane conduct,
he characteristically assumes — to paraphrase Montaigne — a "supercelestial mien" to conceal "subterranean behavior." The sonorous tones
of his judicial dignity carry undertones of a snarl; this fleeting moment
of *alla breve* scansion carries, like the glint of light on a drawn sword, its
own special threat. Susanna, quick to catch its import, exclaims "O

cielo! un precipizio/Qui certo nascerà."[26] An F-sharp wedged against the A-flat (m. 91) tilts toward the dominant of C, and at once we are back in imbroglio, with a literal repetition of the remainder of the exposition.[27] The turn to the subdominant has, however, carved out a special place in C major for the Count; it has a lingering and disturbing effect.

The Finale to Act II

The finale to act II of *Le nozze di Figaro* is perhaps Mozart's greatest single piece of dramatic composition in all the operas. It is, on the simplest level, a consummately entertaining work; around every corner there lies another felicitous turn of action or of phrase. Furthermore, it unites this string of diverse comic moments into one single conception — a lively *commedia* which at the same time penetrates far beyond the *buffa* conventions which seem to dominate it; at certain sublime moments it seems to speak directly to the nature of true nobility, and to that of friendship and loyalty.

In form the finale consists of eight smaller pieces laid out in a large key-area plan. They move from E-flat major to the dominant, then through an "X-section" (G, C, and F major) to the dominant again, and finally return to the tonic. This key scheme shapes a closed form with its own harmonic drive and dynamic curve. Although the action of the finale is confusing, and constantly turns back on itself, its reversals are carefully plotted in a dynamic curve with a gradually heightening tension: they are ordered in four waves, only three of which crest and break (see fig. 3). Each wave begins with the revelation of a new crisis, and closes with a feeling of resolution which the cresting of the next wave will belie. Each wave gathers momentum toward the final climax, the *buffa* windup by the full ensemble. The dramatic apogee of the first

Figure 3   *The Dramatic Curve of the Finale to Act II*

I	V		X				I
E♭maj.	B♭maj.	B♭maj.	G maj.	C maj.	F maj.	B♭maj.	E♭maj.
$\frac{4}{4}$	$\frac{3}{8}$	$\frac{4}{4}$	$\frac{3}{8}$	$\frac{2}{4}$	$\frac{4}{4}$	$\frac{6}{8}$	$\frac{4}{4}$
march	minuet	Allegro	passepied	gavotte	buffa figures	gigue	march
crisis	resolution	triumph	Figaro enters	crisis & resolution	crisis	resolution	crisis…

Wave I | Wave II | Wave III | Wave IV

wave occurs near the middle, with the discovery of Susanna in the closet; here the psychology of the situation is developed in a leisurely fashion. Each of the last two waves gains in impetus by means of an increase of action (as opposed to a lingering attention to a character's inner feelings or to his particular public stance), a later climax, and a generally shorter time span.

The topical contents of the four waves are dance rhythms, and the pendulum motions of the reversals shape a "dialectic of dance." At either end of the finale the conflict is between duple and triple dances: the first and last trios of pieces each consist of two fairly well-developed key-area forms in duple meter enclosing one dance movement in triple. In both groups the triple meter accompanies the resolution of a crisis, while the crisis itself develops in the duple meters more comfortable to the Count. The central group of the finale consists of two dance movements, one in triple meter and the other in duple. The second contains both crisis and resolution in it, and is a gavotte. While it contains a metrical argument just as do the opening and closing groups, the contest is not, in this case, between triple and duple, but over the proper nature of the *mezzo carattere* gavotte; the struggle is resolved in favor of the heroes. The gavotte movement is the storm center of the finale and, appropriately, the point of furthest remove from the tonic (C major in an E-flat key scheme). It terminates in the quietest moment of the finale, in a mood both exalted and tender, on a plane far removed from the tone of comic melee which dominates the remainder of the piece. To bury the most serious and tender moment of a composition in its center, as Mozart does both here and in the fourth act finale, may seem an odd procedure, for it runs the risk that the memory of the moment will be blurred or even obliterated by the comedy to follow. It is, however, in keeping with both the nature of *buffa* conventions and the modest and unpretentious manner with which this opera proposes its vision of a possible earthly paradise.

Because of the nature of the events in the finale — the defeated of one moment are the triumphant of the next, and one crisis is averted only to have another arise — the action within individual movements also moves by short thrusts and constant shifts of focus. Rather than a continuous and lyric development of themes one finds a mélange of short broken motives, recitativelike material, and *buffa* patter; the occasional lyric passages provide their own shift and contrast. Da Ponte supplied a key word — *confuso* — for the finale, and Mozart points it up several times in prominent and appropriate settings.

The first piece in the finale is an angry duet between the Count and the Countess; it has as its metrical foundation a duple meter (4/4), which is inflected as a march, a bourrée, and even as a tentative gavotte.

Example 4-10

The Count begins with a sturdy and stubborn dotted-rhythm march accompanied by strings, and by a little wind band which punctuates the first and third beats of every measure. The Countess answers with a more florid line (without the winds), which comes to resemble an ornamented gavotte in measures 9–13. The passage reminds one of the masculine-feminine contrast between bourrée and florid gavotte in the first piece of the opera, the duet between Figaro and Susanna. As the argument grows more heated (with the Count's angry questions the piece moves into the second key area), the Countess takes a firmer stand: setting her posture is a bourréelike melody (mm. 24ff) which hardens into a march in measure 35. The Count set the march topic at the beginning of the movement; it is properly his idiom. Goaded into anger, the Countess now takes to it splendidly, using the Count's material (dotted rhythms and triadic motives), but more spiritedly than he: her anger takes wing in the exalted style and provides the consolidating and cadential material for the end of the "exposition" (ex. 4–10). Mozart invests the Countess here with a noble *forza* which is absent from her bearing in Beaumarchais's version of the scene.[28] Forced into an alien idiom, she exhibits for the first time a capacity for the fiery dignity characteristic of Donna Anna or Konstanze. The Count can only follow her lead; together they bring the second key area to a close.

With one brief measure of lead-in, the piece returns to the tonic. Almaviva peremptorily demands the key to the door (m. 55). The Countess gives it up[29] amidst protestations of Cherubino's innocence, which send the Count into further transports — an F-minor passage in exalted-march rhythms (the harmonic digression occurs here, rather than in a proper X-section). The Count's anger reduces the Countess to pleading her own innocence instead of Cherubino's. Then, claiming for evidence against her her very perturbation ("Vel leggo in volto"[30]), Almaviva launches his most bitter invective at the final consolidation of E-flat — "Mora, mora, e più non sia/Ria cagion del mio penar!" These words are cruel beyond any due measure, and must be remembered against him; significantly, they represent one of da Ponte's interpolations in Beaumarchais's text.[31] They must have a serious effect on any estimate of the Count's character. A more decent man, bearing in the back of his mind his own guilt, would try to be temperate and conciliatory when he has the upper hand. To a bullying temperament, however, the reminder of

personal guilt is only a spur to more remorseless bullying. As Almaviva
faces his Countess, the improbability of her guilt must cross his mind
for a moment. But the renewed shame which this reflection costs him
only increases his wrath, and his intention to make the charade as ugly
as possible. There is something unbalanced in this behavior, whether or
not the command can be taken seriously. It must not only wound the
Countess, but also arouse in her a fearful sense of isolation. She is
sequestered from the society which she knew before her marriage (she
was, after all, a city girl, a native of Seville), with a husband who has
ceased to love her. Her husband, moreover, is trying to convince
her that she is a literal outlaw of that society, indicted by it of immoral
conduct and condemned by it, in the person of her husband, to die.
Then he could continue to behave as he pleased; the tribunal is above
suspicion.

The music of the return is cleverly constructed to catch at once the
Count's arrantly pompous anger and the Countess's frightened innocence. It makes palpable the progression in the Count's anger during
the movement: from ordinary ire to a guilty wrath which deals hys-
terically in thoughts of ultimate punishments. The material of the first
key area was inchoate; it portrayed two people uneasily jockeying for
position, and the Countess the first to find any stable indignation. The
harmonic return, as so often in the operas, is not accompanied by a full
melodic return: only the Countess's exalted march is retained (mm. 91
to the end). The diffuse motives leading into her march are omitted, and
the return is consolidated by new material with a sharp profile for both
characters. On the imperative "Mora" the Count sings whole notes in
an *alla breve* "white-note" cantus firmus — a return of the threatening judicial posture which he mimed so effectively in the trios of acts I and II.
The Countess answers with a florid phrase much like the ones she sang
in the exposition before finding the strength for indignation. And
Mozart adds a strange and telling touch over the Count's cantus firmus.
As counterpoint to it the clarinets and bassoons have ascending and descending scales in parallel thirds — the sonorities associated with the
Countess in her moments of quiet reflection, when our sympathies were
enlisted in her behalf (ex. 4–11). *Amoroso* winds are also Cherubino's

Example 4-11

Example 4-12

Molto andante

music (the word *mora* is an anagram for *amor*). The juxtaposition of mock species counterpoint and the instruments associated with a noble human passion makes a judgment on the exalted style, at least as it is found in *Figaro*. The Count's affecting of divine rhythms is not a noble gesture but debased, partaking not of the celestial but of the demonic: high passion when misdirected or cruel is no longer exalted, but merely feverish. In an opera where our shared humanity is most highly valued, the ecclesiastical style will necessarily appear perverse, and this juxtaposition of topics provides a convenient perspective for the recognition. When the march of the second key area returns in the recapitulation, it is disturbing to hear the Count sing it first (m. 91), claiming as his music the motive which was so eloquently introduced in the exposition by the Countess. The worst has happened: the Count has succeeded in crushing his gentle wife's spirits.

The march comes to a strong cadence in E-flat major with sixteenth-note string flourishes on the strong beats of the measures: ♪♩ 𝄽 ♪♩ 𝄽 ♫ ♩ Drawing his sword the Count walks deliberately to the closet. The flourishes turn into the tread of an attacker on his guard; reminiscent of the flourishes in the exposition and recapitulation of the act I trio, they turn the key to B-flat major at the same time as they bring the Count to the closet door. "Susanna," he gasps, *con maraviglia*, as the stage direction has it.[32] *Molto andante*, in 3/8 time, and *piano*, the strings play the unadorned accompaniment to a paradigmatic late eighteenth-century stage minuet, the most graceful and the noblest version of the dance (ex. 4–12). Susanna's minuet has no melody: the strings instead project a concentration of the characteristic qualities of the minuet — an "essence of minuet." As Susanna gains strength from her triumph, her line gradually takes on more articulation and ornament (mm. 134ff). The instruments support her with a carefully orchestrated crescendo: first the horns join the strings with the accompaniment figure (m. 133), and a measure later the clarinets and bassoons enter to double her melody. The minuet is perfectly symmetrical — sixteen measures grouped by fours (the final four-measure cadential phrase is repeated for a total of twenty). The twenty measures stay close to B-flat, with no real cadence on the dominant; the point is not to depict a dramatic action, but to freeze action for a vignette of confrontation — a *tableau vivant* of triumph and surprise. The moment is dreamlike in its deliberate grace; the Count must be experiencing that torpor of limb and mind which overtakes one in a nightmare.

The trancelike quality of the movement does not abate after the first cadence of the minuet (m. 145). The basses strike a B-flat pedal and the Count and Countess slowly express their amazement in asides; Susanna looks on with pleasure, perhaps rather enjoying the effects of her surprise even on the Countess. The pedal makes the section more static, halting the articulation of the dance rhythms and providing a point of reference for a wandering harmony and phrase structure. Even the *buffa* patter which Susanna takes up while not under observation is denied its flash and glitter; it floats in dreamlike space as she sings with delight "*Confusa* han la testa"[33] — the first pointed setting of that emblematic word. After the section ends with a half-cadence on the dominant the minuet figure returns, tossed antiphonally from choir to choir — from horns to strings and back again. As the Count awakens from his daze, he hears no measure free from the insistent ♩ ♫♫ of the essential minuet figure.

Susanna has done what Figaro only imagined doing — teach the Count how to dance. Like Figaro she chooses the Count's proper music as the tune, although even a more aristocratic version. "The queen of all dances," one dancing-master called the minuet;[34] here no one could think it otherwise. Susanna's triumph is complete, her sarcasm serene. The moment effects a startling transmutation of roles: we accord Susanna her minuet with absolute justice. Not merely the clever servant reveling as she beats her master at his own game, she is nobler than Almaviva. The minuet is not his proper music; it has become hers.[35] The Count dimly perceives her nobility and is shamed by it. Circumstantial evidence tells him he has a right to be jealous, but the characters of the women confronting him tell him he does not. Circumstances may have driven Rosina to form a friendship with her servant girl, but now that servant is her equal and the Count does not measure up. Moments later the women will force the Count to his knees, and he will gasp out in supplication "Rosina." He has momentarily been affected by their nobility, or he would not leave himself thus exposed. The fevered duple meter has been vanquished by the tranquil triple gesture — again the triumph of the more human passions over the exalted (in this opera better styled the *exalté*).

A frozen moment of confrontation is not long supportable. The orchestra swings into a gay *buffa* motive in duple meter,[36] calling all three back to normal time. Questions, explanations, and recriminations fol-

Example 4-13

Example 4-14

low while the effects of the minuet are being calculated and put into perspective. The long key-area piece in B-flat which absorbs the minuet's impact is a wonderful construction. In it ready-made motives presented like precut swatches of material are pasted along various plateaus of tonality in a complex key-area layout.[37] Two motives predominate, both open-ended "vamp-till-ready" figures which can be closed off at any juncture (ex. 4–13). Transitions between keys are effected not by the development or transformation of motives, but by short breaks in the regular rhythmic and harmonic action established on each plateau; the breaks are often abrupt bits of recitative.

This patchwork method of construction lends itself well to the present situation. Each character is trying to assume the posture most advantageous for him; all three have their masks on and deliver their sayings in clipped cadential formulas. The Count, still suspicious, wants to appear repentant. Susanna and the Countess, seizing the moment, put on a public *buffa* face, delivering mock moral aphorisms in patter parallel thirds (ex. 4–14).[38] Shrill-voiced and cautionary, they rather resemble comic harpies, trying to batter the Count to his knees with their epigrams.

But cracks do appear in the masks, of the Count and Countess at least, the Count when he cannot control his suspicion of being had, and the Countess when she allows her real sense of betrayal to rise to the surface. She preserves the somber mood of "Porgi, amor"; it often breaks through the *buffa* atmosphere of the section. The most moving moment occurs when the Count "in atto di preghiera"[39] gasps out

"Rosina," and the Countess is moved to real anger. "Crudele!/Più quella non sono"[40] she cries, in recitative. She moves the harmony from an E-flat major plateau to the dominant of C minor. After a fermata, a deceptive cadence (A-flat momentarily functions as the sixth degree in C minor) slips the tonality to the next plateau, on A-flat major. It curtails the modulation process, up till now a series of mechanical moves in continued proportion (B-flat : g :: E-flat : c), by skipping the C-minor plateau — an ironic pun on the words "Più quella non sono." The Countess's pain is deep, and not to be assuaged by the pat resolution of this lesser imbroglio.

She is, however, to be admired for the resilience she displays in the face of her suffering. Although the brittle *buffa* is hardly her idiom (nor is it in fact Susanna's — she plays a caricature of herself in this trio), the Countess is capable of assuming it in order to regain her husband's love. And part of the delight of this movement is the ambiguity of her outbursts. The bitter anger of her exclamation at the Count's "Rosina" seems entirely spontaneous, and so also do similar interjections in measures 199–203 (the move to B-flat which begins the X-section) and measures 211–18 (the first cadence in the first E-flat modulation).[41] But at other moments — in the patter epigrams, for example — she seems to be composed, and coolly pressing her advantage. Surely her last moment of pathos (mm. 280–87) is premeditated; one sign of this is that it is in rhythm rather than declamatory, moving against the background of the "vamp-till-ready" music. It is also in a key (C minor) rather than being an agent of key change, and spoken to Susanna, her buffer, rather than directly to the Count. The minor inflections in her melody, to the words "Ah, quanto, Susanna,/Son dolce di core!"[42] strike a note of conventional pathos. But if some of the Countess's anger is affected, her ability to dissemble in the service of her love is a welcome sign that she possesses, in addition to the gentle dignity of her demeanor, a measure of true spirit.

The two women manage to force the Count to his knees, and he gasps out "Ho torto"[43] over a melodramatic augmented sixth, just into the tonic return. Open-ended (coming to a half-cadence), it occasions a sublime cadential phrase to close the movement, one which speaks of reconciliation and future understanding.[44] A near-rhyme with an A-flat cadence deep in the X-section (mm. 247–53), where Susanna playfully urges the Countess to have mercy on the Count, it pulls a cadence out of the syncopated "vamp-till-ready" music (see ex. 4–13b, p. 125), and depends for its effect on the lovely chromatic harmony arising from the deceptive-cadence relation of V of vi moving to IV (mm. 247–48, 250–51, 320–21, 323–24), and on the beauty of Susanna's soaring melodic line. Thus the first wave of the action in the finale comes to an end.

The close of the second key area (in the large-scale key scheme; see fig. 3) has settled a problem, and the dominant has been gained with a strong sense of arrival. This resolution, however, is as temporary as the dominance of the new tonic.

Figaro's entrance at the beginning of the finale's "X-section" (G major) immediately undermines the stability attained with great effort by the Countess and Susanna; the plot "rethickens." Figaro too puts on a *buffa* mask, maintaining the impression that the scene is a *commedia* staged by the characters for each other's benefit. He chooses a dance from the far right of the metrical spectrum for his entrance—a passepied or triple contredanse (the two were closely associated). Its light meter (3/8) and strong downbeat epitomize the nimble-footed, carefree servant's posture. Figaro humbly requests all those present to help celebrate his nuptials "tra canti, tra balli/De' vostri vassalli."[45] Again the expert stage manager, he has brought the musicians with him; they are waiting outside, he announces, and their flourishes can be heard in the orchestra (mm. 335–37, 339–41). Again the formal structure of the event is meant to impose: the movement stays carefully within the bounds of dance structure, beginning with a four-measure flourish and *riverenza*, and continuing in four-measure units thereafter until the Count intrudes on the symmetry.

Figaro moves adroitly here from miming the aristocrat (as in "Se vuol ballare") to playing the buffoon. He has come to clear up trouble, not to get into it, as he would were he to adopt the posture of his sardonic minuet. Assuming his proper place, he plays the role of respectful servant cheerfully, tugging his forelock with a vengeance. But the Count knows Figaro too well to take this masquerade at face value. He collars Figaro with a "Pian piano, men fretta,"[46] characteristically inserting a long-held note and odd measure to destroy the dance rhythms momentarily (ex. 4–15). Figaro tries to wiggle away with more of the passepied, but the Count suggests that he has a small doubt he would like to see relieved. The new crisis underway, the passepied closes with the Count crowing as the rest of the ensemble expresses fresh fears.

The Count obviously considers himself clever in his choice of rhythm for the confrontation with Figaro. Desiring to exhibit his own competence at the dance game, he moves away from the march, his natal rhythm, to don a mask himself—the mask of the *mezzo carattere* gavotte; he thinks it is just the posture for the role he wants to play. He turns out, to his misfortune, to be wrong. The clue to his misapprehension lies in the nature of the gavotte, and of its companion topic, the pastoral.

In the stereotype of the pastoral the sophisticate assumes an innocence and simplicity which he cannot actually possess: in the court of

Example 4-15

Marie Antoinette the nobles who played at love as shepherds and milkmaids were attempting in their artificial world to mimic a lost naiveté. Of the dances available for use in re-creating the pastoral world, two, the siciliano and the pastorale, were believed to be renditions of real shepherd music, and thus were "raw material," the artifacts of *temps perðu*. The gavotte, on the other hand, is not raw material, but a direct reflection of the estate of the sophisticates themselves; it is a result of play with the pastoral convention rather than, like the pastorale or siciliano, material at the source of it. In those two dances multiple layers of reference are not available; to perform them is to suggest innocence itself. In the gavotte, the artificial rearrangement of the 4/4 measure, which creates its coy, "beating" affect, suggests instead a sophisticate feigning innocence, a self-consciousness which is demure, or possibly sly.

In the Count's hands the gavotte is to be, of course, the latter; at the start of the movement the gavotte rhythms suit his insinuating tone admirably. But its double layers turn out to defeat him in the end. Shamed but not repentant, he tries to use the dance ironically. His question is on the surface of it innocent, but with a barely suppressed edge of knowing menace. The strings support him with an Alberti bass, the characteristic gavotte accompaniment (ex. 4–16). The first reprise of the dance is a formal antiphonal battle between the Count and the two women over Figaro, whose decision to feign ignorance (mm. 403–6) throws the heroines into a panic. The strings double the tempo of the Alberti bass ($\flat$ instead of $\flat$), as the ladies' "Nol conosci?"[47] carries the piece into the second key area. Once there, Susanna begins the questioning with the Count's original music, attempting to put truthful words into Figaro's mouth. Now the gavotte phrase is divided into four parts, one fragment for each member of the quartet: first Susanna, then the Countess, followed by a prod from the Count and a final cadential denial from Figaro (mm. 411–15). The section is repeated twice, the second time gaining greater urgency from the divisions added by the women to their line (eighth notes are subdivided into sixteenths in mm. 415–19).

The second key area ends with two cadential gavotte motives, the first the Count's and the second Figaro's. Because of its dynamic markings (*sforzando* on the first beat of the gavotte pattern, *piano* on the second), the Count's new "gavotte" (mm. 419–25) is in effect an exalted march, with undertones of rant; this scansion is heightened by the orchestra, which in its strict imitation of the motive applies upbeat flourishes to the first beat of the gavotte pattern, effectively moving the barline to inflect the 2/4 as an exalted march: ♩♪ ♩♪ instead of ♫♫ | ♩♪♩♪ Figaro deftly fields the Count's last words—"Il tuo ceffo già t'accusa;/ Vedo ben che vuoi mentir"[48]—at the same time reinstating the gavotte inflection with its air of feigned innocence. "Mente il ceffo, io già non mento"[49] is the literal-minded answer of a bumpkin or the hedging of a skilled equivocator (ex. 4–17). Figaro's drawling gavotte has the canny man playing the fool in a game of one-upmanship, using the Count's material. His feigned foolishness distresses Susanna and the Countess, however; they take up his tune to implore Figaro to stop fencing and admit the truth (since they have already been forced to "explain" the incriminating letter Figaro had sent to the Count, they see no reason for further prevarication, but Figaro is unaware of the situation). Puzzled,

Example 4-16

Example 4-17

he takes refuge in noncommittal answers. The movement returns to the
tonic with the two women in patter assuring Figaro that "La burletta ha
da finir." [50]

Again choosing to pun rather than answer directly, Figaro seizes on
the word "burletta." Back in the tonic with the Count's opening gavotte
motive (see ex. 4–16, p. 129), he makes, as it were, a formal announcement; to finish the farce happily, as is usual in the theater, the characters will perform an "azion matrimoniale." [51] Two horns in horn fifths
add the flavor of the ceremonial to his music. One more layer has accumulated in the dance and in Figaro's posture: playing the innocent, he
has taken up the Count's own music of pseudo-innocence, eliminating
the Count's snarl. Playfully proposing the marriage as a continuation of
their pretended play, Figaro takes the Count aback with the diabolical
impermeability of his surfaces. The Count thought himself protected by
the mere assumption of a civilized veneer to cover his malice. Figaro, by
admitting that both their postures are theater, brings the proceedings
within the proscenium arch and under the sanction of its conventions.
His confession of being at play ensures that the drama, granted a life of
its own, can play itself out. The Count is a mere actor in the *commedia*;
Figaro has again become its playwright.

Again events threaten to pass the Count by as in a dream. The three
protagonists rush to take advantage of his discomfiture: they pick up
Figaro's cadential gavotte and join together in a prayer for the marriage's happy consummation. The entire movement until now has been
preparation for this moment of conciliation. Here the teasing, many-
layered gavotte is transformed into a soaring hymn, a celebration of the
unity of the heroes. Previously comic, the gavotte is now sung in close
harmony with suspensions, echoes of the exalted style. To the accompaniment is added an unmediated pastoral element — a drone-bass
pedal with deep *forte* entries (see ex. i–1, p. 2). In turning the gavotte
into a musette-gavotte, the humble drone effects a transformation of startling beauty; it grounds the dance, giving it unsuspected depths. Even
the Count's muttered patter at the repeat ("Marcellina, Marcellina,/
Quanto tardi a comparir!" [52]) is assimilated into the affect of this pastoral hymn; with its divisions of the beat it has the effect of a decorative
double, the crowning ornament of the cadence.

The musette-gavotte was not a creature of Mozart's invention, nor
was he the only artist to transform the pastoral genre for his own purposes. Usually, however, the popular song texts set to musette-gavottes
(as in ex. 2–30, p. 55) reflect the rather wearisome naiveté of a *raffiné*
idealizing the hypothetical simple life. Those poets and painters from
Virgil to Watteau who did turn the pastoral to higher ends were giving
expression either to a repugnance toward their present life and a long-

ing for a golden age, or to a weary and elegiac nostalgia at thoughts of mortality. It is unusual to use the genre as Mozart does in *Le nozze di Figaro*: not as a retreat from life but as a shelter for a living compromise. He transforms the otiose nostalgia of typical pastoral music into a profoundly devout, though secular, confession of faith. The elevation of a genre does not necessarily entail the destruction of its sources and limits; Mozart joins the other artists in seeing the pastoral as a place out of time, where Eros presides. But the nobles at the court of the Petit Trianon found their pleasure in pretending to be what they were not, whereas pleasure for Susanna and the Countess lies precisely in their enjoyment of the particularity of each other's being. They use the pastoral as a meeting place because there neither woman will have to deny her nature in its separateness; notions of class do not obtain in the remove of the pastoral, and each woman can address the other openly without at the same time submerging her essential attributes. A later duet (III, 20) will reveal how the two women behave toward each other when alone together in a pastoral place. Now they draw Figaro in with them, and the essentially private place becomes a public stance. The Count failed to transform the *mezzo carattere* gavotte into his own idiom, the exalted march. The proper expression for the exalted in *Le nozze di Figaro* is not ecclesiastical, but pastoral — that strange, half-lit, classical place presided over by Cherubino as tutelary deity. The very music cunningly chosen by the Count for disguise is the only ground where his three opponents can stand united. Worse is to follow immediately for the trio. Nevertheless, the extraordinary beauty of the transformed gavotte lifts this moment out of time into enduring significance; throughout the imbroglio it will remain indelibly with us as an image of an abiding relation among three undeniably noble people.

From C major to F major, II in E-flat, is but a simple drop down by fifth, and ♪ *Andante* smoothly becomes ♩ *Allegro molto*. But the change in temperature is radical — from the exalted hymn of the three conspirators to the *buffa* patter of the drunken gardener. The rapid-fire *buffa* quintet which begins the imbroglio of the third wave is another large key-area form, covering a great deal of dialogue in a simple 4/4 meter. In it Antonio enters, announcing that someone has leapt from the balcony into his carnations and brandishing papers which fell from the culprit's pocket. Figaro, quickly sizing up the situation with the help of whispered hints from Susanna and the Countess, devises a clever solution. For once the product of his ingenuity meets their immediate approval, and they exclaim "Che testa! che ingegno!"[53] The situation requires a quick and radical remedy, and Figaro's dramatic imagination comes brilliantly to his rescue.

At the end of this movement Figaro, using his talents as a mime, announces that it was indeed he who leapt from the window, and that he has strained a nerve in his ankle in the process. The orchestra follows him *ad libitum* as he slows to a tempo which will suit the moment to come, singing a comic chromatic descending line to mime his descent from the window. At the bottom he "picks himself up" from his leap (which is accompanied by a modulation down a fifth, in B-flat major), and appears to have developed a limp. The new 6/8 meter, with its stress on beats 1 and 3, 4 and 6, is a fine foil for him as he demonstrates his sprained foot—a slow "limping" gigue. The last movement's F tonic is retained as a dominant pedal in the upper voices, making *terra firma* seem a little shaky, and appropriately so. Antonio immediately produces papers which turn out to be Cherubino's commission and Figaro is, in his own words, in a trap.[54] He manages to have Antonio silenced by the end of the second key area, but the problem of the commission remains: Figaro needs the right answer, and quickly. Susanna and the Countess recognize the paper as Cherubino's commission and alert Figaro, who begins the X-section pretending to curse his bad memory ("Che testa," the head which the women have just been praising) on an augmented sixth in G minor—another comic chromatic moment (m. 650).

The gigue figuration and dominant pedal now become more than just a mime of Figaro's antics: they are used to build up an unrelenting X-section tension. The figuration—a staccato repetition of a three-note rising line—elaborates a series of modulations by thirds (ex. 4–18). The dominant pedal rides over the figuration, preventing any of the cadences from breaking the tension, at the same time as the modulations are accomplished by the simple device of transforming the third of the old tonic into the dominant pedal of the new key. The pedal device permits Mozart to move to a new key at each turn in the action without ever interrupting the suspenseful figure. Figaro sings in D minor, but when the Countess and Susanna give their whispered hint the key changes to the E-flat major of impending deliverance. Figaro's puzzlement matches a turn to C minor; he mutters "È l'usanza . . ."[55] strug-

Example 4-18

gling to find the proper words to spring the trap. Now the tension reaches a climax: the orchestra crescendos and the skeletal line is deflected from the expected A-flat major toward B-flat major, via a G-flat and an A-natural.[56] When Figaro supplies the right answer, "il suggello" ("the seal," mm. 670–71), the tension "resolves" to a strong half-cadence.

In keeping with the deft understatement of this movement, the tonic returns in an undertone (m. 672), at first with the limping figure in the orchestra alone; it depicts both triumph and disgust interiorly, pent inside the characters — who speak in asides — rather than exploding as it will at the finale's end. The Count destroys the commission in quiet chagrin, and Susanna expresses her relief with a reticently triumphant stylized B-flat fanfare, culminating in a long-held high F (mm. 674–79). The movement succeeds by way of a clever economy: a rhythm and harmony used to choreograph a special posture for a character at the outset of the piece are seized on to create a psychological climate which dominates its remainder. Figaro the dramatist proposes and Mozart disposes.

Lorenzo da Ponte, in a frequently quoted passage in his memoirs, styles the composition of a finale as a librettist's bête noire:

> This *finale*, which must remain intimately connected with the opera as a whole, is a sort of little comedy or operette all by itself, and requires a new plot and an unusually high pitch of interest. The *finale*, chiefly, must glow with the genius of the conductor, the power of the voices, the grandest dramatic effects. Recitative is banned from the *finale*: everybody sings; and every form of singing must be available — the *adagio*, the *allegro*, the *andante*, the intimate, the harmonious and then — noise, noise, noise; for the *finale* almost always closes in an uproar: which, in musical jargon, is called the *chiusa*, or rather the *stretta*, I know not whether because, in it, the whole power of the drama is drawn or "pinched" together, or because it gives generally not one pinch but a hundred to the poor brain of the poet who must supply the words. The *finale* must, through a dogma of the theatre, produce on the stage every singer of the cast, be there three hundred of them, and whether by ones, by twos, by threes or by sixes, tens or sixties; and they must have solos, duets, terzets, sextets, thirteenets, sixtyets; and if the plot of the drama does not permit, the poet must find a way to make it permit, in the face of reason, good sense, Aristotle, and all the powers of heaven or earth; and if then the *finale* happens to go badly, so much the worse for him![57]

One suspects that da Ponte enjoyed meeting the challenge posed by the conventions of the finale as much as he enjoyed complaining about them. Excessive as they may seem in description, their effects cannot be explained away as merely conventional; sound eighteenth-century

musical habits produced them, and Mozart always tailors them ingeniously to meet the immediate needs of the drama. The slam-bang
strepitosissimo close to the finale is a musical necessity, for its final cadence puts the period either to the whole, or to a considerable section,
of the opera. The 158 measures of E-flat cadences which close this finale
(from the *Più allegro*, m. 783, the return of the tonic in the finale's last
movement) are not excessive, but obligatory, if a proper dynamic balance is to be struck. An area of such harmonic simplicity demands, of
course, correspondingly simple melodic material and a forthright meter.
The characters must be painted with broad strokes, and all their characteristic gestures subsumed under the common denominator of a
single duple meter, the quick march. Happily, the march is a fully appropriate topic for the close of both of *Figaro's* grand finales. In the
fourth act the march will accompany a public celebration of dilemmas
successfully resolved; here in the second-act finale it choreographs the
frenetic triumph of the wrong side. In the larger scheme of the finale it
closes the last round in the contest between duple and triple meters, the
dramatic "dialectic of dances" which gives the piece its shape. After
Figaro's triumph in his characteristic triple, the Count and his party go
him one better in the duple of the Count's exalted-march style. Against
its background all the characters are viewed at a distant perspective,
moving in choirs or teams, and only occasionally doing a solo turn.

   Marcellina, Bartolo, and Basilio all have solos in the same style — a
mincing gavotte made tipsy by string flourishes, and dissolving after
four measures (or two steps) into *buffa* patter (ex. 4–19).[58] The gavotte
rhythms and their dissolution into patter suitably portray characters

Example 4-19

whose thin veneer of sophistication thinly veils a rather crude natural temperament. The same gesture recurs at the opening of the third-act sextet (III, 18), the endearing moment when Marcellina and Bartolo embrace Figaro as their long-lost son. There they both sing gavottes accompanied by the characteristic Alberti bass, Bartolo's over a musette-like pedal. Basilio's "In quegli anni" (IV, 25) also begins with the same gavottelike figure. The gavotte motive is a happy rhythmic tag for cartooning the old *précieux ridicule* — the fulminating Bartolo, or Marcellina ostentatiously preening her thinning plumage. The gesture catches the characters' self-parody, their attitudinizing; they manner their movements, and the double-layered rhythmic artifice of the gavotte mirrors these harmless affectations. It is not necessarily meant to make them dislikable: Marcellina and Bartolo sing gavottes both when they are the newly arrived villains of the piece and when we hold them highest in our affections. When Marcellina minces in here to the rescue of Almaviva, the spectacle of a tarnished old *poseur* daring to reveal such a vengeful nature is slightly repellent, but when later she shows herself capable of maternal affection, her mannerisms become instantly lovable; she seems an eccentric but amiable old dear.

After each of the conspirators' gavottes there follows a burst of startled questions from Susanna, Figaro, and the Countess, and the Count enters with his characteristic *alla breve* style, imposing a half-note beat over the quarter notes of the gavotte, to cry "Olà, silenzio:/Io son qui per giudicar"; [59] as always he is the stern voice of judicial piety. In the *più allegro* and *prestissimo* sections the triumphant Cheshire-cat grin of the conspirators is portrayed by more *alla breve* cantus-firmus music, moving in whole and half notes, and accompanied by choirs of wind instruments which give the slow-moving harmonies a special ethereal sound.[60] These smugly ecclesiastical snippets send a verbal glance heavenward: "Qualche Nume a noi propizio/Qui li (ci) ha fatti capitar."[61] Since the advantage is the Count's, Susanna, Figaro, and the Countess must perform on his ground; their most profiled music resembles species counterpoint with syncope, providing an elaboration of the cantus firmus of the other characters.[62] It properly sets, for the third and final time in the finale, the word *confuso*, sung now wistfully by the three; it applies no longer to the Count, but to them. These passages suggest again the deep connection between the march and the ecclesiastical style. But, as happens throughout *Figaro*, the poses of factious, unloving characters reveal the ecclesiastical stance not as the extreme of nobility, but as smug presumption and infernal piety.

The subject of finale conventions illuminates a question which was raised earlier — why some of the most moving and meaningful moments of the opera are buried in imbroglio and rapidly passed over. The C-

major gavotte movement in the middle of this finale is one of those moments. It is Mozart's first revelation of a possible resolution of the
opera's central concern — the staking out of the grounds on which two
characters of disparate social backgrounds can meet and come to one
another's aid. The opera does not end with the answer to the question or
emphasize it by some other conventional spatial accent, and the notion
of mere convention is often invoked to explain this apparent defect or
others like it: since Mozart was forced by contemporary operatic practice to write frenetic finales, he had to bury the matters most important
to him in somewhat unlikely places.

It is possible, however, to take another view of conventions both social and musical, as it seems to me that Mozart did. The vision which
gave shape to the music of *Le nozze di Figaro* is neither revolutionary nor
Romantic, although both interpretations are current and popular. Conventions must prevail, both in the world abroad and in music; there is
nothing "mere" about them, for they form the sturdy superstructure
which makes things work. If a man has some apprehension of a deeper
and more enduring truth about how to live his life, there is no efficacy in
asserting it directly and openly against convention. Instead one drops
occasional hints of other possibilities — the private proprieties which
can successfully exist within convention's frame. To the lingering sound
of the gavotte the audience will attach other memories in a tissue of in-
terconnected moments: the surface incongruities in the characterization
of Cherubino, the text's constant classical and pastoral references, the
deepening pastoral atmosphere of the last two acts. Together they trace
out a shadowy outline of another shape, which while intersecting with
the public moments of the opera forms a wholly different plane. The
musical conventions invoked in the opera are definitive in that they lay
down the boundaries within which the characters must move. The special out-of-time moments, on the other hand, are cumulative, and their
sum is a private vision of how, given the necessity of limits, one may
best live one's life.

CHAPTER FIVE

Act III

The Count's Scena

As the climax of the mad day draws near, the pastoral affect will grow more prevalent, confirming the plethora of allusions one finds to it in the first two acts. But the beginning of the third act is the Count's, just as the beginning of the first belonged to the betrothed couple and the Countess inaugurated the second. "Vedrò mentr'io" (no. 17), an accompanied recitative and aria, is the Count's one great set piece in the opera, and it follows on an equally important duet between the Count and Susanna. The *scena* which the two pieces constitute is one of Mozart's best moments of psychological portraiture. His Almaviva is no mere cardboard heavy; a villain who is beneath contempt would cast no real shadow, and there must be no illusion about the nature of the menace to the apparently pacific comedy of *Figaro*. The pity and sympathy which the Count arouses here by a fleeting moment of human behavior qualify him for a more serious judgment against him when he ceases again to honor human ties.

Its minor key (A minor) is the first of the special qualities of the duet. Only two pieces in the opera actually begin in minor, the other being Barbarina's little cavatina at the beginning of act IV; even the Countess's moments of intense and private grief are cast in major. Dramatic recitativelike chords begin the piece, and the Count takes up an expanded version of them in a declamatory style, each accent of which is supported by the orchestra after the manner of accompanied recitative (ex. 5–1). The entire *scena* has an archaic flavor, beginning with these opening chords with their augmented sixth expanding to a half-cadence

Example 5-1

—a conventional *accompagnato* opening for a high-tragic recitative in *opera seria*. The Count's breathy pause after "Crudel!" and his suspended C anticipating the orchestra's repetition of the augmented sixth add to the conventional pathos of the declamation. Four more measures of arpeggiated dominant follow, punctuated with staccato pleas from the Count. Then suddenly, with the flick of a chromatic scale (m. 10), the declamatory style is banished, not to return until the next aria, the Count's "Vedrò, mentr'io."

The anomalistic style of these first ten measures of the duet concedes to the Count a flicker of honest passion. The big man's hoarse ardor here is moving; he is in an erotic daze, trembling from the impact of Susanna's youthful charms and her astonishing air of capitulation. He is also pitiable because we know that Susanna is about to tell him a dreadful lie, capitalizing on his tremulous passion — the cardinal sin for a true lover. And she is going to bring off the lie by willfully perpetuating a myth which the opera is dedicated to exploding — that a woman's words are written on water, "la donna è mobile."[1] The pathetic A minor of the opening allows the periods of the two characters to be juxtaposed directly, without transitional material, but with the maximum contrast between the Count's distracted eros and Susanna's pert assurance: to slip from minor into the relative major is a simpler harmonic move than the modulation up a fifth to the dominant, yet the consequent change in tonal color is much greater. To the Count's ardently interrogative E-major triad (V of A minor) is directly juxtaposed the cool C major and the blasé flirtatiousness of Susanna's rejoinder: "Signor, la donna ognora/Tempo ha di dir di sì."[2] Third-related harmonic progressions effectively reveal two different tonal worlds which are connected only by a common tone and a common moment in time. This particular version of the progression resembles the terrible bland sweetness of Don Giovanni's drop from E major to C major in his second seduction of Donna Elvira, where with cruel insouciance he sings a snatch of a love song he will use a moment later for the seduction of Elvira's maid (*Don Giovanni*, II, 2, 32–46). The fall from the E-major reflections of Elvira and Leporello down to the troped love song is chilling, and Susanna's answer to the Count has something of the same effect, augmented by the clever way in which she smoothes the Count's rocky declamation into a trim four-measure bourrée. (The orchestra helps by ceasing to double the melody, and punctuating instead the strong beats of the dance; in m. 12 it turns its own dramatic augmented sixth of m. 5 into a remarkably coy version of that chord.) The audience must have an ambivalent reaction to Susanna here; she is almost too accomplished in the role of the ingratiating tease. She is protected from disfavor only by the prior evidence of her good character, and the response to her indifferent perkiness is a corresponding wave of sympathy for Almaviva, for an instant portrayed as a victim struggling in the snares of love. Later, however, this intimation that the Count has a soul will do him no good.

Rarely does Mozart write such a compact "exposition." The greater strength of the major mode relative to the minor, and Susanna's neat capping of the Count's uneasy rhythms, make her four measures sufficient answer to the Count's ten. In them the second key is established, and the next fourteen measures are merely a slow lead-in to a dominant pedal for the return of the home key. Contrary to the usual practice in instrumental music, Mozart returns to the major, not the minor, tonic. A minor is not the key of the movement in a symphonic sense, that is, it does not dominate the tonal argument; here the "key" of the movement is only the key to the first gesture, and A major prevails for the last forty-four measures. Recovering from the shock of Susanna's sudden acquiescence, the Count slips into his first *mezzo carattere* gesture of the opera — a charming A-major bourrée with a real tune (ex. 5–2). He is still a sympathetic figure; stripped of his arrogance and of reminders of his power, he is simply a man enjoying a moment we all long to experience, when the object of one's fondest desire first shows signs of an answering passion. His throaty measures of subdominant opening out to a high-E appoggiatura on the word *gioia* (mm. 30–31) are joy untrammeled. Susanna, being indeed the woman we thought she was, sings as a contrapuntal aside a prayer for absolution from her lie; addressed to "Voi che intendete amor,"[3] it thus invokes the protection of Cherubino

Example 5-2

COUNT

Mi　sen - to ＿ dal con - ten - to ＿　　　Pie - no di gio - ia il　　cor. ＿

and the special circle of "donne che hanno intelletto d'amore." The piece ends with the two singing in parallel thirds — an ironic "love duet" in which only one partner truly participates.[4]

The first and second reprises of this duet achieve an ingenious rhythmic equilibrium. Against all common practice, the forty-four measures of expansive A-major bourrée suffice to provide a proper balance for the clipped fourteen measures of "exposition." Those fourteen measures are marked by clock time — the time it takes to speak lines of dialogue without repetition — while the forty-four measures with their constant repetitions of text and music are opera's more usual elaborated expansion of a moment's dialogue. But the musical images presented in the opening are fresh, and powerful particularly because of their compactness; the reflections stimulated by their juxtaposition so weight the opening that only a long-spun-out close will sufficiently balance it. Here, as in so many of the numbers of *Figaro*, the new Classic freedom to give action a musical resonance stands behind the originality of Mozart's conception. In other hands the first exchange between the Count and Susanna would probably have been relegated to the preceding *recitativo secco*, forcing these most important revelations under the counter, so to speak. And the admission of action into the musical continuum of an opera in the supple and adaptive key-area plan does more than bridge the chasm between action and reaction: it leaves us with a suggestive impression of the ethos of the action — the mode in which it is taken — which makes a powerful contribution to the ever-increasing stock of the opera's musical metaphor.

The Count need only overhear one exchange between Susanna and Figaro to realize that Susanna's capitulation was feigned. His immediate response is to plan revenge,[5] in a dramatic *recitative accompagnato*. Then in an impassioned aria, *Allegro maestoso* and *alla breve*, he vents his spleen. He has received a cruel blow, and any show of dignity on his part as he retires to lick his wounds ought to increase the modicum of sympathy which he gained just now. But his response fails of nobility; the text of his aria reveals his old self again, in all the arrogance of its limitations:

> Vedrò, mentr'io sospiro,
> Felice un servo mio?
> E un ben che invan desio
> Ei posseder dovrà?
>
> Vedrò per man d'amore
> Unita a un vile oggetto
> Chi in me destò un affetto
> Che per me poi non ha?[6]

The Count is a man in whom loss stirs not sadness or despair, but grim envy: it merely wounds his vanity. He mentions the object of his desires only impersonally, as "un ben," who has moved him while herself unmoved. First on his mind is his "rival," who as a mere servant has no rights except those of punishment and deprivation. (Were he to remember Figaro's role as go-between in the courting of Rosina, it would only make the situation more intolerable.) The vision of this "vile oggetto" besting and mocking him torments the Count, as he reveals in words which become the centerpiece of the aria:

> Tu non nascesti, audace!
> Per dare a me tormento
> E forse ancor per ridere
> Di mia infelicità.[7]

Generations of arrogant assumptions about the absolute privilege of rank lie behind the verb "nascesti," and explain the Count's edgy tone as he envisions the derision of his energetic and clever challenger.

"Vedrò, mentr'io" is a grand vendetta aria in a mixed mode. The prevalent style of the first key area is declamatory: the Count's opening music, although cast in four-measure phrases, joins its motives in a loose and unperiodic relation while the orchestra actually organizes the energies of the period. In the vocal line two measures of a dotted and descending motive yield to two measures undotted, and ascending to a snapped-off octave leap (mm. 45–48). Measures 52–55 begin as a repetition of the phrase, but a sudden influx of bile at the thought of Figaro possessing Susanna causes the Count to substitute for the original measures 3 and 4 a typical question cadence from accompanied recitative (an augmented sixth moving to the dominant for a half cadence; mm. 54–55). The *alla breve* style does not take wing until measure 66 and the arrival in A major.

Even that firm rhythmic footing, however, is short-lived. The new line of action which begins in measure 66 is not developed, but peters out into uneasy exclamations of "Vedrò? Vedrò?" over a V-i oscillation in D minor (through m. 87). The *Allegro assai* and return to the tonic (mm. 88ff) provide a new and vigorous beginning, but after four measures the stride of the march is broken again by a series of five three-measure groupings, which set the important stanza "Tu non nascesti, audace!" This stunningly extended phrase, which in closer conformity to periodic norms would amount to ten or eleven measures, not fifteen (see ex. 5–3 for both the "normal" and the "abnormal" — actual — version) is the critical moment of the aria. Afterward it makes its cadential drive, ending in a *bravura* mini-cadenza in measures 145–55.

The extensions of the "Tu non nascesti" phrase must be examined

Example 5-3

closely, for they reveal the near-dementia of Almaviva's jealousy, and its source deep in his *amour-propre*. The first extensions lay bare the extent of the Count's malice toward Figaro. The phrase "Tu non nascesti, audace!" receives a vengeful caress, its first three words lasting two measures rather than one (the proper duration if the sentence were to fit into a four-measure period). The snapped-off "audace!" forced now out of rhythmic proportion with the first part of the phrase, makes the utterance all the more arresting and peremptory:

The words "Per dare a me tormento" receive the same caressing attention, to form a third three-measure phrase (the "nascesti" phrase is repeated), rising a menacing chromatic third where the "paradigm" has two measures and a more forthright diatonic ascent.

The treatment of the next words, "E forse ancor per ridere," reveals Mozart's sense of the Count's present state of mind. They could have been set in two measures — the pace of the normalized version, and an effective angry quickening after the previous three-measure phrase — and then have been followed directly by the reach up to the high D for the broad "operatic" cadence figure.[8] But Mozart chose instead, by unexpectedly repeating the word "ridere," to fashion another triplet, actually a two-measure unit with the rhythm of measure 2 repeated (1–2–2 rather than 1–2–3, with the numbers representing entire measures). The three previous triplets were duplets stretched out of shape: quarter notes become half notes, dotted quarters become dotted halves. This fourth triplet, however, has a true extra measure: at the mere thought of Figaro's derision, the Count gives an involuntary *frisson* of horror, adding two beats to the phrase. The dominant harmony of the last beat of measure 8 (11) of example 5–3 lasts one full measure more, emphatically darkened by a B-flat chromatic appoggiatura postponing the dominant in the bass line[9] and by the orchestra's *sforzando* (in the "paradigm" the dominant harmony would resolve to I$_4^6$ in m. 9 and return for the final cadence in m. 10). All this attention focused on the one measure lends it a strong thetic accent, beside which the high D of the cadence figure pales. The word "ridere," surfacing the second time in this moment of unsuppressible panicked anger, almost overwhelms the conventional musical climax of the phrase. Figaro the dancing master stalks the Count's nightmares, even though Almaviva has not actually been present to witness the mocking challenge which Figaro delivered to him in "Se vuol ballare." A repetition of the long phrase (without the

first of the two "nascesti" groupings) makes clear the obsessive quality
of his vision. But this moment of inadvertent self-revelation is fleeting;
the Count recovers himself, and the aria ends with a Handelian cadenza
on the word "giubilar."

The nature of "Vedrò, mentr'io" invites comparison with other moments of high tragic style in the opera. The *recitativo accompagnato* and
aria of this choleric soliloquy intentionally announce themselves as a
troped aria convention from an archaic style. The convention with its
recognizable edges is meant to be suggestive: it calls attention to the
exalted formality of the Count's stance, and recalls other instances in
the opera where opera's odd habit of singing one's speech suddenly
ceases to be invisible, bringing into special prominence the provenance
of the singer's song. Only two other characters in *Figaro* ever approach
the *opera seria* vein in their music. The Countess's lovely "Dove sono"
(III, 19) has some of the hallmarks of the high tragic style, namely
its dramatic *recitativo accompagnato* introduction and the exalted-march
style of the *Allegro* (mm. 77ff). But although her soliloquy retains the
shape of "Vedrò mentr'io," echoes of the lyric mode of "Porgi, amor"
soften its conventional outlines, turning an unassimilated trope into a
characteristic figure.[10] The most striking similarity is with Bartolo's revenge aria in act I; in fact "La vendetta" (I, 4) was probably planned as
a foil for "Vedrò, mentr'io." In addition to the fact that both are revenge
arias, there are other similarities. Both are in D major, *alla breve*. Both
use trumpets and timpani in their orchestras, a special effect usually reserved by Mozart for the marching bands and *finalissimos* of the operas.[11] Both are at some distance from the *alla breve* paradigm, consisting of a proliferation of figures arranged by shifts and wrenches, and
often slipping into pure declamation. Bartolo's senatorial stance is undermined by his sudden lapse into the bathetic accents of *buffa* patter (I,
4, 58–66). He is by nature a buffoonish character; the distance between his pretensions and his person makes his version of *opera seria*
convention effectively a parody of the convention. Koch, in his *Journal
der Tonkunst*, complained of the debasement which the comic style had
effected on the conventions of *opera seria*:

> Ever since they began to dress up buffoon ariettas in the form of
> broad-scale arias, the serious arias have necessarily declined more and
> more in value; for as soon as the humorous masters the form of the
> serious, the serious takes on features of the humorous.[12]

While Koch was certainly correct in assuming that the serious style (at
least in eighteenth-century Italian opera) would never wholly recover
from this devaluation, he was apparently unaware that he had described

precisely the birth of a new convention. The role of the *vecchio prepotente* is as old as comedy, and the flexible rules of the new comic opera allowed the introduction of a hybrid aria which borrowed from *seria* idiom in order to capture the fulminations of this stock character. Bartolo's style — this unlikely fusion of patter with the exalted — was already well on its way to becoming a comic cliché.

Edgy, bellicose, and vain, the Count's white-note music lacks the superb and natural haughtiness, the classical purity, of Donna Anna's "Or sai chi l'onore." The comparison implied by setting "Vedrò, mentr'io" in the same formal mode as Bartolo's vengeance aria helps to clarify these puzzling imbalances in the Count's *ancien régime* nobility. Before Almaviva enters to utter clichés which are properly his, the exalted style has already been given a dangerously comic critique by a minor character; thus the nobleman cannot escape being tarred with the brush of the buffoon. Unlike the disreputable old lawyer Bartolo, however, the Count is not to be dismissed with a laugh; he is a man to be reckoned with, someone who has the power to harm decent people. The anomalies in his stance — the declamatory bombast, the vengefully distorted march, the edge of rising panic — have the effect of cartoon, but not of comedy. When the exalted and noble show a hysterical underside, disturbing cracks appear in things which are usually considered worthy of respect. The Count is a nobleman somehow dislocated from the limits which define noblemen as good men. He displays a capacity for excessive and erratic behavior which is not contained within the confines of the noble code of conduct. His *alla breve* stance, undermined by Bartolo's fulminations and by its own disturbing air of manic decay, becomes a flawed and unsettling gesture.

The Pastoral: Duet and Chorus

The duet between the Countess and Susanna, "Che soave zefiretto" (III, 20, in B-flat major),[13] supplies the first hints of that peculiar quality of color and light which will soon dominate the opera — the gloaming tints of the pastoral. Twilight is the emblematic time of day for the pastoral, "Finchè non splenda in ciel notturna face,/Finchè l'aria è ancor bruna e il mondo tace."[14] It is the time of day when Susanna, in the most eloquent of pastorales, "Deh, vieni" (IV, 27), will sing to entice her lover to a hidden grove whence time is barred, and where nature arranges all to please. Twilight is a dim and uncertain light under which familiar objects and persons present only shadowy, half-distinguished outlines, and may appear to be quite other than they lately seemed under the unremitting light of day. An elegiac and reflective time, it frightens narrow-spirited people, threatening to loosen their grip on the reassuring routines of day and night. Yet it is grace to others, who make their escape through it to a gentler world free of the limits imposed by daytime necessity. Twilight's half-light bathes the final scenes of the opera. Even Figaro, usually better at creating atmospheres than at sensing them, is moved by its special quality. Pausing to reflect on the evening, he describes himself with apt irony as Vulcan preparing to trap Venus as she cuckolds the faithful husband with Mars.[15] His moody sarcasm is comic, but its classico-pastoral frame of reference reveals the influence of the crepuscular atmosphere on his private musings. The gloom of twilight is, of course, ideal for an imbroglio consisting of seven cases of mistaken identity.[16] But the imbroglio itself, revolving as it does around questions of identity, has a deeper significance: the success of the two women in their exchange of roles drives home with a particular force how much by nature they have in common.

Susanna and the Countess are looking forward to twilight when they sing their duet. The Countess is dictating to Susanna a letter for the Count, which will suggest an evening rendezvous for him, ostensibly with Susanna, in the garden. The Countess intends to go herself, disguised as Susanna. She deliberately chooses a bucolic text for her letter. Wishing to make it allusive, a hint rather than an open invitation, she sends only a short poem which is the lyric of a song:"Che soave zefiretto/ Questa sera spirerà/Sotto i pini del boschetto."[17] The duet is cast as a pastorale.

With the coming of twilight the music of the pastorale also comes to dominate the opera: it is the topic of five of the remaining seven numbers. "Che soave zefiretto" is a typical pastorale, with its 6/8 meter and *allegretto* tempo marking, its even legato style, and the delicate simplicity of its design. Winds in parallel thirds and a flat key (B-flat major) have been borrowed from earlier music of the Countess and Cherubino to mark the pastoral place. Flat keys are especially suited to the pastorale because of their soft, mellow sound and their slanting relation to the main and public key of the opera—D major. The first thirty-seven measures of the duet have a simple two-reprise form, cadencing on the dominant in measures 16–17 and immediately returning to the tonic. Changes of harmony, staged by the eighth-note bass on the first and fourth beats of each measure, are leisurely, not dramatic. Steady legato arpeggios in the strings provide continuity. The two women sing short phrases, primarily arpeggiated in imitation of the accompaniment. The Countess almost seems to be listening to the accompaniment, as if to receive from it the proper cues for her composition. Susanna repeats each phrase of the text reflectively, to assure herself it is penned correctly. When the note is completed, the Countess says "Ei già il resto

Example 5-4

capirà."[18] "Certo," answers Susanna. Together for the first time, in parallel thirds, they repeat the phrase cadentially (m. 34).

Now the Countess leans over Susanna's shoulder and they read the text together, each taking a line. The music (mm. 37ff) repeats the I-V-I layout, but much truncated (the strong cadence on the dominant is omitted). Susanna starts off with the first phrase, to the Countess's original music. As she is finishing, the Countess overlaps with the beginning of the second, to Susanna's original music. Susanna overlaps with her for the last phrase, singing a line which had originally belonged to the orchestra, now slightly altered.[19] The technique resembles a rhythmic and melodic stretto, but without stretto's dramatic urgency. Instead the interweaving of the arpeggiated patterns in the two voices casts an atmosphere of unanimity and intimacy. An extended recapitulation of the phrase "Ei già il resto capirà" follows to intensify the feeling. First Susanna imitates the Countess at a measure's distance. When next, one at a time, each does a measure of ornamental divisions—the first sixteenth notes in the piece—the effect of the echo is breathtaking (ex. 5–4). They close with six more cadential phrases, mostly in parallel thirds, on the same line of text: in all, the phrase "il resto capirà" is heard twelve times.

The text used by the Countess for her note is a continuation of the mood she expresses in the preceding "Dove sono," with its elegiac sigh for "i bei momenti di dolcezza e di piacer,"[20] and her choice of the pastoral mode to address her husband further reflects that nostalgic state. But at the same time the pastoral text and music figure the classless, timeless meadow where two women ordinarily separated by circumstance can meet and stroll quietly together. The duet's Arcadian music is very different from the rhythms of the sophisticatedly naive gavotte: its 6/8 meter evokes the bucolic spirit directly, deliberately eliminating any courtly frame. The duet is the eye of the opera's storm, showing Susanna and the Countess calm and secure in their friendship. Their mutual trust and affection are all the more remarkable in this moment of the Countess's greatest humiliation when, all else having failed, she is

Example 5-5

reduced to ignoble plotting with her servants to win her husband back.
Yet the two women are in perfect unanimity; saying little, and nothing
which notes the difficulties of the circumstances, they comprehend each
other completely. Their gentle but emphatic assertion of the phrase "il
resto capirà" is emblematic of their unity; its repetition forces the casual
phrase to significance. The Count will understand the implications of
the note, as the third-act finale will attest. But the luminous understanding between the two women has its own aura, and will later bring
the Count to a more serious intelligence — of the power of love to humble the arrogant and to elevate the humble. Right now, although the
situation is deadly serious, the two women seem at play together in a
sheltered and intimate place, a place which bears the same oblique relation to the public world of the opera as B-flat major does to D major.
Like the C-major gavotte (which is to E-flat major, the key of its finale,
as B-flat is to D major), this pastoral duet, its serenity indelibly fixed in
the memory, stands out above the imbroglio of the opera, joining that
collection of impressions which serve to sketch out the nature of Mozart's
shadowed Arcadia.

This intimate moment is buffered from immediate collision with the
imbroglio by the entrance of a chorus of peasant girls. They come to
present flowers to their *padroncina* "per monstrarvi il nostro amor."[21]
Barbarina leads them, and Cherubino is among them, still disguised as
a girl. The chorus's chosen meter is again a pastoral 6/8, but now in the
key of G major, only a simple harmonic move away from the bright colors of the opera's public key. They sing in legato parallel thirds and
sixths, with a musette-style tonic pedal in the first and second key
areas.[22] Although most of the chorus is cast in the even legato rhythms
of the pastorale, an occasional dotted figure in the orchestra[23] suggests
the more sprightly gigue (ex. 5–5). The chorus is a mean between "Che
soave zefiretto" and the renewed imbroglio of the third-act finale. G major mediates between B-flat major and the bright C major to follow. The
giguelike turns of phrase slipped into the pastoral affect bridge the gap
between the gentle legato of the previous duet and the martial strains of
the band march opening the finale. The peasant girls' tender homage —
assuring the Countess of the affection of her subjects and thus frustrating the Count's efforts to cut her off from an important source of self-

respect — confirms and recasts as a public stance the pastoral image. It also triggers the next crisis, when Cherubino is discovered hidden and blushing in the midst of the peasant girls.

The Finale to Act III

The ceremony of the third-act finale would in ordinary circumstances be the culmination of the dramatic trajectory — the celebration of the nuptials of Susanna and Figaro, Marcellina and Bartolo. In *Figaro*, however, the festivities are merely the cover for more intrigue, and a continuation of the tracing of the real trajectory of the work, one which is longer and higher-arched, and finally culminates in the confusion of the fourth-act finale.

The finale begins with another ingenious use of "real" music — a march played by an approaching band of castle musicians. They enter just in time to save Figaro from another embarrassing situation: Antonio and the Count are pressing him to admit to his lie about jumping from the window, and his admission would incriminate himself and all his allies. Figaro seizes on the approach of the march to cut off all further conversation. Unlike Cherubino's "ballad" or the passepied of Figaro's quickly summoned dance band, the march exists independent of the volition of any one of the characters: the paraphernalia of ceremony are merely arriving at the appointed time. By the end of the finale, however, the protagonists have turned the march to their own advantage and it has been absorbed into the opera's structure of metaphor.

The march is an utterly charming one, in a sturdy dotted style with pseudo-Turkish inflections before the cadential section of each reprise (the minor turn of the triad on the supertonic, preceded by its dominant, and with grace-note flourishes in the oboes on strong beats; ex. 5–6). It is also an ingenious creation, which fully meets the particular demands of this situation. It displays its formal nature as an actually performed march by beginning *in medias res* on the dominant, as if the marchers were coming from a distance. An attentive listener will discover that the distance is indeed considerable: in order to support the

Example 5-6

effect of approaching musicians, the repeat of the second reprise of a fairly lengthy march actually begins the finale:

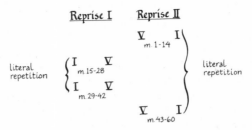

Strings, a full wind complement, horns, trumpets, and timpani constitute the orchestra, and they are introduced slowly, also to increase the effect of an approach from the distance: strings, flute, and horns in the first and *pianissimo* measures, oboes added in the first Turkish turn (*piano*), bassoons in the second, trumpet and timpani in the first runthrough of the first reprise (again *pianissimo*), and finally clarinets in the repetition of the first reprise, *forte*.

Beginning the march *in medias res* poses a problem for a careful composer. Since the proper climax of the march has been dismantled, and sections of it placed at both beginning and end, a new curve will have to be superimposed on the old if the disarrayed march is to have a proper dynamic arch. Mozart's solution to the problem is to make the second reprise uncharacteristically less interesting than the first, building the more complex part-writing and climactic phrasing into the move to the dominant rather than into the return to the tonic. The first eight measures of the second reprise are a broad cadential formula with G major as tonic: I IV (VII) II V I, in clipped two-measure phrases. The return to C major as tonic is then achieved by the Turkish music in two offhand three-measure phrases, almost as an afterthought. In the first reprise the move to the dominant (the second four-measure group) is achieved in a burst of rhythmic and melodic energy. The rhythm ♩ ♫♩ ♩ is repeated at the critical moment in the phrase, whereas in the second reprise it continues to alternate with measures of rhythmic stasis:

Example 5-7

The rise from G to D in the treble instruments is dramatized by the counterpoint of contrary motion in the bass line (ex. 5–7). The casualness of the second reprise makes this move to the dominant all the more dramatic, causing a curious imbalance which allows the disordered march to retain the dynamic curve that a grand motion of return to the tonic out of order in the first fourteen measures would have denied it. The terracing of instrumentation and dynamics over the four sections brings the orchestra to the highest dynamic level of the piece (full orchestra at last) and its most dramatic moment (the second rendering of the energy-charged first reprise) just when the whispered conversations taking place under cover of the march are over and the ceremonies are about to begin. The second reprise's leisurely cadence leaves the close of the piece with a stubbed-off ending, but Mozart makes it work for him by adding a four-measure extension of tonic fanfare (mm. 57–60). In a concert march the little appendage-coda would be ungainly; on the stage it only points up the essential *Gebrauchsmusik* nature of the march. It sounds like a short bit of cadential cliché habitually saved up by the practical castle musicians for putting the final period to their *ad libitum* repetitions when they see all the participants mustered to begin. This coda also serves as a beginning — a formal fanfare to call the attention of the gathering to the first performance of the ceremony (the two maidens singing a chorus of praise to the Count). Mozart's skill in turning conventional structures on their ear, only to make the attendant problems into advantages, shows itself clearly in the attention to detail lavished on this "occasional" piece. Practicing structural sleight of hand he has created out of the sections of an ordinary march an extraordinary one which sounds, in the circumstances, perfectly ordinary.

This finale marks the flowering of a metaphor for which Figaro himself planted the first seeds — in another march, in a previous finale. At the end of act I Figaro's march was in praise of Cherubino, apostrophizing him as the god of amorous warfare, and musical references to the erotic and the military continued to be bound together in gentle union throughout the opera. Now the march comes just in time to rescue Cherubino (and Figaro). Figaro's fine hand is obviously behind the performance of the two maidens and chorus who salute the Count for his abolition of the much resented *droit de seigneur*; he enters during the recitative preceding the march in order to collect them.[24] A small entanglement postpones his departure with his band, but when he hears the march he exclaims in fanfare style "A' vostri posti, o belle, a' vostri posti."[25] Against the background of the march his words have the snap of a military command. One can picture his small troop smartening up with mock salutes and marching off, swept away by the approaching music, to leave the Count outfoxed and impotently angry. Cherubino giggles among them, dressed now after his unmasking half in girls' clothing, half in boys', to underline his androgynous nature. Cherubino's presence among the choristers gives the military metaphor all the more force: the masculine part of his dress is the three-cornered hat of his soldier's uniform, which was presented to him with ironic ceremony before the march by the Count and Antonio (who found it in his cottage where Cherubino was hiding with Barbarina). The peasant girls are young Lysistratas mustering for a battle on behalf of Eros. Disguised as singers and dancers, they will hold down the front lines in the confrontation with the Count, the palace troops of the circle of *donne*, advancing in the cause of its amorous campaign.

Figaro has given his performers a poem to sing, effusive in its praise of "Sì saggio signor,/A un dritto cedendo/Che oltraggia, che offende."[26] At first two girls sing alone and the company dances to their contredanse melody (m. 74). Full orchestra accompanies them, while horns, trumpets, and timpani punctuate the cadential rhythms of the third and fourth measures of each four-measure phrase. The duple contredanse with its rhythmic and topical neutrality is a good choice for the chorus's rustic encomium (instead of their habitual pastorale-gigue rhythms) because barely suppressed under the contredanse scansion are the accents of a cocky march, which emerges when the duet moves to the dominant. The bass drops out and the trio of military instruments comes into prominence, playing horn fifths (ex. 5–8a) while the singers have fanfares (ex. 5–8b); both are military motifs. The horn fifths help to turn

Example 5-8

the contredanse scansion into a military gesture by doubling the rate of change of the harmonic rhythm: eighth rather than quarter notes (the contredanse scansion) become the level of the beat:[27]

The contredanse returns with the return of the opening material and the tonic (m. 106). But when the rest of the chorus joins the two girls for a choral coda, the military topic returns for a grand climax — sixteen measures of vociferous drum tattoo (mm. 117–32).

Although the march is inflected over the contredanse rhythms and the singers seem to be blushing country girls (who earlier played soldier), it is proper to remember that march rhythms also introduced the finale — and will close it — and to think of the girls as soldiers who in the contredanse impersonate maidens demurely dancing a rustic chorus. Their fulsome poem is a gauntlet thrown down before the Count, challenging him to go back on his word in public. He cannot resist them; after the dancing of a fandango he is forced to play the benevolent lord and announce a *festa nuziale* open to all in his domain. The chorus then repeats the contredanse-march in shortened form: the original ratio of 44:27 (contredanse:march) is strikingly reversed to 16:28, the twenty-eight measures largely consisting of the drum-tattoo section broadly extended. The hymn of praise has become a triumphal march.

The triumph, however, is not complete, since a public renunciation is hardly sufficient. Mozart uses the fandango specified by Beaumarchais (act IV, scene ix) to introduce an uneasy note into the triumphant C major. It provides authentic local color for the first and only time in the opera, yet its very authenticity strikes an outlandish note. The compositional premises of the fandango are diametrically opposed to the polar symmetries of the French court dances which constitute the vocabulary of *Figaro*. Spun-out, open-ended, and irregular, Mozart's version of the dance consists of sinuous permutations and combinations of five short motives, grouped here by measure for convenience:

Motive a is a head motive which begins all but the last phrase of the dance. Motive e is cadential, closing all phrases ending on the tonic. Both a and e mark time by signaling beginnings and ends of phrase groupings. The other motives are organized additively, strung like beads on a string, avoiding the symmetries of an antecedent-consequent relation. The additive construction and the irregular placement of the floating caesuras obscure any sense of ordinary two-measure dance-step groupings. Predominant instead is the inexorable march of eighth notes brought to the surface by motive b, and never far below it. The fandango's harmonic scheme is solar, rather than polar, as in most dance pieces: it explores first the dominant minor and then the relative major, returning to the tonic in between. The tonic harmony at the beginning and end is nailed down by two four-measure groups, one riding on the dominant and one cadential. They consist of almost the same combination of motives, for a near end rhyme. The other keys by contrast are explored by longer phrases, forged into units by the repetition of motive d across the natural seam of the four-plus-four:

measures:	4	4	4	8	2	4	6	4	4	3
motives:	abcc	abbe	abcc	abdddb¹b¹e	ab	abcc	adddde	abdd	abbe	b¹b¹e
harmony:	V/a	a	V/e	e	V/a	V/C	C	V/a	a	a

(cadential measures and the two long modulatory phrases are underlined)

The tonic is never squared off by a I-V-I period. Instead the dance begins on a first-inversion chord and moves through IV to the dominant, where the harmony rests, touching on the tonic only on weak beats and measures, except for cadential measure e. All the characteristic fandango elements — the minor tonality, the frozen tilt of the ubiquitous dominant harmony, the steady eighth-note pulse, and the open-ended, spun-out phrases — lend an air of elegant and static suspension to the dance, a stylization of tension. The Count reads Susanna's note under cover of the strange and foreign dance, while Figaro cynically observes him, little suspecting the pain that same note will bring him in act IV. The brittle, edgy tension of the fandango, framed though it is by the bright C-major marches, reaches past the march into the next act to be confirmed and intensified by the F minor of Barbarina's cavatina.

The finale to Act III is difficult to stage well. It is the opera's only "crowd scene"; orchestra, chorus, and actual dancing receive the principal emphasis, and singers hitherto individualized become part of the mass. All the main characters are on stage, along with the chorus (the women who serenaded the Countess before the finale have been joined by their men). The stage directions for scene xiv, beginning halfway

through the march with the presentation of the nuptial couples to their
padron and *padroncina*, call for

> Cacciatori con fucili in spalla; gente del foro; contadini e contadine;
> due giovinette che portano il cappello verginale con piume bianche; due
> altre con un bianco velo; due altre [con] i guanti e il mazzetto di fiori;
> due altre giovinette, che portano un simile cappello per Susanna, etc.[28]

Too often in performance a token peasant or two stands in for the intended gay throng of participants and onlookers. The spotlight then
will fall exclusively, in the contredanse, on the two peasant girls, and in
the fandango on the Count and Figaro — a mistaken rendering of the
action. Crowd scenes in operas are traditionally the locus for a furtive
action surreptitiously carried out under cover of the general bustle, de-
lighting the audience with a sense of being in on a maneuver which is
invisible to most of the participants. The Count's fumblings with the assignation note and Figaro's sardonic asides to Susanna should not take
place on a sparsely occupied stage center.

At least some sense of population is also necessary for the central
effect of the finale — its impassive ceremony. Ceremonies, once initi-
ated, overwhelm the will of any individual and must be allowed to play
themselves out. When the ceremony is controlled by music its formal
symmetries parcel out time inexorably, insisting on consequents for all
antecedents and returns for all departures. Furthermore, this ceremony
is being stage-managed by some of its participants; its ostensible and its
intended ends are not the same. A good production should catch the
theatricality of the conspirators' game — a *commedia dell'arte* playlet invented as a snare to catch the conscience of the Count. The conspirators
are the players, a ragtag company, masking their shrewdness by mas-
querading as fools and *naïfs*. They strut in jauntily to the strains of the
marching band (one nice touch would be to have a *commedia* clown with
a bass drum miming the strokes of the timpani). The phrasing of the
march suggests a tutti-solo choreography: the first eight measures of
each reprise for the entire group, and special solo turns for the six measures of Turkish music, divided three-plus-three between two small
bands, which vie with each other to see who can achieve the most comic
parody of soldiering. The girls carrying the bridal gear could be young
Colombinas, carrying out their duties in the presentation ceremony
with an exaggerated flourish. They grow demure for the contredanse,
but when the march resurfaces the whole company can barely suppress
its delight in its own cleverness and wit. The clown beats out his drum
tattoos with extravagant enthusiasm, and the others struggle to hide
broad smiles as they strut about the stage. Even the fandango is meant
to be danced by the group, since the stage direction at its head reads "I

figuranti ballono."[29] The company turns its hand to miming the elegant Spanish turns as well as they play soldier, in stiffly slinky gestures with only a tinge of parody about the edges. Their irresistible exuberance bursts out again at the return of the march, at once a proper conclusion to the ceremony and a celebration of its success. The Count stands by chagrined; he knows their exultation is really self-congratulation, but the *double entendre* of the public ceremony renders him helpless. One cannot take vengeance on a pack of clowns, fools, and waifs paying homage to the beneficence of their protector.

A *commedia* choreography for the finale is appropriate to more than the immediate situation. While the rogues with coxcombs take the Count by storm, their performance also makes an important connection between two images developed throughout the opera: Eros militant and the eroded grandeur of the exalted march style. The ragged band of soldiers fighting for the rights of love wins its battle by a parodistic rendering of a noble march. The Count loses his gavotte in the second-act finale, and here he finds his grandiloquent march no longer viable. The instinct for play, for mimicry and parody both of oneself and of others, is pitted against the monolithic mask of self-absorption. The one is agile, imaginative, and generous; the other is stolid and literal, and buttressed only by the arrogance of *amour-propre*. Bedroom soldier and canny fool, two paradoxical couplings so often the butt of comedy, turn into substantive figures in *Le nozze di Figaro*. There are heroism and generosity in their self-deprecation, and hidden reserves of intelligence in their antics.

CHAPTER SIX

Act IV

The Pastoral: Barbarina and Figaro

Much of the last act of *Figaro* concerns a new complication — Figaro's conviction that Susanna has actually betrayed him with the Count. The complication seems at first glance entirely superfluous; enough already remains to be accomplished before the plot can grind to a halt. And is Figaro plausibly credulous enough to imagine that his beloved could suffer the slightest pang of desire for the Count? So it would seem within the limits of a conventional social comedy where, the battle between the servants and their master being the principal theme, Figaro's error would only muddy the waters, placing him momentarily on the wrong side. But Mozart's opera is not such a comedy, as Figaro's fall from grace makes clear. Placed in the last act, it draws a final distinction between Figaro and the women in the opera, a distinction which was hinted at earlier but is to be clarified only at the last, because it is more subtle than the opposition between the three heroes and the Count and closer to the themes at the opera's core. The circle of "donne che hanno intelleto d'amore" is finally closed, showing that Cherubino's Dantesque references in "Voi che sapete" were not mere ornament. The creatures who rightly comprehend love are the women, who view the world with a gentler and more compassionate vision. Figaro's bold nature is too mercurial to be open to their kind of seeing. He, like the Count, must learn how to "be affected." He is quicker than the Count at the lesson: the mere sound of Susanna's normal voice in the fourth-act finale reveals the entire hoax to him, and he knows immediately that she could not have been untrue. But first a distinction must be made between him and the women, for the natural receptivity of their nobility is a trait which Figaro can only cultivate.[1]

Barbarina's miniature cavatina is an appropriate curtain raiser for act IV. It is another pastorale, with all the usual hallmarks of the dance. In 6/8 meter, *Andante*, with even, legato figuration, it consists of the simplest of two-reprise constructions: an orchestral introduction moving to the dominant and mimicked by Barbarina, a brief X-section on the dominant (mm. 15–19), and a return to the tonic with cadential figures. Barbarina is a child rapidly becoming an adolescent. There is talk of her "education" in the opera, most of it uttered with a slight leer.[2] She seems, however, to have learned also from some worthy grown-ups: in choosing pastoral rhythms for her cavatina she imitates the Countess and Susanna. Her little-girl anguish at losing the pin is caught by the F-minor tonality of the piece and by its frequent pathetic accents; it is an essay in the mock-tragic genre. Chords of the diminished seventh prevail, especially in the orchestral introduction: the plangent accents in measures 4 and 12 are particularly striking.[3] The introduction closes with a four-measure half-cadence on the dominant featuring a regular alternation of V and vii^7 of V over a V pedal, as the figures in the treble spiral higher and higher in the purposeless circles of someone searching in vain. Barbarina shortens the introduction by omitting this phrase, making her move to the dominant instead by a fervid augmented sixth on the words "Ah, chi sa dove sarà?"[4] She repeats this half-cadence — a typical *opera seria* model which she probably learned from the Countess, who moves into "Dove sono" from the preceding *recitativo accompagnato* by one very much like it[5] — at the end of the aria, just before Figaro interrupts her. This would suggest that Barbarina had intended her cavatina to be a composite aria: here she would swing into a new section in A-flat major, perhaps cast in exalted-march style like the second part of "Dove sono." But other elements of the piece militate against grand passion: Barbarina's wavering child's voice,[6] the thin texture of the reduced orchestration (strings only), the nursery-rhyme simplicity of the phrase structure. While aping the manners of the Countess and Susanna, Barbarina cannot assimilate them into her childish habit, and this makes for delicate comedy.

Barbarina's pastorale also reaches out to rhythms and themes occurring both earlier and later in the opera. It confirms the note of unrest at the end of the third-act finale, both in its minor tonality and because at its close Figaro learns what he thinks is the true version of the events which transpired during the fandango. It reaches forward by establishing the pastoral tone for the rest of the act. But Barbarina's is a pastorale with an important difference — its minor tonality. Her version of the affect, associated always with the unpleasant shock of revelation, will figure the pastoral mood for Figaro until the fourth piece of the last-act finale. Twilight seems threatening to him as a result; all forms loom deceptively large and misshapen. Overhearing Susanna's pastorale, "Deh, vieni" (IV, 27), just before the finale, he exclaims "Perfida! e in quella forma/Meco mentìa? Non so s'io vegli o dorma."[7] His first words impute a treacherous pseudo-innocence to the pastoral gesture: it cloaks wolves (*donne*) in sheeps' clothing. Yet in remarking his strange and ambiguous state of mind, he bears unconscious witness to the power of the pastoral: he does not now appreciate its transforming grace, but it holds him in thrall. He does sense that Eros reigns there, but his is a dark satiric vision, of Venus and Mars cuckolding the clumsy Vulcan (and perhaps in their adulterous union giving birth to an illegitimate Cupid). He is not released from his misapprehension until in the finale, from beneath her masquerade, he hears the healing sound of Susanna's voice. Then the tranquil B-flat pastoral music returns (IV, 28, m. 275, *Andante*), reaching back to act III and the letter duet to complete the circle. In between Mozart has rung the changes on the pastoral affect in the versions of Barbarina, Marcellina, and Susanna, and finally of Figaro himself (in his E-flat minuet just before the final pastorale, sung as a self-styled Vulcan); Figaro's sarcastic adaptation is framed by the real place itself in the two B-flat versions. In defining Figaro's view of the pastoral by Barbarina's cavatina, Mozart is subtly mocking him. The malevolence he senses lingering in the twilight is imagined, not actual, unlike the real menace of the *bujo loco* in *Don Giovanni*.[8] Figaro takes himself seriously, but we understand his posture as a pseudo-tragic stance; his grim anger and heavy sarcasm, since inappropriate, become part of the comedy.

The Pastoral: Pro Marcellina (IV, 24–26)

The two arias which follow Barbarina's pastorale — Marcellina's "Il capro e la capretta" and Basilio's "In quegli anni" (IV, 24 and 25) — have been given short shrift in *Figaro's* recent performance history; they are consistently omitted from productions of the opera. Few commentators on the opera have granted that these numbers have anything to recommend them; most follow Edward J. Dent, who argued that they were probably added merely to give each singer his "statutory rights in the matter of arias" (neither Marcellina nor Basilio has a solo aria elsewhere in the opera).[9] One argument used against them has been the alleged deficiency in construction of act IV: since it consists of a sequence of five arias and a finale, breaking with a principle which the three previous acts would seem to have established of locating a major ensemble somewhere near halfway through the unit, the act has drawn criticism on the grounds of lack of parallelism, as well as for the weakness which a chain of solo arias allegedly introduces.

This criticism is easily disposed of. It is possible to argue, on the grounds of construction alone, in favor of the retention of both arias. Rigid parallelism is rarely a feature of Classic "symmetry" because it weakens a sense of the period, and periodicity is by far the more important quality of a phrase, an act, or an opera. While the ensembles midway through the other three acts function as secondary climaxes, shaping for each act a graceful curve, a simple succession of solo arias has the advantage of throwing the weight of the final act on the finale itself; the resolution of the imbroglio has the more impact for not following close on the dazzle of a full-blown ensemble.

Another serious charge levied against these two arias is that they are extraneous, and add nothing either to the plot or to the central themes of *Figaro*.[10] But happily this charge can be refuted with hard evidence. The arias of Marcellina and Basilio in act IV form an important preface to Figaro's angry soliloquy "Aprite un po' quegli occhi" (IV, 26). Viewed in this light both arias — Marcellina's especially — are crucial to the theme of feminine friendship which is the matter at the opera's heart.

An unspoken assumption behind the omission of Marcellina's aria is that once she is discovered as Figaro's mother she is of no more interest; that she is a character of little weight, introduced to complicate the plot, and expendable after the act III sextet. Her creator, however, thought more of her. In his description of the characters of *Le mariage de Figaro* Beaumarchais portrays Marceline as "une femme d'esprit, née un peu vive, mais dont les fautes et l'expérience ont réformé le caractère."[11] Taking up the cause of women in his play Beaumarchais made Marceline, seduced and abandoned by Bartholo in her youth, his chief crusader. In his preface to the play, in speaking of the recognition scene, he demonstrates his sympathy for her plight:

> Saisissant l'aveu naïf de *Marceline* au moment de la reconnaissance, je montrais cette femme humiliée et *Bartholo* qui la refuse, et *Figaro*, leur fils commun, dirigeant l'attention publique sur les vrais fauteurs du désordre où l'on entraîne sans pitié toutes les jeunes filles du peuple douées d'une jolie figure.[12]

He gives Marceline a diatribe which moves right to the point,[13] and the ingenuous selfishness of the Count's cruel remarks about wives (made unknowingly to his wife, who he thinks is Susanna, at the end of act V) provides illustration if one were needed.[14] In act IV Marceline becomes a quasi-heroine of the piece. She apologizes to Figaro for having misjudged Susanna, and Figaro assures her that he is incapable of jealousy — an "impulsion féminine"[15] — even if Susanna should prove momentarily unfaithful. Immediately thereafter Figaro meets Fanchette (Barbarina) and hears circumstantial evidence of Susanna's infidelity. Marceline witnesses their encounter and his angry outburst, and afterwards can throw his proud words about jealousy back in his face. Her reasonable defense of Susanna calms Figaro, and he leaves her, "lui baisant la main avec respect,"[16] in order to find out exactly what's up. In a brief coda to the scene Marceline determines to warn Susanna of Figaro's suspicion, both because she is such a handsome creature and because *if one's own interests don't countervail*, women should always defend their sex against "ce fier, ce terrible . . . et pourtant un peu nigaud de sexe masculin."[17] The feminists carry the day here, but Beaumarchais, with his usual ironic detachment, gently mocks Marceline's declaration of solidarity, suggesting by the proviso that he has her insert (italicized above) just how easily expediency could prevail over principle; her self-righteousness is not entirely free from self-delusion.

Da Ponte (and Mozart his collaborator, of course) made few alterations of substance in the first two acts of *Le mariage*, the most significant among them being the postponement of the Countess's entrance until act II and the invention of "Voi che sapete" with its allusions to the poetry of Dante.[18] On the last three acts of the play, however, da Ponte worked more independently, combining three acts into two by cutting, condensing, and rearranging. He excised the trial scenes (III, xii–xv), Bartholo's refusal to wed Marceline (III, xiv) and Bazile's attempts to do so (IV, x), and most of Figaro's famous *tirade* on the fickleness of women and the inequities of the social order (V, iii), while adding the arias for Marcellina, Basilio, and Susanna which precede the fourth-act finale. Some of his changes were necessitated by the excessive length or operatic inconvenience of a sequence: he omitted entirely IV, xiii, Figaro's first conversation with Marceline about jealousy, both because it would have required an excess of uninterrupted recitative and because Barbarina's cavatina would make a better curtain raiser for the last act. (With it, however, had to go the joke of Figaro's gainsaying himself about trusting Susanna — an example of the way librettists must streamline their original sources.)

Other changes da Ponte made were, however, more significant. The most drastic and telling one — major surgery on Figaro's philippic — will be taken up shortly. But even though da Ponte retained much of act IV, scenes xv and xvi of the Beaumarchais (Marceline's rebuke of Figaro and her comments after his departure), he made changes in these scenes which underline the considerable shift in focus which occurs from *Le mariage* to *Le nozze*. In the play the harsh lot of women takes its place alongside other injustices which Beaumarchais desired to see set right; he left its exposition to a secondary character in order to keep it properly subordinated to the central issues of the play. In da Ponte's libretto, on the other hand, the "feminine question" crowds out these other issues; in his greatest show of independence from his original he substitutes for one hero — Figaro — two heroines, or Susanna and the Countess. The scene which shows their recent archenemy, Marcellina, joining the charmed circle of *donne* at the very moment when Figaro is defecting becomes far more important to the opera than it had been to the play. Da Ponte alters it to make Figaro come off a poor second to Marcellina, at the same time turning the attention of the act away from Beaumarchais's universe of particular social injustices to the individual and yet more universal question of relationships between the sexes.

The first important change is in the nature of Figaro's exit (*Le nozze di Figaro*, IV, iii). Receiving his mother's rebuke[19] ungraciously, without the sweet reason which Beaumarchais allows him, he answers Marcellina's "Dove vai, figlio mio?" with the curt response "A vendicar tutti i mariti," and "parte infuriato."[20] Thus da Ponte's Figaro is more stubborn and suspicious, and less open to persuasion, than Beaumarchais's, while the words which da Ponte gives Marcellina after Figaro's departure make it even clearer that she is a convert:

> Presto, avvertiam Susanna . . .
> Io la credo innocente: quella faccia . . .
> Quell'aria di modestia . . . È caso ancora
> Ch'ella non fosse. . . .[21]

She too knows that bearing is character, and is moved by Susanna's evident *noblesse*. Her words are a self-paraphrase, of one of her sarcastic rejoinders to Susanna before their act I duet of mutual distaste (I, 5):

> Brava! questo è giudizio!
> Con quegli occhi modesti,
> Con quell'aria pietosa,
> E poi. . . .[22]

Significantly, both passages are da Ponte's additions, and they underscore the abrupt nature of Marcellina's about-face. Yet however abrupt the metamorphosis, it is utterly believable. In losing her infant son Marcellina was deprived of a proper object for her maternal affection, and it is no wonder she has gone about for several decades making trouble for others. With her son revealed (having at least the instincts for the right man she had chosen him for the wrong role, and was about to become a comic Jocaste, a joke of dubious taste), she is completed. Beaming on all the formerly ugly objects in her purview, she is delighted to marry the man with whom a few moments ago she was only an uneasy and resentful conspirator. Her description of her new son as "il dolce frutto dell'antico amor nostro"[23] is funny, but at the same time touching. Although Marcellina remains a comic figure, first Beaumarchais, and to an even greater degree da Ponte, make her a lovable one; her maternal advice is sound and compassionate. Figaro should have taken it.

The aria with which Marcellina consolidates her gains in our sympathies is the disputed "Il capro e la capretta." For its text da Ponte makes one more change in Marcellina's role: he adapts her feminist diatribe, originally delivered after the recognition scene to a sympathetic Figaro about the wrongs she suffered at Bartolo's hands (see p. 160 and p. 356 n. 13), to a soliloquy occasioned by her concern about Figaro's own sudden abandonment of Susanna. He condenses them into one sentence,[24] which becomes the text of the second half of a composite aria. The text of the first half, entirely da Ponte's invention, posits as a paradigm for human relationships the behavior of the beasts of the (Arcadian) field. It is a parody of pastoral poetry, a near-quotation from Ariosto's *Orlando Furioso*:[25]

> Il capro e la capretta
> Son sempre in amistà;
> L'agnello all'agnelletta
> La guerra mai non fa;
> Le più feroce belve
> Per selve e per campagne
> Lascian le lor compagne
> In pace e libertà.[26]

With her pretensions to scholarliness Marcellina fittingly does not speak directly but quotes, and quotes poetry with a long and special tradition behind it; her erudite version of pastoral is right in character for the *vecchia pedante*.[27] The act of quotation and her particular sources place her in company with Cherubino, who with his schoolboy quoting from Dante and pastoral poetry in acts I and II first introduced the image of the circle of *donne* into the opera. Marcellina's conversion ensures our comprehension of the importance of this image; when Figaro defects she is delightedly engaged in coming over, and in this aria she gives the pastoral her bluestocking blessing.

Previously Marcellina has often moved to the mincing gavotte rhythms suited to the *vecchia prepotente*. Here she makes her first appearance in triple meter, abandoning the duple identified with the Count and his followers (ex. 6–1). Although her text is self-consciously pastoral, Mozart avoids giving Marcellina the *echt* 6/8 pastorale; to parade her in panniers and bonnet would be too much of a burlesque for his purposes, and the *Tempo di Menuetto* gesture actually is more effective here. It is striking that, although dance patterns abound in the arias

Example 6-1

Example 6-2

of the opera, this aria and Basilio's which follows are the only two to specify a dance rhythm by name. In Marcellina's case, Mozart must have intended by the appending of the label to suggest a special manner of performance: calling attention to the minuet rhythms makes the aria more self-conscious — not just "minuet," but "minuet-as-posture." Marcellina's conversion is of heart, not of manner; she cannot be expected to have found her way out of the layers of preening and pretension which have aged along with her, even though they are now revealed to hide a good soul. Her minuet is fustian and affected, antique — quite different from the muscular rhythms of "Se vuol ballare" or the tranquil and dignified minuet assumed by Susanna in the second-act finale. It is an ordinary Classic minuet with a graft of archaic clichés from *opera seria*; they are fancy ornaments, unassimilated. The orchestra is of strings only, and frequently sounds like the *tutti* of a *concerto grosso*. The orchestral introduction consists of an eight-measure expository period elided at measure 8 with a five-measure Baroque-style cadential formula. Measures 10 and 11, with their constantly moving bass, Italianate string figuration, and hemiola, have an especially old-fashioned ring to them (ex. 6–2). Measures 21–24 display more of the concerto-style figuration in the strings. When, arriving at the dominant, Marcellina breaks into a long coloratura embellishment with divisions to the thirty-second note (on the syllable *-tà* of *libertà*, m. 32), she might be envisioning herself as the heroine of a Handelian *opera seria*. The second half of the aria — the contrast and moral to her pastoral text — starts as a bourrée with characteristic upbeat and syncopated rhythm, ♪♪ ♩ ♩, but quickly degenerates into vocal fireworks with three separate coloratura cadenzas (mm. 70–74, 82, and 84). The old coquette can't help striking attitudes, yet underneath it all she now displays such goodwill that she seems wholly warm and endearing. Her conversion by their grace points up with a special force the nobility of Susanna and the Countess.

The text of Basilio's aria is the next of da Ponte's interpolations, and it supplies a further critique of Figaro's behavior vis à vis the opera's heroines. Basilio tells a rather repellent story about the skin of an ass, with the moral that one can escape any peril by playing the fool. When I was young, he says, I was gay and passionate, but Dame Caution (*donna flemma*) equipped me with an ass's hide and sent me into the world; when I was attacked first by a storm and then by a hungry beast, the hide provided me with shelter from the rain and its stench drove off the animal. Again da Ponte has drawn on Italian sources for his text, not here Ariosto or Dante, but the *commedia dell'arte*, and on the more cynical and scatological side of its tradition: a spell which turns a man into an ass was almost *de rigeur* in the pastoral farces of the *commedia dell'arte*, and ravening beasts frequented its woods.[28] Basilio's cartoonlike predator seems intended for contrast with Marcellina's Arcadian flocks, and the same is true of their two versions of *flemma* — her prudence[29] and his pusillanimity. Her lofty pastoral style, for all its mannerism, is much to be preferred.

The music of "In quegli anni" is a string of grandiloquent but empty postures which Basilio strikes to illustrate his jaded tale. In contrast to the converted Marcellina's essay into triple meter, Basilio's first few measures use the gavotte of the *vecchio prepotente*, the type he and Marcellina shared with Bartolo in the second-act finale (ex. 6–3). After a patter section (mm. 26–32) and a quick inflection of bourrée rhythms (mm.

Example 6-3

33–37), he turns to an unctuous *Tempo di Menuetto*, more in Figaro's rhythms than *à la* Marcellina:[30]

But his minuet soon degenerates into a crude madrigalism — the kind of word painting Mozart rarely resorts to except in parody. At the words "Rimbomba il tuono,/Mista alla grandine/Scroscia la piova,"[31] there is an abrupt modulation to G minor (m. 52) and string tremolos and rapid scalar upbeats obliterate the minuet rhythms. The passage resembles the dramatic imitation of storm sounds in the operas of Rameau and Gluck, whose tempests served to set the tragic stage; here their incongruity is comic. The minuet returns with the discovery that the ass's skin will provide effective shelter (m. 57), but is scared away forthwith by the arrival of the beast (species unspecified) whose menace is represented by alternating *forte* and *piano* ascending and descending chromatic scales — another mock-tragic gesture (mm. 70 ff). Minuet and tonic return at the words "Ma il fiuto ignobile del mio vestito,"[32] making the joke of the fastidious minuet celebrating the coward's refusal to discriminate (ex. 6–4). Final tonic cadences are achieved in a new section with a third meter and gesture — a march in 4/4 (the gavotte was in cut time, the minuet in 3/4), with dotted rhythms and horn fifths (mm. 110–14).[33] The text of the march is Basilio's summing-up, his enunciation of the *sententia* which constitutes his "philosophy of life":

> Così conoscere
> Mi fe' la sorte
> Ch'onte, pericoli,
> Vergogna e morte
> Col cuoio d'asino
> Fuggir si può.[34]

Example 6-4

Basilio chooses his musical clichés well, the march for elevation as well as the minuet for repose. He is an accomplished narrator in the grand style, expertly doling out action, color, and moral lesson, but the content of his narrative stands in comic contrast to his smooth and grandiloquent gestures. His tale is distasteful and craven; rescue lies in a vile stench, salvation in the hide of an ass. His music mocks the moral vocabulary of the opera: the minuet's noble serenity and the arrogance of the march both ring hollow here.

Surely da Ponte meant the text of "In quegli anni" to be applied as an involuntary critique of Figaro's behavior. The moral of Basilio the pander's tale is obvious: it's always wise to hide your light under a bushel, or any other camouflage at hand, no matter how ignominious. His story blackens the character of the canny fool celebrated in the third-act finale. Arlecchino's diamonded livery turns into the hide of an ass, and camouflage — the canny fool's spirited means of self-defense — is shown up as an act of abject cowardice; the real menace of human viciousness becomes the empty threat of a comically ferocious lion. Text and music combine, in this position as prelude to Figaro's antifeminist diatribe, to point out that playing the fool is finally a dangerous game. The role was once good protection for Figaro, but he has played it too long and the ass's skin threatens to become his natural vestment. It colors his estimate of the people closest to him, and leads him to enunciate a cynical chain of paradoxes to describe human behavior: the donkey human, the innocent traitor, the enchanting witch, the thorny rose, the spiteful dove.[35] All surfaces betray; all realities are brutish. Figaro has become enmeshed in the very paradox he plays.

Da Ponte made his most substantive revision of *La folle journée* in Figaro's famous soliloquy. Although it occurs in about the same place in the opera as in the play, da Ponte's alterations and Mozart's music turn this speech to entirely different account. Figaro remains the hero and center of Beaumarchais's play. His soliloquy upon discovering Susanna's putative betrayal mentions her only at beginning and end; her supposed treachery figures merely as a springboard for Figaro's invective. His real anger is directed against the Count as the representative of a repressive society which wastes the life of any clever man who looks beyond his class (or lack of it — part of the point in the play of the peculiar history of Figaro's birth is to make him an outcast, living on the fringes of society; that point is blunted in the opera since its concerns are not with social reform). His bitter recital of his scrambles merely to subsist leaves us full of admiration for the toughness and wit of the survivor and anger against the orders which have tried to break him down.

The subject which obsesses Figaro in the opera, on the other hand, is

not injustice but indignity — the humiliating affront to a man's self-
esteem which is cuckoldry:

> . . . Buia è la notte . . .
> Ed io comincio omai
> A fare il scimunito
> Mestiero di marito. . . .[36]

His *recitativo accompagnato* and aria ("Tutto è disposto . . . Aprite un po'
quegli occhi" — IV, 26) form a *scena* in the high style which has already
been debased in earlier acts by the performances of Bartolo and the
Count, also trapped in their obsessions with cuckoldry in one form or
another. Figaro's grim reflection on his new role as husband is a line
adapted from the original soliloquy,[37] but it is one of the few which da
Ponte borrows. Omitting several pages, and all the social criticism of
the original, his version leaps to Beaumarchais's closing sentiment, in
the play muttered by Figaro almost as an afterthought: "Suzon, Suzon,
Suzon! que tu me donnes de tourments!"[38] Da Ponte uses this exclamation as the headline for a freewheeling diatribe against women, a "catalogue aria" of the sins of that treacherous sex. The next lines are his first
original ones in the new soliloquy, and the third and capping comment
in a series of remarks which he has carefully prepared by the interpolations he gave to Marcellina in act I and at the beginning of act IV:

> Con quell'ingenua faccia,
> Con quegli occhi innocenti . . .
> Chi creduto l'avria! . . .[39]

First Marcellina maliciously supposed a paradox between Susanna's
bearing and her character with words very like these. Later she admitted her mistake and resolved the paradox, again with words like these
(see p. 162). When Figaro, using nearly the same words for a third
time, makes the same invidious mistake as Marcellina did at first, a
comparison between the two of them is unavoidable. Figaro now comes
off a bad second to the old reprobate: at a time when his trust is wavering, even she has learned to give good character its due. His last line in
recitative is an epigram whose falsity the opera has already taken great
pains to demonstrate: "Ah, che il fidarsi a donna è ognor follia!"[40]

While Figaro's words in his recitative force a contrast between him
and Marcellina, the text and music of his aria cannot help but connect
him with Basilio. He has in fact purposefully allied himself with Basilio
for the moment, choosing him to be part of the gallery which he has
concealed to witness the assignation of Susanna and the Count.[41] The
role of the canny fool travestied in Basilio's "In quegli anni" has been
Figaro's camouflage and delight throughout the opera. The paradoxical

metaphors for the brutishness of women which run through the text of Figaro's aria are inspired by Basilio's image of the sage in beast's clothing.[42] And the two men have exchanged rhythmic gestures: in IV, 25, Basilio takes on Figaro's act I minuet, although without its stiletto wit, and now Figaro assumes the duple meter and *alla breve* gesture which have hitherto characterized the Count and his henchmen. Transformed by unheeding anger, he has momentarily changed sides.

"Aprite un po' quegli occhi" begins as an exalted march: despite its 4/4 time signature, the dotted rhythms of the vocal line and a strong bass punctuation on the first and third beats effect a broader scansion of 2/2 over the violins' angry strumming sixths (ex. 6–5). But Figaro's obsessive jealousy breaks through in his long-spun-out list of paradoxical epithets for women. Here (m. 49) the march dissolves into patter — lists are endemic to the patter style (ex. 6–6). The last two-thirds of the aria

Example 6-5

Example 6-6

Example 6-7

consists of the list, its almost literal repetition, and ten measures of additional cadence, the repetition and cadential formulas functioning as an extended coda.[43] This coda brings back the march style with horn fanfares, alternating with Figaro's suggestive "Il resto nol dico,/Già ognuno lo sa."[44] The horns translate his allusion into sound: the rest will be cuckoldry, and not of the Count (ex. 6–7). The cuckoldry pun, borrowed from "Se vuol ballare," undergoes a transformation here at the opposite end and pole of the opera. No longer an elegant and fleeting allusion to that ancient sport, tactfully underlined by a play on the word *capriola*,[45] it has become the punch line of a dull joke, forcefully rammed home by Figaro's less-than-veiled insinuations. (In performance he should cock his ear and point at each entry of the horns, accompanying the tedious joke with as exaggerated a dumbshow.)

"Aprite un po' quegli occhi" is a brilliant and sardonic aria, but its anger is not heroic, nor does it share the subtle invention of "Se vuol ballare." The obsessive character of the list with its patter, the crude and repetitive pun on *corno* and *cornuto*, are hardly exalted. For much of the aria Figaro's idiom is that of the stock comic servant, and his jokes are blatant and crude, delivered with the scurrilous leer of the lowest orders of comedy. His logic has taken Basilio's conceit to an excessive position: if all appearances lie, then all women are only invidious paradoxes. To play out the role of buffoon to its logical extreme is to cease to be fully a human being. If a man comes entirely to trust in disguise as a means of survival, all the good things of life eventually come to seem mere deception as well. Passion, commitment, and trust have no place in the world of one who willingly wears a coxcomb.

This chain of three arias at the start of act IV, far from being a weak spot in the construction of *Le nozze di Figaro*, represents a thoughtful rewriting of the conclusion of *Le mariage de Figaro*. By turning away from the social to the personal, and changing a political broadside into an analysis of sexual warfare, da Ponte and Mozart explode the particular issue of injustice to women into a more profound question, ethical in the deepest sense, and beyond the topical limits of the original play — how one should live one's life. Looking back from act IV, one can make out other delicate alterations worked by composer and librettist on their French model which confirm the change in subject matter. For example, his glinting *alla breve* moments make the Count appear more vicious, more of a "heavy," lacking some of the social grace and charm of his prototype in Beaumarchais. What is more important, the virtues and claims of the band of *òonne* are strengthened. The Countess is made less flirtatious, her interest in Cherubino more distant, and never explicitly sexual (see p. 104). Marceline's youthful seduction and fall from virtue are glossed over without remark, and Bartolo, who compounded the cruelty in the play by refusing for some time to marry Marceline and legitimize their offspring, pledges himself to her immediately and willingly in the opera. The focus on women is no longer suggested by one particular case, as Beaumarchais made Marceline its only spokesman in *Le mariage*. As if to announce the central theme, women are first mentioned abstractly, by Cherubino in "Voi che sapete," setting the stage for this moment of chiasmus in the fourth act where one of the more unattractive figures of the opera gravitates into the heroines' sphere of influence, while Figaro, its hero, detaches himself from them. Both were, for the first three acts, anomalies in their chosen surroundings — Marcellina in the men's world and Figaro in the women's. Here where the one becomes more lovable, the other momentarily more callous, each seems to receive his new character in renewed association with his own sex.

This eleventh-hour chiasmus points out where the crucial distinction of the comedy lies — not between servant and master, but between men and women. *Le nozze òi Figaro* celebrates a special kind of eros, for which the blushing adolescent Cherubino is the figure — an eros which seems paradoxically passive because its defining quality is its openness. Women are the natural residence for this gentle eros; receptive to the impressions of all good things, they are moved by them, toward them. Men must act, rule, and make things, a necessity which enforces on them a circumscribed and idiosyncratic view of the world, impenetrable to ways of being foreign to their own. Women, on the other hand, move in the background, the penumbra of life; they are not defined, as men are, by being counts or music masters, but by being women. They watch and wait, observing the cosmos entire, and are the ones to demonstrate the final and proper relations between things to the men around them. Figaro is coarsened for a moment at a crucial point in the opera because the disguises he has been forced to adopt to survive in the world of affairs have almost become his second skin. Susanna, in a loving and utterly characteristic way, will pull him back.

This view of the relation between men and women found expression in the work of other eighteenth-century writers, including one novel which could more strictly than *Le nozze òi Figaro* be termed a pastoral. In 1787, one year after *Figaro* was first performed, Bernadin de Saint-

Pierre published a book which rather more explicitly articulates the
same sentiments. His *Paul et Virginie*, which he styles an "espèce de pastorale,"[46] postulates an eros which is "le lien de tous les êtres, . . . le
premier mobile de nos sociétés, et l'instigateur de nos lumières et de nos
plaisirs."[47] In the novel's naive plot two women, ostracized from the
rigid and unforgiving society of eighteenth-century Paris, bring up
their two children in a tropical paradise sheltered from the corrupting
habits of Europe. The virtue of the two mothers and the daughter Virginie (and of the son Paul, by virtue of the constant guidance of the
women) is so great that all noble people who meet them recognize their
excellence and are drawn into their circle. The pastoral ends in tragedy
because this community of innocents cannot help but be bruised by its
first jar with "civilization." When Virginie perishes in a shipwreck, indirectly at the hands of a cruel Parisian relative, the force of her loss is
overpowering; one by one the others quietly follow her to their deaths.

In a *préambule* to the novel published in the new edition of 1806,
Saint-Pierre identifies the source of his eros with women:

> Les femmes ont contribué plus que les philosophes à former et à ré-
> former les nations. . . . Ce fut dans leurs bras qu'elles firent goûter aux
> hommes le bonheur d'être tour-à-tour dans le cercle de la vie, enfants
> heureux, amants fidèles, époux constants, pères vertueux. Elles pose-
> rent les premières bases des lois naturelles. La première fondatrice
> d'une société humaine fut une mère de famille.
>   . . . Les hommes naissent asiatiques, européens, français, anglais; ils
> sont cultivateurs, marchands, soldats; mais par tout pays les femmes
> naissent, vivent, et meurent femmes. Elles ont d'autres devoirs, d'autres
> occupations, d'autres destinées que les hommes. Elles sont disséminées
> parmi eux pour leur rappeler sur-tout qu'ils sont hommes; et maintenir,
> malgré les lois politiques, les lois fondamentales de la nature. . . . Ainsi
> les femmes n'appartiennent qu'au genre humain. Elles le rappellent sans
> cesse à l'humanité par leurs sentiments naturels et même par leurs
> passions.[48]

In short, women are the universal principle, men its individual emanations; the "weaker sex" has a secret knowledge and a quiet but charismatic presence on which men are profoundly dependent if they are to
remain human beings. This sweeping rhetoric articulates the principle
which tacitly animates *Le nozze di Figaro*, a work exceedingly different in
tone and style from Saint-Pierre's romance. In both works women are
the exemplars of how one best may live one's life. In both works women
must be endowed with a special place in which to move, beyond the
ordinary limits which men, strenuously occupied by their particular
callings, mark off for their own convenience. In both works that place is
the same — the pastoral.

But the differences in tone between the two works are more striking

than their thematic similarity. *Paul et Virginie* is artificial and sentimen-
tal, a sigh for a nonexistent world, while *Figaro* is a vivid and compelling triumph of compromises. Saint-Pierre's tale bears its moral message
close to the surface: his pastoral is a real garden peopled by cardboard
characters. Those innocent paragons, set in motion to proclaim the doctrine that "notre bonheur consiste à vivre suivant la nature et la vertu,"[49]
are remote and unbelievable. Moreover, because their pastoral paradise
is a real place with a geography and topology, it is tenuous and open to
destruction by the encroachments of nonlovers. The novel is a confrontation between the perfect and the corrupt, and must end badly; the
reader is to weep for what ought to but cannot be. The very unreality of
Mozart's pastoral place, on the other hand — it is an imaginary garden
with real creatures in it — is a guarantee of its possibility. It is merely a
state of mind, called into being by a tacit understanding and defined by
a nostalgic and otherworldly musical gesture. But its shelter is still substantial, precisely because it can coexist with the harsher realities of the
daylight world. That the comic figure of the converted Marcellina is
chosen to put the seal of approval on the intimacy between Susanna and
the Countess, and on their pastoral retiring-place, is part of the delicacy
of the comedy, and part also of its considerable power. Deny this demi-
mondaine her statutory aria, and you deprive the opera of a demi-
heroine in the process.

The Pastoral: The Private Finale

The second- and fourth-act finales are alike in one element: in both
the moment of greatest significance (in act IV the reconciliation of Susanna and Figaro) takes place in the key most distant from the main key
of the movement. The fourth-act finale consists of three carefully articulated sections — an intensely private episode framed by two more public ones. These three sections, containing six movements in all, are in
part defined by differences of key and meter: the outside movements,
all four in duple meter, move from D to G major at the beginning and
from G back to D major at the end, while the two inner movements,
both in triple (3/4 and 6/8), are in E-flat and B-flat major respectively.
Most of the company participates in the "public" sections, but the two
interior movements belong to Susanna and Figaro alone. While their
private interlude dovetails naturally with the plot of the rest of the finale, at the same time its distinctive affective profile throws it into sharp
contrast with the surrounding pieces. In climate and topic it is the
proper resolution of a separate and transcendent line of action, which
began to take shape in act III with the pastoral letter duet, and which
merits a climax separate from the more orthodox working-out of the
comic imbroglio. The line to this climax plots out its own key-area plan

in B-flat, arching from the B-flat letter duet through to the pastoral fourth act, where Barbarina's F-minor cavatina and Susanna's F-major aria "Deh, vieni" stand both in key and in tone as a kind of dominant to the final B-flat resolution — the pastoral reconciliation of the happy couple (IV, 28, 275–334).

"Deh, vieni" is on the surface of it Susanna's retaliation for Figaro's mistrust of her. Aware that he is watching her in the darkness, she whispers to the Countess "Il birbo è in sentinella/. . . Diamogli la mercè de' dubbi suoi."[50] She pretends to sing with tremulous expectation of her tryst with the Count, knowing full well the effect her words will have on Figaro. The text she chooses is a sensuous invitation, firmly committed to the pathetic fallacy of the pastoral:

> Oh, come par che all'amoroso foco
> L'amenità del loco,
> La terra e il ciel risponda!
> Come la notte i furti miei seconda![51]

Later the breeze "teases" ("scherza"), the flowers "laugh" ("ridono"): all nature "speaks" in response to the passions of a lover. But the pathetic fallacy also works in reverse. Because all natural elements in the magic garden take on human habits, humans merge naturally with the landscape. Susanna seems to be a nymph or dryad, some minor local deity murmuring incantatory promises: "Ti vo' la fronte incoronar di rose."[52] Her "punishment" for Figaro is also a generous invitation for all true lovers to shrug off the compromises of the noonday world and join her in the twilight and uncorrupted garden.

Of course Susanna chooses the meter and tempo of the pastorale for her apotheosis — 6/8, *Andante*, and legato, with occasional dotted rhythms reminiscent of the siciliano (mm. 28 and 51–52, for example). "Deh, vieni" is intended to be a performance, a serenade like Cherubino's *canzonetta* in act III; many of the devices used in "Voi che sapete" recur here. The strings, carrying the accompaniment, are *pizzicato* throughout, until the lovely moment just after the return of the tonic when off-the-beat pulses are written *arco* for the first time (m. 56). The *pizzicato* suggests a guitar accompaniment, perhaps the same guitar Susanna used in act II. The poetry is set essentially in syllabic fashion, each line ending with a lingering feminine cadence which stresses the rhymes:

m.33 bel - la

m.36 t'ap-pel - la

m.47 L'au - ra

m.50 ri-stau - ra

Example 6-8

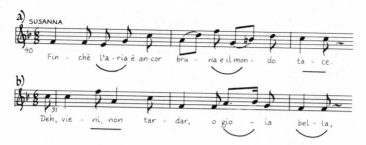

Line length also dictates the unusual three-measure units which constitute all phrases until the last eighteen measures. Again, as in "Voi che sapete," the emphasis is on singer and song: the rhythmic regularity and discreteness of the lines, and their singsong end rhymes, suggest a literary rather than choreographic source for their musical shape. Cherubino's otiose pastoral poetry has become a powerfully seductive force in Susanna's hands.

Again as in "Voi che sapete," fidelity to the repetitive lengths of poetry poses a problem for the end-oriented drama of the harmonic process, and again Mozart solves the problem ingeniously. Since three-measure phrases do not admit of a two-plus-two antecedent and consequent division, most of them have instead of melodic curves a simple melodic descent or ascent. Phrases which rise from a low note generate some energy with their roughly anapestic shape (the melodic peak is the "thesis" of each anapest), and are used to move to the dominant (mm. 34–36, 40–42; ex. 6–8a). A melodic descent, on the other hand, lends the line a dactylic effect, and makes it suitable for phrases of resolution (ex. 6–8b). Joining the lines in pairs, one of each foot type, shapes rhythmic energies in tune with the requirements of the harmony:

m. 31-36:	I	$-\cup\cup$	$\cup\cup-$	V
37-42:	I	$-\cup\cup$	$\cup\cup-$	V
45-50:	V	$\cup\cup-$	$-\cup\cup$	V
51-56:	V	$-\cup\cup$	$-\cup\cup$	I

The first two pairs of lines are less tightly yoked because the harmony requires a rhythmic thesis (for the firm tonic) first and arsis second (for the move to the dominant).[53] The third pair is forged into a real period — an expansion of the dominant area — because thesis follows arsis. Two dactylic phrases provide a cadential thesis at the return to the tonic.

Since the dactyls of the thetic lines echo the double dactyls and trochees of each 6/8 measure, the macro- and microrhythms of the piece employ the same poetic feet as a basis. The rhythms of the dactyl, front-stressed and enervating rather than climactic, mime the falling gesture of the hand leisurely strumming the guitar. The events of the key-area plan of "Deh, vieni" are treated not as dramatic gestures, but as gently, almost idly inflected nuances. The isolation and rhythmic completeness of each line give the aria a feeling of suspension rather than of drama, despite the care with which the harmonic process is worked out. It requires only a new melodic inflection of the original rhythmic rhyme to turn the piece to the dominant, and another bending of the same phrase slips the harmony back to the tonic; the regular cadences of the poetry are never disturbed. The graceful and hypnotic feminine cadences float on the air feather-light. One holds one's breath waiting for the next phrase, all the while expecting the repetitions to spin out endlessly.

The enervated, swooning rhythms of the aria require a counterweight if the piece is to effect a proper final cadence. Mozart builds the material for the counterweight into the aria's orchestral introduction. There the strong-weak rhythm is balanced by its reverse — an iambic foot in the second half of the introduction, consisting of a staccato scale passage in the winds ascending to a leading-tone just before the cadence. The measure of scales (29) has an upbeat function and moves to a strong tonic downbeat in measure 30 (ex. 6–9). Mozart uses this embryonic iambic cadence sparingly, calling on it only four times: first here, then after the move to the dominant (mm. 42–44), before Susanna's lovely "cadenza" (mm. 60–62), and as a final cadence (mm. 72–74). Each instrument takes half a measure of the scale, and they overlap in stretto for the collective effect of one large iamb:[54]

flute: ∪   —
oboe: ∪   —
bassoon: ∪ │ —

At each appearance the scale cadence gently secures the new harmonic position. Susanna's cadenza is a giant iamb also, fashioned from fragments both of her vocal line and of the instrumental figures. By a simple turn of *ars combinatoria* the opening measure of the melody, and arpeggiated tonic triad, is arranged second in order in the cadenza and is approached by two rising scales. Since the melodic peak of the phrase occurs near the end of its arch instead of at the beginning, as in the original dactyls, the dactylic opening becomes an iambic close (ex. 6–10). The repetition of this phrase with a two-measure extension of

Example 6-9

Example 6-10

the stressed foot makes the principal tonic cadence the emphatic gesture of the entire piece.

"Deh, vieni" pictures Susanna in repose for the first time in the opera, confirming the virtues which have shone through her roles in the past. If there was any fear earlier in the opera that her pert resilience could turn into a shrewish indifference, "Deh, vieni" removes it, showing her warmheartedness to be only tempered by her wit, not overwhelmed by it. She cloaks her passion in sport, to avoid dull sentiment, but the sport is clearly a loving gesture to Figaro if he could but recognize it: with her "vieni, non tardar"[55] she is willing him to shake off his heavy anger and enter the pastoral garden. The F major of her invitation dispels the F-minor darkness of Barbarina's pastorale. To Figaro's credit, he will understand "Deh, vieni" later, when all disguises are removed. The pastorale is the couple's true nuptial song, and he will finally need no prompting to join Susanna in it. Now, however, after witnessing her performance, he is left in a trancelike state between trust and suspicion, intensely moved by Susanna's beauty and grace, but stung to the quick by what he supposes to be her intentions.

After the preliminary maneuvers at the beginning of the fourth-act finale, the crowds disperse momentarily, leaving Figaro and Susanna alone (Figaro thinks he is alone with the Countess). In the next two pieces (IV, 28, 109–334) he moves from sardonic anger to dizzy joy to a blissful reconciliation with his beloved. In gesture the two pieces move from a slow and elegant minuet like Susanna's in the second-act finale, through a burlesque of the quicker minuet style, to a graceful pastorale. The double-minuet movement is a complex and skillfully organized key-area layout in E-flat major, and the B-flat pastorale a more relaxed and orthodox version of the same. Transitions between movements are accomplished smoothly by the substitution of one note value for another: *Larghetto* ♩ roughly equals *Allegro molto* ♩. equals *Andante* ♩.

Figaro intends high sarcasm in his choice of the *Larghetto* minuet, the noblest of the opera's minuet gestures. Even Susanna's noble triumphal minuet in the second-act finale was cast in a light 3/8 meter, and marked only *Molto andante*. The slow 3/4 of Figaro's minuet draws out the ♩ ♫♫ rhythm into self-parody, while his words (quoted in n. 5–15) are a bitter paraphrase of Susanna's pastoral poetry. Susanna is Venus to Figaro's Vulcan, a wave of self-pity causing him to liken himself to the cuckolded crippled smith. Horns in parallel thirds and sixths and triplet figures in the inner voices suggest the twinned topics of hunt and court: Figaro-Vulcan as huntsman, his voice a declamatory fanfare, proclaims the arrival of the hunted with the elegant and prepossessing gesture of a court herald (ex. 6–11). As he describes the cuckolding and his trap, the chromatic bass and the turn toward subdominant harmony have a slippery, insinuating quality about them (mm. 116–19). The elision of the two fanfare phrases, $^{\text{m. }109}$ $^{1\,2\,3\,4}_{\quad\ 1\,2\,3\,4}$, is balanced by the extension of the last phrase into six measures, in groups of two. The *Larghetto* ends with a typical minuet cadence (mm. 120–21), which is elided with the beginning of the *Allegro molto* (ex. 6–12). Figaro's bitterly elegant parody, although misdirected, is a controlled and imaginative set piece.

The *Larghetto* forms an expansive first period for the first key area of the E-flat movement. This movement is among the more interesting

Example 6-11

Example 6-12

treatments of dramatic key-area form in the opera. One problem Classic opera poses is how to integrate a chain of complex and varied events, affects, and textures into a unified structure which retains a sense of balance overall, and of tension resolved. The problem is especially acute here: Figaro's opening *Larghetto* minuet is, as the first period of a key-area layout, radically unassimilable. Although only a first period, in time it constitutes a little under half the duration of the entire first reprise.[56] Its tempo and affect are at variance with the rest of the movement, and its complete harmonic closure also sets it uncompromisingly apart. To make the dominant area an effective counterstatement to the first eleven measures will require time and a strong cadence.

Mozart's first move is to blur slightly at beginning and end the hard-edged outlines of the *Larghetto*. The hunting triplets in the inner voices at the opening weaken the force of the tonic (E-flat is only sounded in the bass on the first beat, and the triplets are the expansion of a first-inversion position; see ex. 6–11). The first strong and stable tonic occurs at the *Larghetto*'s close, giving the period a slight harmonic and rhythmic tilt toward the *Allegro molto* despite its seeming squareness.

Mozart smoothes over the join at the end of the *Larghetto* by elision, and by using material reminiscent of it to begin the *Allegro molto*. Susanna (as the Countess) interrupts Figaro, telling him to lower his voice. Thinking her indeed to be the Countess, Figaro loses his previous control and blurts out a warning about the betrayal she is about to witness. Surprised in the middle of a cool private fantasy of revenge, he slips from his elegant gesture into a flustered and prosaic explanation—a breathless *Allegro molto* travesty of his original fanfare, oscillating between I and V. The change in style is psychologically apt, while the similarity in motives eases the transition from a slow to a quick tempo (ex. 6–13).

The clipped and syncopated motive which Figaro uses for the last cadence in the first key area (mm. 135–39) becomes a landmark in the movement (ex. 6–14). Except for this cadential phrase the *Allegro molto* has no distinctive material of its own until after the "exposition" (m.

Example 6-13

Example 6-14

Figure 4 The Shape of the *Larghetto, Allegro Molto* Movement

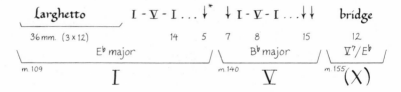

* Single arrows indicate syncopated cadences, double arrows the syncopated cadence preceded by the phrase of syncopated counterpoint.

169; see fig. 4 for a chart of the entire movement). Were the second key area to have another closed period with its own topic, its formal symmetry would be bulky and redundant in the face of the symmetries of the *Larghetto,* and would impede the strong drive to a successful close which is necessary for counterbalance. Instead Mozart sets up passages of tonic-dominant oscillation to fill in the time between cadences. After Figaro first uses the distinctive four-measure cadence, Susanna immediately counterstates it, moving the harmony to the dominant (mm. 135–46). Agitated, she speaks by mistake in her natural voice. Figaro immediately recognizes her, and in the space of a measure everything becomes clear to him: he'd been the one to initiate a plot calling for disguises, a trap for the Count, not for him; Susanna sang that lovely pastorale for him and not for the Count. Without skipping a beat he takes up a new role: he'll tease Susanna with some of her own devices. For his music Mozart uses more of the oscillating measures, extending the second key area (mm. 146–54). He then appends four preliminary measures to the original syncopated cadence to make it a strong close for the dominant material. In a phrase which moves from I to V through subdominant harmonies Figaro takes his motive from the strings in the oscillating passage while Susanna sings a syncopated counterpoint over it (ex. 6–15). Because of these syncopations the new material blends naturally into the syncopated cadence figure to form a snappy and effective eight-measure cadential period (mm. 161–69). The "exposition" ends with the two asserting in asides how they'll outfox the other; Figaro has the advantage, because for once he knows more than Susanna.

The syncopated cadences at the beginning and end of the second key area by framing it provide a counterweight to the framed formality of the *Larghetto*, without having a formal content of their own. In the return to the tonic even more serious problems arise. The return must be dramatized, but not in the usual way, by the recurrence of the opening material of the first reprise; something new and of equally sharp profile is required. Furthermore the second reprise must be at least as long as the first, and a flurry of syncopated cadences will not suffice to fill it. The cadences will supply an end rhyme, but material of some formal substance and striking gesture must be found to balance the monolithic *Larghetto*. Mozart invents as a solution a quick minuet for Figaro (ex. 6–16). A minuet with the selfsame intent as Susanna's pastorale, it is in fact Figaro's counterstatement to "Deh, vieni" —both sport and declaration. Knowing he is addressing Susanna, Figaro pretends to be addressing the Countess:

Example 6-15

Example 6-16

Figaro: Eccomi ai vostri piedi . . .
                Ho pieno il cor di fuoco.
                Esaminate il loco . . .
                Pensate al traditor.
Susanna: E senza alcun affetto? . . .
Figaro: Suppliscavi il rispetto.
                Non perdiam tempo invano,
                Datemi un po' la mano . . . [she slaps him]
                Oh, schiaffi graziosissimi!
                Oh, mio felice amor! [57]

All Figaro's lines are double-edged, meaning more actually to Susanna than to Susanna as the Countess. He is at her feet with contrition and passion. She is to think — kindly — of the erstwhile traitor Figaro. She won back his love, and a new respect, in measures 139–46 when the latest events of the mad day suddenly became explicable. But Figaro would no more express passionate sentiments directly to Susanna than she to him. Both choose as a more comfortable mode of expression the *double entendre* — although not in order to mask or evade strong passions. The mute offering up of oneself in act can be a far more reverberant declaration of love than any number of ardent speeches.

Figaro's minuet ends as a near-burlesque of the quarter-note minuet style. It is filled with minuet traits and figures — even quarter-note motion (at least at first), horns and clarinets in horn fifths at the outset (mm. 182–83) and in punctuating chords (mm. 184–85, 188–89, 192–93), and a meager orchestra (no low strings, emphasis on brass and winds) like a court dance band. The text fits the music awkwardly, increasingly so as it nears an end (the slurs on "schia-af-fi" and "gra-a-ziosissimi," mm. 255 and 256, for example), tilting the minuet toward a waltz, with its characteristic ♩ ♩ measure. This equipoise of two dances results in a swoony minuet of slurred dignity. The trick of having Figaro sound as though he were sloppily improvising words to a preexisting tune (an effect of the awkward text setting) is a clever way of showing his delight in his amorous sport. We are aware that Figaro is aware that he is playing a role, that he is playfully continuing in it without bothering to hide his joy at the revelation of Susanna's faithfulness.

The minuet is a felicitous solution to the construction problems caused for the second reprise of the *Larghetto-Allegro-molto* by the unassimilable *Larghetto*: its melodic profile plainly marks the return of the tonic, and its closed formal structure and regular phrases are an effective counterpart and counterweight to the long period of Figaro's Vulcan minuet. But forty-four measures of minuet[58] cannot in themselves form the second reprise; they are too sedate and static to provide a final strong tonic cadence for anything but their own closed form. So Mozart pulls the minuet apart to embed parts of it at crucial moments in the second reprise. His solution is dramatically apt because it allows the lovers to alternate between asides and disguises — the formal minuet serving as disguise, the more amorphous material a vehicle for asides. The first interpolation of minuet material (mm. 182–96) merges with the syncopated counterpoint and cadence from the end of the movement's first reprise (mm. 204–13). From here on the cadences grow more emphatic. The minuet's second key area, which moves through subdominant harmony to the dominant (mm. 215–26), provides the wedge for a new buildup of energy for the final line of action. This leads to a "false recapitulation" of the minuet theme (mm. 227–32; see ex. 6–16) wherein Figaro tries to take Susanna's hand and she slaps him. The minuet breaks off, the oscillating material returns, and she slaps him again and again (mm. 232–46). Figaro, more blissful with each slap and proof of Susanna's love, praises the slaps with the real return of the minuet (mm. 247ff.) while Susanna fills up the rests between its phrases with angry fanfare counterpoint. This newly energized version of the embedded dance merges naturally into the syncopated counterpoint and cadence, making the final drive to the tonic cadence twenty-eight measures long. The longest of the cadential drives in the piece, it provides a necessary and sufficient release from the tension built up earlier by the anomaly of the *Larghetto*.

The powerful clash of forces in this duet suggests the importance Mozart attached to Figaro's reconversion. It is the most elaborately worked-out piece in the finale, containing a wealth of material in a consummately skillful arrangement. Although an extensive movement, it needs no extended X-section because of the special tension introduced at the beginning. All "development" (here rearrangement and recombination of material and harmonic drops to the subdominant to start a new trajectory) is concentrated on one objective — building a hierarchy of cadences of increasing strength to tug against the stable and squared-off nuggets of dance material which comprise Figaro's two roles — his "before" and "after."

The energies generated by the E-flat movement spill over into the B-flat pastorale for their final resolution; it celebrates the unity of the two lovers. Like the other pastorales in the opera it is *Andante*,[59] in 6/8, and legato. The pace of the movement is relaxed; it uses little other material beside the opening motive — fanfarelike triads over tonic and dominant harmonies. A little later this opening is made cadential (for the end of the first period, second key area, and entire movement[60]) by the addition of a syncopated cadence figure (ex. 6–17). Figaro begins the piece with his rapturous confession:

> Pace, pace, mio dolce tesoro:
> Io conobbi la voce che adoro,
> E che impressa ognor serbo nel cor.[61]

Susanna, like Figaro in the preceding movement, needs no time to contemplate the new development. She joins him immediately in parallel thirds, and together they bring the period to an end. They are given little private time in which to enjoy their reconciliation; straightaway the Count arrives on the scene and they decide to continue the charade, repeating the same material on the dominant in making their decision. The Count, thinking he is surprising Figaro on his knees before the Countess, vents his anger in a small X-section which passes through G minor to V[7] of B-flat major (mm. 314–26). Susanna and Figaro depart

Example 6-17

arm in arm during a brief recapitulation, which consists only of the opening material — the pastoral affect concentrated into one eight-measure phrase. Their parting words are both a final irritant for the enraged Count, and the proper sentiment to put the period to their reconciliation scene: "Ah, corriamo, mio bene,/E le pene compensi il piacer."[62] They are reconciled just as they courted one another, with passion, but under the guise of play.

This pastoral duet is in one sense the end of the opera. Of course the opera cannot in fact end with Figaro making love to Susanna disguised as the Countess in order to humiliate the Count. But untangling the imbroglio is not the opera's only concern. It has already been pointed out how in the last two acts the metrical and gestural content of certain numbers superimposes on the ordinary shape of the opera another harmonic arch defined by the repetition of the pastoral affect: B-flat major (no. 20), F minor (no. 23), F major (no. 27), E-flat major (no. 28C), and now B-flat major (no. 28D). These moments prick out another closed form, with all the necessary harmonic events: B-flat the tonic, tension provided by the minor dominant and then cleared to F major, E-flat to outline the dominant seventh, and finally a return to the tonic. The new grouping is organized like a finale — that of the second act, for example — but its movements are not contiguous. They are instead points which lie also in the surface of the public plane of the opera; the pastoral close cannot exist independent of the public common. Since the only evidence for the existence of the private world lies in the configurations of its points upon the public surface, the pastoral must remain a veil of illusion cast about the opera. *Le nozze di Figaro* portrays only two enduring human relationships — that of Susanna and the Countess, and of Susanna and Figaro. The pastoral exists to protect these relations, and is viable only as long as it is unspoken. Susanna and Figaro put trust in the value of ambiguity, and play at being what they are. Such psychic address is more than camouflage: it is evidence for the nobility of modesty and the glory of the tacit.

Alla Breve: The Public Finale

The events surrounding the core of the final finale are both more public and less intense than is the reconciliation at its center. In the pastoral which is the emotional focus of the end of the opera we experience the happiness of the lovers directly, through their music; they move in harmony and in step in a moment of intense and intimate delight, unconscious of any audience. In the twin pieces flanking the center, however, the participants are constantly aware of their roles as they share in the mechanical winding-down of the comedy. The "ceremony" of the Count's seduction of Susanna (the Countess) at the finale's opening is balanced at its close by the "ceremony" of the reconciliation of the noble couple. These are outcomes forced not by a newly shared passion and commitment, but by the pressures of previous events. The sight of the Count and Countess reconciled in anything but a bright public light would misleadingly suggest that the Count was moved deeply, when he is probably only moved by a momentary sense of choreographic decency.

Key relations in the finale also suggest a winding-down. While the keys of the second-act finale shape a well-plotted key-area layout with a thrust to the dominant and point of furthest remove from the tonic, the keys of the fourth-act finale are grouped in pairs:

D maj. G maj	E♭ maj. B♭ maj.	G maj. D maj.
PUBLIC	PRIVATE	PUBLIC
duple	triple (pastorale)	duple

The center pair stands to D major as Neapolitan to tonic, and is not established by any motion of harmonic grammar. Its real justification lies in its function as final cadence of the B-flat pastoral "ghost-form" reaching back over two acts, and thus its emotional intensity is due in part to the connections of the flat keys with earlier moments. The keys of the outer pieces skirt tonic-dominant relations; both are plagal and falling — the playing-out of energies generated earlier, the aftermath of objectives already gained.

The motions of the first two pieces of the finale are scattered and diffuse; characters jockey for position, preparing for the funnel of the G-major movement on the other side of the pastoral, when the Count will drag them out of the shadows one by one. Now like fish in a pool they swim about in the twilit murk, one or another occasionally rising to the surface. In the first piece, the D-major movement, Susanna (the Countess), waiting in the darkness for the Count, is assailed by Cherubino who thinks of himself as flirting with, and frustrating the Count's lascivious designs on, Susanna. At the climax of the movement he manages to kiss the Count by mistake (a playful conceit of Beaumarchais's, to have the Count vaccinated by Eros?), and then to step out of the way adroitly so that Almaviva can as mistakenly slap Figaro. The movement ends as Cherubino exits, leaving the others to comment on the confusion.

As background for the incessant motion of the movement Mozart provides a neutral measure in a slow four with no gestural content of its own. The "real" beat and measure shift constantly throughout as various characters step to center stage. An opening D-major *forte* chord an-

Example 6-18

Example 6-19

Example 6-20

nounces the underground beat, but the orchestra's first phrase changes
the surface beat to eighth notes, picking out a misbarred gavotte (ex.
6–18). Tension between the two "beat 1's" will continue until the final
cadence of the movement. Cherubino, in his public role as the mis-
chievous boy-god, sings the gavotte first, and it remains for the most
part his rhythm. The piece has two other clearly identifiable gestures —
a second gavotte and a bourréelike motive. Gavotte 2 begins on the
same beat as gavotte 1 and serves it as counterstatement or consequent
phrase. Because the second gavotte has a cadential tilt, it establishes the
dominant in the second key area. It is distinguished from gavotte 1 by
an Alberti bass and slurred sixteenth notes — *gavotta tenerella* to *gavotta
smorfiosa* (ex. 6–19).[63] The third "tune," the bourréelike motive, fills up
the measure after gavotte 2 in the second reprise in order to return the
stress to beat 1 of the 4/4 measure and to engineer a strong masculine
cadence. Like the gavottes, however, it comprises only half of the slow
4/4 (ex. 6–20). In between these dance fragments is rhythmic imbroglio.
   One wedge out of periodicity into imbroglio comes, paradoxically,

from a device built into the trim symmetry of gavotte 1. Cherubino's two-measure [64] answer to the orchestra's two-measure gavotte phrase is extended to four by a deceptive cadence on B, the sixth degree (on the first beat of m. 3). After the orchestra repeats its phrase the Countess takes up the gavotte, but moves instead to B-flat, the lowered sixth — the thin end of the wedge of an augmented sixth pointing to A as dominant — and in her desperation at Cherubino's interference unexpectedly broadens her gesture to a declamatory measure with string tremolo, using the full 4/4 measure (m. 6). Her outburst subsides immediately, and with gavotte 2 her emphatic dominant (A) becomes a tonic. The pointing of the augmented sixth is forgotten, and the measure of declamation seems in retrospect a parenthesis, not an integral part of the harmonic grammar. This alternation of declamation and dance occurs twice more, imposing a rondolike motivic organization on the harmonic structure of the key-area plan:

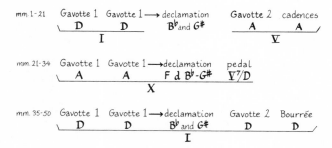

In the X-section the Count and Cherubino share the consequent of gavotte 1 (mm. 22–23, 25–26), and the declamatory passage (mm. 26–33; it is much extended, in order to provide X-section turmoil) expresses the company's indignation at Cherubino's continuing mischief. In the return (m. 34) Cherubino sings the original orchestral incipit and the others take the consequent for a chorused aside (manipulation of texture is one means by which the movement reaches a climax — at each recurrence more voices take the two gavottes). The crisis of the movement occurs in the return when gavotte 1 is repeated (m. 37). Cherubino administers the fatal kiss, Figaro steps nearer as Cherubino impishly darts out of the line of fire, and the Count slaps, instead of the page, Figaro. Rhythmic condensation serves to quicken the pulse here. The four gavotte measures are divided among the company and are considerably shortened, with the declamation limited to one measure of patter for the Count which completes the augmented sixth (G-sharp in m. 39). Gavotte 2 enters straightaway in the next measure. Previously only heard in the orchestra, here it is a song of relief and triumph for Susanna, the Countess, and the Count:

> Ah! ci ha fatto un bel guadagno,
> Colla sua temerità! (curiosità!)[66]

By occurring so much closer to gavotte 1 than it did in the first reprise, it brings the two separated halves of the gavotte together to tighten the second reprise, making them the beginning of a strong iambic cadence. The stressed part of the iamb is provided by the new bourrée, whose entry resolves the ambiguity about downbeat (though not about level of beat) prevalent since the beginning of the piece.[67]

It is rather startling to note about this movement that its proper 4/4 measure is used only for its out-of-the-ordinary moments — its outbursts of indignation and surprise — while the dance measures-within-the-measure establish the regular pulse. The moments of high passion and rhythmic imbroglio, kept in their place by the trim dance fragments, seem frozen and stylized gestures, as much a mask as Cherubino's teasing gavotte. This structure suggests a particular style of performance for the movement. Cherubino is its gadfly, up to his mischief while the rest of the company alternates between the measured gavotte and outbreaks of indignation. A good performance should catch the stylization of the abrupt shifts: the ensemble, made one by their annoyance at Cherubino (who the Count thinks is Figaro), should wheel stiffly and formally as a body, while the page skips around and through them. Eros is the catalyst of the public as well as the private contretemps.

Mozart realizes the tempo designation of the next piece — *Con un poco più di moto* — by making the gavotte beat (♪ in the slow 4/4 measure) the beat of a contredanse. ♪ equals ♩, and since the contredanse moves primarily in eighth notes, one level below the beat, the result is a feeling of compression, of a quickening of the pulse of the imbroglio. Again the dance pattern is half the length of the measure, with the difference that the downbeats of the contredanse and the 4/4 measures coincide every two contredanse measures (ex. 6-21). This opening contredanse motive with its typical half-cadence (the feminine ending in m. 53 below) occurs only once, serving simply to set the contredanse beat. After it

Example 6-21

Example 6-22

cadences Figaro is given a new and mocking contredanse motive, resembling the first one inverted (m. 57; see ex. 6–22). Because of its
insistence on the fifth degree, it moves the piece easily to the dominant.
The second key area comes to a cadence with the Count's declaration of
love:

> Che dita tenerelle!
> Che delicata pelle!
> Mi pizzica, mi stuzzica,
> M'empie di un nuovo ardor.[68]

From his first words in this movement the Count has been distinguished
from the others by his use of the full 4/4 measure.[69] As the others sing
their clipped contredanse phrases he stumbles obliviously about, his actions layered against the rhythms of their moves. For this libidinous exclamation Mozart gives him a two-measure motive which consists of a
subdominant fanfare for the onomatopoetic *pizzica* and *stuzzica* followed
by a smooth legato cadential formula; the motive is superimposed for
purposes of comparison, in example 6–22, over the four measures of
contredanse. Almaviva's long measure of stable subdominant and subsequent fevered rise to the tonic are a parody of amorous ardor. Mozart
has him repeat them twice, ending the section with more of Figaro's
contredanse, a consequent phrase finally added to make a strong tonic
cadence (mm. 102–6).

The Count's ardor could touch us here, as did his earnest act III duet
with Susanna. Again he appears to be expressing himself without calculation, in direct and sincere response to the stimulus of another human presence. Unfortunately, the hands he admires so immoderately
are not his lover's, but his wife's, and his language is that of the discriminating libertine, not the heartfelt lover. Obviously his lovemaking is
stimulated by boredom, and he is blind to the particular object of his
amours. His mistake makes him immediately comic, and in a deeper
sense repellent. A new situation or the dimly perceived outlines of an
attractive young figure will whet his jaded appetite, and he remains un-

moved by another person's singularity — in this opera the only admissible ardor.

The contrast between public and private in the finale is pointed up by the transition — or lack of it — from Susanna's and Figaro's pastorale to the *Scena ultima*. Immediately after the pastorale's B-flat major cadence the orchestra strikes a *forte* G-major chord, and the Count starts his hue and cry. The two third-related triads connect with one common tone (D) two disparate and obliquely related tonal worlds. The juxtaposition of the soft and mellow flat key with the hard-edged and brilliant sharp key makes clear how much ground has been traveled in one brief moment.

The ensuing *Allegro assai* begins as a conventional key-area plan in the Count's own duple dotted rhythms. Its time signature is 4/4, but the Count's rhythms and the quick string figuration suggest instead an *alla breve* scansion. The Count drags Cherubino, Barbarina, Marcellina, and Susanna out of the shadows while the rest of the company begs pardon for them. This action occupies the entire first reprise until the long dominant seventh before the return of the tonic (mm. 394–98). The Countess, appearing out of nowhere to unravel the plot with one sentence (m. 398), sings a bourréelike melody for the first tonic cadence of the return (ex. 6–23). The Count will in a moment beg somber pardon in an *Andante* version of this bourrée melody (the original ♩ roughly equaling ♪). But first a dreamlike deceleration, harmonically a brief X-section just after the first tonic cadence, prepares the halved beat, as the Count, Basilio, and Antonio absorb the new development. The deceleration has two parts — a chromatic progression from G minor rationalized by a descending bass line, and then a quicker move by fifths up to E-flat. E-flat becomes the lower note of an augmented sixth opening out to the dominant. The deceleration, a super *alla breve*, keeps half notes as the beat but groups them into 4/2 measures. It serves to make rhythmically acceptable the Count's solemn bourrée, even though that phrase moves at exactly half the tempo of the Countess's original music. If the fermata in the score over the rest in measure 420 before the Count's *Andante* solo is performed to prolong the quarter-note rest to two half notes, they will, along with the cadence note "so" and the two-

Example 6-23

Al - me - no io per lo - ro per - do - no ot - ter - rò.
pp

Example 6-24

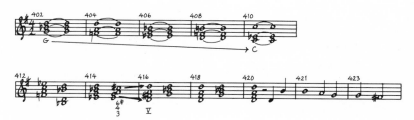

Example 6-25

quarter-note upbeat of the Count's "bourrée," fill out another 4/2 measure (ex. 6–24). In other words, the *Andante* marking for the Count's solo does not indicate a fresh start in a new and slower tempo, but renders in a more conventional notation than a 4/2 measure the slowing to a tempo precisely half as quick as before.

The actual reconciliation scene is an extraordinarily poignant moment, hushed and solemn, when the Count seems to rise for the first time to the dignity of his regal wife. But it is nevertheless hedged about with qualifications. The Count's supplication is brief, the Countess's answer (the consequent to his antecedent, with a two-measure extension) only a little more fulsome (ex. 6–25). The Countess's words and gesture have about them a gentle imperiousness which is not native to her. Had they been alone, the Count might have been able to bully her into a state of submission, but in a public ceremony she slips naturally into the queenly gestures necessary to lend her appearance weight. As a result of the slow braking of the deceleration — the previous long-breathed chords of surprise, floating in harmonic limbo — their music retains a quality of trancelike suspension. The super *alla breve* is a meter imposed for an inordinate amount of time onto a more lively gesture. It gives this music, and the hymnlike chorus which follows it, an air of exalted control — of borrowed and unnatural circumspection — which is appropriate to the quality of the reconciliation. Although the symmetries of the slow bourrée leave no sense of imbalance or incompleteness, its position in the finale as a sudden slow gesture in the midst of a lively drive to the final cadence generates a curious tension between the proper tempo and the present tempo. This tension, meant to arouse expectations for the seventy-four measures of final D major cadence, at the same time cannot help but impart to the scene some feeling of the impermanence resulting from behavior not from the heart. The Count's "Perdono" seems heartfelt and is moving, but it is hard to forget that *alla breve* caught the rhythm of his hypocrisy earlier in the opera. Furthermore, the mere fact that it must be public forces a contrast between this controlled pageant and the thorough intimacy of the B-flat pastoral reconciliation of Susanna and Figaro. There is little reason given to hope that Almaviva's public apology will affect his actions in private. The mad day has brought the servant couple through a crisis to establish a firmer foundation for their marriage, but the noble couple is repeating, not for the first or last time, a ritual act of apology and forgiveness.

The spring of tension is coiled to its tightest by the three-measure lead-in to the final *Allegro assai*—a fall to the dominant of D major which is necessitated by the plagal relation of G and D (if an artificial dominant were not introduced, D major would sound too much like the dominant of G major). Whereas the broad key-area plan of the second-act finale required 244 measures of E-flat cadence to round off its long harmonic period, the last finale, because of its segmental nature, localizes tension: the coiled spring of the *alla breve* explodes into a brief, quick-tempoed march. After a dominant pedal and a touch of the tonic minor to drive the wedge deeper (and to catch the tone of the line "Questo giorno di tormenti,/Di capricci e di follia"[70]) the tonic bursts triumphantly forth on the words "In contenti e in allegria/Solo amor può terminar."[71] The sentiment is an appropriate motto for the opera, and the rest of the finale (after the dominant cadence, m. 471) translates it into sound. The singers drop out for four measures while in the distance, *piano*, the full orchestra (with timpani and trumpets as in the end of the third-act finale) strikes up a march. The company hears it too, and cries "Ed al suon di lieta marcia/Corriam tutti a festeggiar!"[72] Not the exalted march claimed in the opera by passion perverted, but a modest soldierly one,[73] it belongs to Eros militant. Akin to the marches ending the first and third acts, it appears here in the opera's proper key, D major. The role of Cherubino d'amore has been almost entirely subsumed by his faithful courtiers, Susanna and the Countess (and lately by Marcellina and Figaro). The boy is now free to abandon the strange androgynous state of adolescence and become a man, to court a real woman, and perhaps even to feel the pangs of love betrayed. Yet he has been a touchstone without whose charismatic presence the transformations wrought during the mad day would never have taken place. Under his aegis Susanna and the Countess have drawn closer together, Figaro has learned to listen as well as to act, and the Countess has faced out the Count to bring him back to her, for at least a moment reconciled. Cherubino is emblematic of the fragile traits possessed by some humans which enable them to discover a special place, a "room of their own," a tranquil refuge to which they may also draw fellow seekers less well endowed than they. The opera, filled with joy and wit, and yet a certain resignation, is not a revolutionary's manual, nor a facile witness to an aphorism about true friendship knowing no bounds. Mozart had no desire to obliterate class distinctions, because for him the way to the most important truths lay through the surface of things as they are. The attempt to shrug off one's skin is a vain and ultimately circumscribing act of violence; one struggles impotently, caught in the coils of the unwilling self. True freedom begins with carefully articulated orders, true knowledge with the patience of the receptive eye.

PART THREE

DON GIOVANNI

I am strangely at a loss what to think of this man. He is a perfect Proteus. I can but write according to the shape he assumes at the time. Don't think *me* a changeable person, I beseech you, if in one letter I contradict what I wrote in another; nay, if I seem to contradict what I said in the same letter; for he is a perfect camelion; or rather more variable than the camelion; for that, it is said, cannot assume the *red* and the *white*; but this man *can*. And though *black* seems to be his natural color, yet he has taken great pains to make me think him nothing but *white*.

Samuel Richardson, *Clarissa Harlowe*, letter 28, Clarissa Harlowe to Miss Howe.

CHAPTER SEVEN

Overture and Introduction

The world of *Don Giovanni*, although nocturnal and ominous in its atmosphere, is not entirely removed from the luminous space inhabited by Susanna and the Countess. The seeming difference in tone between the two operas is at first so striking that it claims all one's attention. Yet the things which distinguish them are not primary, but superadded, and cause a shift in perspective rather than a change of scene. The first thirty measures of the overture left aside, *Don Giovanni* begins in essentially the same way as does *Figaro*. The *Molto allegro* of the one and the *Presto* of the other are virtually interchangeable, with their *galant* fanfares, marches, hints of noble bourrée, and flourishes of concerto style. Even the *Sturm und Drang* turn to minor in the overture to *Don Giovanni*, just before arrival in the second key area (mm. 67–76), has its analogue in an only slightly less flamboyant gesture in *Figaro*'s overture. There are differences between the two passages,[1] but they serve the same formal function.

The change in emotional climate from the one opera to the other, that quickening of the pulse which one inevitably experiences at the outset of *Don Giovanni*, is effected entirely by the overture's first thirty measures. They belong to the genre of the *ombra* scene, in which, according to operatic tradition, striking and solemn music evokes the domain of the shades.[2] The musical elements of the *ombra* style here are purposeful unorthodoxies: a minor key (always in the musical language of the late eighteenth century the signal of unusual and portentous events); an antique chaconne bass and the ponderous dotted rhythms of an earlier style; chains of syncopations, with no resolution provided to the rhythmic imbalance which they provoke; frequent assertion of the Phrygian half-step; sideslipping chromatic progressions and a major place in the harmonic events conceded to the Neapolitan sixth; a handful of disconnected "filler" figures, the most distinctive of all merely a minor scale ascending through the octave and descending again slowly from a point a chromatic crack higher; sudden *sforzando* shocks in an otherwise *piano* and muted uneasiness. Figures are laid into the larger structure in chunks, open-ended and repetitive rather than symmetrically rounded off in the departure-return sequence of the dance. Yet all the *ombra's* unorthodoxies are embedded in a harmonic plan which is only deceptively complex, and ensures the maximum local mystery and indirection with the minimum sacrifice of broad cadential muscle.[3] Furthermore, a fantasialike slow introduction was hardly a novelty in itself. Mozart had just supplied the *Prague* Symphony, K. 504, with a slow introduction resembling this one on almost all counts except for its beginning in a major key.[4] The construction and locus of the introduction are not mysterious, nor is the piece *sui generis*, as some fervent admirers of *Don Giovanni* would have us believe.[5] The D-minor section is carefully fashioned to pose a diametric opposition to the material of the main body of the overture, or human movements caught by the rhythms of dance: *alla breve* is the logical meter for the supernatural component in this confrontation. The *ombra Andante* is *alla breve* as *alla capella*, the slow and somber meter of church fugues and choruses, slowed past the tempo of even the exalted march, and loaded with heavy figuration and complex rhythms. The substitution of a tempo twice again as fast (the *Molto allegro's* ♩ roughly equals the *Andante's* ♪) eases us into the gestures of the sunlit *buffa* world without skipping a beat.

By invoking the superhuman and supernatural at the outset of the opera, Mozart does more than simply prefigure the celestial will and the power of its censure. He also invites the listener to view the familiar *buffa* world at a new remove. The *ombra* music gives the world Mozart created in *Le nozze di Figaro* a further moral dimension; it suggests a new height for aspiration and a new capacity for cruelty and wrongdoing, both of which were unthinkable before when one's vision was bounded by the limits of the terrestrial social hierarchy. It expands our perspective on the world to include the penumbra above and below the human order, suggesting that what is about to be encountered is a kind of human action which is either too noble or too base to be encompassed within the narrower limits of merely human judgment. Whatever one may decide to be the nature of the transgressions of the *dissoluto punito*[6] (a task of considerable difficulty, to judge from the thousands of labored and inconclusive paragraphs concerned with spelling out precisely the error, or the glory, of his ways), the word "transgression" is clearly an apt one in the context: the Don's sins involve a "crossing beyond" the proper limits of human experience, and in order to secure his punishment, the purview of the opera must be widened to include the realms of the only authority capable of judging him. In accommodating the divine perspective the opera has somewhat to distort our view of that small part of the world where we were formerly at home: to gain the new dimension the vivid planes of *Figaro's terra firma* must be compressed into a caricature of themselves, a shadow play.

Thus all that seems different in the domains of the two operas becomes a matter merely of a different stance toward the conventions of a single world. In *Figaro* the conventions which support human relations are plastic in Mozart's hands; he expands and redefines them, finding happy places within for unconventional behavior. In *Don Giovanni* the conventions have become rigid and chilling — grim truisms rather than growing-spaces. Masetto is a stock peasant character, and Donna Anna moves in her noblewoman's habit with the taut hysteria of the caged. The characters who do live beyond the boundaries of convention deserve some admiration, but it must be mixed — with pity, for Elvira, and for Giovanni with a measure of horror. The warmth and subtlety which informs the relationship of Susanna and the Countess are impossible in a world whose human inhabitants are necessarily diminished in complexity by the overshadowing presence of the superhuman and daemonic. If there is some note of solace, it must not be embraced over-quickly; only a hard look at the opera can assure that we do not grasp at straws.

CHAPTER EIGHT

The Opening Scene

The Structure of the Drama

One striking feature of *El Burlador de Sevilla y convidado di piedra*, the first Don Juan play,[1] and of many versions thereafter, is its beginning *in medias res*, with cries of rape, and hot pursuit in the darkness. In the earliest versions of the first scene none of Don Juan's women victims are identifiable precisely as Donna Anna, and in Tirso's version the routed authority turns out to be Don Juan's uncle, who benevolently permits the seducer to escape into the night. Nevertheless all the openings share the same silhouette, and for good dramatic reasons. The story itself has the thinnest of plotlines: Don Juan is a libertine, so Heaven punishes him. For a successful presentation of the plot on stage two scenes alone are indispensable, one to make a compelling display of the depth and depravity of Don Juan's crimes, and another to bring the final vengeance of Heaven down on his head. In between these pivotal scenes the author is meant to improvise, inventing as large and varied a bouquet of seductions and confrontations as may please him; he is free to improve upon the fancies of others or to compose fresh histories himself. Tradition, however, has fixed the outer scenes firmly in place in order to ensure a modicum of dramatic power and coherence in a work which could easily be weakened by diffuse and errant improvisation in its episodes. Final vengeance has to take the shape of the "Stone Guest," whose visitation became the hallmark of the legend. The opening and indicting scene, with Giovanni bursting from a darkened house pursued by an outraged noblewoman, provides evidence of at least one sin commensurate with the high degree of celestial attention manifested by the statue's visit, gives the play a dark and galvanizing opening, and in some versions, Mozart's included, furnishes an outraged father of the outraged gentlewoman as a handy candidate for murder and petrifaction.

By the time of Giovanni Bertati's libretto for the composer Giuseppe Gazzaniga, *Don Giovanni o sia Il Convitato di pietra,*[2] the traditional breathless opening had been supplied with a brief upbeat — a monologue by Don Giovanni's comic servant Pasquariello as he keeps watch outside the house of Donna Anna. *Opere buffe* often begin with a soliloquy by a comic servant; a monologue-beginning works well in opera, since a few nicely conceived reflections by the protagonist's *alter ego* can provide the exposition which would occupy several scenes of a straight play's spoken dialogue. It was left to Mozart, however, to bind the two traditions, of low comedy and high tragedy, together into what is perhaps the most stunning opening scene in operatic literature. The comic-servant routine and the passionate chase and duel, while serving as introduction to the business of the opera, in their confluence take on a far deeper meaning. The brilliant characterizations of Leporello, Don Giovanni, and Donna Anna, laden with ambiguity and irony, establish musical metaphors thematic to the entire opera. Furthermore, the daring combination of disparate styles into an apparently seamless and unified whole itself projects the opera's central theme: the rhetoric of *Don Giovanni*, and perhaps its final blackness, is figured by the act of setting the high pathetic style in the unlikely and antic foil of *buffa* comedy.

"Notte e giorno faticar"

Leporello's "soliloquy" masquerades as a simple foursquare march. Yet some subtle rhythmic imbalances and clever inflections of the stock march affect invade its apparent straightforwardness, sketching in with darker strokes the dubious qualities submerged in the role of the stock buffoon-servant. Leporello has no malice, no true diabolism in his nature. He's only good-humoredly vulgar, a touch greedy in his discontent, inattentively cruel, a little slow to draw a moral consequence.

"Notte e giorno" is a study in the art of articulating one simple meter into a series of varying rhythmic gestures. The aria is set in 4/4, a rhythmic modulation to ♩ from ♩ , the *alla breve* of the overture. Each different scansion of the 4/4 is part of the mimetic account of the subject matter of Leporello's complaint. At first he is merely himself, the flat-footed sentinel, executing a frankly pedestrian march. Mozart's articulation of the simple 4/4 march seems curiously labored at first glance, since he phrases the four beats across rather than within the barline:

usual march: 1 2 3 4

this march: 3 4 1 2

In Leporello's version beat 3 is stressed because it begins the phrase, beat 1 because it begins the measure. The march is distinctly more pedestrian when the two halves of its 4/4 measure receive nearly equal weights; an ordinary stride becomes the stiff-legged gait of a tin soldier, a *soldat malgré lui*. Facing about in comic annoyance Leporello executes a formal infantry maneuver, drawing himself up to reconnoiter at the flourish on the first beat of every other measure:

left   right   left   feet together, attention!
3   4   1   2   3   4   1   2

The unconventional gavottelike barring of the march also positions just before the barline the sixteenth — and thirty-second-note upbeat runs which suggest Leporello's salutes, assuring them a strong accent. If the runs were arranged as upbeats to beat 3 of a conventionally barred march, as they are in measures 1–4 of example 8–2 below, they would be merely pallid decorations, no longer serving to direct the marcher in the execution of his military figure.

Leporello marches in sturdy distraction, preoccupied with his angry resentment against his master. A check on the expected march period structure catches his bemusement. Mozart makes all the two-measure units of the eight-measure phrase antecedents, repetitions, that is, of the eight-beat opening motive. He organizes the repetitions on a rising line from F to B-flat, to portray both Leporello's concentration on his rising anger and the growing distance between the sentinel and his post. By its third instance the eight-beat figure begins to sound clumsy and overdrawn. By its fourth repetition the sentinel's four-step maneuver has transported him too far from his starting place, obliging him to break ranks and scurry back, a "choreography" which is suggested by the bustling sixteenth-note descending scale which ends the phrase (ex. 8–1). A lesser composer, attending to the conventional expectations for meter and period structure, would have fashioned something like the following unexceptional little march period, whose four-measure consequent returns the marcher neatly to his starting place (ex. 8–2). Its trim march symmetries suffice to set the comic stereotype. Mozart's version, with its stilted "gavotte" rhythms and the overstrained stretch of

Example 8-1

Example 8-2

the figures toward the dominant seventh, makes the stereotype larger than life and thus renders it particular.

Leporello's silent motions on stage are revealing enough; when he turns to sing to the tune of his march, he gives away even a little more. The repetitive figuration is now with equal appropriateness brought to the service of a list, the usual chain of servants' complaints:

> Notte e giorno faticar
> Per chi nulla sa gradir;
> Piova e vento sopportar,
> Mangiar male e mal dormir.[3]

It arrives on the dominant again, where the grand flourish of scales on the dominant seventh demands an equally portentous event to follow. Leporello's fancy, piqued by visions of his master's activities in Donna Anna's chamber, conjures up an apt musical metaphor for what his master represents to him — a full-fledged cavalry march (m. 20). It begins vigorously on the dominant with a string flourish, a horn call in parallel thirds, and arpeggiated triplets in the middle strings, this last the conventional evocation of riding at a gallop.[4] Since the 4/4 measure is no longer mechanically articulated, it has a broad and heroic sweep (ex. 8–3). The notion of a cavalry march as a metaphor for the gentleman — the *cavaliere* — takes off from a direct contrast with Leporello's foot march: gentlemen ride to hunt and to war, while servants follow on

Example 8-3

Example 8-4

foot. But the prerogatives of a gentleman transcend the trivial matter of
better transportation: they also grant him license for seduction. The
horseman is also a bedroom soldier, says Leporello with a leer at Donna
Anna's house; the evidence is inside. The orchestra puts the sexual *dou-*
ble entendre over succinctly, using hunting horns to suggest cuckoldry
and the equestrian imitation for an even bawdier dig — it translates the
time-honored pun on the word "mounting" (It. *montare*) into music to
emphasize the dual nature of the *cavaliere*'s pursuits.

The rhythmic sweep of the cavalry march's phrases is striking because while each of the phrases is an irregular three measures long, this
irregularity makes no claim on our attention. It might be more notice-
able if the figures in the foot march were not also drawn out past normal
expectations. A simple recomposition of the cavalry march (to the state
of the foot march of ex. 8–2, p. 203), punctures its blown-up phrases
(ex. 8–4). The result is another period of a simple march for a *buffa*
servant's lament, which works well enough to have been the skeleton
Mozart considered at the start, but lacks all his jokes. Once one com-
mences to play with the skeleton, each broad stroke necessitates an

Example 8-5

other. The infantry march fails to find its consequent phrase after nineteen measures, and requires an answer equal to its own extravagant extension. The necessity of a strong tonic chord on the first downbeat of the consequent introduces the extra measure into each phrase of the cavalier's march, helping to give it the expansive "die-Jagd" tone which is contrasted so successfully with the stiff-legged gait of Leporello's march. The settled contrast of foot and cavalry marches (mm. 1–25) demands yet a new inflection of gesture for the cadence, so Leporello comes by his low half-note refusals alternating with clipped "no's" in patter for a seven-measure cadential figure (mm. 26–32). Mozart's version is better music as well as better comedy: it evolves from three pale and choppy eight-measure phrases of equal weight[5] into two broader phrases, which, while spun out to thirty-two measures, are still bound together in antecedent-consequent relationship. For the characterization of Leporello, at any rate, broad comic strokes are the more precise ones; by stretching the simple rhythmic conventions of *buffa* rhetoric Mozart substitutes profile and character for the prosaic homogeneity of caricature.

The possible inflections of the supple 4/4 are not exhausted yet. After Leporello's patter cadence the horns enter on a long F (m. 32), making the cuckold joke again in order to direct attention back to the clandestine activities within. Strings and bassoons take advantage of the gavottelike barring of the opening march to inflect a real gavotte in its place (ex. 8–5). Its skeleton of descending parallel sixths touching on the tonic every first beat, and the characteristic ♩. ♫ figure which further energizes the downbeat, shape the gavotte's miniature rhythmic arch over the barline. (Leporello's foot march fails to be a gavotte because the same rhythmic event keeps being repeated: the unadorned and mechanical alternation of F and C at the opening of the march forms caesuras at the half-measure and every two measures, making a two-measure grouping the first full member of the phrase:

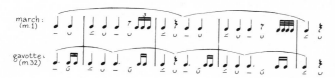

The triplet flourish over the barline to measure 2 punctuates the two-measure unit, and the first harmonic change occurs immediately after that cut to give it final confirmation.) This little orchestral gavotte-phrase mimes Leporello's *frisson* of delight mixed with envy as he imagines what he is missing by his enforced sentinel duty. The flirtatious rhythms and amorous associations of the dance suggest the love play transpiring inside between "il caro galantuomo" and his "bella."[6] The sarcastic endearment *caro* is a natural concomitant of the gavotte: with a heavy exaggeration of salon preciosity Leporello imitates the gentleman lover at work.

The gavotte and Leporello's response to it are a gloss on his earlier manifesto — "Voglio far il gentiluomo."[7] The horns for cuckoldry and horses for mounting in the accompaniment to his cavalry march have already demonstrated the privileged life of a *gentiluomo*, and the gavotte spells the associations out for anyone dim enough to have missed these musical puns. A gavotte inflected over a march rhythm is used to somewhat the same effect by Figaro in "Non più andrai," to the text "Narcisetto, Adoncino d'Amor." There the joke is gently affectionate, figuring young Cherubino as a blushing soldier in the war of Eros. Leporello's version takes a cruder turn. Seduction in *Don Giovanni* no longer has the expanded meaning it takes on in *Figaro*, that of forging bonds of affection between human beings who rightfully bear the name of lover. Seduction to Leporello is merely a means of garnering pleasure for oneself; capitulation demeans, if it doesn't ruin, the seduced, while enhancing the confidence and repute of the seducer. In Molière's *Don Juan* the servant Sganarelle, offended by his master's deceiving love play, wants to restrain the Don, yet fears him too much to make more than a feeble and easily silenced protest. Leporello is no Sganarelle; far from disapproving of Don Giovanni's actions, he wants to belong to the class which holds them as prerogatives. Like Sganarelle, he is afraid. When the clamor of a chase sounds in the background Mozart shows up his braggadocio by having him substitute to the music of his proud "E non voglio più servir" the muttered "Non mi voglio far sentir"[8] as he hastily hides in the shadows. His fear, however, usually restrains him not from lecturing the Don on his depravity but from getting a bit of the action for himself. Molière makes Sganarelle's weakness a quality endemic to servants: the role of masters is ruthlessly to prevail, of servants ruefully to have their scruples trampled. Leporello, on the other hand, has no scruples about following in his master's footsteps; a servant's nature is to be a cruder model of his master, and finesse and opportunity are the only barriers raised by class.

"Notte e giorno" is the equivalent of a vulgarly hearty smack of appreciation for Don Giovanni's mode of conduct, delivered with rolling eyes and an occasional leer. The consequences of the chase for hunter or victim the aria conveniently ignores. Although Leporello is comic, and can even generate some sympathy in his audience, his unabashedly prurient account of what it means to be a gentleman is a little chilling. Whereas in *Figaro* the word "noble" in "nobleman" expands to include the virtue as well as the rank, in *Don Giovanni* the word is contracted to a mean and narrow range, all the more debased because a servant in wholehearted approval unconsciously delivers the indictment.

The Nature of Don Giovanni

The high passion of the chase is grafted directly onto Leporello's final cadence: his F becomes the bottom of a tremolo run up through E-flat to B-flat, and thus a dominant instead of a tonic. This effortless modulation compels a new rhythmic gesture and a new emotional climate. From F major — the *buffa* face of its relative minor, the grim D opening the overture, and Leporello's key throughout the opera — we move to B-flat major, D minor's sixth degree. The new rhythm, although not indicated by a change of signature, is unmistakeably *alla breve*, and the new gesture is another version of march time — a slightly accelerated exalted march (ex. 8–6).[9] Anna's *opera seria* indignation betrays her immediately upon entrance — "come furia disperata,"[10] she characterizes herself — and so does the ambiguity of her first words to her seducer, "Non sperar, se non m'uccidi,/Ch'io ti lasci fuggir mai!"[11] It would be merely insensitive to accuse Donna Anna of real ambivalence toward her enemy in her present fury; yet later, when she persists in directing all her ardor toward the pursuit of her seducer rather than toward marriage with her affianced lover, these words will afford a second meaning. Here she has the bearing of a classical tragic heroine; moving fiercely to what will become her characteristic *alla breve* gesture, she sees her vengeful anger as divinely inspired. Nobility is as full-blown and majestic in this opera as *buffa* is salacious.

Giovanni, on the other hand, wants only to identify himself as No-

Example 8-6

Non spe -rar,— se non— m'uc - ci - di, Ch'io_ti   la - sci_ fug·gir_   mai.

Man. The stage direction describes him as "cercando sempre di cel-
arsi,"[12] and his response to Donna Anna's challenge is oddly oblique:
not "You shall not detain me," but "You shall not find out who I am."[13]
He also conceals himself in his music, adopting for his first utterances
Donna Anna's vocal line, and never in the remainder of the trio (Leporello supports the duo throughout with patter imprecations about approaching trouble) originating any of its rhythmic or melodic material.
It is hardly surprising that a pursued seducer should try to conceal his
identity from his intended victim. Yet although Tirso's Don Juan, pur-
sued by Isabella and several Spanish nobles, also at first calls himself
No-Name, he finally cannot resist revealing himself, crying out "Fool!"
I'm a gentleman!"[14] (nor could Odysseus bear to leave the Cyclops
without at the last informing him proudly that No-Man was Odysseus,
son of Laertes[15]). Giovanni is strangely free from this besetting vanity.
Chameleonlike, he doesn't even betray himself in speech, but borrows
Donna Anna's music and a combination of Leporello's and Donna
Anna's words.[16] The most striking thing about him is that he sees
nothing demeaning in escaping, pursued and nameless, into the darkness; he feels no need to regain his public dignity. His retort to Anna's
wrathful epithet "scellerato" ("villain") is a cool "sconsigliata" ("rash
woman") — "you're ill-advised to make a fuss." In fact if the music of the
movement were not so elevated, Don Giovanni's first appearance on
stage would amount to a simple sight gag. The musical imagery of
"Notte e giorno" made the hunt a live metaphor for seduction. Now
suddenly the gentleman hunter sprints out, determinedly stalked by his
erstwhile prey — "exit, pursued by a bear."

In other eighteenth-century versions of *Don Giovanni* the chase scene
might well have been played for laughs. Don Juan Tenorio had fallen
into disrepute in the eighteenth century. His story belonged primarily
to the popular theater, where it had degenerated into the spectacle of a
comic gentleman scrambling out of windows, inventing adroit lies to
cover misdemeanors, and taking the occasional pratfall. There are, beside Mozart's, only two eighteenth-century versions of the tale of any
reputation, and neither one takes it very seriously. Goldoni's *Don Giovanni Tenorio* is merely, on his own account, an undercover attack on a
lover who has spurned him. And the Bertati/Gazzaniga opera views the
story from a certain remove, bracketing it neatly in ironic quotation
marks. It is presented as the second act of a two-act opera, the first act
of which portrays a debate among the members of an Italian opera company traveling in Germany about what work they should produce; they
finally decide on *Don Giovanni* despite the fact that all of them agree it to
be a vulgar farce.

Indeed, in his choice of libretto da Ponte was perhaps less to be praised for prescience than he was to be censured for pandering to low tastes. For the eighteenth-century audience the subject of hellfire and damnation had lost both its dignity and its shock value. Consider, for example, Henry Fielding's wry remarks in *Tom Jones* on the status of hell as a literary subject matter:

> "Had this history been writ in the days of superstition, I should have had too much compassion for the reader to have left him so long in suspense, whether Beelzebub or Satan was about to appear in person, with all his hellish retinue; but as these doctrines are at present very unfortunate, and have but few, if any believers, I have not been much aware of conveying any such terrors. To say truth, the whole furniture of the infernal regions hath long been appropriated by the managers of playhouses, who seem lately to have laid them by as rubbish, capable only of affecting the upper gallery — a place in which few of our readers ever sit."[17]

And to the refined libertines of the Enlightenment, seduction as Grand Guignol must have seemed merely adolescent. To be caught out in attempted seduction was ridiculous and unmanly, behavior beneath a gentleman's dignity; the preferred sport was drawing-room intrigue with the tacit consent of the seduced. Most eighteenth-century works which are notoriously about seducers turn out under closer scrutiny to be about something quite different. The burden of Richardson's *Clarissa Harlowe* is the unflagging virtue of the heroine, and the role of Lovelace her seducer is principally to make it manifest. Tom Jones is a doughty adventurer whose amorous interludes overtake him because of his winsome beauty and sheer niceness. Even the archrogue Rousseau of the *Confessions* is passive in his escapades; he makes a point of describing his frequent amours as the result of his weakness, and not as a matter of premeditated pursuit.

In fact, although there is much talk about the "Don Juan type," it is difficult to name another representative of the class beside Don Juan, in his various manifestations. When dealing with such a character, writers seem to have been drawn exclusively to the Don as *sui generis*, the full and sufficient expression of a creature who, although encountered frequently enough in ordinary life, does not cut a very attractive figure as the center of a play or novel. For the straightforward seducer is a difficult literary hero in any era; depending on the sophistication of the audience his exploits will be either too horrible or too banal to be witnessed with approval. The reason for the extraordinary popularity of the Don Juan figure prior to the eighteenth century may have been that

he was inextricably paired with as galvanizing a figure invented for his
despatch — Tirso's Don Gonzalo, the famous Stone Guest. When sin
was punished by damnation, the audience need not be uneasy about enjoying either.

But to an audience for whom hellfire had been emasculated, and
rapine reduced to a vulgar and demeaning pursuit, a morality play
could provide little interest. In eighteenth-century works where the
theme of sin and damnation was retained, it was usually so thickly
veiled as to be unrecognizable: the seductions in Choderlos de Laclos's
Les liaisons dangereuses[18] are cerebral campaigns of the utmost refinement, and the seducers are punished by natural rather than supernatural causes — a duel for the Vicomte de Valmont, and for the Mar-
quise de Merteuil a disfiguring disease. In the face of these fashions it is
surprising that da Ponte retained the traditional armature of the Don
Juan story, even discarding the disclaimer that Gazzaniga's ironic introduction would have provided, and that Mozart played the chase scene
seriously. Of course the one elevated gesture belongs to Donna Anna,
while Giovanni remains almost a cipher in the scene. But the potential
joke of the hunted turning tables on the hunter must have been intended to comprise a more significant image. Given Mozart's vignette of
the hero locked in ungraceful flight from a bristling fury, we must
somehow assimilate this rather ridiculous behavior into the account of a
man who, variously damned or worshiped for the past two centuries,
was termed in Kierkegaard's famous essay on the opera the "expression
of the daemonic."[19] The extraordinary reputation of Giovanni the *Über-
mensch* must be squared with the thin melodrama of his story, the insig-
nificance of his introduction, and the banality of his pursuits.

The conclusion of this first scene reveals more of the Don. The Commendatore enters[20] to challenge Don Giovanni to a duel. Giovanni
refuses, having no desire to cross swords with an old man, but the Commendatore persists, and Giovanni finally accedes in exasperated decision ("Misero! Attendi,/Se vuoi morir"[21]). He battles with and kills the
Commendatore. Then, with Leporello gaping from a nearby hiding
place, he stands over the old man as he dies.

Musically the five throughcomposed sections comprising the overture and first scene are arranged in a symmetrical hierarchy of gesture.
From the supernatural heights of the D-minor *ombra* fantasy introduction the affect declines to the bright clarity of the D-major *galant*,
touching bottom with Leporello's ribald *buffa* grousing. The high *galant*
with Donna Anna's stirring exalted march begins the reascent and now,
at the entrance of the Commendatore, the scene returns to the somber
pathos of the fantasy style:[22]

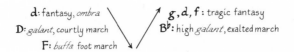

d: fantasy, *ombra* \
D: *galant*, courtly march \
F: *buffa* foot march \
g, d, f: tragic fantasy \
B♭: high *galant*, exalted march

In this fantasy section time is taken in very special ways. The fantasy gesture is suited to the depiction of high tragedy because, unlike the *galant* and *buffa* styles, it is free of the normal gestural and temporal restraints of the dance and of the period.[23] Here the fantasy communicates both the immediacy and the enormity of the event, first by a pantomimic choreography of the actual challenge and battle — a literal representation of time's passing — and then by a surreal distention of time to mark the Commendatore's death throes. Time is taken first below and then above the threshold of periodic dance structure, the normal time element of the opera. The fantasy and its temporal distortions cause a sense of the portentousness of these events to pervade the scene, fulfilling the less specific portent of the overture; its tone is not matched again in the opera until the Stone Guest appears in the next-to-last scene (notice that whereas at the opening of the opera the *buffa* and *galant* styles are set in the frame of high fantasy, at the close of the opera the reverse is true — but more about that later).

Giovanni's behavior throughout the challenge and battle is marked by an insouciant and natural nobility; it is honorable and properly formal. The Commendatore's first challenge is portrayed musically by one formal antecedent-consequent (command-refusal) phrase (mm. 139–46), which is not set in a continuum of ordinary periodic rhetoric, but is meant to be directly mimetic of the ritual formality of the meeting. Giovanni's refusal is tossed off with a i⁶-iv-V-i cadence in G minor. The Commendatore delivers a second, more peremptory challenge ending on the dominant of G minor (m. 149), and when again refused repeats approximately the same phrase in D minor, his increased urgency expressed by the inflection of a G-sharp to form a penultimate augmented sixth.[24] After a decisive measure of silence, Giovanni accepts the old man's challenge. Refusal to do so would be an insult, a violation of the code of honor. That Giovanni is acting from the sense of a nobleman's necessity and not from viciousness is made clear by the detachment of his death knell for the Commendatore after the fatal blow is struck; his words — "Ah! già cade il sciagurato,"[25] are reportorial, coolly free from either triumph or regret. He couches his acceptance in an eight-measure cadence (mm. 159–66, including the measure of rest), using the antique formula i-VI-iv-V-i, a harmonic version of the descending-tetrachord or "chaconne" bass (ex. 8–7). A critical theme also in the overture and second-act finale, here this portentous formula puts the

Example 8-7

brakes on the semiregular rhythm of overlapping fours which was set up at the outset:

	m 139		($\underline{V}/g$)	($^{6\sharp}_3$, $\underline{V}/d$)	(d minor cadence)
COMMENDATORE:	1 2 3 4		1 2 3 4	1 2 3 4 1	
DON GIOVANNI:		1 2 3 4	1 2 3	1 1	2 3 4 5 6 7 8.
LEPORELLO:			1 2 3 4	1 2 3 4	

It lends Giovanni's assent the stern and ceremonial flourish appropriate to the occasion of a formal calling-out, and brings the first section of the fantasy to a close on a strong D minor cadence.

The remainder of the swordfight is choreographed with graphic literalness. The brief back-and-forth of sword strokes is hung on a descending chromatic line, itself organized into three two-measure lengths by a counterpoint of tritone and resolution. The combat culminates in Don Giovanni's final lunges, which are directed by a complementary chromatic ascent (see ex. 8–8 below). The sword reaches its mark on a thrusting diminished seventh (of V in F minor). The Commendatore, mortally wounded as the harmony touches a dominant of a dominant (an overreaching of the dominant which had previously been prepared by the augmented sixth and i⁶₄ accompanying Giovanni's preliminary lunges), falls back to his death agony as the harmony slips back to the dominant (ex. 8–8).

At the moment of the death blow, time and pantomime are arrested by a fermata. The new signature, *alla breve*,[26] and the instruction *Andante*

Example 8-8

Example 8-9

slow the tempo by half, making the previous ♩ roughly equal 𝅗𝅥 . The strings mark time with gravely ticking triplets over a dominant pedal; they measure out the precious seconds of life remaining to the Commendatore. The very deliberateness of their ticking puts the scene out of time, for time passes normally only when attention is not called to it, leaving the shapes of events themselves to measure its passing for us. The monotony of the measured triplets is temporarily open-ended, fixing on the bare phenomenon of time's passage to make the present moment seem capable of enduring forever. Over the ticking of the triplets the low murmurs of Don Giovanni and Leporello seem automatic, elicited from them involuntarily. They are not singing to us or to another character, but are transfixed and private in awe of the moment at which "the vital spirit leaves the throbbing breast."[27] Giovanni's first music is again not of his own invention, but is Donna Anna's "Come furia disperata" of the chase music, cast in F minor and slowed to twice its original tempo (ex. 8–9). Hearing the familiar figure in slow motion and in the minor heightens the dreamlike effect of the scene. Giovanni's voice emerges occasionally from the sepulchral mix of bass tones to sculpt a phrase with a plangent dissonance[28] or a reach for a high note. His torpor underlines the preternatural quality of the moment: "real" time has been suspended so that the audience may be made to recognize the grave import of the Commendatore's death.

Harmonic procedures are simple in the fantasy. The harmonic rhythm is slow-moving, consisting of three oscillations of V to i_4^6 (all but the last i_4^6 over a pedal, and each filling one measure) and two i-iv-V-i cadential phrases. An air of suspended animation is maintained in the measure-to-measure relation by the avoidance of a strong tonic, and of most of the secondary articulations implied by the harmony.[29] The first i-iv-V-i phrase (mm. 181–86) includes the austere pathos of a VI-ii⁶-V⁷ "deceptive cadence" after the dominant is first attained.[30] The omission of this VI-ii⁶ parenthesis shortens the second i-iv-V-i phrase by one measure: circumventing the possible monotony of repetition, Mozart at the same time catches poignantly the Commendatore's dying breath. Giovanni

Example 8-10

Example 8-11

begins the repetition by leaping up to his pathetic E-flat on "già" (m. 186). The Commendatore, growing rapidly weaker, can only manage one note to three of Giovanni's, so the two men engage in a momentary "hocket." The Commendatore moves, in an open space in the texture, to the flatted second degree G-flat, forming a Neapolitan sixth which, followed by i$^6_4$-V-i, is another poignant cliché for cadences in minor. The Commendatore's halting line, its barely audible Phrygian inflection fainting toward the tonic, hauntingly evokes the utter weakness prior to death. Example 8–10 compares his last two phrases (contiguous in the score).

A chromatic line in the oboes descending from the dominant marks the flight of the soul from the body (ex. 8–11) and returns us to familiar measured time. By supplying the implied resolution of the chromatic line which ordered the swordplay, and by turning directly mimetic again (although now of a "supernatural" event — the hushed gravity of the death scene makes such a fancy possible), this second chromatic descent puts time back on the track, heightening the fantasy's quality of parenthesis, of a moment frozen in time. But returned to ordinary time Giovanni is impatient of last rites, and forestalls the anticipated tonic by hissing out for Leporello. The drop from high fantasy to the lowest *buffa* dialogue in *recitativo secco* ("Leporello, ove sei?"/"Son qui, per disgrazia . . ./Chi è morto? voi o il vecchio?"/"Che domanda da bestia! i vecchio."[31]) is immediate and stunning. It only underlines Giovanni's polymorphic nature: a gentleman when answering the Commendatore's challenge, at his opponent's death he slips back into the seamy behavior of an arrant blackguard. He wears no mask in either episode; he is never "playing a role."

It is precisely this perplexing contradiction in his nature which brings many delineators of the character of Don Giovanni to elevate him: George Bernard Shaw's counter to Ruskin's outraged attack on the libretto of the opera[32] cheerfully embraces the prodigy of the Don:

> As to Don Giovanni, otherwise The Dissolute One Punished, the only immoral feature of it is its supernatural retributive morality. Gentlemen who break through the ordinary categories of good and evil, and come out at the other side singing *Finch'han dal vino* and *Là ci darem la mano*, do not, as a matter of fact, get called on by statues, and taken straight down through the floor to eternal torments; and to pretend that they do is to shirk the social problem they present. Nor is it yet by any means an established fact that the world owes more to its Don Ottavios than to its Don Juans.[33]

Attacking Ruskin for prudishness, Shaw displays his own habitual reverse prudishness as far as the question of the existence of the Divinity is concerned. A visit from a stone *deus ex machina* (or *machina dei*) may be a bad way to solve the "social problem" posed by Don Giovanni, but Shaw clearly does not consider the Don to be one. In the "Don Juan in Hell" sequence of *Man and Superman* he ultimately installs the Don in heaven, there to ponder through his high intellect a mysterious quantum called "Life: the force that ever strives to attain greater power of contemplating itself"; his task in heaven is to be "the work of helping Life in its struggle upward."[34] For Shaw, Giovanni's intent pursuit of earthly pleasures is merely a passing phase in the evolution of a superhuman intelligence.

Indeed, many versions of the Don Juan story make the protagonist into a heroic freethinker — a contemner of social hypocrisies, like Molière's Don Juan or, like the Don of Shaw, E. T. A. Hoffmann, and other nineteenth-century writers, a man prey to a metaphysical vision of the ideal which leads inevitably to a *taedium vitae*. It is obligatory for this Don to be articulate and to give a reasoned account of himself; he must always have a creed. Shaw takes this loquaciousness to extremes in "Don Juan in Hell," but even the bloodthirsty Don Juan of Thomas Shadwell (*The Libertine*, London, 1676) — a proponent of a hedonism which permits under its name every sadistic excess — gives a defense of himself in ringing Lucretianlike tones after the arrival of the statue:

> There's nothing happens but by Natural Causes,
> Which in unusual things Fools cannot find
> And then they style 'em Miracles. But no Accident

Can alter me from what I am by Nature.
Were there
Legions of Ghosts and Devils in my way,
One moment in my course of pleasure I'd not stay.[35]

As Shaw's sequel makes plain, hell is an inappropriate dwelling for a man of such philosophic powers.

Among the subsequent admirers of Mozart's Don Juan, the aesthete-essayist of Kierkegaard's *Either/Or* is one of the few to heed the peculiar inarticulateness of the character, understanding it as central to his being. He sees the Don as a life force, a power of nature — "primitively controlled life, powerfully and irresistibly daemonic."[36] Yet this word "daemonic" still imputes a surpassing worth to Giovanni's nature, and the word has since become the adjective most commonly associated with encomiums of the Don. Its orthography is intended to recall its derivation from the Greek δαίμων — divinity, genius, or tutelary deity — and to extend its implications beyond the limits of the field of Christian demonology;[37] "daemonic" signifies the supernatural not as above the natural, but as quintessentially natural — "the power of nature, the daemonic, which as little tires of seducing . . . as the wind is tired of blowing, the sea of billowing, or a waterfall of tumbling downward from the heights."[38] And since the life force cannot sin, Giovanni's cruelties and vulgarities are to be excused, or veritably embraced: "His passion sets the passion of all the others in motion. . . . The existence of all the others is, compared with his, only a derived existence."[39] The daemonic man's sins are sins only in the eyes of the *petite bourgeoisie*, whose restricted vision is mean and crippling. The daemonic man is above the morality of the vulgar, and properly the only moral being: as Shaw has the Devil observe after Don Juan departs for heaven, "To the Superman, men and women are a mere species . . . outside the moral world."[40]

The music of Mozart's opera will not, however, suffer a similar apotheosis of the character of the Don. Let us for the moment characterize as "natural" the mode of behavior appropriate to the *galant* and *buffa* worlds which form the full and resonant cosmos of *Figaro*, and which reappear in *Don Giovanni* more narrowly circumscribed. Giovanni then is a man whose behavior is both super- and subnatural. The opera's mélange of musical styles, and more particularly the brilliant mobile inverted pyramid of social gestures which constitutes its overture and first scene, carries the theme of the opera with it. The hero is a buffoon; the buffoon is a hero. By being both he is fully neither. Were he only an obsessive seducer he would be of no interest, but he can behave like a Don as easily as not. He redeems himself from mere vulgarity in the battle with the Commendatore, acting with a clean and spirited *disinvoltura*: he accedes with all proper formality to the challenge but without undue alacrity, waiting until the Commendatore has made it a matter of honor, and he displays neither dismay nor pleasure at his opponent's fall. He is secure in the propriety of having granted Anna's father an opportunity to avenge the insult to his daughter: "L'ha voluto: suo danno,"[41] he says indifferently to Leporello afterward, his elevated disinterest degenerating into a careless flippancy. He is a galvanizing and disturbing figure — daemonic, if you must — because his sphere of action encompasses the highest and the lowest possibilities of human behavior. Rarely does one encounter a man at once of such silliness and such intensity, such spirit and such utter lack of humanity.

Nor can it be said — although it might save the notion of the dark hero — that Giovanni runs the moral gamut in a conscious or willful manner. There are some striking similarities of attitude between Don Giovanni and the notorious seducer of *Les liaisons dangereuses*, but one crucial difference separates Giovanni from the Vicomte de Valmont: Laclos's protagonist is all self-consciousness and calculation,[42] while Giovanni's conduct cannot be explained by recourse to any principle or deliberate intent; he is not purposefully anarchic, or involved in a willed rebellion against ordinary moral standards. Early in act II, in response to Leporello's importunities, Giovanni makes an insouciant defense of his way of life:

Gio: Lasciar le donne! Pazzo!
Lasciar le donne? Sai ch'elle per me
Son necessarie più del pan che mangio,
Più dell'aria che spiro!
Lep: E avete core
D'ingannarle poi tutte?
Gio: È tutto amore:
Chi a una sola è fedele
Verso l'altre è crudele.
Io, che in me sento
Sì esteso sentimento,
Vo' bene a tutte quante.
Le donne, poi che calcolar non sanno,
Il mio buon natural chiamano inganno.[43]

He delivers his sophistical argument with an easy indifference to its truth or falsehood, taking the lazy pleasure in casuistry that a child might display. And Leporello, easily giving up the protest, answers him in the same spirit: "Non ho veduto mai/Naturale più vasto e più benigno."[44] But Giovanni's first lines state the truth of his case: to him women are like food[45] and the air he breathes; he pursues them at the command of a stimulus-response mechanism as natural to him, and as automatic, as the instinct to maintain one's life by taking nourishment. He is merely inexplicable — a *monstrum*, a prodigy, spontaneously at the service of an obsession. Questions of morality can have no relevance to his actions.

Although one function of the role of Leporello in the opera is to project, as a pale double of Don Giovanni, the trivial vulgarity of incessant womanizing, it also serves to provide a realistic moral standard for the measure of base behavior. It helps us to remember that most ordinary men cleave to one woman, with occasional lapses, and fear God, although an occasional touch of pride may make them forget their proper place; their sins are committed, judged, and shriven in a familiar moral sphere. There are certain depths beneath which even Leporello refuses to sink. He probably regards his own flirtations as bachelor's license, the customary preface to settling down with some Giannotta or Sandrina. When Giovanni flaunts his seduction of one of Leporello's girls, Leporello asks in an aggrieved tone:

> E mi dite la cosa
> Con tale indifferenza?
> . . . Ma se fosse
> Costei stata mia moglie? [46]

And although he comes to take a certain delight in playing the stand-in for Giovanni with Elvira in act II, he is moved to pity for her in the finale of the opera, when Giovanni pitilessly mocks her efforts to make him repent. [47] That his attempts to reform Giovanni or to leave the Don's service [48] come to nothing, does not change his function as moral measure. We are not concerned to find in Leporello a model of perfection, but merely to discover in him some vague consciousness of a moral imperative no matter how feeble or fleeting. In self-indulgent self-defense he pleads subornation: Giovanni has robbed him of his innocence. [49] His besetting sins are all too human, his very moral weakness an acknowledgment of a nodding acquaintance with the way things ought to be.

Don Giovanni's actions, on the other hand, are characterized by a moral neutrality: he is not evil but banal, not noble but punctilious, and without fear where true courage would discern what properly is to be feared. His "baseness" amounts to a trivial obsession with seduction, his "nobility" to mere freedom from the passions of hate and fear. The obsession and the freedom are opposite sides of the same coin — a habitual disposition which forfeits the right to be judged as excess and thus traps him outside, not above, the limits of human virtue and vice.

The moral world of the opera is delineated by the familiar *galant* and *buffa* — courtly and peasant — dance gestures. To be fully human in the opera is to move in such-and-such a way, to be defined by a particular

Example 8-12

gesture or stance. In the anonymity of his moral void, Giovanni is strangely denatured. Moving across the hierarchy of classes quickly established by the opening music he gives allegiance to none, although he partakes of them all by imitation; he is truly No-Man.[50] Mozart marks his nonparticipation ingeniously; almost every solo song of Giovanni's is a conscious performance or disguise. He woos Zerlina in the guise of a nobleman in "Là ci darem la mano" (I, 7), serenades Elvira's maid with a *canzonetta*, providing only his voice for Leporello dressed as Giovanni (II, 3), and sings to Masetto and his band disguised as Leporello (II, 4). This last piece, "Metà di voi qua vadano," one of the cleverest *buffa* numbers in the opera, is actually premised on the theme of disguise and concealment. Giovanni is dressed in Leporello's *buffa* key of F major. His aim is to disperse the troupe of peasants Masetto has gathered for the purpose of punishing him so that he can take on Masetto alone. Adroitly he sends them off in all directions on a fictitious trail, which the opening of the aria mimes. A syncopated F pedal marks the actual position of the quarry (Giovanni beneath his disguise as Leporello), while under the pedal tritones pick out first the fourth degree, then the third, and then the second, closing in on the F which, after one feint with a deceptive cadence (m. 8), finally becomes a proper tonic on the "quà" of "Lontan non sia di quà" (ex. 8–12).[51] Some measures later Giovanni dressed as Leporello describes the noble quarry (himself):

In testa egli ha un cappello
Con candidi pennacchi;
Addosso un gran mantello,
E spada al fianco egli ha.[52]

As he makes the picture more vivid ("Addosso un gran mantello . . ."), he slips into a courtly march with fanfares (mm. 24 ff.) — Giovanni playing Leporello playing Giovanni, a moment with parodistic echoes of Leporello's parody of a gentleman's habit in "Notte e giorno." Layer piles on *buffa* layer in this convoluted situation, where the only thing certain is that the "true" Giovanni is not to be discovered in any of them.

Giovanni does, however, have a "theme song," sung in a private moment, when he is giving Leporello orders for the peasants' ball — the famous "Champagne" aria,[53] "Fin ch'han dal vino." Mozart makes a telling choice of gesture for Giovanni's sole unguarded moment — a rapid and feverish contredanse. The contredanse had no place in the hierarchical vocabulary of eighteenth-century social dance; it was a new dance, a "danceless dance," and hence the true dance of No-Man. The text and the macrorhythm of "Fin ch'han dal vino" expand the social connotations of the contredanse into a thoroughgoing metaphor for Giovanni's nature. In the text Giovanni commands from Leporello the very anarchy which the contredanse had introduced into the orderly cosmos of the social dances:

> Senza alcun ordine
> La danza sia:
> Chi'l minuetto,
> Chi la follia,
> Chi l'alemanna
> Farai ballar.[54]

Leporello is an obedient servant: this is precisely what transpires in the famous ballroom scene of the first-act finale, where three stage orchestras play at once each a different dance while under the cover of this rhythmic and social anarchy Giovanni procedes on his second attempt to seduce Zerlina.

Not only does Mozart perceive the contredanse as generally appropriate to the nature of the Don, he also makes the formal organization of "Fin ch'han dal vino" reflect on Giovanni's character. Another antithesis of hierarchy is the famous list which Leporello keeps for his master; Giovanni mentions it in the aria also:

> Ah! la mia lista
> Doman mattina
> D'una decina
> Devi aumentar.[55]

The insatiable cry of "just one more" grants the preceding units no particularity, and hence no dignity or worth; the counter is interested in the counted only insofar as they resemble each other, and thus deserve a place in the list. The contredanse is a listlike dance — an additive dance in which phrase piles on phrase as the dancers intemperately improvise yet another figure. Mozart manages to make this manifest in "Fin ch'han dal vino" by superimposing on the essentially dramatic plan of the Classic key-area movement with its clearly delineated beginning, middle, and end an impression of additive or chain construction. To

Example 8-13

bring this about he builds with clear-cut and even-measured units, repeated without alteration. The staple of the aria is a "tonic phrase," consisting of a two-measure unit repeated three times, once each on the three notes of the tonic triad, and then punctuated by a V-I two-measure unit (ex. 8–13). This phrase is deployed as a stabilizer, whose mere recurrence marks the aria's major hinges. It begins the piece (with two strains), shapes the return to the tonic (with four strains, separated by two extended cadential phrases consisting only of two-measure units of I_4^6-V), and anchors the coda (with one strain as part of an orchestral postlude); figure 5 is a detailed map of the deployment of the tonic phrase. The remaining material of the aria is also shaped into two- or four-measure units, so that even the twenty-four-measure phrase forming the second key area drives to its cadence on the dominant by dint of repetition (of units which grow from two to four measures) rather than by means of a more organic form of development. Only four times are there phrases which contain other than an even number of measures. The extensions to phrases in the X-section and return (mm. 65–69, 93–96, 116–19), because they begin as incessant four- or two-measure repetitions, sound more like the musical equivalent of "and so on" than the climactic exclamations which extensions usually provide. And the elisions in the coda (mm. 127 to the end) are in the service of avoiding threatened cadences in order to add another repetition, in a relentless *moto perpetuo*. In short, lost in the incessant repetitions, we only know where we are when we hear yet another tonic phrase; even the tonic return has an additive effect. In the columnar contredanse or "longways," our Virginia reel, the dance comes to an end not as a result of some climactic maneuver, but when yet another do-si-do happens to deliver the lead couple back to their proper place — a choreography as arbitrary as the shape of a list.

Since the list as a form of ordering is in truth an analogue of anarchy, it is akin to the middle-class contredanse, which is placeless and in a special way classless. From ancient times the placeless had been considered to bear a peculiar menace: the Greek word ἄτοπος , literally "without a place," came to mean "strange" or "paradoxical," and, particularly when extended to human beings, "repugnant" or "harmful." Giovanni's menace seems to be of the same nature. Just as the contredanse cuts across the established orders of dance gestures, so does the Don cut

Figure 5   "Fin ch'han dal vino"

Phrase	# of measures	Key Area	Groupings	Type
1	8	I	2+2+2+2* (I .... V, I)	tonic phrase (Orchestra only)
2	8		2+2+2+2	tonic phrase
3	8	↓	2+2+4	
4	8		2+2+2+2	
5 a)	24 { 4	V	2+2	
b)	8		2+2+2+2	
c)	12		4+4+4	
6	13	X	4+4+5 (i_4^6, V...)	extension
7	8		2+2+2+2	tonic phrase
8	8		2+2+2+2	tonic phrase
9	11	I	2+2+2+2+3 (i_4^6, V...)	extension
10	8		2+2+2+2	tonic phrase
11	15		2+2+2+2+2+5 (i_4^6, V...)	extension
12	8		2+2+2+2	tonic phrase
13	15	Coda	1234123(4) 12121234(5) (5)	extension and elision
14	18		1212121(2) 12121234567.	tonic phrase elided with extended phrase – orchestra postlude

*Underlining indicates tonic phrase.

across the world of Donna Anna and the other characters, threatening to subvert it. What has brought this rootless creature into being is left unexplained. He is merely a phenomenon whose nature has been molded not by the proper moral orders, but by an illusory liberty whose obverse is an *idée fixe*. Although he is hardly aware of the threat he poses, its power to destroy the world of the other characters is unmistakable.

To counter Giovanni's anarchic contredanse no human music will suffice. Only divine justice can take on a man for whom there is no judgment on earth, and only the superhuman rhythms of the *alla breve* pathetic fantasy can be measured against the breathless, intemperate music of the "danceless dance." Yet — and this is symptomatic of the Don's moral neutrality — the instrument of his punishment must issue from a situation which is related only indirectly to the crimes he is to be punished for — a situation in which, according to some criteria, he can be said to have acted well. The murder of the Commendatore, by redeeming Giovanni from the perpetual venality of a career of seduction, makes him worthy of punishment on a celestial scale. Giovanni's transgressions are all concentrated into that one stroke of the sword. The spectral hush of the Commendatore's requiem music raises the moment out of the opera's time, to compel recognition of the horror and pathos of the act itself, free of any moral palliative (Giovanni's quasi-decent behavior, for example). It renders inexorable the ultimate arrival of the divine avenger: his retribution will be postponed only until Giovanni has thoroughly demonstrated the mean and trivial preoccupations of the dedicated seducer of women.

Giovanni and the Other Characters

Although the first scene of *Don Giovanni* sets the trajectory of the opera's action, most of the main characters will wait until after the death of the Commendatore to reveal themselves fully, and three of them — Elvira, Zerlina, and Masetto — are creatures without a connection to this central line of action (the murder of Donna Anna's father and his return for vengeance). Irrelevance to the "plot" is not the only dissimilarity between the dramatis personae of *Don Giovanni* and their counterparts in *Le nozze di Figaro*: they are furthermore a radically homeless tribe, without the well-known personal histories of the *Figaro* characters or their local connections to one another, and this lack of a past, plus the musical modes in which they are presented, makes them seem to be statically conceived class-types rather than creatures of flesh and blood. The characters of *Figaro* show themselves in multifaceted surfaces as the opera unfolds. Central to an understanding of them are the duets, six in all, each featuring its heroine Susanna, in delicate interplay with her fiancé, with the Countess, with Cherubino, with Marcellina, and with the Count. The characters in *Don Giovanni*, on the other hand, are presented in their separateness: the opera has fewer duets, four instead of six (two of them among the less memorable pieces in the opera[56]), the proportion of solo arias per character is higher than it is in *Figaro*,[57] and several of those arias are formal *da capo* set pieces. In the matter of rhythmic gesture the sphere of *Figaro* is almost entirely *di mezzo carattere*: its noble-born heroine, the Countess, adopts a mixed lyric style that might be dubbed *amoroso-heroico*, and beside its noble refinement high passion dwindles into rant. In *Don Giovanni* only Ottavio inherits the *stile amoroso-heroico*, and the lofty and fulminating *alla breve* is the opera's predominant meter.[58]

These are some of the musical reasons why the characters other than the Don in *Don Giovanni*, while casting longer shadows than their predecessors in *Figaro*, still seem fixed and immobile, presenting not faces but masks. That the gentle *mezzo carattere* center of *Figaro* can be discovered only in the stance of the most ineffectual actor in the drama of *Don Giovanni* is emblematic of the difference between the two operas. *Le nozze di Figaro* studies the luminous possibilities of a web of ordinary human relations — the tender pleasures of friendship and courtship. *Don Giovanni* often concerns the posturings of an unrequited and hermetic passion, and the relations of all the main characters are almost exclusively with one man — the Don. In *Either/Or* Kierkegaard's essayist sees Giovanni as a transfiguring force that brings to fruition the potential for beauty latent in all women. Dealings with the Don in reality, however, seem to have the opposite effect: they fix a character immobile, like a butterfly fluttering on the head of a collector's pin. Paradoxically, Giovanni collects by eluding, and in their efforts to lay hold of the protean Don his "victims" are frozen in near-cartoons of their own natures. Circling around the vibrant nonentity which is No-Man, they are locked in an unceasing struggle merely to retain some dignity for their place.

CHAPTER NINE

The Noble Lovers

Donna Anna

Each of the two pairs of lovers in *Don Giovanni*, noble and peasant, shares a certain style of solo music (Elvira falls into a class by herself). Donna Anna's characteristic idiom is the *opera seria scena*, her proper gesture the *alla breve* march. Her brilliant recitative and duet with Don Ottavio following the death of the Commendatore are cast in the exalted style at its most intense. She opens the D-minor duet with a phrase cleverly extended into a super *alla breve*. Only its third member satisfies ordinary periodic expectations; the normal version would be one measure shorter, but, lacking the stirring syncopations over the barline which open the first two phrases, would render the exalted-march affect in a more prosaic style (ex. 9–1[1]). Mozart's syncopations protract the natural grammatical accent into a written-out pathetic one,[2] giving the phrase an expansiveness which justifies extending the

Example 9-1

225

last member from two measures to three. Both the syncopations and the extension are emotionally apt: the syncopation as an expression of Donna Anna's intense distress (according to the stage direction she should act *disperatamente*), the extension a tender lingering over the words "Chi a me la vita diè" (mm. 69–72), stirred by the image of her murdered father.

Against Donna Anna's intensity Don Ottavio is gentle, and slightly bumbling. In the recitative he calls breathlessly for help in reviving his fiancée, only to be rewarded on her waking by being mistaken for someone else (the killer? or merely a passing stranger?) and brushed aside imperiously.[3] In the duet he answers Anna's nine measures by a move from D minor to a pacific F, D's relative major. His response is a version of her line, but recast in a style more appropriate to him. Her syncopated phrases sound extended, but all except the last are not, thus retaining the rhythmic snap of two-plus-two symmetry. Don Ottavio smoothes them into true three-measure units for an even but flowery line with none of the tight power of Donna Anna's delivery; he "waxes lyrical" (ex. 9–2). The third member of his phrase is unextended, as Donna Anna's was, and the last is a close verbal and rhythmic rhyme with her plangent three-measure half-cadence, but considerably softened in its detail—major rather than minor, and legato where her phrase was clipped. Twice Ottavio closes the first reprise (mm. 90 to the end of the second key area are in essence repeated) with the heartfelt, although perhaps overavuncular, pledge "Hai sposo e padre in me."[4]

Ottavio's promise seems to inflame Anna rather than soothe her. She brushes his comforting words aside with a dramatic recitative (which serves as an X-section), demanding that Don Ottavio swear an oath of vengeance. And so he does, turning her peremptory recitative into lyrical arioso sequences in the process (mm. 130–34). Returning to the tonic the couple commemorates the moment with some stirring passages in D minor, the fits and starts of the earlier phrases smoothed out

Example 9-2

Example 9-3

now by their newly achieved singleness of purpose. The return consists of one long-lined phrase which has been forged out of several shorter ones by an inordinate dominant tension. Overwhelming several rhythmically weak tonic cadences, this phrase moves to a stirring climax on a startling harmonic unorthodoxy (ex. 9–3). Exploiting the Phrygian relations inherent both in the Neapolitan and in the lowered sixth degree,[5] Mozart makes the G which has figured as the highest melody note of the previous measures sound like a new and even higher pitch; the couple, touched by a divine frenzy ("Che barbaro momento!"), is lifted out of itself, and beyond the limits of the diatonic order.[6]

Like the second key area the X-section and return are repeated twice, the X-section/oath-swearing varied slightly and the final cadences of the return expanded by some thirty-three measures. The key-area plan in minor provides a dynamic scheme admirably suited to the musical portrayal of an action. Donna Anna's opening material is inchoate — halfway between arioso and melody. To Don Ottavio are consigned the hopeful and consolatory modulation out of the minor and the clearer articulation needed for the second key area's cadential phrases. Donna Anna's break into recitative obliterates Don Ottavio's placid thoughts of a future spent ministering to her needs, along with any traces of the recently established relative major. In the return both D minor and the couple's resolve are consolidated by one long sweeping phrase and a coda of cadences.

Donna Anna's first solo aria is another *opera seria scena*: an accompanied recitative — "Don Ottavio . . . son morta!" — and the splendid *alla breve* exalted march "Or sai chi l'onore" (I, 10). Anna has finally identified Don Giovanni as her attacker, having heard something familiar in his tone of voice when he tried to silence Donna Elvira in the previous trio.[7] In a state of shock she spills out to Don Ottavio the story of Giovanni's nocturnal visit to her chamber, her struggles to free herself, and her pursuit of the seducer into the darkened street where he met and murdered her father. Facing Don Ottavio with the evidence, she again demands him to avenge her, in an aria which is the prototypical exalted march of the *opera seria* heroine; the rhythmic gesture of her aria, "Or sai chi l'onore," has already been discussed (see pp. 19–22). Perhaps with the purpose of underlining its source, the scheme of "Or sai chi l'onore," is closer to a *da capo* than to a key-area plan.[8] It is monolithic in its grand simplicity. The A-section consists of a single broad period. Anna's passionately disjunct intervals are hung on a smooth rising line, which organizes them to a climax (see ex. 1–2, p. 21). The aria has many similarities with the couple's revenge duet: the *alla breve* style, the shared keynote D (with a strong inflection of D minor in the B-section of "Or sai chi l'onore"), the four-plus-two-plus-three opening phrase, and the brief break into recitative. Anna's emotions and gestures are as noble — and as monochromatic — as the affections of the most queenly of *seria* demigoddesses.

Her narrative of the midnight visit is often cited as evidence for present-day arguments that Giovanni has been successful in his seduction, and that Donna Anna is actually pursuing the man she loves. E. T. A. Hoffmann's fiction about the opera, *A Tale of Don Juan*, contains the most famous statement of this position: Donna Anna and Don Juan are counterparts in "all natural endowments." When they meet, however, it is too late, for the Don has "reached the height of infamy," and can only wish to corrupt her:

> When he fled the deed was done. The fire of a superhuman sensuality
> . . . had been infused in her and made her powerless to resist. Only he,
> only Don Juan, was capable of rousing in her this erotic madness.

Afterwards, racked with love for the Don, she prods the "frigid, unmanly, commonplace Don Ottavio" to revenge, she requests time from him — another year for mourning — but, destroyed by this mortal passion, "she will not survive that year."[9]

If, however, one pays close attention to Donna Anna's actual narrative of that fateful evening, the seeds of this fantasy are contained only in a careful ambiguity. After Don Giovanni seizes Donna Anna:

> Alfine il duol, l'orrore
> Dell'infame attentato
> Accrebbe sì la lena mia, che, a forza
> Di svincolarmi, torcermi, e piegarmi,
> Da lui mi sciolsi.[10]

Ottavio takes Anna to mean that she escaped before consummation of the "infame attentato" and breathes an expansive sigh of relief; it is cleverly set as the deceptive resolution of Anna's A-minor cadential formula to a major triad on VI (Ottavio's comforting F major again — mm. 52–53).[11] But the text would allow us to suspect that her escape occurred afterward. We are not to know; it hardly, I think, matters. On Anna's face is frozen an ambiguous grimace. The victim turned huntress, the "assaulted turned assailant," as she describes herself,[12] pursues her prey in an access either of righteous anger or of unholy passion. It will always be a question whether her outstretched hand is a sign of menace or of desire. If desire, its urgings are buried too deeply within her for her to admit them even to herself. Certainly she thrusts Ottavio away both often and instinctively. "Non mi dir," her last aria, and a singer's showpiece,[13] is a chilling affair. In the recitative which precedes it she murmurs unconvincing excuses mostly to do with respectability ("Ma il mondo . . . oddio . . ."[14]). While she adopts for the first of the two parts of the aria Ottavio's own lyric *amoroso* style in 2/4, engaging in dialogue with a complement of wind instruments, the text of the second part presents a non sequitur to her assurances of love for him — the self-occupied prayer, "Forse un giorno il cielo ancora/Sentirà pietà di me."[15] Her aria superficially resembles the Countess's "Dove sono," but the divergent texts of their two second parts[16] make the Countess's coloratura an integral part of her passionate 4/4 march affect, leaving Donna Anna's as mere icy ornament.

In general, however, Donna Anna's music has real splendors; there is no greater aria of exalted wrath than "Or sai chi l'onore." Only the most disingenuous reading between the lines can indict her for hypocrisy; her character read in isolation, both in her words and in her music, must remain unimpeachably what it seems. Any doubts which arise concerning her character and motives must be attributed not to her music itself, but to the musical frame in which it is set. Comedy is not merely less serious than tragedy (or high melodrama, as the case may be here); it can also be more supple, and at its best — in Leporello's "Notte e giorno," for example — it subtly undercuts the monolithic intensity of the heroic style. *Buffa's* wit and irony give one a sense of hidden powers held in reserve, whereas tragic heroines tend to pull out all the stops at once. In the meantime, balancing the potency of *buffa* at the other end of the affective spectrum is the terrible gravity of the fantasy style, in which the judgment of seriousness is omniscient — the composer himself counts every heartbeat for us. It sets a standard for the tragic affect which is more elevated than that to which the *alla breve* gesture can attain. The old-fashioned purity of Donna Anna's gestures sets her off from the other characters; in her single-minded dignity she is unapproachable, and also less interesting than the others, for there is less to know about her. The *alla breve* style in *Don Giovanni* is not passion perverted, as the gentle light of *Figaro's mezzo carattere* gestures makes it appear, but passion staunched. Even if her contact with Don Giovanni has unsettled Donna Anna she will conceal it; she knows best how to hold herself erect.

Don Ottavio

Judgments of Don Ottavio's character fluctuate wildly between charges of insufferable nastiness and insincerity and a praise which champions him as the type of eternal faithfulness.[17] Always it is his passivity which is the focus of attention; even writers who take the middle ground gently mock him, writing him off as a cardboard character and one of Mozart's few failures. A good deal of the blame is laid at the door of *opera seria*, whose intrusive conventions are said to make of the character of Don Ottavio a dramatic impossibility,[18] however beautiful his music. Yet no one expresses disappointment at Donna Anna's *seria* set pieces, or at the Count's formal *scena* "Vedrò, mentr'io" (*Figaro*, III, 17), even though it intrudes on the generally *mezzo carattere* texture of *Le nozze di Figaro*; instead the use of the convention is in both instances considered deft musical portraiture. That he is a *seria* character is as intrinsic to Don Ottavio's characterization as it is to Donna Anna's. But while Anna is a tragic queen, a creature of righteous anger and furious sacrifice, Ottavio's gentler moral virtues would figure best in tales of constancy, renunciation, and elegiac grief. He sings in the tender *amoroso* style of the Countess: both "Dalla sua pace" (I, 10b) and "Il mio tesoro" (II, 8) are *arie d'affetto*, and bear some resemblance to "Porgi, amor" and "Dove sono."

"Dalla sua pace" shares the slow 2/4 lyric vein of "Porgi, amor" and its wind complement, in this case flutes, oboes, and bassoons. They are most prominent as a delicate solo windband for six measures in the codetta (mm. 64–69), where they are set against Ottavio's cadenza on the words "Morte mi dà."[19] The military topic featured in "Porgi, amor" is muted here to courtly punctuating chords on the horns (mm. 13–15, for example). The two arias are also laid out on slightly different plans. "Porgi, amor" is a short key-area form with a subdued outburst of grief at the return, while "Dalla sua pace" is a *da capo* aria: a formal, closed A-section in G major gives way (m. 17) to a mid-section with a quickened pulse and darker tonalities (G minor, diminished-seventh chords), and the *amoroso* A-section is repeated, with minor changes in orchestration, for the close. The *da capo* form is clearly meant to remind us of Ottavio's *seria* provenance; a formalized presentation of emotions is part of his habit, while the Countess's more spontaneous reflections follow the key-area plan — the natural and therefore less self-conscious lines of Classic harmonic procedure.

Heavy weather is often made of the fact that "Dalla sua pace" was composed as an afterthought for the Vienna performance of 1788; some writers want to omit it from the opera altogether. But in itself the aria does not conflict with what we know of Ottavio's character; instead, with its reminiscences of the Countess's style, it rounds him out. It is admittedly an anticlimax after "Or sai chi l'onore," but anticlimaxes can serve a dramatic purpose. By its placement the aria reinforces the *seria* theme (one by one the characters depart the stage via "exit arias"), leaves the right character alone on stage (Ottavio is reflective like the Countess, and sings one of the opera's three soliloquies; only the nature of the opera makes his reflectiveness seem fatuous rather than moving), and solves the staging difficulty posed by "Or sai chi l'onore" — after Anna's fierce challenge to a hesitant Ottavio, the couple can hardly leave the stage hand-in-hand.[20]

"Il mio tesoro" is an *alla breve da capo* aria, cast as a slow march with a *bravura* B-section (mm. 29–48) and cadenza (mm. 71–end). *Amoroso* and military elements alternate, although they are not as subtly wedded as they are in "Porgi, amor." Clarinets and bassoons play a prominent solo role in the *amoroso* A-section, and return after the long and fiery coloratura cadenza for a summing-up in the nine measures of orchestral postlude (mm. 96–97). Ottavio's second aria is the most formal *da capo* of the four in the opera[21] — an elegant and old-fashioned *opera seria* set piece.

It is difficult to make out exactly what elements in Ottavio's music might suggest that Mozart was parodying "tenor love" in the character of the gentle Don, although that frequent judgment must depend on his two solo arias. Perhaps the coloratura passages scattered through "Il mio tesoro" are one source of the opinion. But nothing about Ottavio's coloratura *per se* suggests a takeoff; good tenors are well able to negotiate the aria's roulades, Francesco Morella notwithstanding,[22] and eighteenth-century audiences did not giggle at tenors as easily as do audiences today. The high voice was for a long time the hallmark of heroes, while the lower registers were relegated to villains and old men; in Gazzaniga's *Don Giovanni* the Don is a tenor. Nor do the beauties of "Dalla sua pace," the Viennese substitute for "Il mio tesoro," in themselves provide anything to laugh at. Mozart clearly did not think it incongruous to give Ottavio a variant of "Porgi, amor" in the place of his original aria cum *bravura* cadenza. "Il mio tesoro" also has echoes of the gentle nobility of the Countess's lyric vein: its close reminds us that this character, although momentarily delivered over to exalted wrath, is essentially a pacific creature with only occasional aspirations to the heroic. Should the Ottavio simply play his role straight, the darker passions of the opera will do the job of parody. Our discomfort with him does not stem from a sense that *seria* conventions have been left unabsorbed or even caricatured; it comes about because in *Don Giovanni* the tender virtues all are savaged. Ottavio is the last among *gentle*-men, saddled with the innocent expectation that noble-born means noble and the conviction that hasty judgment is a sin.[23] In both *Figaro* and *Don Giovanni* Mozart fashions a moral perspective for the spectators by the judicious weighting and juxtaposition of various musical styles. In *Don Giovanni*, unlike in *Figaro*, we are meant to find the music of artless goodness embarrassing; outdistanced by the sharper, swifter passions, mere decency appears effete. It remains, nonetheless, true decency. Because we are disquieted to find ourselves embarrassed by good character, we prefer to assert instead that Don Ottavio is a pious hypocrite or a dramatic failure. Rather than acknowledge our equivocal sentiments, we accuse Ottavio with the cynical words of the Vicomte de Valmont, the seducer of Laclos's *Les liaisons dangereuses*: "Voilà bien les hommes! tous également scélérats dans leur projets, ce qu'ils mettent de faiblesse dans l'exécution, ils l'appellent probité."[24] It is only this easy disparagement of uprightness which allows us to retain any optimism in the face of Mozart's clearer, and (in this opera) blacker, view of the world.

CHAPTER TEN

Donna Elvira

"Ah! chi mi dice mai"

Donna Elvira makes her first entrance (I, 3) heralded by Giovanni's goatish hiss: "Zitto: mi pare/Sentir odor di femina! . . ."[1] Demeaned even before her entrance by this crude comparison to a bitch in heat, she lurches in to the accompaniment of a stiff and archaic ritornello. Donna Anna's *seria* style has a dignified and classic air to its intensity: "Or sai chi l'onore" is streamlined, with no ritornelli, and a rising line tightly organizing the sweep of its gesture. Elvira's *seria* frame is rather more eccentric; Mozart takes pains to imitate the details of the style as well as its broader outlines. Formal and independent ritornelli are rare in the arias of his later operas, although an aria may frequently begin with an orchestral tag consisting of several measures of its "main tune"; the habit is, rather, Handelian. The ritornello of "Ah! chi mi dice mai" is made up of two sets of unrelated and unperiodic "doodling" string figures forced to a period by a three-measure fanfare cadence (ex. 10–1). The orchestra has an unwonted independence: none of its material is employed in Elvira's vocal line. This ritornello could be reworked along the lines of normal late eighteenth-century period structure into a brief orchestral incipit that might open a less remarkable aria in march style (ex. 10–2). In this recomposed version the two measures of introduction, after unostentatiously establishing the march gesture, immediately relinquish control to the singer. In Mozart's version the framing gesture of the orchestra propels Elvira; she seems not to be mistress of her own movements. The harmonic rhythm is very slow in the first four measures (only one change of harmony per two-measure unit), and the tri-

Example 10-1

Example 10-2

adic string flourishes are only the most perfunctory filler, making the approach of the marcher jerky and spasmodic. This overdrawn and awkward gait is reminiscent of the gesture opening Leporello's foot march, and not by accident, since the two, Elvira and Leporello, are frequently paired off in the course of the opera. The fancy French string work in the ritornello and elsewhere (large leaps, dotted rhythms, richly decorated upbeats) is also overornate and exaggerated. In relation to the beginning of the orchestra's repetition of the ritornello Elvira's first vocal entry is askew — one measure late — giving the impression at least of distraction, if not of dementia.

The text of "Ah! chi mi dice mai" is a hysterical mixture of shame, chagrin, and bitter jealousy:

Ah! chi mi dice mai
Quel barbaro dov'è,
Che per mio scorno amai,
Che mi mancò di fè?

Ah! se ritrovo l'empio,
E a me non torna ancor,
Vo' farne orrendo scempio,
Gli vo' cavar il cor.[2]

Elvira is pursuing Giovanni determined either to recover the man who once called her his "sposa"[3] or to exact the penalty for his desertion. As punishment she intends nothing short of bloody slaughter, personally executed. As the aria moves to a cadence on the dominant of the conventional key-area layout,[4] Elvira takes the last two lines of the text, "Vo' farne or*ren*do scempio,/Gli vo'ca*var* il cor," in manic leaps of sevenths and octaves.[5] Mozart makes this fiery passage-work (vocal fireworks that can so easily sound strained and harsh in the leaps to the lower register) into a material element in Elvira's characterization. At the same time he turns to good use another oft-criticized *seria* habit — the penchant for repetition of words in arias, which had been a prime target of reformers' criticisms. Obsessively, twelve times in the aria's simple two-part form she repeats the phrase "Gli vo' cavar il cor," in two of the last four repetitions with passages of fervid coloratura on the syllable -*var*, as though in simulation of the twist of the knife.

"Ah, fuggi il traditor"

Donna Elvira's second aria, "Ah, fuggi il traditor" (I, 8), is also an Handelian *tour de force*. Again Mozart takes the greatest care to make the aria seem odd and old-fashioned; again the primary agent is a rhythmic one. With the intent of catching the motoric rhythms of a Baroque aria, and simultaneously making Elvira's gait appear lurching and awkward, Mozart constructs the aria of two short rhythmic motives. The first, of three measures, has an accented note on the second beat which lasts just short of a measure's length: ♩ ♪♩ |♫♩ ♩ |♩ This curious rhythm is both extremely clumsy (it leaves one struggling valiantly to find the downbeat) and strongly end-oriented (in that it has no downbeat, it has no proper beginning). The second motive is a simple two-measure "consequent" which sets the phrase back on the normal rhythmic track: ♩ ♪|♫♩ ♪|♩ These two motives in various permutations and combinations constitute all the material of the vocal line of "Ah, fuggi" until its final cadence, where Elvira lets loose with what has by now become her habitual coloratura. An incessant rhythm in the

Figure 6 The Motivic Structure of "Ah, fuggi il traditor"

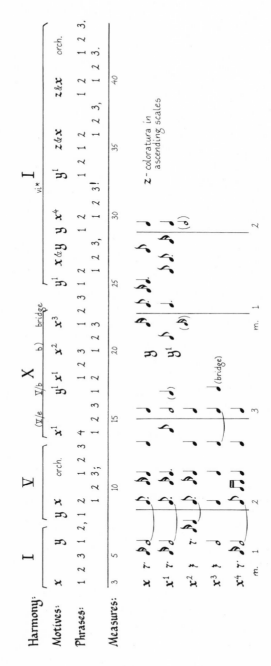

Example 10-3

strings — ♪♪♩ ♩ — marks the downbeat, supplying a fairly regular pulse; it or a variant — ♪♪♪ | ♩ — (see for example the second violins, mm. 6 and 8) occurs in every measure except at the few important cadences, where the forward motion has instead to be retarded.

The various devices which Mozart uses to maintain this headlong motion must blur the outlines of the key-area layout, although, as figure 6 illustrates, he manages nevertheless to emphasize its crucial junctures. The complexity of figure 6 is a reflection of the fluid motivic disposition in the aria. Clearly articulated cadences occur only on the dominant and at the end; the X-section is elided almost imperceptibly with the return. The five-measure phrase constituted by the two rhythmic motives x and y frequently turns into a four-measure version, most easily when the y member precedes the x member so that the two can dovetail neatly (ex. 10–3). Although the undovetailed, five-measure phrase appears in its entirety only twice, at the opening of the first reprise and of the X-section (mm. 14–18), there is still little sense of periodicity in the aria. The cockeyed syncopations, the occasional five-measure phrase, the many variants of x and y, and the several types of elision make every cut seem different, and the perception of larger relationships difficult. There prevails instead a sense of a quasi-mechanical deployment, in various combinations and over various harmonies, of two virtually irreducible "rhythmic cells." The effect is eccentric, to say the least — a "conceptual" aria, cleverly working the archaic technique of *Fortspinnung* into a periodic setting. The reduced orchestration — strings only — also contributes to the aria's deliberate air of obsolescence.

Its eccentricity makes "Ah, fuggi" a tremendously effective aria. Because it is short and, with its rhythmic elisions, feels as though it were throughcomposed, it is the ideal choreography for Elvira's breathless dash to snatch Zerlina from the clutches of the archfiend Giovanni. In its brevity it provides a dynamic upbeat to the more fully-worked out explanations of the quartet which follows it; a full-blown aria for Elvira here would be redundant. The bridge, with its sideslipping chromatic syncopations and inflection of the minor, gives one a momentary glimpse of Elvira's pain as well as of her urgency (ex. 10–4).

But the aria's *stile antico* is not affected merely out of a desire for rhythmic urgency; surely it is intended as a musical expression of per-

Example 10-4

sonal eccentricity. Mozart may well have had in mind the lines which Molière gives Don Juan when he sees Elvire approaching in the distance: "Est-ce folle, de n'avoir pas changé d'habit, et de venir en ce lieu-ci avec son équipage de campagne?"[6] Elvire's inappropriate attire is to Don Juan of a piece with an eccentric mind, out of season, and a personality sure to be annoying; he suspects she'll be excessive as usual, and make a scene. In place of country clothes Mozart gives Elvira her singular Handelian style in both "Ah! chi mi dice mai" and "Ah, fuggi." The particular eccentricity in Elvire and Elvira which gives rise to the edginess of Don Juan and Don Giovanni is an ecclesiastical one: while Donna Anna fancies herself a fury, Elvira truly is one, or its Enlightenment counterpart, a Christian *dévote*. Her original in Molière's *Don Juan* had been stolen by the Don from a nunnery. Although da Ponte for some reason omitted the convent from Elvira's preopera background (in his version Giovanni is said to have seduced her in her house[7]), the present Elvira, coming like Molière's Elvire to comprehend the equivocal sentiments animating her lust for revenge,[8] tries to bring Giovanni to repentance, and then declares at the end of the opera her intention to immure herself in a convent for the rest of her life.[9] No mere voluptuary, to her the crux of Giovanni's crime is not the assault on her body but the seduction of her heart.[10] Like Elvire, Elvira has the air of a *dévote*, a spiritual zealot. High-strung and high-minded, she pursues the "barbaro" Giovanni with the same fanatical ardor she will later turn to doing Christian penance. She is a woman of great passion and not a little madness; she is completely vulnerable because she looks to Heaven for her principles, yet cannot control her willful and susceptible heart. It is a measure of the bleak perspective of *Don Giovanni* that such high excesses are rendered as near-comic idiosyncrasies by the stiff-gaited rhythms of an antique style.

Elvira, Giovanni, and Leporello: "Ah! chi mi dice mai" Revisited

Continually throughout the opera its most passionate and vulnerable character is submitted to relentless mocking and humiliation. Elvira is the only character who wears her heart on her sleeve and, to misquote Iago, daws do peck at it. When the question is raised of what is the most perfidious act committed by Giovanni the libertine, one searches in vain for a clear candidate among his more obvious crimes. The attempted seduction of Zerlina singles out apparently the most helpless victim, and it takes place right before our eyes; but Zerlina's several happy recoveries muddy those waters by robbing the crime of its consequence. The murder of the Commendatore is the one successful act we witness, and vengeance finally arrives through his agency; yet Donna Anna is a chilling figure, and the Don honorably gives the old man a chance to beg off from their duel. But there is one act which, although it has no place under the rubric of seduction and the announced themes of the opera, we are forced to witness over and over again, and which in the sheer cumulative weight of instances of inhumanity must have the most unsettling effect on the spectators — the constant savaging of Elvira. Separated from her own kind by her overflowing passions, she is continually thrown into the company of Leporello and the Don. If the characters of *Don Giovanni* were imagined as arranged in a frieze, the two pairs of lovers, high and low, would take their places at the two sides, and Leporello, Donna Elvira, and Don Giovanni in the middle; this uneasy trio of nonlovers is the centerpiece of the opera.

Even Elvira's first appearance on stage is in their cruel company. "Ah! chi mi dice mai" has been spoken of previously only as a solo, and as an astute piece of characterization. But by a further brilliant stroke Mozart manages, while creating his fury, at the same time to demonstrate her impotence: he makes the piece into a trio. A trio, that is, which is not properly *à trois*, for the two musical styles joined in it are mutually exclusive; like oil and water they are never meant to come to that happy union of separate entities which usually characterizes Mozart's writing for ensemble. Don Giovanni and Leporello are concealed to one side of the stage, and after Elvira's first jagged cadence, Giovanni, not for the moment recognizing her, comments appreciatively on the windfall fortune has set before him: "Udisti? Qualche bella/Dal vago abbandonata."[11] The largely stepwise motion of his recitativelike *buffa* patter is in suave contrast with Elvira's vocal histrionics (ex. 10–5). The Don takes advantage of every inflection of her passion. Even at her most dramatic

Example 10-5

DON GIOVANNI   DONNA ELVIRA

U - dis-ti? Qual-che bel-la__ Dal__ va- ga ab-ban- do - na- ta.   Vo' far-ne or-ren-do scem-pio,

moment — a series of cadential sequences in octave leaps to V of vi (mm. 41–45) — Giovanni comically enervates her fury, interjecting "Poverina, poverina"[12] in mock-pathetic accents over her minor triad.

Giovanni's and Leporello's interruptions in the trio are limited to five interjections.[13] And since Giovanni, not recognizing Elvira, has no reason to be of a mocking turn of mind toward this new beauty, he cannot intend his commentary to be ironic or derisive beyond his usual habits. Nor can it have an effect on Elvira, since she is completely unaware of it. It is aimed solely at the audience, and has a devastating effect on our view of this passionate woman: it prevents us from ever taking her seriously. Once more *buffa* undercuts the sincere and the serious; all earnest ardor is merely grist for its mill. In *Les liaisons dangereuses* the Vicomte de Valmont calls the devout and upright woman he seduces and ruins both *la belle Dévote* and, as though the two words were synonymous, *la Prude*. But "prude" in Valmont's amoral vocabulary is far from being a term of opprobrium denoting a nature of offensive moral stiff-neckedness. To his jaded appetite prudery is merely a new titillation, an untried affect:

> J'aurai cette femme; je l'enlèverai au mari qui la profane: j'oserai la ravir au Dieu même qu'elle adore. Quel délice d'être tour à tour l'objet et le vainqueur de ses remords! Loin de moi l'idée de détruire les préjuges qui l'assiègent! ils ajouteront à mon bonheur et à ma gloire.[14]

Similarly Molière's Don Juan, confronted with the righteous figure of Elvire announcing her new dedication to God's service and the reprobate's salvation, tries vainly to persuade her to spend the night with him; after her abrupt exit this inveterate student of his own tastes is given to a moment of quizzical musing on her newfound attraction for him:

> Sais-tu bien que j'ai encore senti quelque peu d'émotion pour elle, que j'ai trouvé de l'agrément dans cette nouveauté bizarre, et que son habit négligé, son air languissant et ses larmes ont réveillé en moi quelques petits restes d'un feu éteint?[15]

Giovanni looks at Elvira with the same amused and tolerant interest; he finds her fury ravishing, her conviction adorable. The aria's E-flat tonality may be intended to suggest the fool's paradise, at odd angles to the "real" (D major) world, which such an earnest nature inhabits when men like Giovanni are around. It is the final and most ruinous indignity to render another human being's passions impotent by one's amusement. With Enlightenment emancipation we too give a little smirk at the fulminations of *la belle Dévote*; we are caught by the same seductive rhetoric which brings us to enjoy as comic spectacle Don Ottavio's steady probity.

The "Catalogue" Aria

Giovanni carefully sets up Elvira's next humiliation, delivering her to Leporello for an account of the Don's desertion of her in Burgos. If ever the hero of the opera were to give an account of himself the moment is now, when he is cornered by an angry victim. But Giovanni neatly and cruelly steps aside, leaving his lieutenant to "explain." Accounts don't interest Giovanni, and he is in fact incapable of giving one. Obsessive natures don't have insights; they can hardly be said to have sight, insofar as that sense is a human faculty. Thus Giovanni fails to recognize Elvira until forced into direct conversation with her. The objects of his obsession swim into his ken conducted by one or another of the senses — he picks up a scent, he pricks up his ears at the sound of a woman's voice, he sights the movement of a blurred female form at a distance — but he lacks the impulse to combine these impressions into the articulated whole which brings men to the threshold of a moral world. Leporello is Giovanni's double and the articulator of his experience, and he has in that capacity a more complicated nature than his master. Their relationship is of course symbiotic; Leporello's aspirations are not very high. He is content when in his role as interpreter he is provisionally accorded the patent of a gentleman and allowed to live a full, albeit vicarious, cavalier's life. Yet he does possess the ordinary man's minimal capacity for reflectiveness, which enables him to observe his master, and also separates him somewhat from Giovanni. Leporello is bound to treat Elvira both kindly and cruelly. He is capable of feeling pity for her, in the second-act finale for example (see p. 365 n. 47), and here he gives her paternal advice which is both expedient and sympathetic.[16] Furthermore, it is probably an ultimate kindness to Donna Elvira to spell out to her just how foolish and misguided was her love for Giovanni. But Leporello cannot help relishing the task of delivering that harsh news, and he shapes his account to expose Elvira to maximum humiliation.

The "Catalogue" aria is *buffa* at its best — a subtle and exquisitely calculated piece of rhetoric. The first reprise of the aria is unusual in its departure from the customary rhythmic vocabulary of the opera: instead of projecting its affective stance through the mediation of the social dances, it is directly mimetic of an action. Leporello takes on the *persona* of Harlequin stage-managing a harlequinade. His vocal line is merely declamatory, while the action, of a hypothetical troupe of acrobats perhaps, is choreographed by the orchestra. Forced to articulate what in the orchestra is mere playful suggestion, I would characterize the subject of the mime as something like the eternal and circular pursuit of male and female — a conceit suggested first by the rhythmic motive tossed continually from upper register to lower and back again (ex.

Example 10-6

Example 10-7

10–6).[17] Flourishes and scales follow the sixteen measures of preliminary footwork (mm. 16–17, 20–21, and 24–25), calling for some sort of
acrobatic turn or caper. They are succeeded each time by a two-
measure snatch of exuberant fanfare-march (ex. 10–7). Only at measure 28 does Leporello cease his declamatory commentary to join the
orchestra, as if to cluck in agreement with it about the incredible number 1003; the orchestra greets the exclamation ("Ma in Ispagna son già
mille e tre"[18]) with more string fanfares (mm. 33–37). An enumeration
of kinds —

> . . . Contadine,
> Cameriere, cittadine,
> . . . contesse, baronesse,
> Marchesane, principesse — [19]

accompanies the move to the second key area; as the list rises through
the social ranks, the bass line rises to the accidental for the new key, G-
sharp (m. 44). When the bass postpones the first A-major cadence, falling back to E or V/V, the dialogue between masculine and feminine recommences with staccato scales alternating in the high strings and basses
(ex. 10–8). Again Leporello is merely commentator until the accolade
for 1003, where he joins the orchestra for the first emphatic cadence of
the second key area (mm. 64–71). The orchestra's mime (the flourishes
and scales begun in m. 16 and repeated here on the dominant) and
Leporello join forces for the second and concluding set of cadences
(mm. 71ff.; see fig. 7 for a diagram of this "first reprise").

Direct mimesis is not Mozart's usual idiom.[20] Although Figaro too is a Harlequinlike figure, who with vivid dramatic imagination mounts his own harlequinades, he still moves with dance rhythms as his medium, invoking both their primary meaning as social furniture and their extended function as part of the language of the affections. Figaro is further from Harlequin than is Leporello,[21] for he is less in need of Harlequin's disingenuous foolishness to survive. Basilio is as close as *Le nozze di Figaro* comes to an unrefined *commedia* character — his aria too contains direct mimicry of nature in its echoes of storms and lions roaring — and Figaro turns momentarily brutish when allied with him. The pantomime of the "Catalogue" aria enters directly into the spirit of bawdy cruelty of the Comedy of Masks, where love is generic, and the reward for swooning lovers is apt to be a pratfall or a kick in the pants. The "objectivity" of Leporello's surefooted barker's patter as he conde-

Example 10-8

Figure 7   The Key-Area Plan of the "Catalogue" Aria

I		V	
$\frac{4}{4}$ Allegro			
2 periods mime	V/V cadence list	1st V cadence	firm recap. of list
m. 1-16 17-37	37-49	49-71	71-84

			I			
$\frac{3}{4}$ Andante con moto						
⌐I V¬	⌐X—⌐	⌐I¬	(X)¬		⌐I	
minuet to V cadence	list V I V V	minuet to bvi cadence	d minor	list, V I V I	minuet,	cadences
4 4 4 4	5 10 8	4 4 (1 2 3 4 1 2 3 4 5)	4	7	4	4 4 4...
m. 85-100	101-123	124-130	131-135	136-172 (end)		

The diagram represents approximately the relative lengths of the first and second sections. Although the first section contains almost as many measures as the second, the 4/4 measure stands to the 3/4 measure in a rough 2:3 ratio (4/4 ♩ = 3/4 ♩).

scendingly invites the "madamina" ("little lady") to observe this phenomenon of nature, the dedicated seducer at his work, is disingenuous,
and a mean piece of art.

In the second reprise of the "Catalogue" aria — the enumeration of
qualities — Leporello drops his air of disinterested observer and broadens the comedy still further. Succumbing to the temptation to "fare il
gentiluomo," he takes on a dignified and sonorous minuet, its periods
punctuated by horn fanfares — the proper music of an amorous Don
were it to be found in any other eighteenth-century opera. There is no
real X-section before the minuet; Mozart seems to be fashioning a composite aria, using a simple two-reprise dance form as the return to the
tonic (see fig. 7). But the demand for some development after the
lengthy first section puts pressure on the chastely articulated periods of
the minuet just as Leporello's fancy extends and extends the list.

The minuet begins with a sixteen-measure "first reprise," which ends
with the subject of "la bianca" and her "dolcezza." [22] Then, given an introductory measure of orchestra to show that the list is open-ended and
thus endless, Leporello does "la grassotta" and "la magrotta," "la grande"
and "la piccina" [23] (the last two in appropriately mimetic fashion). With
the return of the minuet after this short X-section he turns to the topic
of age, and seems to be about to bring the minuet to its proper period
when a dark thought intrudes. A deceptive cadence on B-flat, the lowered sixth degree, sets a D-minor frame for Leporello's suddenly sinister
patter, "Ma passion predominante/È la giovin principiante" (ex. 10–9). [24]
Staccato eighth-note arpeggios in the bassoons underline the menace of
this chilling touch of D minor, the opera's key of the supernatural and of
high tragedy. Musically the D minor provides a disturbance in the minuet return, which is a requisite if the closing D-major cadences are to be
lengthy enough to serve also as closure for the entire piece.

Dramatically the sudden dark tone of the passage has been interpreted by some as Leporello's sudden realization of his master's wickedness. [25] But Leporello is too knowing a type to be overcome by sudden
illuminations: the fact of his master's "wickedness" is already a working
premise for him. Superficially the D-minor turn is in fact just in character for Leporello — the ill-suppressed gloating of a (vicarious) libertine
on arriving at the most delicious part of his list of delights, the seduction

Example 10-9

of innocents. Furthermore, as it turns out, Leporello has enough self-knowledge to have called on these very expectations of his character in plotting his punch lines: he has merely feigned an oblivious delight in playing the gentleman. The D-minor leer is in fact a means of galvanizing Elvira by showing her her own place on the list. Although she may by now seem old and used, Donna Elvira is still in fact a young girl (as, indeed, is Donna Anna); she was a novice in both senses of the word when Giovanni met her in Burgos. Like a skilled orator, with a wave of his hand Leporello directs his discourse back to the particular case just when his listener might be allowing herself to forget that she was the occasion of it. The gesture should invoke in Elvira painful memories of life in all innocence pre-Giovanni; they are humiliating ones too, for in being shown her own classification she is exposed to the brutal shock of seeing herself as a statistic. After undergoing the annihilation of this quintessentially modern experience, it is merely embarassing to remember how one thought one's passions mattered. (The chilling D minor also has a further repercussion, although one which is not necessarily within the compass of Leporello's intentions: it sets the seduction of innocents apart from the fall of contessas and brunettes, to connect it with the high seriousness of the tragic mode. The scene changes just following this aria to a stock vision of rustic Arcady, and in its frame Giovanni promptly attempts to seduce the peasant-bride Zerlina.)

Elvira's new vision of herself brings her a new kind of pain; the satisfying pangs of unrequited love give way to a nagging chagrin at having been a fool. Successful, Leporello prepares to drive his humiliating lesson home. His strategy is to move swiftly to strip not only Elvira, but all women, of their dignity. To close his interrupted period he takes up again the list music of the X-section (mm. 100–105), his language casually praising his master's thoroughgoing indiscriminateness ("Non si picca se sia ricca,/Se sia brutta, se sia bella"[26]). Onto its studied nonchalance Leporello grafts the four-measure minuet phrase which opened the section, now become a consequent to the list's antecedent (mm. 135–46). The phrase which results answers a musical problem at the same time as it makes Leporello's point, extracting the utmost in both cadential drive and salacious humor from the little minuet. The material which provides the close of the aria must be long enough to function as cadence not just for the second reprise of the 3/4 music, itself already swollen beyond reasonable minuet proportions, but for both of these large sections of Leporello's grandiose creation (see fig. 7). The additive seven measures of list impose a greater breadth on the final period than the simple symmetries of the minuet could have enforced. Working *ars combinatoria*[27] on the level of phrase members, Mozart reverses the order of the list and minuet phrases, reversing their functions at the same time. The list music becomes a strong phrase of return and half-cadence, while the minuet turns from a generative head-motive into an answer to the list's half-cadence, and thus into a mere component of the powerful rhythmic sweep to closure.[28] Its new musical position gives it new dramatic impact. Prim-and-regular now follows expansive-and-casual, the refined balances of the dance providing a strange under-lining for the lewd, almost aphoristic "Purchè porti la gonnella,/Voi sapete quel che fa."[29] In dulcet tones, and with meaningful glances at Elvira, Leporello warbles his final and cruellest punch line, one which he set up from the opening of the second section when he allowed us to think that he had forgotten himself. His aristocrat's minuet has become the vehicle for an insult — "Purchè porti la gonnella" — which reduces all the particularity of womankind to a mere sign of sexual difference. Women are convenient receptacles for the lusts of a ruttish male — women are "skirts."

Because the neat four-measure minuet phrase will not suffice as consequent to the energy released by the list's seven-measure antecedent, the phrase is driven to a deceptive cadence on the sixth degree (m. 146), one which is parallel to the D-minor deception (m. 131) in all but mode. Two more cadential formulas, the first again deceptive, wind the period to a close in measure 154. Leporello has shot his bolt, and can conclude his sentence ("Voi sapete quel che fa") with the studied casualness of IV-V-I cadential clichés. At the same time the orchestra gives the aria a final pat into shape by taking up the bassoons' ominous staccato arpeggios from the D-minor passage and turning them into D-major cadence ornaments (mm. 150–54: vi, V/V, I$_4^6$, V, I; ex. 10–10). This musical end rhyme to the D-minor section resolves that passage's questionable modality while coloring the close with its mocking echoes — the orchestra's ratification of Leporello's gentle devastation. An eighteen-measure coda consisting of various types of denied D-major cadences puts a firm period to the bulging list.

The "Catalogue" aria is the opposite of what its name implies: it is not

Example 10-10

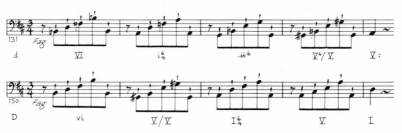

a mere list, but a well-formed piece of periodic rhetoric, an exercise in the art of persuasion. Although he may ultimately be doing Elvira a calculated kindness, the first impact of Leporello's demonstration can only be utter humiliation for *la belle Dévote*, reared as she must have been from a tender age by the twin lights of *cielo* and *core*. This confrontation between the monolithic passions of *opera seria* and *buffa*'s cynical, mocking wisdom leaves Elvira exposed, raw, and mortified. And although the audience may feel a moment's lingering sympathy for her, it soon turns to side with Leporello's irresistible and velvet bullying; the temptation is always to place oneself under the protection of the worldly wise, even if their position smacks of cheap cynicism. The wit and flexibility of *buffa* continue to erode all seriousness, developing an ambiguous moral point of view from which decency and passion appear fatuity. Mockery is more persuasive than passion; it easily makes cynics of us all. Exposed to Leporello's suave patter, one would need all one's moral courage not to string along.

The Ensembles: "Non ti fidar, o misera"

Between the murder of the Commendatore and the damnation of the Don, much of the requisite "filler" action in *Don Giovanni* is provided by a theme and variations on Elvira's separation and humiliation. For instance, the events at the beginning of act II — Giovanni's reseduction of Elvira and subsequent substitution of Leporello for himself in the lovemaking — are mere repetitions of the action in act I which culminates in the "Catalogue" aria (and lacks only an exchange of identities between servant and master). By the time this elaborate joke has played itself out it has involved a trio, a lengthy recitative, a short song, a major ensemble, and an aria for Leporello.[30]

But also earlier on in the opera, in act I, the types of music allotted to the characters suggest Donna Elvira's alienation from her own kind and her entrapment in unholy fellowship with a seducer and a buffoon. The similarities in the overdrawn entrance marches of Elvira and Leporello have already been pointed out (see p. 234). The musical point of the "discovery quartet," "Non ti fidar, o misera" (I, 9), where Donna Anna and Don Ottavio first begin to doubt that all noblemen are honorable, is a contrast between "normal" and "abnormal" styles. Elvira begins the piece with the super *alla breve* rhythms which Donna Anna adopts in her moments of sharpest grief (at the opening of her revenge duet with Don Ottavio, I, 2). Marked by jagged leaps of a seventh and an octave, they are regularized into a smooth *alla breve* by the end of her phrase (ex. 10–11). Commenting on the noble bearing of the distraught woman,[31] Donna Anna and Don Ottavio take up her cadence figure. Its placid

Example 10-11

Example 10-12

Example 10-13

alla breve rhythms strike the social norm for the entire quartet. Giovanni's entry is in sharp contrast to the thoughtful serenity of their utterances; his patter shifts the duple scansion to a flurried 4/4 across the barline, barely socialized into the *alla breve* by the end of the phrase (ex. 10–12).[32] Giovanni's intent is to separate Elvira from Donna Anna and Don Ottavio before she is able fully to reveal his perfidies to them. Lacking his usual cool control, he takes up Elvira's syncopated half note himself for his final cadential phrase, an agitated "Forse si calmerà."[33] Against its half and sixteenth notes is set the orchestra's *alla breve* cadence figure, which has come to be the normal heartbeat of the quartet (ex. 10–13). In her subsequent entry Donna Elvira takes up Giovanni's 4/4 in a rousing arpeggio, which whips up the energy necessary to move the piece to the dominant while linking the exalted anger of the "pazzarella"[34] Elvira with Giovanni's low patter (he answers her phrase with patter 4/4).

Example 10-14

DONNA ELVIRA

Sde-gno, rab- bia, dis-pet- to, spa-ven-to

The quartet continues in the same vein. Elvira's signature music for the entire opera might be her convulsive outburst of "Sdegno, rabbia, dispetto, spavento,"[35] in a strange wedding of coloratura and patter; it plays consequent phrase to the smoothly swelling triplets of the other three voices (ex. 10–14). There is something rather comic in the noble couple's placid and insulated caution while they debate the merits of the unfortunate woman's case. "Incomincio a dubitar,"[36] they agree soberly over a dominant pedal (mm. 66–68), while the melodic lines of Giovanni and Elvira swirl around them in unmistakably violent conflict. The final period of the recapitulation (mm. 79 to the end) sums up the contrasts: Ottavio and Anna move serenely to the close repeating the *alla breve* cadence figure while Giovanni and Elvira admonish and fulminate in rapid sixteenths.

The link which is made in this quartet between idioms of the sublime and the debased is a crucial one for the opera. Elvira tells Giovanni he can no longer control her, for she has lost all prudence.[37] Tight-lipped *prudenza* is what keeps Donna Anna moving through the even paces of the noble *alla breve* while the rhythms of Elvira and Giovanni surge above and below its proper levels. Anna's *alla breve* does soar in the next piece, her passionate "Or sai chi l'onore." But a distinction is still preserved between the "classical" *alla breve* of that aria and Elvira's mannered and "neurotic" entrance march or her patter coloratura. Don Giovanni and Elvira are both beyond the pale, and in that sense fitting associates. In the great sextet of act II (II, 6), Elvira's exclusion from her rightful world is made painfully apparent when all proper society (the two pairs of lovers) is grouped against her, adamantly refusing the pardon she is so far gone as to beg for her dissolute lover. There again, after an *alla breve* set-piece conversation between Donna Anna and Don Ottavio,[38] Elvira enters with an over-the-barline dotted 4/4, the same metrical contrast as is developed in this first-act quartet. The tense descending chromatic scales of her pleas for mercy are confronted by the simple diatonic chorus of "No"'s from the righteous avengers, and then debased to Leporello's cringing mock-pathetic chromaticism as he throws himself on their mercy. Although Elvira is returned to the vocal fold at the end of the sextet, it is only after melodramatic shame has turned to comic humiliation: the wicked lover she has wantonly been sheltering turns out instead to be a lowclass rascal, and Elvira a dupe, not a sinner. Again, as in the "Catalogue" aria, the movement is from a pain which can be borne with conviction to a weary consciousness of being an object of ridicule: the others say nothing, but what must they think?

The Ensembles: "Ah, taci, ingiusto core"

Yet the uneasy trio of Donna Elvira, Don Giovanni, and Leporello comes together in act II to sing some of the most beautiful music in the opera. "Ah, taci, ingiusto core" (II, 2) sets up a situation which is not intended to have its culmination until the painful sextet (II, 6) when Elvira discovers her "lover" is not Don Giovanni, but Leporello. But in this trio and in the subsequent recitative, Elvira shows herself in the most attractive light heretofore, at the same time as she is treated, all unknowingly, with callous indifference. As the trio opens she appears on her balcony in the gathering dusk, unaware of the presence of two auditors, Leporello and Don Giovanni, and tranquil for the first time in the opera. To the gentle 6/8 rhythms of a pastorale, crepuscular and contemplative music here as it is in *Figaro*, she admonishes her heart for the motions it insists on making toward an "empio," a "traditore," since "È colpa aver pietà."[39] Making her out in the dim twilight, Giovanni, dressed as Leporello in preparation for his attempt on Donna Elvira's maid, hides behind Leporello-dressed-as-Don-Giovanni, and begins to serenade. The trick is a vivid stage image for Giovanni's habit of psychic concealment; chameleonlike as always, he copies Elvira's music also, making it his own. In fact, the material for the second key area (m. 19) is simply the music of the opening period (mm. 1–14); it is repeated on the dominant after four measures of transition, with Giovanni singing Elvira's opening phrase. He rewrites only her cadence, in order to make it more seductive: using the same number of measures, but one I-IV-V-I formula instead of two, he substitutes for the first formula two measures of ardent subdominant harmony (ex. 10–15). (Note the end rhyme between the motives on "pietà" and "carità" which unites the first and second key areas. Giovanni's more urgent version also provides the firmer cadence, which suits the needs of the move to the dominant as well as the importunities of his wooing.) The Don has slipped on his serenader's mask; the orchestra begins to imitate the mandolin-strumming figure which later accompanies his *canzonetta* (II, 3).

Since we know Giovanni's plans, the indifferent cruelty of his blandishments makes us suffer for Elvira. Warming up, he begins the X-section with a vertiginous drop in harmony from E to C major, and a fervent trope, which calls into service a fragment of the *canzonetta* he is about to dedicate (in II, 3) to Elvira's maid (ex. 10–16).[40] The slip to a

Example 10-15

Example 10-16

third-related triad gives the song a fresh and earnest ardor, while at the same time framing it to underline that it is a song and a performance. The fiendish efficiency of the man is notable here: Giovanni likes to get the most out of his material, wasting nothing. Seeing Elvira's conflicting emotions at the return (m. 54), he congratulates himself on his talents.[41] Leporello, who has found the travesty hopelessly funny,[42] at the same time is not wholly indifferent to its cruelty, and frames a prayer for the protection of Elvira's confiding nature.[43] The same mixture of sympathy and barbarism characterizes Leporello in the recitative which follows. Although he straightaway chides Giovanni for his treatment of Elvira,[44] the Don soon has him making burlesque love to her, and enjoying it. Even Giovanni is a little surprised at how quickly Leporello takes to his work: "Il birbo si riscalda," he says in a wry aside.[45]

The scene intensifies certain impressions from act I — Giovanni's chameleon nature, Leporello's equivocal moral character, Elvira's susceptibility — while adding one new perception. Elvira is presented in a contemplative moment; the audience is made privy to her interior struggle with her desires. She is the only person in the opera whose inner conflicts we are allowed to witness, and in the process she becomes less of a caricature. "Ah, taci, ingiusto core" has certain similarities with "Ah! chi mi dice mai," the trio in act I in which Donna Elvira fulminates while Don Giovanni and Leporello comment in amused delight on her distress. But the striking contrast between Elvira's music in the two trios — a tragicomic exalted march in the one and reflective pastoral music in the other — is a sign that *la belle Dévote* ought perhaps to be taken seriously.

"Morte" and "Pietà": The End of Act II

The pathos of Elvira's lonely meditations deepens with the deepening twilight of act II. At the opening of the sextet (II, 6) she finds herself in a "bujo loco," and is seized with a melancholy fear of death:

> Sola sola, in bujo loco,
> Palpitar il cor mi sento;
> E m'assale un tal spavento,
> Che mi sembra di morir.[46]

The key is E-flat, the "fool's paradise" of Elvira's first-act entrance march. But whereas the E-flat of "Ah! chi mi dice mai" was framed by pieces in D major, the tonal colors of act II are generally darker, and E-flat does not bear that anomalous Neapolitan relation to the surrounding keys (now C and G); it is not at odds with the tonality of the act. Furthermore, in the sextet itself it is the E-flat which frames D major, and not the opposite. After Leporello, feeling his way about the dark courtyard, carries the piece to the dominant, B-flat becomes the bottom note of an augmented sixth, and pushes the key to a surprising D major. The X-section begins in D, with a troped duet between Donna Anna and Don Ottavio (mm. 28–61). The noble pair is dressed in mourning,[47] and their entrance is heralded by a formal fanfare with horns and drums — a sudden bright change of color which helps to set the hard edges of the trope. The stances of the two lovers have suffered no change since the revenge duet of act I; they seem to be caught in the middle of a continuing conversation (which they will still be engaged in just before the second-act finale — there it occasions Donna Anna's "Non mi dir" — and again when all the characters speak their last at the end of the finale and of the opera, II, 11, 712–40). Here Don Ottavio's ardent but relatively amorphous D-major phrases are briskly overlapped by Donna Anna's strong *alla breve* D minor. Her music is veritably statuesque in its grief. It modulates first to B-flat major and then, by means of a chromatic descending line and a dramatic one-measure extension, to C minor (ex. 10–17). Donna Anna appears here in her most tragic mode.

Example 10-17

But these measures of music, which are, in Donna Anna's case at least, particularly beautiful, suffer in juxtaposition with the intimate glimpse we have just had of Elvira, gravely and honestly examining the dark places of the heart. Both women speak of "morte" (Anna swears to Ottavio "Sol la morte, o mio tesoro,/Il mio pianto può finir"[48]), but their accents differ. On Anna's lips the word is part of a high-flown cliché about grief, and is raised as an excuse, to stave off further importunities from Ottavio. But the thought of death intrudes itself unwelcome on Elvira's delicate sensibilities; she absorbs it from the night air. The stage setting sets the psychic climate of the opera at this moment: in the meditative twilight of the "bujo loco" E-flat is the tonic and D the unstable degree; Ottavio's and Anna's public tableau of wooing and withstanding is the mode which strikes a false note.

Late in the second act the word "pietà" provides another occasion for comparing the sentiments of Donna Elvira and Donna Anna. Both women are given virtuoso arias preceded by a dramatic *recitativo accompagnato* (Elvira's was added at the request of the singer for the Vienna performance of 1788). Neither *scena* adds materially to the characterization of the two women. Elvira's — "In quali eccessi, o Numi" and "Mi tradì" (II, 8c) — involves essentially a formal development of the "contrasto d'affetti" which she feels stirring within her at the thought of Giovanni's inevitable damnation.[49] The same clash of sentiments has just been developed in a more dramatic fashion in the trio "Ah, taci, ingiusto core." Anna's "Non mi dir" is one more barrier raised against Ottavio's wooing. Both women speak of "pietà," but Anna invokes it in cool and distant self-interest,[50] while Elvira is describing feelings stirred in her heart both by and for another: "Ma, tradita e abbandonata,/Provo ancor per lui pietà."[51] Although Elvira's passion is without doubt foolish and undignified, her capacity to be moved and to act on her emotions is still more attractive than Anna's icy refusals of either passion or solace. Yet this openness and almost willing loss of dignity also make her *déclassée*, an outcast from the proper orders and a constant companion-victim of the classless opportunist Don Giovanni. Significantly, she is the only one of the three women who follows Giovanni into the second-act finale, where her beseechments meet their final rebuff. To complete

Example 10-18

the portrait of Elvira it is necessary to examine her encounter with him there.[52]

Elvira bursts in on Don Giovanni and Leporello as they are tranquilly wrangling at dinner, the Don as usual getting the best of it. The initial pastiche of D-major social music — a march and some *musica da tavola* played by a windband — emphasizes the rhythmic anomaly of Elvira's tempestuous B-flat entry: her quick-tempoed 3/4 has no proper place in the metrical spectrum (ex. 10–18). At times it is scanned as a waltz, but the accompaniment is overfreighted with details like the *fortepiano* eighth-note tremors in the strings at the opening, and the phrase structure is frequently irregular. For example, Elvira's second phrase consists of ten measures ending anomalously on an open cadence decorated by a coloratura turn ("Pie*ta*de io sento," mm. 215–18; see ex. 10–19, p. 256). Measures later, as the dominant begins to tilt back to the tonic, she repeats the same eccentric figure in response to Giovanni's query, "Che vuoi, mio bene?" giving as her answer "Che vita cangi" (mm. 263–66; see p. 374 n. 53). The figure occurs only twice, both times riding aloft over an ambiguous dominant (one which is not clearly either a new tonic or the fifth degree of the old). The second instance of the figure is introduced only in response to the first, and is without rhythmic connection to the surrounding periods. Thus the two phrases stand out from the established fabric of the piece as cries from the heart.

It is well worth repeating all of Elvira's exhortation:

Elv: L'ultima prova
Dell'amor mio
Ancor vogl'io
Fare con te.

Più non rammento
Gl'inganni tuoi;
Pietade io sento . . .

Da te non chiede
Quest'alma oppressa
Della sua fede
Qualche mercè.

. . . . . .

Gio: Che vuoi, mio bene?
Elv: *Che vita cangi.*[53]

Clearly Elvira has undergone some manner of conversion, or at least a reversion to the training of her girlhood. Leporello, by showing her her proper place among the ranks of the seduced and abandoned through the painful device of the "Catalogue" aria, has brought her to see her frenzy for revenge in a new light: the bloodlust she confidently thought was the will of Heaven[54] has been shown up as merely her own attempt to retain a hold on Proteus. After the honest and touching reflections of "Ah, taci, ingiusto core" and "Mi tradì," she has managed to bring her heart into line with the dictates of her faith; she has recognized that the true object of a lover is not to possess the beloved, but to endeavor to bring him into a state of grace. Now the fulminations of *la belle Dévote* have found their proper focus, guided by the realization that the believer will always be misled unless in the orders of love she puts God first, not man. Elvira is here to offer herself as a scapegoat, a victim, rendering up the last shreds of her pride in order to save her beloved. She has done what Donna Anna could not — find a resolution to the sterile conflict between passion and pride which has held both women inert throughout the opera.

The answer is a swift but incontrovertible "No." Giovanni sardonically cries "Brava!" and Elvira recognizes his response for what it is — one with Valmont's titillation at the spectacle of female piety and Don Juan's lust pricked by Elvira's unconsciously becoming *désbabille*. "Cor perfido!" she cries, over essentially the same V/V-V progression as set her two previous exclamations (mm. 269–70). But one small alteration in the progression changes the tonal world: the G in the bass of the previous V/V becomes G-flat, the lower note of an augmented sixth, making the originally ambiguous F-major triad clearly V and a prelude to the return of B-flat (ex. 10–19). Elvira's proposal to Giovanni and her defeat have been swift and tacit. In six words and seven brief measures of music the transformation wrought so easily by G-flat's alteration of an uneasy tonic into a certain dominant catches the final hardening of Elvira's knowledge of Giovanni and of herself in relation to him. It is a knowledge which she finds she has possessed all along, of his arrant insouciance and her own hopeless impotence. The brevity of its

Example 10-19

Example 10-20

dismissal is illustration of the utter futility of the attempt. Leporello, a little slower-witted, needs to hear another "Brava!" from Giovanni (m. 272) before he takes the point and joins Elvira in her last shrill cry of "Cor perfido!" (mm. 275–78). The grace of a Christian disciple, which in a well-ordered world should be the ultimate and saving power, loses its efficacy in the face of Giovanni's paralyzing aura. With the Don in the world salvation is beside the point; the dining-salon has become a private limbo in which all three characters are eternally joined in barren but immutable relation.

Mozart skillfully emphasizes the hopes dashed in this harsh moment of recognition by recomposing the return (mm. 280ff). In place of Elvira's tumultuous assault which opened the exposition, he has Giovanni start off with a trivial waltz tune. Impatient with the interruption now that its novelty has worn off, Giovanni turns back to his dinner with the words "Lascia ch'io mangi."[55] His waltz is cool and detached, properly beat by the measure instead of the quarter note (the beat of Elvira's entry music); (ex. 10–20). After four measures of rest he adds as an afterthought "E, se ti piace,/Mangia con me."[56] The tune of this indifferent invitation later sets the last words of the toast with which Giovanni closes the movement:

> Vivan le femmine!
> Viva il buon vino!
> *Sostegno e gloria*
> *D'umanità*! (ex. 10–21)[57]

Example 10-21

(The finale of the Bertati opera opens with Giovanni making a toast to the women of Venice; rather than employ it merely as social background, da Ponte puts the device of the toast to more telling use as a cruel mockery of Elvira's passion). Several claims have been made as to the provenance of this scrap of a tune. The most interesting suggestion, which applies to the toast music alone, is that it is couched in galliard rhythms; it would be characteristic of Giovanni's courtly disinterest for him to transform Elvira's turbulent and anomalous 3/4 into the antique rhythms of conviviality and good cheer.[58] At any rate, waltz and toast set the tone for the return, and Elvira's original entry music reappears as a jeremiad[59] set in a satirical frame. (Leporello remains coupled with Elvira for the rest of the movement, exclaiming over Giovanni's "heart of stone"; in order to emphasize their coupling, Mozart has Leporello sing the string accompaniment to Elvira's entry music when it first reappears, mm. 296–98.) Once again in this opera *buffa*'s ironic trivialities manage to mock and unman the accents of righteous anger. The strange amoral perspective which the opera enforces makes it impossible to take Elvira's preachments seriously. Her self-immolation is finally absurd and meaningless; passion and openness, or the willingness to be vulnerable — the cardinal virtues of *Le nozze di Figaro* — turn to comic hysteria in the face of Giovanni's prodigious indifference. There is to be no more satisfaction for *la belle Dévote* than there was for the classical statue.

CHAPTER ELEVEN

Zerlina and Masetto

"Giovanette" and "Ho capito"

Of the three women in *Don Giovanni* Zerlina is appropriately the one to be introduced last. Appropriately so for several reasons: because she is the fresh young novice whose seduction has already been darkly bruited as the most terrible,[1] because she is the only woman whom Giovanni actually attempts to seduce before us on the stage, and finally because she is the only character who finds a viable answer to the question of how to live in a world which is under Don Giovanni's shadow. First, however, she must make the discovery that it does contain him, a bitter and tantalizing truth which the other women were already in possession of before we encountered them.

In keeping with the opera's distant perspective on its characters — its habit of introduction by near-caricature — Zerlina is first shown at play in an idyllic vision of rustic Arcady; we single her out only slowly from a throng of peasants in pastoral poses. The chorus "Giovinette che fate all'amore" (I, 5) is cast in 6/8, a gay country gigue with occasional musette phrases (mm. 11–13 and *passim*). Its opening material is distinguished by a cleverly cockeyed period structure — a phrase of seven measures articulated into three plus four. The "extensions" are actually just repetitions of brief gigue fragments; underneath there lies a vague nonentity of a gigue tune, once the repetitions are stripped off to expose the regular period structure (ex. 11–1). The substance of the tune lies in these repetitions, which are carefully balanced against each other to assure a firm final punctuation to the phrase. The head of the three-measure phrase is repeated, but the tail of its four-measure consequent,

Example 11-1

Example 11-2

and the second repeated motive is a slightly longer unit which ends on a strong beat:

The genesis of the repetitions becomes obvious when the singers join the orchestra. They are the echoing fa la la's of a typical peasant chorus, which sound faintly vacuous on strings, but perfectly justifiable when vocalized. Zerlina and Masetto are singled out as soloists and thus leaders, at least on their wedding day, of the rustic gathering. Zerlina is further distinguished from Masetto because she sings the more articulate solo, while Masetto's consists of the bottom or "harmony" line of a series of parallel thirds (ex. 11–2). "Giovinette" is the lightest froth of a country gigue, its art carefully concealed.

As the chorus ends Giovanni and Leporello enter, with backward glances to make sure Donna Elvira has departed. Giovanni is charmed by the embarrassment of feminine riches before him, and immediately singles out the bride. He offers the couple his protection (Leporello straightaway putting "protection" to the mock by flirting with other *contadine* and calling it by the same name[2]), and orders Leporello to take Masetto off to his *palazzo* with the rest of the peasants for a *festa*. When Masetto protests, Giovanni first promises that "La Zerlina/È in man d'un cavalier,"[3] which line Zerlina blithely parrots,[4] and he finally threatens Masetto with a menacing gesture at his sword.[5] Masetto, defeated, assents under protest to be removed from the scene in the *buffa* aria "Ho capito" (I, 6).

The opening words of Masetto's aria, loosely translated "I get it," pick up on an exchange between Giovanni and Leporello in the preceding recitative. Giovanni, having given Leporello a command to divert Masetto, asks "Hai capito?" and Leporello answers "Ho capito."[6] Sullen sarcasm is about the only weapon Masetto has against Giovanni. Quickness is a quality he lacks, and so it is of paramount importance to him to show that he knows what is going on. The word "capisco" (the verb of which "capito" is the past participle) is Masetto's slogan. Later in the first act Zerlina has almost won him back after her first disappearance with Giovanni when her consternation at the sound of the Don's voice in the distance brings back Masetto's suspicions and he challenges her:

> Ah! *capisco,*
> *Capisco*, bricconcella:
> Hai timor ch'io comprenda
> Com'è tra voi passata la faccenda.[7]

He forces her to show herself to Giovanni while he hides in the shadows, saying "*Capirò* se m'è fedele,/E in qual modo andò l'affar."[8] When he reveals himself to Giovanni, the Don with his characteristic adroitness brushes off his first surprise, and quotes back to Masetto, with mock-pathetic embellishments, Masetto's words at their first encounter: "La bella tua Zerlina/Non può, la poverina,/Più star senza di te."[9] Masetto answers, just as characteristically, "*Capisco*: sì, signore." Zerlina's concern all along, since Elvira made her aware of Giovanni's perfidy with her stunning "Ah, fuggi il traditor," has been only for Masetto's safety; she knows he's the kind of hothead that Giovanni can crush effortlessly. But Masetto's compulsion not to be hoodwinked makes him overly suspicious and an easy mark. He's duped because, needing to be in the know, he identifies "knowledge" with the worst he can imagine; if "capisco" is his byword, it's because he never does seem to understand well enough.

"Ho capito" is straightforward *buffa*, without the feverish invention which characterizes Leporello's two solos in act I. It is cast in F major, the *buffa* key. Most of its simple figures come in two-measure units and are repeated several times. As a result, the *Allegro molto alla breve* is actually rendered as a flat-footed, pacing 4/4 (counting two measures as one), a foot march like the opening gesture of "Notte e giorno" (ex. 11–3). Unlike the variety of gesture in Leporello's comic masterpiece,

Example 11-3

Example 11-4

MASETTO

Fac - cia il nos-tro ca-va-lie-re, Ca - va - lie-ra an-co-ra te,   ca - va - lie ra an co-ra te.

however, the foot march remains the sole gesture of "Ho capito"; Masetto is a very simple fellow.

The accompaniment of the aria is thin-textured, the strings playing in unison more often than not. A brief bridge leads back to the tonic at the end of the first reprise (mm. 34–38), and the material of the return is considerably curtailed, consisting only of the first nine measures of the opening (here mm. 39–47) and a new figure for the cadence (mm. 47–55). The text of the new figure is Masetto's own salacious *double entendre* on the word *cavaliere*: "Faccia il nostro cavaliere/Cavaliera ancora te!" (ex. 11–4).[10] The phrase is the equivalent of "Surely our horseman will mount you!" and Masetto grimly runs it into the ground, repeating the words "Cavaliera ancora te!" eight times. He goes through the entire second reprise a second time (with the bridge altered to ride on I rather than on V, mm. 55–61), tacking on a hard-driving series of two-measure figures for a coda, to the same text; Masetto likes to make sure people understand his ironies. Its very simplicity makes the aria rhetorically powerful; it has the single-minded drive of sulky, impotent anger, and after his ill-treatment at Giovanni's hands surely no one would grudge Masetto that passion.

There is, however, a tendency among modern writers to find in the anger of "Ho capito" an embryonic political consciousness, "the herald of the upheavals of the French Revolution."[11] A superficial glance at *Le nozze di Figaro* might lead to the erroneous conclusion that the work contains revolutionary sentiments, since its original was a subversive document which delivered a strong and deliberate indictment of social injustice. But finally even in *Figaro* a purely political analysis is a Procrustean bed; certain pointed variances with the Beaumarchais play suggest that da Ponte and Mozart deliberately took a new direction in their opera.[12] It is even more difficult to discover a celebration of revolution in *Don Giovanni*. If any character is a threat to the fabric of society it is not Masetto, but the Don himself, who moves outside the proper orders, and cries "È aperto a tutti quanti;/Viva la libertà!"[13] The little band of peasants which Masetto organizes to crush Don Giovanni is not preparing for armed revolt against an oppressive upper class,[14] but hunting down an outlaw. There are good aristocrats in the opera, and they act in concert with the peasants throughout. Twice they save Zerlina, and near the end of act II a pathetic band of members of both classes — Donna Elvira, Zerlina, and Masetto — huddles around its protector, Don Ottavio, as he finally decides to call in the authorities.[15] Furthermore, Masetto would be the most ineffectual of sans-culottes. His blundering suspicions are ultimately of greater peril to himself than to his enemy: Giovanni hoodwinks him with ease, and his world is put right only by the tolerance and good sense of his bride. *Don Giovanni* is indeed an opera particularly about the social orders, but it is not in any usual sense a political work. Any further consideration of this question will more appropriately be left to the discussion of the finales, where all the orders come together. From the characterization of Masetto, however, one thing is made certain: in the world of the opera anarchy is a threat, and not a cherished promise.

Zerlina's Music

Leaving aside the large ensembles, Zerlina's appearances are three: a duet with Giovanni — "Là ci darem la mano" (I, 7) — and two solo arias, one in each act — "Batti, batti" (I, 12) and "Vedrai, carino" (II, 5). The three pieces have some striking resemblances: all three consist of two contrasting sections (the first two with contrasting time signatures also), all three inflect for some time a pastoral affect, and all three treat the key-area layout in similar fashion. Certain dissimilarities in detail, however, build to a narrative climax by the final aria, and they eloquently relate Zerlina's history.

"Là ci darem la mano"

"Là ci darem la mano" is the sweetest imaginable of love duets. It is Giovanni's proposal of "marriage" to Zerlina, which carefully leaves open, of course, the question of whether the joining of hands will be under sacred or merely secular auspices. But all irony and cynicism must be suspended in the face of the sheer beauty of this dialogue of seduction and acquiescence. A real melody, completely fulfilled and not divisible into constituent figures, is rare in this opera; even the "tune" of Giovanni's *canzonetta* in act II is rather the elaboration of an eloquently sensual guitar progression — an improvised melody riding over the blocked-out chords of the mandolin figuration in the background. Furthermore, it is subtly brought to our attention in "Là ci darem" that Giovanni is singing a song. Voice and accompaniment begin together, without the formality of the framing measures of orchestral introduction habitual to an "aria." The slow 2/4 measure is articulated so simply that it tends to fall into two equal halves, with the even "pluck-strum, pluck-strum" of a guitar accompaniment as rhythmic skeleton (ex. 11–5).[16] The rhythm of the vocal line follows the plucked accompani-

Example 11-5

ment with little variation, and only the punctuating winds and brass in measures 4 and 8 point up the shape of the entire 2/4 measure. Although Giovanni's rhythms could be taken as a slow and stylized bourrée, and sometimes contain hints of a slow gavotte,[17] the opening of "Là ci darem" is in essence a lover's serenade.

There is an eminent and persistent tradition, probably emanating from the famous essay about this opera in Kierkegaard's *Either/Or*, that Cherubino is Don Giovanni as a boy[18] (it is sometimes further elaborated, by a sly twist of logic, into the syllogism that since Mozart resembles Cherubino, and Cherubino is a young Don Giovanni, Mozart must be Giovanni as well). What would seem to be supporting evidence for the notion is the fact that, whereas most other characters in the two operas move to the rhythms of social dance, both Cherubino and Don Giovanni have in their arias the habit of appearing to sing. The lyrics to Cherubino's songs are clearly "texts," one of which he has composed himself, and I have already pointed out how the music of his two famous arias is a conscious setting of these texts (see pp. 84–88, 104–111). Twice in act II Giovanni is called on to perform — in his *canzonetta* (II, 3), and in the quotation from it in the preceding trio — and the opening of "Là ci darem" is a subtle attempt to suggest a performance. But there is little else in the natures of the two characters which supports the conceit. Cherubino is essentially a passive creature, a *tabula rasa* to be writ upon by the women drawn to his beguiling adolescent openness. It is an important part of the charm of Mozart's conception that the adolescent will grow up into a normal young man. Adolescence is a special time, and Cherubino the adolescent assumes a special importance as the presiding god Amor. But part of the delightful pain we experience in watching Cherubino would vanish if he were drawn as a special adolescent who bears the seeds in him of a *monstrum* of a man. It is hard to credit Mozart with so cynical a teleology that the god of love must mature into a loveless betrayer.

Internal evidence is also against the relationship. The texts of Cherubino's songs are boyish effusions in a long literary tradition of apostrophes of Love. The Don's love songs are occasional pieces, tailored to the moment — rather crude and overperfumed for Elvira's maid, full of promises and assurances for the suspicious Zerlina. Singing is further-more Cherubino's natural medium, whereas Giovanni in his only self-revelatory moment is given not a "song," but the middle-class con-tredanse as theme-rhythm. He is a user of song as a public mask for seduction, and cunningly so, since song is the distillation of the seduc-tive powers of a human being. Singing the eight bars Giovanni ad-dresses to Zerlina at the beginning of "Là ci darem," the performer stands at two removes from the actual object of his mimesis: he is imi-tating the performance of another skilled performer (Giovanni), who is himself imitating the state of being of ardor. It is the singular delight of opera that the audience can apprehend this imitation of an imitation at the same time that it is being moved by the direct experience of a lover's tender expression of passion.

The 2/4 section of "Là ci darem" is constructed to move in waves of increasing urgency to Zerlina's acquiescence. The contrast between Giovanni's and Zerlina's fully rounded opening periods is first off one of "masculine-feminine." The rhythmic simplicity of Giovanni's line is set against the embellishments of Zerlina's version: she adds an initial up-beat, a dominant appoggiatura (m. 12), and an extended cadence (mm. 16–18; ex. 11–6). But these small rhythmic alterations work more than a change of gender on Giovanni's simple melody. The new sixteenth-note upbeat forces a lengthening of the first beat of the first full mea-

Example 11-6

sure; with the upbeat but without the lengthening, the rhythm ♪ ♫ ♫ | ♪♩ would set a far different tone, of jaunty triviality. Continuing the upbeat to each phrase, Zerlina fills in Giovanni's measure 2 with an eighth note on "Mi" and this more legato and continuous line restores the full 2/4 measure as a unit in place of the half of it, overriding the divisive effect of the guitarlike accompaniment. Song gives way to dance — a slow stylized bourrée with syncopation measures. The performance frame has been subtly dissolved and we are back in the normal idiom of opera, where singing is the equivalent of the talk in a spoken drama, and not a special medium; Zerlina is addressed by a troubadour, but she responds in normal accents. Thus even across the two nearly identical periods urgency builds, by means of devices which double the metrical foot and suggest a change of climate from the cool melos of an accomplished wooer to the anxious reflections of a woman in perplexity.

The question inevitably arises, just how perplexed is Zerlina in her perplexities? The responsory beauties of the duet, abstracted from the situation on stage, tend to make one forget the oddity of its "dialogue": although its periods consist of impeccable antecedent-consequent phrases, the "lovers" are not actually engaged in face-to-face conversation. Giovanni's lyrics are directly addressed to Zerlina, but her words are an aside, "fra sè," the outward reflection of an inner struggle:

> Vorrei, e non vorrei . . .
> Mi trema un poco il cor . . .
> Felice, è ver, sarei:
> Ma può burlarmi ancor." [19]

Although Zerlina's words and the nature of her first phrase suggest that the primary contrast of the opening eighteen measures of the duet is between experienced courtier and innocent victim, there are difficulties with this straightforward interpretation. Zerlina's natural idiom is a rustic 6/8, the peasant gigue of "Giovinette," and yet she is right at home in the *mezzo carattere* 2/4. Giovanni's next two phrases — a bold triadic fanfare riding on the dominant (mm. 19–20, 23–24) — are all courtly invitation and promise, and her yielding sigh motives are no less suitably ladylike and refined as answers. Any analysis of Zerlina's character must start from the fact that she is tempted. She has a sense of her own attractiveness, and some pretensions; she is probably not innocent of girlish fantasies about precisely the opportunity Giovanni is offering her. The preceding recitative gives evidence that she was not without expectations about the habits of the nobility: the line "Io so che rado/ Colle donne voi altri cavalieri/Siete onesti e sinceri" [20] is a shyly flir-

Example 11-7

ZERLINA

Pres - to non son_ più_   for - te,non son_ più_   for - te,non son_ più_   for - te.

tatious demand for some tender of good faith — if she's to compromise
herself, let it not be as it was with other girls whom she's gossiped
about. There is perhaps room for the suspicion that her apparent conversation with herself is intended to be overheard, that she deems it
both decorous and expedient to hold out and let Giovanni witness it.
"Presto non son più forte"[21] is deliciously ambiguous, both a lament and
an invitation. Its three measures of chromatic sigh motives are, whether
intentionally so or not, a relentless tease (ex. 11–7). If we grow too
cynical about Zerlina, however, we are ourselves no more percipient
than Masettos. Her adaptability ought not to be mistaken for the instruction of experience, or her instinctive femininity for the designing
coyness of an accomplished coquette. Girls in the village do gossip, do
learn about other ways. But if one of them were actually to compromise
herself, the village would be bound to find out and would punish its
own. Masetto would not be so jealous of his bride if he did not feel he
still had something to protect. It is a mistake to portray Zerlina's hesita-
tions as coy simperings, and to belie by overclever stagecraft the relative
innocence of her temptation.[22]

The switch from eight-measure to two-measure phrases for the second exchange between the Don and Zerlina (m. 19) has already increased the sense of urgency about the duet, and with the return of the
tonic (m. 30) come two-measure units which seem even shorter, since
they are antiphonal fragments of the original eight-measure phrases. In
measure 40 a true stretto effect is achieved when the voices begin to
enter at one-measure intervals, overlapping each other's phrases, and
the Albertilike bass supporting Giovanni's phrases increases the intensity. At the climactic moment Zerlina's "Non son più forte" suddenly
stands out alone, sinking to the subdominant adorned with chromatic
"sigh-motive" appoggiaturas, and with a minimal accompaniment.
Giovanni, sensing that she is now ripe to be plucked, cries "Andiam,"
and finally, on the dominant (V_5^6), Zerlina addresses her first words
directly to him: "Andiam!" (mm. 48–49). The 2/4 dissolves into a 6/8
pastorale, almost in gigue tempo, with a musette bass supporting the
"skirl" of the lovers' voices in parallel thirds. Unanimous at last, they
sing a fittingly pastoral text: "Andiam, andiam, mio bene,/A ristorar le
pene/D'un innocente amor!"[23] After two periods the sweet pastorale is
transformed into less static closing material by the dots, trills, and flour-

Example 11-8

ishes of a pert French gigue (mm. 64 to the end), still to the same text (ex. 11–8).

The close of "Là ci darem" is a delectable distillation of love's harmony, and so it should immediately strike the listener. But knowledge of the lovers follows close on this pleasure, to suggest inevitable ironies. The utopian vision of lovers' bliss intimated in the pastoral topic — dreamlike, halcyon, with no limits or consequences, innocent of shame and heedless of the world — is clearly illusory when one of the "lovers" is by nature untrue. Furthermore, the seducer in this case has gradually been betraying his true nature, in images which suggest a sinister analogue to the pastoral: he too is rootless, placeless, a creature of the shadows, yet he offers not freedom from oppressive limits but anarchy — another cage. The pastoral place in "Là ci darem" is not *Figaro's* luminous metaphor for survival, but a cruel joke. The knowing little French gigue at the cadence seems to imply this, gently mocking the heartfelt accents of the simple pastorale.

"Batti, batti, o bel Masetto"

Mozart does not, however, remain cynical about the pastoral's promise; Arcadia's 6/8 meter is also the time signature of "Giovinette che fate all'amore," and thus Zerlina's proper music. The 2/4–6/8 coupling of "Là ci darem la mano" is deliberately repeated in Zerlina's next aria, the charming "Batti, batti, o bel Masetto" (I, 12); it is a companion piece to the love duet. "Batti, batti" takes place just before the first-act finale. Zerlina, in the act of stealing away with Don Giovanni, has been saved by the tempestuous entrance of Elvira who, crowing her warning, "Ah, fuggi il traditor," enfolds Zerlina under her wing and swoops off the stage. Alerted by Donna Elvira's conduct when she reappears, Donna Anna has identified Giovanni as her seducer, and has charged Don Ottavio with the burden of vengeance. Giovanni has given Leporello orders for the evening's *festa*. Now in Giovanni's garden, surrounded by other peasants resting here and there on "sofà d'erbe,"[24] Zerlina attempts to win Masetto back after her abortive defection. Her aria follows the outlines of "Là ci darem" — a key-area plan in 2/4 with expanded pastoral coda (see fig. 8 for a comparison of the layouts of the two pieces).

The opening section of "Batti, batti" is one of Mozart's most clever

Figure 8   The Key-Area Layouts of "Là ci darem" (I, 7), "Batti, batti" (I, 12), and "Vedrai carino" (II, 5)

	I	→	V	(X)	I	⌢	I	"X"	I
I,7 A major *Andante*	$\frac{2}{4}$ 1-18 D.Giov's song, Zer's dance	17-24 move to V	18-28 D.Giov's fanfare, Zer's sighs; no solid V cadence	29 V⁷	30-46 "stretto" version of 1-28	47-49 ascent to V⁵ on "Andiam"	$\frac{6}{8}$ 50-64 pastorale with musette	X contained in IV of French gigue —— PASTORALE	64-end French gigue
I,12 F major *Andante grazioso*	$\frac{2}{4}$ 1-16 gavotte	17-24 move to V	25-34 drive to solid cadence; contredanse scansion	35-36 V⁷	37-52 gavotte with *double*	52-60 V-I oscillation as question	$\frac{6}{8}$ 61-68 V-I oscillation as answer	69-78 IV phrase on "passar," delayed cadences —— PASTORALE	79-end cadences
II,5 C major *Grazioso*	$\frac{3}{8}$ 1-16 siciliano (6/8 scansion)	17-24 move to V	25-32 V cadences —— PASTORAL AFFECT	33 V⁷	34-48 mm.1-23, all on I	49-52 V⁷	$\frac{3}{8}$ 53-63 contredanse	63-85 "beating" on V⁷ and ii⁶	85-end orchestra postlude summing up aria

and playful applications of dance rhythms. His combination of the rhythms of a gavotte with a cello obbligato is at once a character portrait and a lascivious pun. Zerlina's appeal to Masetto here must be couched in a mixture of idioms. She is guilty, but in one sense has nothing to repent of; she refuses to beg, but at the same time knows that Masetto must be cajoled out of his stubbornness. Her solution is an arch parody of submission which is intensely sexual:

> Batti, batti, o bel Masetto,
> La tua povera Zerlina:
> Starò qui come agnellina
> Le tue botte ad aspettar.
>
> Lascèrò straziarmi il crine,
> Lascerò cavarmi gli occhi;
> E le care tue manine
> Lieta poi saprò baciar.[25]

The first line with its plosive consonants is onomatopoeic, and Mozart sets it to a musical equivalent — the gavotte. If we ignore for the moment the cello obbligato, the dance's clear, crisp beating carries the poet's intention over into the music:

The first two lines of the text have gavotte articulations, and the violins are given gavotte bowings. Although later in the section the outlines of the dance are blurred slightly, its clarity at the outset makes it the dominant conceit of the 2/4 section.

The *faux-naïf* gavotte with its sexual overtones smacks of the court and the courtesan. It is as if to mitigate this impression that Mozart introduces the cello obbligato, whose deep sonorities and legato bowings moderate the effect of the usual support of the gavotte, the Alberti bass; rather than picking out each beat distinctly, the obbligato smoothes and softens the mincing rhythms of the dance (ex. 11–9). The obbligato part is a superadded element, grafted onto the gavotte, and plumbing a deeper level of passion. Suggesting perhaps Zerlina's loyalty to and abiding affection for Masetto, which make her perverse little toy of a piece finally right-minded, it resembles the consciously symbolic accompaniments which Bach uses in some of his sacred arias to project the underlying affect of a text.

Like its counterpart in "Là ci darem la mano," the 2/4 section encompasses the dominant (mm. 16–34) and the return to the tonic (mm.

Example 11-9

37ff.), where the gavotte is ornamented as if with a French *double*. Then, as Zerlina utters aloud for Masetto's benefit what she has known all along would be true ("Ah, lo vedo, non hai core!"[26]), a series of phrases oscillating from V to I builds tension as a prelude to the 6/8. Rhythmic activity increases (the violins adopt thirty-second notes at the start, the cello for the last two measures) and the orchestra crescendos to the fermata (m. 60). The pastoral tune comes as a grateful release, not only to the local tension caused by this "bridge" section, but to the many-layered complexity of the gavotte-cum-obbligato. Coquettishness yields to heartfelt joy and promise, and if our judgment of its openness is qualified somewhat by memories of the obvious self-consciousness Zerlina displayed in the gavotte, this fails to dim the pastorale's luminous glow. The cello obbligato continues, but no longer seems superimposed; it is assimilated into the thinner texture of the 6/8 and supports, rather than belies, the structure of the meter. Zerlina's exuberant *passaggi* postponing cadences (mm. 72, 75) match it rhythmically note for note. The underlying harmony is of the utmost simplicity, consisting largely of more pendulum motion between V and I, the tonic now on a solid footing. The 6/8 section is almost entirely innocent of subdominants. There are two of them, only one of which is prominent: the goal of a brief falling-fifth sequence (mm. 68–70), it is the sole harmonic motion-away-from-the-tonic in the 6/8 section (ex. 11–10). The remaining twenty-nine measures serve as a capping cadence for the energy which this progression has generated.

Again the text of the pastoral 6/8 is pastoral in evocation:

> Pace, pace, o vita mia!
> In contento ed allegria
> Notte e dì vogliam passar.[27]

Example 11-10

Again the vision is of a pair of lovers at play in Arcadia, but its groves are much closer to home than were the distant vales of "Là ci darem la mano." In its simple harmonies and repetitive fa-la-la vocalisms the pastorale of "Batti, batti" resembles that of "Giovinette" more than that of "Là ci darem." Zerlina is indeed a pert baggage with some pretensions to attitudes beyond her station, and her seductive sophisticate's gavotte may suggest that she has picked up some polish from her brief association with the Don. But any new knowledge has only embellished her native intelligence: she has seen the truth of Elvira's warning with immediate good sense. The pastorale has before now been used in the opera twice, once as a stock vision of peasant life ("Giovinette"), and once as a stock evocation of idyllic love ("Là ci darem"). With wit and perception Zerlina makes love to Masetto in "Batti, batti" by conflating the two conventions and revivifying them. For the first time in the opera seduction gains a good name. Zerlina is a true-hearted seductress because, unlike Giovanni, she rejoices in acknowledging the necessary human limits of person, place, and time. Her promise to Masetto is a rustic garden, but peopled with real inhabitants. It speaks well for her, and it almost works.

"Vedrai, carino"

Masetto grudgingly begins to yield to Zerlina's charming incantation. "Guarda un po' come seppe/Questa strega sedurmi! siamo pure/I deboli di testa!"[28] he grumbles, feeling better about his capitulation to feminine warmth when he can call it invincible witchery. Were it not for Zerlina's fright at the sound of Giovanni's voice behind the scenes, all would be well between them. But Masetto isn't man enough to trust his own submission; afraid to be caught napping, he interprets Zerlina's fear for their safety as a sign of guilt, and forces her to the cruel test of presenting herself to Giovanni as if alone, in an isolated garden nook. Although she tries to hide, Giovanni finds her, and the trio is swept into the chain of events which leads to the dénouement of the first-act finale — the second attempted seduction of Zerlina. Later in act II the outraged Masetto pursues Giovanni with a band of peasants and meets the Don dressed as Leporello, who divides him from his companions,[29] tricks him of all his weapons, and, giving him a light drubbing, leaves him groaning in the dark. Zerlina arrives with a lantern, assesses his wounds as slight, and promises to nurse her patient back to health if "tu mi prometta/D'essere men geloso."[30] She offers him, in "Vedrai, carino," a salve for his wounds — a "certain balm" which she carries on her person. Enjoining him to feel its beating, she places his hand on her heart.[31]

The music of "Vedrai, carino" is pastoral again — a moderate 3/8, marked *Grazioso*. Like Zerlina's two previous arias it consists of two contrasting sections, although here the time signature remains unchanged throughout. Despite the uniformity of meters over the two sections, a decided rhythmic quickening — from eighth- to sixteenth-note motion — takes place, as in the other two arias, following a fermata after the return of the tonic, and the two sections have different affects (see fig. 8, p. 268, for a comparison of the three plans). The second section has the air of a gay triple contredanse, but its purpose is chiefly mimetic: the sole text of the section is "Sentilo battere,/Toccami qua," and its music features a direct representation of the beating heart. The winds and horns do most of the beating, first with repeated staccato chords (mm. 63–65, 69–71), and later (mm. 76–77) with the winds providing the harmonic "crisis" for the cadence, alternating ii^6 and vii^6_5 of ii, the only moment of real chromatic harmony in the aria. In the orchestral postlude which binds the material of the two sections together into a single closing period, the second section is represented almost entirely by a distillation of the "heartbeat music" (with the subdominant preceding, rather than following, the dominant so as to bring the aria to a cadence; ex. 11–11). Again the word "battere" has been given a musical portrayal, but the mimesis is direct — one might say "heartfelt" — and not a sophisticated pun on the nature of a dance rhythm as it is in "Batti, batti."

The first section of "Vedrai, carino," on the other hand, has a simple gravity which is new to Zerlina, and, indeed, to the opera. Despite its 3/8 meter, the section has the demeanor of a motion *alla siciliana*, and could be barred accordingly except for a few extra 3/8 measures at the

Example 11-11

Example 11-12

two major cadence points. The 3/8 meter must have been chosen for its appropriateness to the movement of the second section; it serves as a metrical lowest common denominator, and is not a true reflection of the first section's scansion. The bass and horns sculpt a broad harmonic phrase out of the opening eight measures: two measures of tonic are followed by a two-measure motion through the subdominant over a tonic pedal, and finally the startlingly evocative horn, almost unsupported, leaps down to the fifth degree (ex. 11–12). The opening five measures (two and one-half in the rebarred version of ex. 11–12) are harmonically static; the real action in the phrase is the motion to the I$^6_4$ appoggiatura to the dominant in measure 6 (m. 3 above). The horns suit the siciliano, the most lofty and noble of pastoral movements; later[32] the strings imitate courtly horn-fifth progressions in brief two-measure phrases.

Zerlina's words, while not contradicting the affect of the music of the first section, do not entirely account for its dignity. They are affectionate and teasingly intimate, almost maternal. The diminutives which she adds to her endearments — "Vedrai, car*ino*,/Se sei buon*ino* . . ."[33] — one might use with a child, and her playful tendering of her beating heart as a medicine is the kind of graphic game one might play with children. Coyly the seductress offers her maternal bosom here, in a style quite different from the erotic nimbus with which she surrounded the word "battere" in her first aria to Masetto. The entire text of "Vedrai, carino" could as well have been set to the playful contredanse rhythms of the second section. The siciliano is instead Zerlina's character shining through her words. Its innocently grave 6/8 is a transfiguration of the gay peasant gigue of "Giovinette," a sure revelation of the intelligence informing "Batti, batti." That her seduction does not attain the tragedy hinted at in the dark D-minor menace of the novice's music in the "Catalogue" aria is due to her own strength and resilience. In her native wit and unassuming dignity she resembles Susanna. She also shares with Susanna and with the Countess that peculiarly feminine intuition of the ways of the world beyond the workaday which is barred to the more circumscribed natures of Figaro and Masetto; her chosen place of refuge is, as it was with the *donne* of *Le nozze di Figaro*, the *mezzo carattere* pastorale.

Yet the two men are also very different in character, and this, along with the darker powers of evil afoot in *Don Giovanni*, distinguishes the two women's situations. Figaro is a figure who is fully worthy of Susanna, and his jealous suspicions distract his trust in her only momentarily. Masetto is Zerlina's proper lover, and she has the sense to know it, but it is a harsh truth of the opera that he is not up to her. She must adapt herself to him covertly, suppressing her deeper intelligence and grace. Recognizing after Elvira's warning how much she is in danger of losing, she must repair things quickly, using all her wiles, whereas Susanna can practice her gentle ruses on Figaro with some leisure and know that he will appreciate the delicacy of her skill. While Susanna at the close of act IV can wait for her own to return to her, Zerlina must return to her own after a daunting excursion into an alien world. The ugliness of the brush with Giovanni will always remain part of the reason for her return. Given the shortcomings of Masetto and the shadow of the Don, Zerlina's solution is not the luminous reunion of equals in an inviolable garden which Susanna effects, but a shaky and somewhat disturbing compromise made with the acceptance of lowered expectations and the knowledge of the everpresent threat of the void. Wit and resilience are not rewarded with plenty in *Don Giovanni*; they are merely the equipment necessary if one is to survive.

CHAPTER TWELVE

The Two Finales

The great finales to acts I and II of *Don Giovanni* bear a peculiar resemblance to one another. They differ from the finales of *Le nozze di Figaro*, in which, following the usual *buffa* habit, a complex series of events prior to the finale has sown the seed for its successive moments of confrontation, revelation and triumph, further revelation and despair (in the finale to act II; the sequence is reversed in the fourth-act finale, of course, so that the heroes' triumph can come last). Any formal similarities between *Figaro's* two grand finales would seem to be merely casual; our interest is in how each finale untangles a particular imbroglio whose patient preparation we have followed over the course of two acts. In *Don Giovanni*, on the other hand, the first-act finale trumps up and untangles its own imbroglio, and not an especially complex one at that; its events are as unnecessary to the "plot line" as are any of the other ad-lib episodes sandwiched in between the opening scene and the end of act II. Neither is the finale to act II a carefully primed comic trap set to be sprung: it fulfills a promise made even by the D minor music of the overture, it is prepared for in moral climate at least by the opening scene of act I, and it is occasioned only by a single aria late in act II ("O statua gentilissima," II, 9), where Giovanni and Leporello meet the statue in the cemetery and extend it the invitation to dine. It depends for its effect on the impact of one prodigiously dramatic event and not, as is so often the rule with finales, on our delight in the smooth workings of a well-oiled machine.

The finales of *Don Giovanni* are both less and more than their counterparts in *Le nozze di Figaro*: they are less of a piece with the action of the

Figure 9 The Scheme of the Finale to Act I

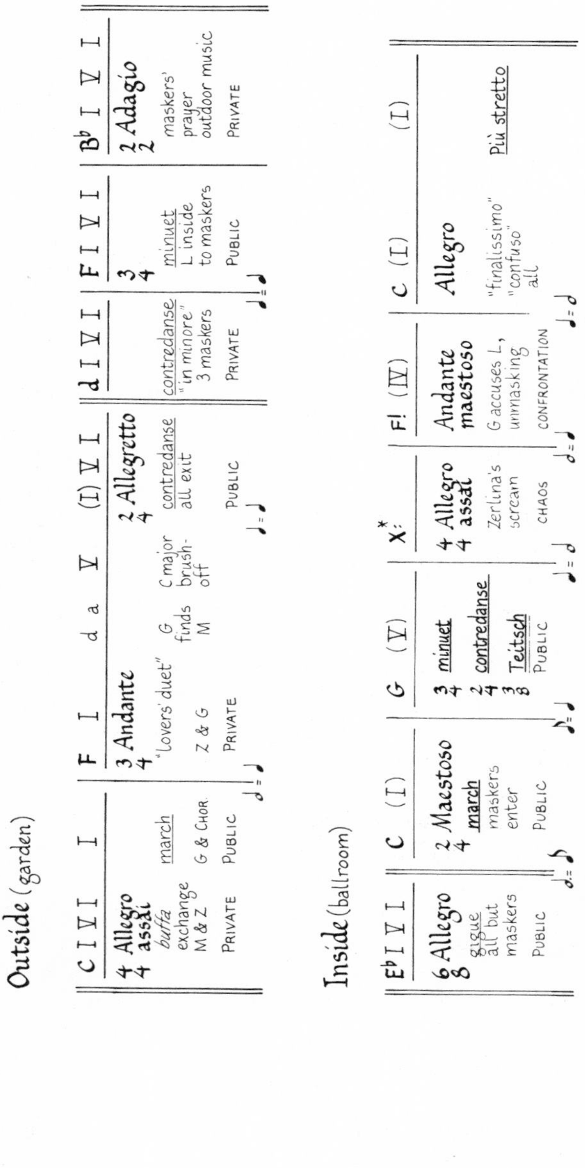

Outside (garden)

C IV I	I	F I	d a	V	(I) VI	d I V I	F I V I	Bb I V I
4/4 Allegro assai	march	3/4 Andante			2/4 Allegretto	contredanse "in minore"	3/4	2/2 Adagio
buffa exchange M & Z	G & Chor	"lovers' duet" Z & G	G finds M	C major brush-off	contredanse all exit	3 maskers	minuet L inside to maskers	maskers' prayer outdoor music
PRIVATE	PUBLIC	PRIVATE			PUBLIC	PRIVATE	PUBLIC	PRIVATE

Inside (ballroom)

Eb I V I	C (I)	G (V)	X*:	F# (IV)	c (I)	(I)
6/8 Allegro	2/4 Maestoso march	3/4 minuet, 2/4 contredanse, 3/8 Teitsch	4/4 Allegro assai	Andante maestoso	Allegro	Più stretto
gigue all but maskers	maskers enter		Zerlina's scream	G accuses L, unmasking	"finalissimo" "confuso" all	
PUBLIC	PUBLIC	PUBLIC	CHAOS	CONFRONTATION		

* See Ex. 12·7, p.

entire work, but in their detachment they bear a more formal and figurative relation to the whole. Furthermore, they beg comparison with one another, and reveal striking similarities in music and in plot. Both have a background of social life, manners, and conviviality, and include pieces of "occasional" music; in both Giovanni makes a toast. Both include a "picture" of the society in microcosm. Both highlight one woman in her relation to Giovanni, and in each that woman's screams shatter apparent tranquility to hasten the dénouement. Both involve a portentous modulation apparently to D minor, followed by the sudden substitution for the expected tonic of a surprise F major, and for the expected figure (the Don in the first and the statue in the second), Leporello, the doppelgänger. The crucial difference between the two finales is that in the first one nothing happens — the aristocrats are impotent and their prey reappears at the beginning of act II merrily unaffected — while the finale to act II finishes him off properly. In the first finale the shimmering mirror which reflects the social order is shattered, in the second the order is painstakingly rebuilt, but in both the theme is the same — the confrontation of the established community of men with a man who cannot acknowledge its limits.

The Finale to Act I: Structure and Styles

The first-act finale is a study in contrasts — of the public with the private, the formal with the intimate, the dark garden with the glittering ballroom. At first its numbers alternate between public and private moments, and then, as the climax approaches, private distress is suppressed beneath a calm public surface, which is eventually shattered by Zerlina's scream. In order to distinguish the public moments from the private, the public are always cast as pieces of "occasional" music — a dance or a march — while the provenance of the gestures of the intimate scenes is more ambiguous.

The finale begins its careful scheme (see fig. 9) with a private moment of easy *buffa* style in duple meter and C major, between Zerlina and Masetto. Zerlina is trying to convince her lover of the threat Giovanni poses to his safety; Masetto's suspicions prevail instead, and he forces Zerlina to remain visible while he slips into a hidden niche to see what she and the Don will do. Giovanni enters accompanied by his servants and a blaze of lights and music, to invite the peasants inside (m. 50). A march with horns, trumpets, and timpani (the latter used for the first time since the overture) marks the cavalier's entrance with full panoply, and serves as an extended coda for the entire C-major key-area movement. When the servants and live music exit, Zerlina tries to hide among some trees. The mood changes with a modulation to the shadowy flat key of F major and a new meter — a gentle 3/4 which is not quite a minuet, not a waltz (m. 92). Again the nonlovers' voices entwine in lovers' music, for a first key area in the tonic (ex. 12–1). Giovanni's surprise in discovering Masetto in the garden moves the piece from its gentle F major to the dominants first of D and then of A minor — "trouble music" with syncopated pedals and augmented sixths (mm. 124, 127). Recovering his composure Giovanni brushes off the minor mode with a drop from the E major triad (V of A minor) to C major — the same sudden movement between third-related triads as will occur in the second-act trio (II, 2; see pp. 250–51). Again Giovanni is quoting (there he will draw from his repertoire of love songs, while here he throws Masetto's fatuous assurance about Zerlina [see pp. 260 and 375 n. 9] back in his face); again the music "hardens" into a perceptible shape (there the tune of the love song, here a triple contredanse with flippant frills tossed between strings and flutes; ex. 12–2). With great presence of mind Giovanni has put on his public face, and Masetto can only answer (after a deceptive cadence, m. 136), parroting Giovanni's cadential phrase "un poco ironico,"[1] "Capisco, sì, Signore."

Unlike his lovesong parenthesis, which begins the X-section of "Ah, taci," Giovanni's clean C major here turns out to be the proper key, the dominant for the second key area. From offstage comes the sound of a small dance band (m. 140) playing a real contredanse in 2/4. The musicians are in the middle of the dance; playing the end of an F-major tonic

Example 12-1

Example 12-2

Example 12-3

period, they move to C for a second-key-area cadence (ex. 12–3). Giovanni calls on the pair to follow him toward the sound. Relieved at a way out of a touchy situation, all three exit to the gay rhythms of the contredanse, Masetto and Zerlina singing with forced cheerfulness:

> Sì, sì, facciamo core,
> Ed a ballar con gli altri
> Andiamo tutti e tre.[2]

The distant contredanse ("sopra il teatro, da lontano"[3]) provides both the area of dominant tension and the tonic return for the F-major key-area plan. The first large section of the finale has consisted of two broad key-area layouts each containing a private and a public moment, closed the one by a march and the other by a contredanse, and all taking place outside.

With the next section our attention turns from the lowborn lovers to the high, and from flirtation with D minor to serious absorption in it. The maskers appear in the garden, F slips into its relative minor D, and the full orchestra takes up a suave *minore* version of the contredanse (the tempo shouldn't change). The maskers express themselves with stiff protocol, one after the other, in a brief movement consisting of three strains. Characteristically, Donna Elvira speaks first, in a D-minor period, encouraging her new friends to persevere in their search for the guilty Don. In a strain which ends on the dominant Don Ottavio seconds her, trying to hearten Donna Anna, who expresses doubts about the enterprise, her music bringing the section back to the tonic with a repeated cadential phrase.

It is period structure which is the oddity in this *minore* interlude. Although there is a mechanical quality about the music of the three maskers, and about the way the three succeed one another each taking a strain, only five of the ten phrases actually consist of the normal four measures. The others contain carefully concealed extensions which give a saving breadth to the clipped dance periods. Don Ottavio and Donna Elvira have nine-measure phrases articulated 2+2+2+3, while Donna Anna's cadential phrases find their extension at the beginning, in a pa-

thetic accent which stresses the word *temo* ("I fear"); they end with regular four-measure phrases for cadential energy. These hidden extensions — just slight distensions in the beginning or end of a phrase —
contribute weight and drama to the maskers' music without detracting
from its dancelike quality. Although the moment is private, the maskers
are caught up in the fevered atmosphere of the public and social part of
the finale; the contredanse *in minore* reflects both their agitation and its
cause at the same time.

   This collection of movements could in fact be seen to constitute a
small dance suite. Straightaway the strains of yet another dance pene-
trate; after what amounts to a *riverenza*, the band, back in F major
again, strikes up the familiar "minuet from *Don Giovanni*" (see ex. 2–2,
p. 34), the quintessence of nobility with its measured tread. Now the
interior and formal intrude on the exterior and intimate: Leporello,
having been instructed by Giovanni to invite the maskers in, opens a
window to issue his invitation, and the maskers accept sedately. The
invitation and acceptance transpire over four strains of the minuet —
two reprises of eight bars each, both repeated. Leporello's aside as he
closes the window explains the intent of Giovanni's invitation: "L'amico
anche su quelle/Prova farà d'amor."[4]

   The shutting of the window encloses the maskers back in their intimacy outside. Drawing together again they address a prayer to heaven
in a solemn *alla breve* (m. 251). The strings drop out, and the voices in-
tertwine in motet style against a background of winds, Donna Anna's
supplicatory coloratura occasionally rising above the other voices in serene slow motion. The out-of-doors (from the cassation-style accompaniment) and the ecclesiastical are strangely bound in this intimate
moment, emphasizing both the isolation and the earnestness of the trio.
It is sublime music, and has its comic side only because we know the
maskers, having had occasion before to judge their earnestness as a stiff
and complacent credulity. Their exit brings to a close a second large
section, of three movements — two intimate exchanges surrounding a
formal dance. These two sections taken together comprise the first half
of the finale, which takes place entirely out-of-doors.

   With scene xx (m. 273) we finally enter the brightly lit ballroom,
where an E-flat gigue tries to recapture the simple merriment of "Giovinette." Inside the private must yield to the public; the anxieties of the
several characters, pent up at first, finally emerge as asides in distracted
counterpoint to the gay surfaces of the gigue. Giovanni and Leporello
give cheerful orders to their peasant guests, enjoining the "vezzose
ragazze" and "bei giovinotti"[5] to make merry. While Giovanni flirts
with Zerlina (on the dominant of E-flat) and Leporello imitates him
with other peasant girls, Masetto growls threats, and Zerlina brings the

Example 12-4

tonic back with the observation that "Quel Masetto mi par stralunato: /Brutto, brutto si fa quest'affar."[6] All the participants recognize the danger to themselves in the gigue's tone of gay abandon. They give voice to their worries in the return, a considerable consolation of the opening, with Zerlina singing descant to the men's ruminations while the orchestra takes up the gigue tune of the original second key area (ex. 12–4). Zerlina's gay lyric scales with their overtones of fever and foreboding catch in this one brief snatch of tune the essence of the party music of *La Traviata*.

With the entrance of the maskers the mood turns *Maestoso* (the 6/8 ♩. roughly equals ♪ in 2/4), the key slips back to the C major of the opening, and the trumpets and timpani return for a dignified processional (m. 360). After a proper *riverenza* Leporello, using the ceremonious language of a host and by now almost indistinguishable, musically, from his master, invites the maskers to step forward.[7] Giovanni seconds his servant with the toast, "È aperto a tutti quanti:/Viva la libertà!"[8] The maskers, thanking him for the welcome ("Siam grati a tanti segni di generosità"[9]), then join with Leporello and Giovanni in the toast. After this anacreontic prelude Giovanni signals for the dancing to begin again, and orchestra 1 (the first of three orchestras gathered on stage) strikes up the stately minuet, now in G major (m. 406). Don Ottavio and Donna Anna are, properly, the only dancers to its aristocratic rhythms, Anna faltering momentarily when Elvira points Zerlina out to her. The minuet plays on mechanically, each eight-measure reprise repeated. When the whole begins again (to be taken this time without repetitions), orchestra 2 enters with a 2/4 contredanse (m. 438), and Giovanni leads Zerlina onto the floor, leaving Leporello to struggle with the recalcitrant Masetto. He finds a bizarre solution to the problem,

Figure 10 The Kaleidoscope of Dances, I, 13, 406–67

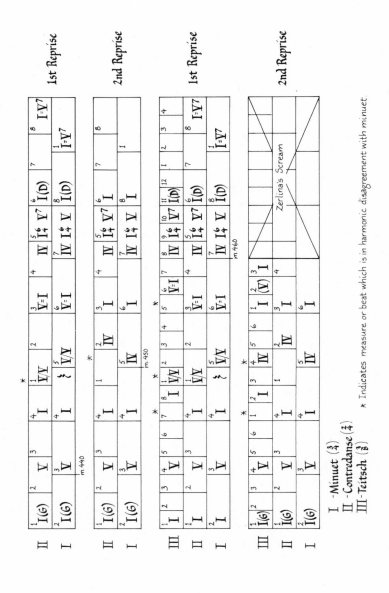

I - Minuet ($\frac{3}{4}$)
II - Contredanse ($\frac{2}{4}$)
III - Teitsch ($\frac{3}{8}$)

★ Indicates measure or beat which is in harmonic disagreement with minuet.

forcing Masetto to dance with him to the music of a Teitsch (a corruption of *Deutsch* — in other words, a "German" or allemande). The rough peasant dance in 3/8 starts up just as the minuet is beginning its third full repetition (m. 455). At the same moment Giovanni leads Zerlina off the stage, "conducendola via quasi per forza,"[10] and Zerlina, speaking for the first time since the dancing began, cries "Oh, numi! son tradita! . . ."[11] Leporello hastens off, leaving the stage to Masetto and the aristocrats, the latter declaring primly to the tune of the second reprise of their minuet that Giovanni is falling into their trap. They are as hypnotized by the relentless stateliness of the dance; their self-congratulation is interrupted rudely by Zerlina's scream — "Gente! . . . Aiuto! . . . Aiuto, gente!"[12]

The famous tour de force of the three-dance ballroom scene merits a digression; it is the occasion of much comment as a landmark of the opera, but no one has actually troubled to point out the handful of simple devices which make the gimmick work.[13] For a man like Mozart, ceaselessly engaged in play with elements, whether numbers, letters, or notes, the "trick" was hardly a difficult one to bring off. Since Classic meters in their simplicity are all factors of twelve or, leaving aside 4/4, of six, in dances of 3/4, 2/4, and 3/8 two measures of the first will equal three of the second and six of the last. Thus three dances in different meters can be dovetailed, if one allows some necessary damage to periodic symmetry. Indeed, the dances in the scene only appear to be separate and equal conceptions: the eight-measure minuet period is set as the standard for one reprise and the other two dances conform themselves to its lengths and harmonies. The only true cacophony permitted in the kaleidoscope of dances should more properly be termed "cacorhythmy"; harmonic disagreement among the dances occurs rarely, seven times to be exact (see the beats with asterisks in fig. 10), and never for more than one-third of a minuet measure, or one quarter note. In all but one of the seven harmonic variances the dissonance is minimized either by a convenient rest in the minuet part (mm. 441, 457), or by the reduction of one of the two dissonant triads to a tone it holds in common with the other (mm. 450, 459, 465, 466).[14] The only actual dissonance occurs on the first beat of measure 457, where the Teitsch rests with a full dominant triad for one minuet beat after the other two dances have moved on to the tonic; it is hardly conspicuous.

The dances increase in rhythmic crudity the more they are forced to conform to previously established period structures. The minuet, since it is the first dance to be played, is a paradigmatic dance form consisting of an eight-measure reprise moving to the dominant and another one moving back (through the subdominant) to the tonic; each reprise is divided symmetrically four-plus-four, and rhyming cadences occur in measures 7–8 and 15–16. The contredanse is forced to a twelve-measure reprise (divided four-plus-eight) in order to cadence in concert with the minuet, it must move through the cadential IV-I$^6_4$-V-I formula at the same time and pace as the minuet, and it is forced to one and one-half measures of tonic doodling at the end of each reprise in order to wait for the more sedate minuet to catch up (ex. 12–5). (Both contredanse and Teitsch begin on the second minuet measure so as not to have to dwell on the tonic at the start of their periods for three, and in the case of the Teitsch six, long measures.) The Teitsch must do most of the compromising. It needs a reprise of twenty-four measures in order to cadence at the same time as the minuet and contredanse. It is also forced to five measures of temporizing on the tonic before its second reprise can begin. Its period structure barely makes sense, at times conforming to the measure of the contredanse (with a first reprise grouped principally, except for the first few measures, in units of two, or one contredanse measure), at times to the minuet (with a second reprise grouped in units of three, or one minuet measure; ex. 12–6). It is a relief when the Teitsch is cut off before it can straggle to its appointed end. Of course the progressive rhythmic awkwardness of the dances suits their ranking in the social scale; the clumsy Teitsch is especially appropriate to the grotesque notion of the coupling of Leporello and Masetto, a pair of dancing bears. The opportunity to imitate some of the badly patched-together dance music he had heard played by humble town bands in village squares must have afforded Mozart considerable amusement.

The C-major processional and toast and the G-major ballroom scene combine to constitute the "exposition" of a broad key-area layout.

Example 12-5

Example 12-6

Example 12-7

Rhythmic tension increases across the second key area as the beat is
further subdivided: the collective pulse of the scene quickens with the
entrance of each new dance, building to a peak of rhythmic intensity
with the frequent sixteenth-note figures in the Teitsch. Zerlina's scream
initiates the X-section, precipitating harmonic and rhythmic chaos. Her
screams can be heard in several keys as she moves behind the scenes
from one side of the stage to the other (ex. 12–7). Meanwhile, the rest
of the characters mill around on stage trying to find the proper door.
Throwing it open on a dramatic V[7] of D minor (mm. 491–98), they be-
hold Giovanni thrusting Leporello forth by the scruff of the neck as the
culprit, to the accompaniment of a surprise F major, the *buffa* key (F
also provides the touch of subdominant often found in finales as a
springboard back to the tonic). The maskers unmask, protesting the
uselessness of his trying to deceive them, and Zerlina sings with clipped
satisfaction "Tutto, tutto già si sa."[15] The *finalissimo* takes up in C major,
with Giovanni singing the key word *confusa*[16] in the usual number of
confused and pell-mell settings. Approaching the *Più stretto* (m. 623), he
pulls himself together to proclaim, as we knew he must:

Ma non manca in me coraggio:
Non mi perdo o mi confondo.
Se cadesse ancora il mondo
Nulla mai temer mi fa! [17]

The Finale to Act I: Libertine and Libertà

In his aria just before the first-act finale Giovanni cries:

Senza alcun ordine
La danza sia:
Chi'l minuetto,
Chi la follia,
Chi l'alemanna
Farai ballar. [18]

The three-dance ballroom scene explains *senza ordine* as "all at once." *Minuetto*, *follia* (actually a *contradanza* [19]), and *alemanna* are jumbled together in a surreal kaleidoscopic landscape of society. This picture of the social cosmos is a harsh and reductionist one — the bemused impotence of the aristocracy, the raw simplicity of the peasant class, and, occupying the center, which in the social hierarchy of *Le nozze di Figaro* is the locus for images of a *mezzo carattere* utopia, a real class that is no class and is thus a threat to all proper orders; it is figured by the merry but limitless contredanse of the bourgeoisie, and the central figure to dance it is Don Giovanni, or No-Man. The threat posed by the middle is demonstrated by the fact that only there does posture explode into action: Zerlina's scream shatters the hypnotic *speculum mundi* stretching into infinity in neat eight-measure periods, and returns us to the more familiar realm of deeds and consequences. But the inhabitants of that world are powerless to act, even once shaken awake. F major is the subdominant of C (the key of the finale as a whole) here, and not the relative major of the punitive D minor, as it will be in the second-act finale. And the bright and neutral key of C major is itself an indication of the inconsequence of the events in this finale: the first is merely a rehearsal for the second, the near-sacrifice of Zerlina is preparation for Elvira's real immolation, and the confrontation between the libertine and humankind is a mere prelude to the surer, swifter visitation of divine wrath.

Giovanni's two toasts constitute another point of contact between the two finales. The aristocrats choose to ignore all but the conventional implications of "Viva la libertà," and respond to their host's "liberality" with the proper forms of *politesse*. Writers on the opera have inevitably treated those words as one more message in the crypto-language of political rebellion which the daring da Ponte and Mozart so carefully concealed in the apparently innocent surfaces of their works. But if this is the case, Mozart's forecast for human freedom is a bleak and frightening one, for Giovanni's toast in the second-act finale tells the banal truth about his toast in the first:

> Vivan le femmine!
> Viva il buon vino!
> Sostegno e gloria
> D'umanità! [20]

"Liberty" is libertinage, "human freedom" the anarchy of individual appetite. The liberty Giovanni intends is *senza ordine*: the Don gives a topsy-turvy party to which he invites only peasants, later including another Don purely as an afterthought, because his attendant women look to be attractive possibilities. "È aperto a tutti quanti:/Viva la libertà." It is important that the Don be pictured as a host, and that his final downfall stem from an invitation to dinner. This detail helps to explain the anomaly in Mozart's particular portrait of a libertine. Unlike the proud and preaching figures drawn by Laclos and the Marquis de Sade, Mozart's libertine is all blind and obsessive appetite, uncalculating and inarticulate, making no distinctions of kind or of class in pleasure. Furthermore, his licentiousness may think itself anarchic, may cry for things *senza ordine*, but it dwells most securely as a parasite on conventions and forms. Giovanni does not see himself as a soldier in the war against repressive institutions, as do so many of the characters in de Sade's writings; he cannot see himself at all. Being a nonperson, dwelling in a moral no-man's-land, he has to adopt the appearances of other customs, other ways. Although he moves through them with cool disassociation, he needs their reflected brilliance. When the doppelgänger Leporello mimics his master in forms of *politesse* his actions burlesque those forms and show their meaningless convenience for the Don. The vitality and spirit which have caused some to see Giovanni as hero, as life force, even as pure Intellect itself, are in reality relentless instinct and a talent for mimicry. Unlike the god Proteus, who, if his captor was patient, would at last assume his proper shape, Giovanni cannot, for he does not have one. A master of the forms, he is also radically dependent on them, for without them he would be invisible.

The Finale to Act II

The Prelude to the Ombra *Music*

The second-act finale opens with more of the social music which forms such a brilliant part of the finale to the first act. A dining room prepared for a feast, tapers lit, musicians on stage — the scene is set for more of the libertine's revels. The first four pieces of the finale comprise a little suite: a gigue (m. 47) and a minuet crossed with a hunting topic (m. 118) are framed by two courtly marches — appropriate *Tafelmusik* for a nobleman's banquet. The only thing missing is the guests. This finale reduces the dissolute life to a figurative onanism — Don Giovanni playing host to himself. His libertine's "philosophy" is summed up in the tawdry maxim "Giacchè spendo i miei danari,/Io mi voglio divertir."[21] For two hundred measures he amuses himself at table by bullying Leporello, and seems to derive no less pleasure from this mean pursuit than he has from his attempted seductions.

Mozart chose for the background music pieces from three well-known operas: Martin y Soler's *Una cosa rara* (the work which drove *Figaro* off the Viennese stage), Sarti's *I litiganti*, and *Figaro* itself. He must have wanted three pieces to balance the trio of dances in the first-act finale (although they occur at an earlier moment in the harmonic arch, since the D-minor *ombra* music must dominate the second finale). He had the famous wind players of Prague at his disposal, and thought to put them to work as a wind band playing *Tafelmusik* on stage; the score hardly taxes their abilities until the third number, an arrangement of "Non più andrai," Figaro's affectionately teasing celebration of Cherubino and *gloria militar* which ends act I of *Figaro*.

The gigue from *Una cosa rara* closes Martin's first-act finale. It is a song of praise for Queen Isabella (like *Figaro* and *Don Giovanni* the opera is set in Spain), giving thanks for the resolution of an imbroglio which in truth will not be fully resolved until the opera's close:

> O quanto un sì bel giubilo,
> O quanto alletta e piace.
> . . . .
> Rendiamo grazie al core
> Di Vostra Maestà.[22]

Taken at a steady pace with full orchestra, it can be rather more dignified a piece than appears here (ex. 12–8). Mozart perhaps enjoyed showing up his rival: bereft of chorus and orchestra the singsong nature of the piece is apparent, and for its lofty vocabulary of rejoicing Mozart substitutes the stage business of low comedy:

Example 12-8

Example 12-9

Ah, che barbaro appetito!
Che bocconi da gigante!
Mi par proprio di svenir.[23]

Thus Leporello, Harlequin to the hilt. When Giovanni asks his opinion of the piece, Leporello the music critic replies, "È conforme al vostro merto,"[24] playing it safe, but certainly intending no compliment either to his master or to the music. It is significant that Leporello is in each case the one to notice and comment on the wind band's selections, while Giovanni is intent on consuming food and drink.

The little hunting minuet from Sarti's *Fra i due litiganti il terzo gode* (first performed in Milan in 1782 and later very popular in Vienna) is another aria of some (comic) pretensions which has been reduced by the wind-band orchestration to a hurdy-gurdy tune (ex. 12–9). Mozart did considerable recomposing, reducing a composite aria of over one hundred measures, with the return to the tonic in a different meter (4/4), to a short and neatly rounded-off two-reprise form in 3/4 alone. Part of the transition to the second key area was also omitted and one of the motives thus excised transferred to the close for a tonic codetta (mm. 150–57). In the original text of the aria a lover gloats over a romantic triumph, describing his rival as doomed to go about the city "bleating like a lamb to the slaughter," while he himself will promenade with his beloved and enjoy hearing passersby praise them as the perfect couple.[25] Instead of the words "Viva la sposa" Giovanni sings "Eccellente marzimino" (*marzimino* is a wine from Trentino, da Ponte's home district). The substitution is pointed and apt: the two come to the same thing for Giovanni, who knows his women as he knows his wine.

Mozart seems to have chosen the pieces more in play than to make a particular point. The title of the Sarti piece, "Come un agnello che va al macello," may have been intended to look forward to Elvira's tempestuous arrival: the description well suits the innocent self-sacrifice of her passionate entry. "Non più andrai" was probably included in part as a graceful compliment to Prague, the city which commissioned *Don Giovanni* because

Example 12-10

here they talk about nothing but 'Figaro.' Nothing is played, sung or
whistled but 'Figaro.' No opera is drawing but 'Figaro.' Nothing,
nothing but 'Figaro.'[26]

Leporello restricts his remarks this time to a dry "Questa poi la conosco
pur troppo,"[27] a charming mixture of embarrassed modesty and pro-
prietary pride on the composer's part.[28] The three quoted works have in
common a recent popularity; they would be recognized without Leporello's identifications. In addition to being very jolly pieces, appropriate
as occasional music for revels, they are also all encomiums touched in
some way by irony, and thus are in subliminal tune with the spirit of the
moment.

During the playing of "Non più andrai" Giovanni tricks Leporello
into revealing that he has snatched a piece of pheasant from Giovanni's
plate. Rather than call his servant down straightaway, he worries him as
a dog might a bone, asking him first with apparent unconcern to speak
up clearly, and then to whistle a tune (mm. 171–86). To hide his mouth-
ful Leporello pleads a head cold, but finally confesses his theft (over the
return of the opening material of "Non più andrai," mm. 188ff). His excuse, an adroit aping of polite dinner-table compliments, is the excellence of Don Giovanni's cook: "Si eccellente è il vostro cuoco/Che lo
volli anch'io provar."[29] His words are set rather clumsily to the famous
music, pointing up the lameness of the excuse and offering a prosaic
contrast to Figaro's charming metaphor of the "farfallone amoroso,
notte e giorno d'intorno girando" (ex. 12–10). The scene from beginning to end has the air of a *commedia dell' arte* improvisation,[30] with the
background music setting the pace and providing the structure for an
ad lib action. It provides us with a glimpse of "Don Giovanni at home,"
framing a seemingly random moment in his life — a kind of vision opera
is not often given to, since lulls in the action are usually for the purpose
of emotional stock-taking — and in the process engrosses us in the
lowest style of comedy, fueled by cruelty and evasion, and using as
stage business the homeliest details of ordinary life, chianti and catarrh

and popular songs. Giovanni's acme may be his audacious refusal to have fear in the face of divine retribution; his nadir is certainly here in the same finale, where his obsession is reduced to a kind of automatic masturbation.

Although the opening scene is unattractive in many aspects, it is nevertheless funny, and once more its crude humor undermines the seriousness of an action of Elvira's. Da Ponte, alive to the comic possibilities in the contrast, underlines it by putting the same word in everyone's mouth. Leporello wants to *test* (*provar*) Giovanni's cook; Elvira wants to put her love for Giovanni one last time to the *test* (*prova*). The words occur a measure apart (mm. 199–200, 202), and as usual the absurd has the edge over the sublime. Elvira is tarred with the *buffa* brush; she appears a *commedia* hysteric, full of ungainly despair. She exits after her B-flat music,[31] discovers the statue, and returns screaming across the stage. Her scream is the chromatically heightened counterpart of Zerlina's in the first-act finale, even to the use of the same A-flat, now as the top note of a darker chord, a vii^7 of C minor.[32] It moves the music from B-flat major to C minor, with an excited augmented sixth from Don Giovanni and Leporello to set the question "Che grido è questo mai!"[33] Leporello goes to investigate as ordered, and a second scream on a diminished seventh (of D minor) is heard offstage. Giovanni, now more agitated, cries with unconscious aptness "Che grido indiavolato!/Leporello, che cos'è?"[34] over a second series of augmented sixths, which properly expand to dominants, all of D minor. Expecting the long-promised doom of D minor, we get instead with the next downbeat, *Molto allegro* and *alla breve*, D's relative major, and Leporello, not the statue. This transition scene is a parody of the one in the first-act finale. Whereas there Zerlina screamed several times, here the screams are divided between Donna Elvira and Leporello, and where before Giovanni dragged forth Leporello at the surprise appearance of his *buffa* key, F major, to answer the D-minor dominants of the company, here at the same confrontation of D minor and F major Leporello enters self-propelled, by his fear of the specter who wants to attend the feast (ex. 12–11). *In extremis* the doppelgänger can only defer doom, not

Example 12-11

deflect it. His brief F-major interlude — the chromatic patter of fear
and trembling — only piques the Don's curiosity, ensuring that he will
face out the danger, whatever it may be.

The Ombra Music: Principles

The 169 measures of music in which the rake meets his final punishment — from the two shattering seventh chords with trombone which
announce the entrance of the Commendatore to the equally shattering
major triad at which Don Giovanni descends to hell — comprise the dramatic core of the opera; they also contain some of the richest and dens-
est music of Mozart's *oeuvre*. Their impact is assured from the very start,
both because the two chords introduce familiar music — the brooding
dotted rhythms in D minor which opened the opera, as the slow introduction to the overture — and because the special sound of the trombones has been added to those measures, bringing to their menace a
clearer significance. The trombones, which are heard first in the cemetery scene (II, xi) accompanying the shade of the Commendatore, are
the most solemn of eighteenth-century instruments. Although they
were instruments of the church, out of place in the usual eighteenth-
century opera orchestra, they had been used since the beginnings of
opera in the early seventeenth century to accompany spectral voices,
solo or choral, in *ombra* scenes. There is a direct line in this respect from
the infernal scene in the *Orfeo* of Monteverdi to the one in the *Orfeo* of
Gluck, and Gluck's *Alceste* and Mozart's *Idomeneo* also use trombones
solely for the accompaniment of the oracular voice. Thus their appearance here would not have seemed unusual to the contemporary opera audience, but would have informed it of the immediate presence on
the scene of a supernatural power.

Along with the three-dance ballroom scene of the first-act finale, the
ombra music is a prime candidate for demystification. Complete and
thorough analyses of it are rare, which is surprising considering the
special significance of the section both to the drama and to lovers of and
writers about the opera. Loose talk about certain aspects of the scene —
about the so-called fate scales and the daemonic, about the saturation of
chromaticism and dissonance, even about "tone rows" (the Commendatore could be said, if one wished, to sing an incomplete row, ten out
of the twelve chromatic notes, in mm. 454–61) — casts a veil of the daemonic about the composition of the work itself, and obscures Mozart's
more palpable and significant musical accomplishment. For the subliminal ordering of what must appear to be an unbridled and chaotic climax — Armageddon forged into an operatic ensemble — he devised a
new musical vehicle. Fusing key-area procedure with the old-fashioned
fantasy style, he invented a hybrid structure which has the advantage of

retaining the taut forensic drama of the key-area layout while introducing *via* the fantasy the maximum local mystery and uncertainty of tonal direction. While the two-part key-area scheme provides a firm harmonic underpinning for the section, the *galant* periodic phrases which usually provide at least a norm for rhythmic action in large key-area movements are absent, except at major cadence points. In their place Mozart uses seemingly diffuse and wandering fantasy material, gestures which are more suited to a slow introduction than to the main body of a "sonata-form" movement. Of course the same material is also found in its proper place, in the slow introduction to the overture of the opera, which is the music of the *ombra* section's first key area and part of its second. Unfortunately, the stress usually laid on the fact that Mozart transported this material from the overture into the body of the opera[35] — a practice which, although infrequent, was by no means unheard of in eighteenth-century music — prevents us from appreciating the far more ingenious permutation of the familiar which Mozart works in the *ombra* scene by transporting the same musical material from one genre to another. The full appropriateness of the fantasy style to the preludial function of the slow introduction, here and elsewhere in the the works of both Haydn and Mozart, might seem to be a sufficient demonstration of its inappropriateness to the broad symphonic movement which this finale requires for a proper close; the qualities suitable to introductory material are generally of a different nature from those which prevail in a fully worked-out sonata movement. Yet, as it turns out, only the unorthodox combination of *galant* harmonic procedure with gestures drawn from an antique and elevated style could generate the air of gravity and mystery necessary to the confrontation of Don Giovanni with his spectral visitor.

To control the fantasy material in the *ombra* music Mozart chooses one particular compositional technique — elaboration in the upper parts against a slow-moving, stepwise bass line. Scales are as crucial to the structural level of the fantasy as they are to the ornamental (where they are most strikingly represented by those famous "fate scales" which in two passages — mm. 462–69 and 479–81 — adorn the Commendatore's line). If the entire bass line of the section is reduced to its essential notes, a boldly simple organizing principle is laid bare (see fig. 11). One single type of motion — scalar, mostly ascending, sometimes chromatic but as often purely diatonic, usually long-lined, but sometimes in brief fragments — leads away from stable areas of strong tonal definition into a dramatic obscurity, and then fetches up again suddenly at the proper tonal place.

Although the choice of scale material to project areas of tonal confusion may seem at first paradoxical, it is actually the inherent logic of

Figure 11 The Skeleton of the D-Minor Music in the Second-Act Finale

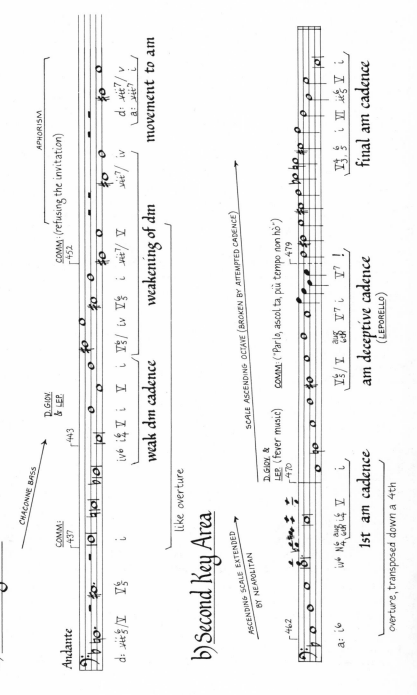

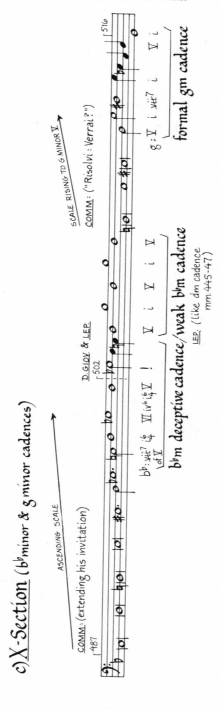

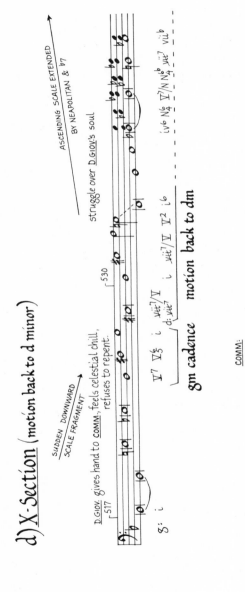

e) Return

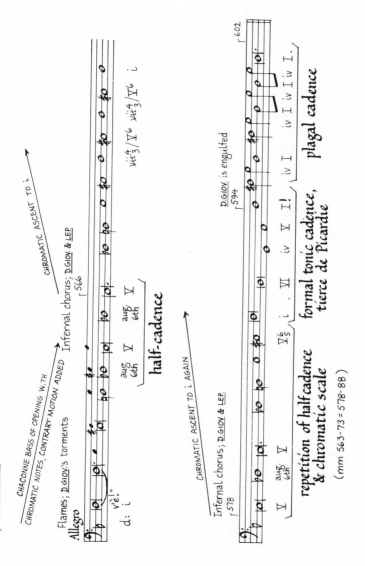

Example 12-12

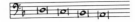

stepwise motion which makes the scale such an effective agent of ambiguity. Each move seems immediately reasonable, no matter what the eventual direction of the line or what harmonies it brings in its train. The scale fragment which Mozart chooses to organize the first key area (mm. 437–61) and the return to the tonic (m. 554) is a traditional formulaic bass which is paradigmatic of this phenomenon — the descending-tetrachord or "chaconne" bass.

Surely one of the reasons for the enduring popularity of the bass known as "chaconne" (ex. 12–12)[36] is the special poetic weight of its first two moves, particularly when heard in the context of tonal harmony. Exploiting the different inflections of the upper tetrachord of the minor scale, and the slanting relation of the triads formed on "tonal" and "modal" degrees of the same scale (the modal degrees are 3 and 6, the latter being the one in question here), the chaconne bass momentarily suspends harmonic discourse: it takes a sudden nosedive the first note out, falling past the pointing leading-tone to the degree of the lowered seventh to open up seemingly uncharted tonal territories for exploration. (In the *ombra* music the drama of this whole-step drop from D to C-natural is accentuated by contrast with the forthright C-sharp leading-tone which has occurred in the bass two measures earlier, as part of the V$^6_5$ which resolves to the chaconne's opening tonic.) The triad apparently formed by the bass's move to lowered 7 is v^6, or the "minor dominant" in first inversion. But the phrase "minor dominant" is a contradiction in terms, since a dominant chord must by nature be a major triad. The triad v^6 has no meaning in the language of harmonic function, and pointing functions must instead be said to be suspended, leaving the listener at the mercy of the leading qualities of "mere" line. This wedge into strange territory is driven further by a second move a whole step down, to the modal degree 6, in minor (here B-flat). The chaconne begins on a minor triad, but its bass has just spelled out a possible 3–2–1 in a major key, and, concomitantly, the triad on the low 6 is major (B-flat,D,F). Although B-flat major is hardly competing to become a key in its own right, the descent of a major third at this moment has a haunting harmonic ambiguity. Far too much space has just been opened up in an area whose topography should have been familiar; the harmonic bottom has fallen out. Just in time the bass makes a third move, down a half-step, a move that turns the crucial corner, explicating the intended syntax of the line by asserting B-flat's Phrygian relation to the dominant. Add (optionally — Mozart omits it in the ex-

position; see ex. 12–13 below) the arresting dissonance of the augmented sixth pointing to the dominant from beneath it (B-flat, G-sharp,
to A,A),[37] and one's sense of place is again complete (ex. 12–13). Such is
the drama of the chaconne bass, set against the backdrop of tonal harmony — a neat definition of place at beginning and end, but in the middle a suspension of functional implications which leaves the listener
briefly without harmonic context, and subject to the quasi-modal "va-
garies" of motion by step.

That Mozart appreciated the special nature of the chaconne bass is
vividly demonstrated in the first movement of the D Minor Quartet, K.
421. There the chaconne is set in the first period against a D pedal in an
upper voice (the violin) for a striking *Sturm und Drang* opening, tied off
by a strong authentic cadence to measure 4 (ex. 12–14). The first measures of the X-section, in E-flat major, start by mimicking the opening

Example 12-13

Example 12-14

Example 12-15

period, but the bass fails to stop on the dominant, or even to rise back up from the subdominant. Instead, extending the scalar motion *ad absurdum*, it continues to slip down stepwise until it has traversed a minor seventh to F. Against the F the treble's E-flat pedal acts like a D-sharp and the top note of an augmented sixth, which opens out to a new dominant on E-natural, a half-step above the original tonic, and to a new key — A minor (ex. 12–15). Thus the most distant key attained in the movement is abandoned in a matter of a few measures by this cool dissolve down the scale to a key a tritone away (a move abetted by the sudden drop in dynamics from *forte* to *piano*, and by the isolation of the dotted figure — its upbeat is lopped off — to attenuate the rhythmic motion). After the seven additional measures it takes to achieve an A minor cadence, the X-section proceeds to a further anatomizing of the figures of the opening period, but in thoroughly familiar keys — the harmonic crisis is over.

Not only does the vertiginous gravity of the chaconne bass provide a stunning opener for the *ombra* music; it is, furthermore, material which in its shapeliness can be recognizably recapitulated, and which has important topical implications. The chaconne is recognizable as an "antique" topic (with an effect similar to that of the learned style on a listener accustomed to the clear and distinct periods of the *galant*), and the haunting descent to 6 in minor has itself an old-fashioned sound — hence the title "modal" degree. (It is interesting that this special poetic move — the fall between third-related triads — becomes a favorite device in nineteenth-century music, for instance at the opening of the Schubert Serenade in D Minor, and that there it has lost its "antique" connotations to become a fresh and powerful progression in the harmonic language of Romantic music.) Not only does this archaic bass make powerfully effective music; because of the association of the old-fashioned with the ecclesiastical, it is as instrumental as the dotted rhythms and the choir of trombones in setting the moral climate of the opera's dénouement.

Furthermore, although the chaconne bass occurs only in the "exposition" and "recapitulation" of the D-minor music, the principle which animates it — that of confusion framed by clarity — also informs the remainder of the key-area plan. Each of its sections is organized by some form of scalar bass, in varying lengths and types; linear motion is the norm for the organizing skeleton of the entire movement. Its important areas of arrival, however, must take another form; they are defined by broad authentic cadences, which cut the seemingly wayward motion with the clarity of their harmonic formulas in order to give the whole its shape. But it is striking that while the solidity of the squared-off rhythms and harmonies of these cadences is the antithesis of the peripatetic habits of pure line, the cadences still echo the special poetic gesture of the chaconne bass, falling a major third from i to VI before turning the corner with a iv-V-i progression (see exs. 12–18, 12–19, 12–23 and 12–27). This powerful and haunting cadence formula has a harmonic effect analogous to the linear gravity of the chaconne's stepwise descent to lowered 6. Indeed, in cases where the repeating element in the chaconne is harmonic rather than linear, i-VI-ii$_5^6$(iv)-V-i is the form which that progression often takes; see, for example, the famous Bach Chaconne in D Minor. (It also becomes the opening material of the Schubert Serenade mentioned above.) This cadence formula occurs four times in the *ombra* music, namely, at every authentic cadence of any significance, and it also figures importantly in the first scene of the opera. In fact the characteristic "chaconne sound" haunts all the high tragic music in *Don Giovanni.*

In addition to the various scalar basses and the "chaconne cadence," only a few other devices of melodic and rhythmic recall are needed in the *ombra* music to confirm the crucial moments in the harmonic argument. Lengthy key-area plans in instrumental music are rarely organized in such a single-minded fashion; it is more usual to draw on a variety of devices, melodic, textural, and rhythmic, to point up the crucial landmarks in the harmonic traverse. In opera, however, the circumstances of the drama often require instead a concentrated focus of musical forces, and nowhere so much as in this famous passage, where the air of anarchy from moment to moment must be balanced by an unremitting march to the appointed end. This cunning union of the grandiose and the efficient makes Mozart's vision of the damnation of Don Giovanni its most unforgettable realization.

The Ombra Music: Analysis

At the opening of the *ombra* music the arresting gesture of the chaconne bass is set with such ponderous grandeur (rhythmically 2+2+2+2) that the half-step of B-flat to A (mm. 442–43) has the feel of a virtual cadence in the Phrygian mode. After this the first key area needs no more material of any profile, and consists merely of cadences —first weak ones in D minor, a key already weakened by a powerful Phrygian cadence, and then a series of secondary-dominant motions

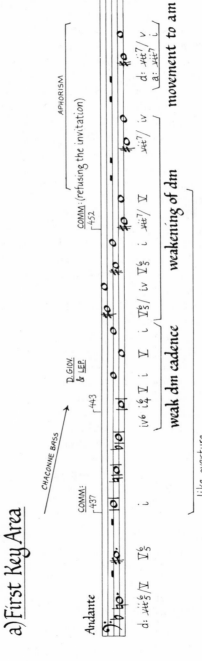

Example 12-16

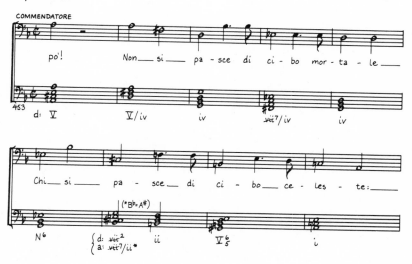

which dissolve D's already weak hold and provide a transition to the key of A minor. The material of this transition is the eight-measure phrase which comprises the Commendatore's famous "tone row" — the setting of his unearthly aphorism "Non si pasce di cibo mortale/Chi si pasce di cibo celeste."[38] These eight measures (454–61) constitute a terse modulatory progression from D minor to A minor, starting with an A-major triad as V and closing on an A-minor triad as i (see ex. 12–16, where the harmonic implications have been supplied in the bass). The Commendatore's tortuously chromatic vocal line — the so-called tone row (of the twelve notes G and G-sharp, although missing, can be accounted for in the bass) — merely follows the implication of that progression, picking out the most "colorful" notes to be flatly juxtaposed without, for four of the eight measures, the accompaniment which would explicate them. (The inner voices of the fully realized accompaniment do provide one spine-tingling touch — the ecclesiastical suspensions in mm. 4 and 8, in the first case with the chromatic passing-tone B-natural increasing the unearthly effect.)

The angular and elliptical style of these eight measures is clearly the appropriate idiom for a shade uttering an aphorism, and the singsong regularity of its four-plus-four phrase structure separates it from its surroundings as if by quotation marks. Although wondrously effective, the passage is not really mysterious, and, since it occurs at a moment of lull in the skeletal motion, it is in fact a bit crabbed-sounding from the necessity of marking so much time with so little essential harmonic

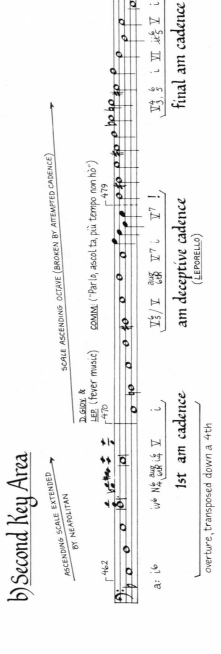

b) *Second Key Area*

change (see fig. 11 p. 302; in over eight measures the only harmonic moves are vii⁷/ᵢᵥ to iv and vii⁷/ᵥ to V, the latter the pivotal relation in the modulation to A minor). The second key area takes off from here, gathering momentum to make its two definitive cadences in A minor.

It is utterly unorthodox, and at the same time wholly reasonable, for Mozart to have chosen A minor, the "minor dominant," as the second key for the *ombra* music. As has already been pointed out, contrast is not the *desideratum* here; a modulation to the relative major, F, as compositional habit directed, would actually have been the unorthodox — indeed the unsupportable — harmonic move. The modulation to the minor dominant is, moreover, entirely in keeping with the "antique" quality of the *ombra* music. A movement in the minor mode in the early part of the century would as often as not have featured a strong modulation to the minor dominant and would also have visited several other keys; for example, every one of Bach's Two-Part Inventions in a minor key has at least one important cadence in the minor dominant. The tendency in the Classic key-area form was of course to set up a strong polarity between two keys rather than to range among many, and the relative major was the most reasonable choice for the "second key" of a movement in minor. Since the minor was no longer considered as parallel to the major, but as a weaker creature, suited to a narrower spectrum of affects, the major provided the satisfying contrast necessary to settle the end of the exposition. Thus the minor dominant in this movement, by harking back to the Baroque "solar" [39] system of keys and to the mono-affective style, contributes both naturally and by association to the air of the venerable and the elevated proper to the visit of the Stone Guest.

The second key area consists of two scales, the first short (four steps) but extended in effect by motions in the upper voices, and the second long (rising a ninth, with four chromatic steps inserted) but broken by a deceptive cadence. The first scale accompanies the Commendatore's announcement that he means business,[40] and it has an unearthly urgency about it, seeming to press past even the limits of the diatonic order. It begins simply, rising by parallel sixths from i⁶ to iv⁶. The bass then rests on low 6, preparing to assert the Phrygian-half-step relation which it bears to the dominant. Meanwhile the upper voices take over the stepwise ascent, moving up first by half-step to an augmented sixth (m. 467, with the E-flat functioning as a D-sharp) and then (with the bass) to a i⁶₄. But on the way to the augmented sixth the middle voice must first move up a half-step from its ⁵₃ position, forming for an entire measure in passing the configuration of a major triad in second inversion on the lowered-second degree — the "Neapolitan ⁶₄" which was involved earlier in the opera in two similar progressions (ex. 12–17)[41]. This chain of

Example 12-17

rather uncomfortable appoggiatura chords, formed merely by passing steps in the upper voices, but each given considerable weight because of the slow harmonic rhythm, has a ghostly effect: the line strains upward seemingly without functional reference, and swollen by the presence of an unnatural major triad (the "Neapolitan $^6_4$"), seems to reach to intolerable heights before subsiding to the familiar — the A-minor cadence. This cadence (mm. 468–70) is the first strong one in the new key, a "necessary but not sufficient condition" for the end of the exposition.

The second scale of the second key area, the longer one, takes up on the last note of the short scale (m. 470) to launch its drive to the exposition's final A-minor cadence. It reaches a hair-raising intensity as a result of the deceptive cadence which occurs after the ascent to the dominant (m. 479) and forces the scale up to the B-natural a ninth above the starting point. For its first four measures the new scale rises diatonically, in parallel $^6_3$ chords (i, vii⁶, i⁶, ii⁶). It constitutes the skeleton of Leporello's teeth-chattering triple-metered fever music,[42] a funereal patter causing a rhythmic quickening which gives a new urgency to the forward motion. Rhythm becomes increasingly an issue as the second key area draws to its close. The exposition is rhythmically continuous for almost its entire length, except for the Commendatore's gnomic modulatory bridge, its only "exposed," or undovetailed, phrase. (The rhythmic clarity of this phrase is feasible only because the harmony is at issue; true clarity in both elements at the same time would put a stop to the inexorable forward motion.) Otherwise, the characters' opening utterances all have an ongoing iambic or amphibrachic rhythm, generally in two-measure units; hence the famous amphibrach of the opera, the Commendatore's paralyzing

Don Gio - VAN - ni

Major cuts are smoothed over by various eliding devices, principally the dovetailing of phrases.[43] The Commendatore's dovetailings here at the critical moment in the exposition take the form of interruptions, covering the thesis of the previous singer's phrase to heighten the tension further. First he interrupts Leporello (m. 474) with the words "Parlo, ascolta: più tempo non ho."[44] Entering over Leporello's last note with the grave dotted rhythms of the exposition, he holds an interior pedal on B-natural while the bass rises step by step past the dominant to F and an augmented sixth, preparing the ground for a cadence. The attendant choir of trombones and the chromatic note over which the Commendatore enters — the first in this hitherto diatonic scale, a D-sharp which is part of a V^6_5 of V — puts his open-ended four-measure phrase in sharp relief (ex. 12–18). Giovanni tries to bring it to a cadence — the first of the formal "chaconne cadences" — parroting the Commendatore's words ("Parla, parla: ascoltando ti sto"[45]) and his dotted rhythms. But his figure is double-time, and overlaps the Commendatore's last measure — Giovanni's insouciant impatience battling with the statue's grave urgency. The one-measure extension which the Don's phrase provides to the Commendatore's uncompromising four measures of spondees is not sufficient for cadence. Leporello's patter line, rising in the accents of irrepressible fear up to the sixth degree, forces a deceptive cadence instead, and marks the recommencement of the skeleton's slow upward motion, on F where it had left off two measures before.

Now the sense of stretto grows very powerful. The Commendatore interrupts Leporello and Giovanni, repeating his four-measure spondaic command on D octaves while the skeleton scale rises chromatically, changing twice a measure now, and accompanied by the insistent "fate" passagework in the strings. It rises above the tonic to 2 as the first half of the scale had risen above the dominant to 6, pressing against the Commendatore's D pedal. The particular harmonies which arise from the concurrence of the bass line with the pedal remain merely acciden-

Example 12-18

Example 12-19

tal formations until the first-inversion dominant seventh on which the Commendatore ends his second four-measure interjection (m. 482). Now finally Giovanni succeeds with his preemptive formal cadence (ex. 12–19). Moving in half notes rather than in the quarter notes of his first attempt (ex. 12–18, above), this cadence balances the quicker (half-note) motion of the second half of the second scale; in the previous ratio of whole to quarter note the effect was mere impatience on Giovanni's part, without the gravity of what must instead appear to be a formal challenge. Furthermore, the rhythmic extension which results from slowing the rate of harmonic change finally provides sufficient breadth for closure:

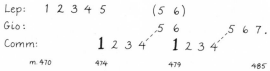

As has already been pointed out, Giovanni's "chaconne cadences" are not the first to occur in the opera: the same grave and measured i-VI-ii$_5^6$-V-i progression graces the Don's challenge to the Commendatore in act I (see ex. 8–7, p. 212). Here the somber and ritual accents of the cadence again make it clear that the challenge has been opened: now the Don will face out the heavenly emissary. As the exposition and first phase of the action comes to its paralyzing close, the absolute certitude of the damned man cuts short all attempts to fear with or for him.

The dramatic contents of the X-section are the Commendatore's actual invitation to Giovanni to dine with him, Giovanni's assent, and the Commendatore's call to repentance. Structurally it falls into two parts. The first one is organized by a long slow ascending scale which superintends a modulation to B-flat minor, the most distant key the X-section will attain, and then, moving up stepwise from B-flat to D, falls into G minor with another of Giovanni's formal cadences. Since G minor is the subdominant of D minor, the second part of the X-section constitutes a staging area for the return to the tonic; it consists of one brief *descending* scale fragment (the only one in the movement beside the chaconne bass), tentative D-minor cadences, and finally a slightly more elaborate version of the first scale of the second key area, which leads into the area of unequivocal dominant preparation for the tonic return.

The first scale in the first part of the X-section is the Commendatore's: as he issues his dinner invitation,[46] for the first time his line doubles the bass (until the cadence figure), rising with inexorable leisureliness from A to the G-flat a half-step above the new dominant, F (see fig. 11c). This scale is one of the few *ombra* scales which is wholly chromatic, and the harmonies which fill it out are also the most intensely chromatic in the movement. Until vii^7 of F minor, the fifth degree (the E-natural in m. 498), the chords make little functional sense, and again are merely the fortuitous embellishments of a rising line (ex. 12–20). Their chromaticism grows particularly intense in the four measures (489–90, 493–94) where the skeletal notes are surrounded by double appoggiaturas (ex. 12–21). The rise of these chromatic appog-

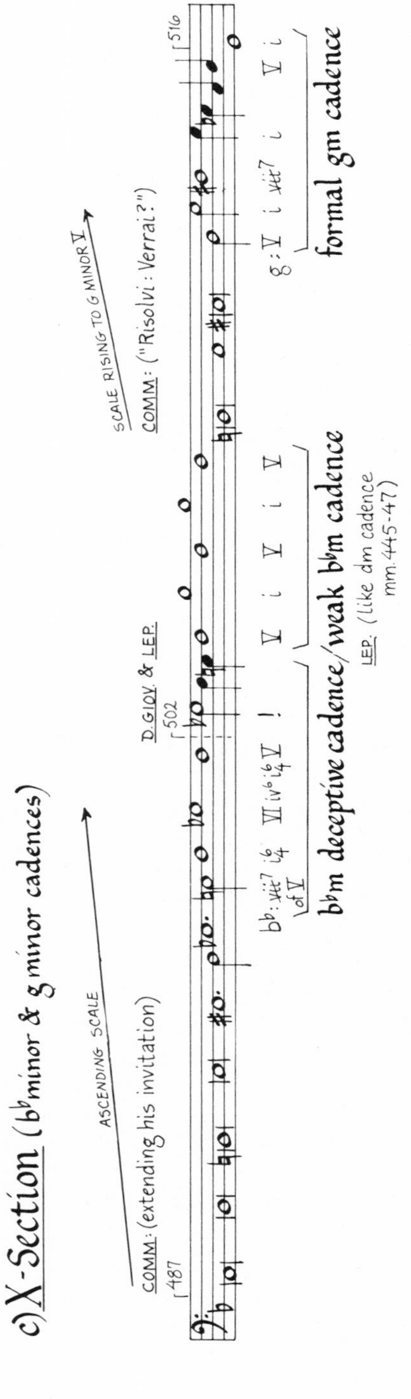
c) X-Section (b♭ minor & g minor cadences)
487
COMM: (extending his invitation)
ASCENDING SCALE
502
D. GIOV. & LEP.
SCALE RISING TO G MINOR V
COMM: ("Risolvi: Verrai?")
516
b♭m deceptive cadence / weak b♭m cadence
LEP. (like dm cadence mm. 445-47)
formal gm cadence

Example 12-20

Example 12-21

giaturas echoes in smaller compass and quickened rhythm the measured ascent of the bass, increasing tension all the more. After two four-
measure units, each graced by these appoggiaturas, the bass itself
begins to change more rapidly, in a dotted pattern, ♩. ♪ ♩. ♪, absorb-
ing, as it were, the energy generated by these chromatic ornaments.
Given the harmonic and linear excitement, phrase rhythm is rather regular—4 4 2 2 3, with the 2's mirroring the stepped-up harmonic rhythm
and the 3 achieving the half-cadence (m. 501; grammatically a proper
question mark for the Commendatore's invitation) on F.

Mozart borrows here, as he does so frequently at the beginning of an
X-section, from the opening materials of the exposition. Both sections
open with grave dotted rhythms and a bass note which changes every
two measures (twice, and at their end four times as slow as the more
urgent scales which close the exposition). Furthermore, after Leporello
makes another deceptive cadence (to the low 6 or G-flat in m. 502, which
by rights should have been the fourth measure and tonic of the Commendatore's cadence figure), an area of B-flat minor i-V vacillation follows which is the counterpart even in texture and figure (the syncopated eighths and running sixteenths in the violins) of the weak D-
minor cadence before the abandonment of the tonic in the first key area
(mm. 445–47; ex. 12–22). Slight changes in the bass figure render it
even more open-ended than is the corresponding passage in the exposition—here the tonic falls on a weak measure, and is surrounded by
dominants in the strong ones—but the reminiscence is sure. F, the dominant emphasized by the weak cadence, is V of VI, the "point of furthest
remove," the habitual goal of the most distant modulation of an X-
section. Above the bass's 5–1 pendulum motion, first Leporello inter-
jects a warning in his usual patter style, and then Giovanni, his line
a grim B-flat minor parody of a fanfare, comes as close to deliberation
as he seems capable: "A torto di viltate/Tacciato mai sarò!"[47] Impa-

Example 12-22

Example 12-23

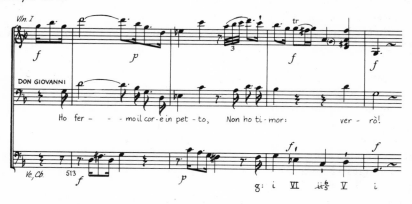

tiently brushing aside the pair's interruptions, the Commendatore recommences his hair-raising scale on B-natural, a half-step above the previous tonic, to press for a decision. The scale rises chromatically to D,
the dominant of the forthcoming new key, G minor (IV of D minor),
where, against Leporello's protestations, Giovanni ties it off with another "chaconne cadence," proclaiming "Non ho timor: verrò!" (ex.
12–23)[48]. The rhyme at this point with the end of the exposition is
hardly accidental; the "chaconne cadence" will occur even once more in

d) X-Section (motion back to d minor)

the *ombra* music, as the final cadence of the section. There, however, it will not belong to Don Giovanni. His formal assent here is his destruction, for it amounts to his final refusal to show by proper fear a proper honor for forces beyond the human. Now the climate changes abruptly and the Don is no longer master of himself.

By way of answer to Giovanni, the Commendatore immediately starts a new line of action, commanding "Dammi la mano in pegno!"[49] On the word "pegno" a sudden *fortissimo* and a timpani roll are meant to suggest the terrors impending. The harmonic function of the *Più stretto* section (mm. 521ff) is to impart the first tentative hints of D minor, while its dramatic charge is to image the terrible knowledge communicated to the Don by the first icy handclasp of death's messenger. It achieves the first, and harmonic, goal by zeroing in on D with approaches of varying intensity, first by a chromatic scale fragment which descends from E-natural to D as dominant (mm. 521–25), and then, after a brief G minor cadence, by surrounding D with its own dominant (mm. 528–32; fig. 11d). Since the sepulchral dotted rhythms have measured normal time for the X-section until now, the abrupt rhythmic quickening of the *Più stretto* (measured quarters and eighths give way to tremolos as the tempo increases) and the sense of vertigo induced by the sudden descending motion suggest the sinner's shudder as he first views the abyss. Giovanni's shock at what may be his first encounter with something unassimilable is expressed in a near-poignant question —

"Ohime! Che gelo è questo mai?"[50] — delivered in his first diminished-seventh harmony of the *ombra* music (vii^7 of F minor, m. 521), against the sinking chromatic bass. The contrast with his imperious cadence formulas is powerful; this is probably the closest the Don will ever come to pathos. But by the time D minor recovers its dominant (m. 528), he is resolute, and the battle for his soul begins.

The scale which provides the battlefield (mm. 533–42) is the D-minor counterpart of the A-minor scale which opened the second key area (mm. 462–69); again it is a scale which seems to press beyond the usual diatonic limits. The Commendatore, calling on Giovanni to repent, is at his most sepulchrally supernatural, supported by the trombones which double the skeleton of the progression. The scale first moves, like its A-minor original, from i^6 to a "Neapolitan $^6_4$" (m. 538). But at this point the upper voices go their own way, ignoring the implications of the would-be augmented sixth which follows (B-flat, G-sharp, spelled B-flat, A-flat) to turn it into a V^7 to E-flat, the Neapolitan, which then partially resolves (to an E-flat minor $^6_4$). After this oscillation in the never-never land of the Neapolitan and its secondary relations, the bass shakes itself loose from B-flat to continue up the scale through B-natural (vii^7 of C) and C (a C-minor triad). This diversion links the unfinished progression to a disjunct and angular line of descending fourths and their leading tones (B-natural to C, F-sharp to G, C-sharp to D, G-sharp to A), which ends the shouting match (ex. 12–24). A slightly shorter version of the same skeleton — a "falling-fourth" sequence — organizes the undermining of the tonic in the first key area (ex. 12–25a), and in the *Più stretto* just before the return makes the first tentative circlings around it (ex. 12–25b). Falling fourths, because they run "in reverse," against the grain of cadential motion (5–1), are a temporizing, neutral sequence (unlike falling fifths, which are forward-moving, each step a minicadence). The crucial degrees of the mode are exposed in a stark landscape, preceded by chromatic tones (in two of the sequences the secondary dominants become the rhythmic

Example 12-24

Example 12-25

focus of the progression). Finally one becomes the dominant, and the direction is reversed, toward cadence. Such a sequence is again old-fashioned, and unusual for the area of dominant preparation in the Classic key-area form. It becomes at the last apocalyptic in tone when it is revealed in its nakedness sung by the Commendatore and doubled by winds, strings, and trombones: "Ah, tempo più non v'è" (ex. 12–25c).[51]

The line which organizes the "recapitulation" is simplicity itself: a scale fragment which moves down to the dominant and back up to the tonic, the ascent being then literally repeated (mm. 581–88; fig. 11e, p. 316). The opening scale is the initial chaconne bass in which a chromatic tone (B-natural) is inserted — often the case with the chaconne — and which is embellished by a part in contrary motion. This "descant" is the skeleton of Giovanni's agonized reports of a "tremore insolito" and "vortici di fuoco pien d'orror,"[52] a skeleton which reaches up to form first an augmented sixth (m. 562) with the chaconne bass and then a dominant octave (ex. 12–26). On the dominant the infernal chorus enters for the first time (m. 563), its charge the warning "Tutto a tue colpe è poco./Vieni: c'è un mal peggior!"[53] The chorus serves the important function of enlarging the sphere of the Commendatore's action, of cor-

e) Return

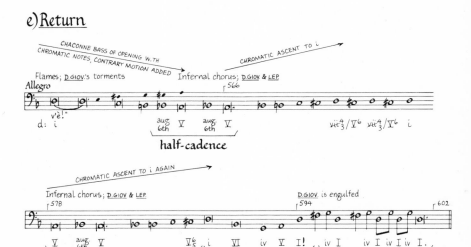

Example 12-26

roborating his authority; we are witnessing not the mere personal revenge of a restless ghost, but a mandate of divine justice. Its line consists only of the half-step B-flat to A, the B-flat treated first as the bass
of the second augmented sixth (m. 565; Giovanni's line forms the first
one), and then as the beginning of the chromatic ascent to the tonic
(mm. 568–70; G-natural, substituted for the previous G-sharp, forms a
G-minor chord instead of an augmented sixth). After assertion of the
tonic the skeleton of measures 563–73 — the oscillating augmented
sixths and the ascent to the tonic — is repeated (mm. 578–88), with the
exclamations of Giovanni and Leporello slightly altered.

The events of the return are extremely compressed and efficient —

first the recapitulation of the material which opened the exposition (the chaconne bass), and then the two strong half-cadences oscillating on that characteristic "corner-turner" of the chaconne bass, the Phrygian half-step, and alternating with chromatic runs up to the tonic. Syncopations, turbulent string figuration, and the dissonances of the descant lend an apocalyptic tone. The *coup de grâce* is delivered at the close of the section, when the tonic of measure 588 becomes the beginning of a final "chaconne cadence," a rhyme with the formal cadences which closed both the exposition and the first half of the X-section. Heretofore Giovanni's property — his punctilious call to arms in act I and earlier in this movement his decisive assents to the Commendatore's challenges — the cadence finally becomes the locus for a stunning reversal: the calling-out is done by the infernal chorus, while the vocal lines of Giovanni and Leporello are mere ornaments of the progression (mm. 588–94). The formula is allotted twice as much time, lasting seven measures as against Giovanni's maximum of three (ex. 12–27). Clearly, the grim punctilio of divine justice has a finality not to be matched by the *politesse* even of the most daemonic of humans; Giovanni has this to learn.

A comparison of the first-act challenge and duel with Giovanni's mortal combat with Heaven's instrument is also suggested by the thirty-second-note scales which the Commendatore's call to repentance shares with the choreographed sword thrusts of the first-act duel (I, 1, 167–74; ex. 12–28). That battle between two mortal men was both cause and prefiguring of this final contest fought on heavenly terms. But the sinner's struggle against redemption is far worse a sin than mur-

Example 12-27

Example 12-28

der; it ensures that Giovanni will have no requiem. The most eloquent — and absolute — single stroke in the opera is the *tierce de Picardie*, the chord of the major tonic which surprisingly closes the final cadence,[54] accompanied by Giovanni's agonizing scream (see ex. 12–27 above). The impulse behind the old-fashioned habit of closing a work with a Picardy third was a theological one — to finish with the greater aural and numerological perfection of the major triad *ad majorem Dei gloriam*. Its ecclesiastical tone is further reinforced by the plagal (minor IV to major I) cadences which then quickly put the period to the section. No further evidence of the swift and pitiless omnipotence of divine authority is needed; Giovanni disappears without leaving a trace.

I have provided this map and guided tour of the *ombra* music in order to explicate the detail of that complex and wondrous construction. Among Mozart's compositions it is *sui generis*, standing out unique and new. In general, nothing is ever wholly "new" in Mozart's repertory, but is instead a brilliant recombination of existing compositional materials. The *ombra* music, however, does seem to merit that adjective, for while it is a combination of preexisting elements, that combination is so tightly welded that it becomes an entity in itself which is not easily dissolved into its component parts; it also has no counterpart elsewhere in Mozart's works. Yet there is a further irony: the elements which are combined, and the new organism which they become, are intended to seem relentlessly "old." Thoroughly antique in tone, the section uses the preluding fantasy, the Venetian trombones, and the chaconne bass and cadence, mimics the monoaffective habits of Baroque composition and its solar key scheme, and closes the whole with the *tierce de Picardie*, which in provenance reaches back to the Renaissance theory of ratios. (Underneath all this, in an unassuming fashion, the "modern" key-area process binds the mixture into a convincing and dramatic whole.) Furthermore, many of these antique elements have actual ecclesiastical references — the original seat of the preluding fantasy and of the trombone choir was the church, and the *tierce de Picardie* brings a composition in line with the perfection of the divine cosmos — and those which have no direct connection with the divine or theological suggest it merely by being old-fashioned (to Classic musicians the *stile antico* was virtually synonymous with the *stile ecclesiastico*). Thus in the archaic musical style of the section lies its meaning: there can be no question that Giovanni's punishment is no mere vendetta, that the "swift sword" is divine.

Perhaps because of the "newness" of its special compounding of old-fashioned stylistic elements, the *ombra* music often seems to listeners to belong more to the nineteenth century than to the Classic style. While the style of the *ombra* music is a singular one for Mozart, meeting a rare affective need, the elements which constitute it became commonplace in much of the symphonic literature of the nineteenth century. Open-ended and formless melodies over broodingly ambiguous harmonies, and apocalyptical climaxes with stentorian brass choirs, barely reined in by reference to a vestigial key scheme — these are a translation of the "antique" elements of the *ombra* music into the standard habits of Romantic musical discourse, the fact of their old-fashionedness forgotten, but the Judgment-Day tone and reference preserved. One degrades the Apocalypse by repetition, however, something which Mozart well understood, for he maintained an ironic stance toward it even in the opera itself: in the epilogue another musical antique, a sprightly fake fugue, burlesques both the supposed moral of the story (the *antichissima canzon*, "This is the end of the evil-doer") and the power of the evil which necessitated it. Such a balance is by nature ambiguous; it is finally this ironic remove which makes this work the *Don Giovanni* of all *Don Giovanni*'s.

Epilogue and Exordium

In extremis the idiom of the opera shifts from the middle ground which would seem reasonably appropriate for a *dramma giocoso* to a strange and disturbing mixture of tragedy and farce. Although the first act is not entirely free from tinges of pleasurable cruelty, nor without its bleak visions, in the end Zerlina is not seduced, Leporello defuses the maskers' tragic key, and the finale closes in the neat and neutral C major of good, clean fun. But the mood of the opera has been darkening since the coming of nightfall at the beginning of the second act. Our sympathies have been seriously claimed by Elvira, only to be wooed away yet again by *buffa*'s engaging ruthlessness. Giovanni's cruelty has become more open, the tension between master and servant aggravated. The dead have been disturbed, and the trombones have sounded their warning. And finally the divine agency has reasserted its ascendancy by condemning the rake to eternal hellfire. Yet the entire second-act finale is suffused with low farce. First there is the eating scene, and then Leporello and Elvira play out their hair-raising parody of Zerlina's screams, farcical in its very melodrama. Leporello's *buffa* patter intrudes itself between Giovanni and his nemesis, and finally provides a rhythmic pulse to support the longer-breathed terrors of the *ombra* music. Some reputable writers have objected to the considerable role played by Leporello in the second-act finale, finding it undignified and distracting — in fact, a dramatic miscalculation, with Leporello managing to steal the scene from the Don. The same and other writers tend to reject the epilogue, also because it diminishes the tragedy or turns it into mere "farce and horror,"[55] and it was frequently omitted in nineteenth-century performances. But while much of the music in the overture, first, and last scenes is cast in the high tragic style, still it would be a mistake to consider the "tragedy" to be Don Giovanni's, or indeed to label the opera a tragedy at all.[56] A tragic hero must be in some way admirable — truly the savior of his people like Oedipus, or once a good, and still a beloved, king like Lear. If there is any pity and fear to be excited in *Don Giovanni*, it is for the lives of the people whom he has left behind him. Their habits and pursuits have been diminished in stature by the mere existence of a man who cannot be touched by the moral order; in this bright commonplace of an epilogue they reappear briefly to repair things as best they can. Not the tragic mode itself, but the mixture of genres, of exalted style and low farce, manifests this diminution to us throughout the opera, in increasingly dark and turbulent colors. The mixed genre has a vision both less noble and more encompassing than that of tragedy: *Don Giovanni* gives us a panoramic view of all the orders of society, showing them stretched to the breaking point.

It might be tempting, then, to look at the opera as a piece of social history, a work which holds up for closer scrutiny the condition of a particular society at a particular moment: the dissolute aristocracy in its decay threatens to destroy the whole fabric of society. There is a serious difficulty with this analysis, however, in that Giovanni, although undoubtedly of aristocratic origin, is not the foremost representative of his order. That function is served by Donna Anna and Don Ottavio, true gentlefolk no matter what else may be said about them. And the aristocratic Don does not adopt the bourgeois contredanse in the first-act finale merely to pander to Zerlina, as some have suggested. It must be in some sense his normal idiom, since he adopts it also when only his double is present (in "Fin ch'han dal vino," I, 11) and disguise is unnecessary. Perhaps, given his idiom, he could be seen as a representative of the rising middle class, threatening with vicious indifference to engulf the moribund régime. The representatives of the old order are Donna Anna and Don Ottavio, Zerlina and Masetto, with their "classic" *alla breve* and *buffa* styles, who are hard put to find a way to stave off deracination and ruin. In the epilogue, a standard *vaudeville* (a finale-type in which each character ritually bids his farewell), Donna Anna and Don Ottavio spend many G-major *alla breve* measures in the stately deferences of noble lovers, and Donna Anna manages to obtain yet another postponement from her eternally "fido amor" (ex. 12–29). Zerlina and Masetto in blithe gavottelike[57] patter — the Arcadian stereotype appropriate to peasants of the *ancien régime* — go off to resume their life as if untouched (ex. 12–30). The survival of these two couples represents the uneasy and contingent victory of the old; it comes at a price.

Elvira and Leporello, with their mannered and indecorous "hyper-

Example 12-29

Example 12-30

Example 12-31

alla breve" and "hyper-*buffa*" styles, have already been uprooted and "declassed" by the sheer attractiveness of No-Man. Cut off from their own kind, they can only cling close to Giovanni. Leporello is the "new" man, shrewd and vulgar, attracted by this novel world of glittering prizes but at heart afraid of the consequences of accepting it, bound at the last by superstition and moral sanctions. He will always equivocate between the old order and the new disorder; an inn is not the place to contract for a job with gentlefolk. Elvira has been spent, the arc of her life played out, by her contact with Giovanni. Bereft of all degree and place, she will go to the only true asylum for the homeless, there to spend her life anonymously in devotion and good works. Her final music, at twice the pulse of the preceding *alla breve*, approaches patter but has the only minor inflection among the four final pronouncements (ex. 12–31). As usual her passion is mocked—this time trivialized by the *vaudeville* form itself, which sandwiches her sad declaration in between the prim accents of the two "normal" couples, equating all fates.

Thus it is only the paradox of the Don himself which makes the opera inadequate as social history: it is not at all clear why a man of rank should be identified with the new bourgeoisie. Since a social account must be precise about just what social phenomenon Don Giovanni represents, the opera must fail in that genre. To absorb the paradox of Giovanni we must ascend to a point of view where explanation of it is not necessary, where it can simply be taken for granted that such men exist — for we know that they do — and try to understand what their existence means for other men. Giovanni is a phenomenon, a *datum* — the rootless, placeless man who gives no honor to the ordinary habits and virtues which keep us all in place, which make us human. His effect is to stun his fellow creatures, who took it in good faith that such a man could not exist. Some, either through *amour-propre* (Donna Anna) or thanks to a saving awareness of their own natures (Zerlina), manage to resist and to stumble back to a rapprochement with their old habitat. Others, either through vanity (Leporello), or through passion and vulnerability (Elvira), have lost their proper place and must inhabit the limbo which surrounds the Don. All pay a price, Leporello and Zerlina the least, and Donna Anna and Donna Elvira the most, although the latter in manners which are radically opposed; all appear in this epilogue as sadly diminished creatures, their lives no longer vivid against the flash of Don Giovanni the *monstrum*. Mozart chose as figures for his vision the available language of social gestures because it caught something about the relation of one strange man to his fellows; this vocabulary does not make his opera sociology or social history, but the work of a man expressing in the language of his time and custom something enduringly true about all men.

Surely, against all efforts to expunge it, the epilogue must stand. There are sound musical reasons to begin with. The E major of the *tierce de Picardie* stands at the end of the E minor chorus which opens Bach's *Saint Matthew Passion* symbolically, its greater acoustical perfection mirroring the perfection of God's creation (the same could be said of Bach's use of the major triad at the close of secular works cast in minor). So too does the D-major triad at the close of the *ombra* music have a symbolic function, as the ultimate sign of God's justice. But Classic composers, with their concern for creating a tonal equilibrium in a work — a strong sense of motion away and return — saw a further question of weights and balances, of having enough measures of tonic to make a convincing close. And since the minor mode was weak, "unnatural," and a special affect, it was not a proper final tonic for an opera. The *tierce de Picardie* at Giovanni's engulfment provides only the first hint of a D-major cadence; its implications must be carried out by a weighty cadential section which will eradicate the uncertainty left by the special D-minor fantasy.

Dramatically also the opera cannot end here. It is a tale of the survivors as much as of the Don; we must see how they are touched by his demise as well as by his existence. The picture, viewed from the distant perspective of the opera's lens, is a strange mixture of celebration and bleakness. A blend of farce and tragedy was appropriate when the Don was enclosed in the terrestrial inferno of the dining salon with his most serious victim, herself farcical because in her passion she failed of the dignity conferred by degree. But now the *dramma giocoso* prevails. The characters mass on stage to go through the rite of the *vaudeville*. All show genteel surprise at the departure of the Don; da Ponte catches the comedy of urbane men trying to assimilate the extraordinary into polite chitchat when he has the company exclaim after Leporello's tale of the proceedings, "Ah, certo è l'ombra/Che l'(m')incontrò!" [58] Each one says his piece, mask in place; performances should be stylized, with a stiff and symmetrical mass choreography. Then Zerlina, Masetto, and Leporello invite the company to sing the moral of the piece. The opera closes with eight lines of doggerel:

Zer., Mas., and Lep.:	Resti dunque quel birbon
	Con Proserpina e Pluton.
	E noi tutti, o buona gente,
	Ripetiam allegramente
	L'antichissima canzon.
All:	Questo è il fin di chi fa mal:
	E de' perfidi la morte
	Alla vita è sempre ugual! [59]

The very moral cockiness of the three-line epigram is testimony to the unreality of the close: the wicked rarely die in a fashion commensurate with their deserts. In the ritual decorum of the moment even the stirring reality of the Stone Guest and Christian hellfire is reduced to a pallid and pastoral vision of Tartarus. The *birbon* is saluted with mock-tragic D-minor *alla breve* flourishes, the *canzon* and *buona gente* by a prim and ticking gavotte (ex. 12–32).[60] The first two lines of the maxim, that "most ancient song," are set to a phony fugue in D major which dissolves after only two real entries into a homophonic setting. (It is telling that although the *buffa* characters call the ensemble to song, it is the two noblewomen who lead off with the first entry of the fugue, invoking the aristocracy of the archaic — and perhaps also the reverse.) The third line, "Alla vita è sempre ugual," is set in the eighteenth-century version

Example 12-32

Example 12-33

of motet style, with the imitation and suspensions of the *stile legato* accompanied only by winds (ex. 12–33). The close is a rousing homophonic D-major cadence followed by a brief orchestral postlude.

The *lieto fine* ("happy ending") was of course habitual in the late eighteenth century; somehow, no matter what the depredations, proper orders were reestablished and their restoration celebrated. This celebration ought not to be considered the result of "mere convention"; it emanates from a distinct point of view which, eschewing satirical or tragical exaggerations of the way the world is, chooses to assert instead the goods of continuity and order, and the equilibrium of good sense. It is a little-remarked habit of much late eighteenth-century opera to make mention somewhere in the happy closing chorus of its musical nature — to call attention to the fact that the participants are singing. This custom may have to do with the fact that many operas were *feste teatrali* commissioned to honor a royal wedding or other ceremony, and were thus in themselves celebratory. Martin's *Una cosa rara* ends with the two women leads dancing and singing a "seghidilla" in honor of their queen, Isabella; the ceremony would have joined fact and fiction when performed on a royal occasion. There are many other eighteenth-century examples of operas in which music itself is made a topic of discourse in the closing chorus of the closing finale — Cimarosa's *Il matrimonio segreto* and Galuppi's *L'amante di tutte*, for example. Closer to home, the Bertati-Gazzaniga *Don Giovanni Tenorio* closes with a comically triumphant chorus in which the survivors all imitate musical instruments, and at the end of *Le nozze di Figaro* the participants, hearing an approaching band play a march, hasten to join it to celebrate the happy ending of the "mad day." When Zerlina, Masetto, and Leporello call on the ensemble to sing their *antichissima canzon*, they are invoking the same tradition. In calling attention to the very artifice of opera — music, that is — the finale becomes the moment when the artificial blurs into the real, when ritual and artful uses of music become one and our life itself is celebrated. Is it not in truth the braver, and the higher, act to to assert that life goes on in the face of cruelty, disorder, and blighted hopes, rather than to delight in the titillation of prevailing melodrama and death?

That statement receives a severe test in *Don Giovanni*.

Afterword

I have throughout these pages intentionally begged one question: I have used the word "Classic"[1] merely as a given, a convenient historical designation, making no attempt to define it in itself or to specify its limits in application to late eighteenth-century music. To do so is a worrisome task which, after having made a survey of definitions offered by representative recent scholars,[2] I am happy to continue to dodge. In the constellation of words usually associated with the label "classic" or "classical," however, one in particular seems to me to be easily applied to the music of late eighteenth-century composers — the word "balance." There is in the music of the Viennese Classic masters a wholly harmonious coincidence of the elements of music, harmonious in the root sense of the word — from the Greek ἁρμόζειν , to "fit"; for a brief moment in the history of music no one of its elements is in eclipse, and no one of them has the leading edge. And certainly, on the stage, one of Mozart's greatest accomplishments was the integration into this happy equilibrium of that constant delight and embarrassment of opera, the dance. Dance had rarely before had a temperate relation with musical works for the stage: it either dominated them, as in the French opera-ballets, or was kept carefully apart, as in the dance-suite overtures and the *divertissements* of *opera seria*. "Dance . . . is . . . nothing better than irrational caprioling from the beginning to the very end, an illiberal skipping about, a perpetual monotony of a very few steps, and of as few figures,"[3] complains the reform-minded critic Francesco Algarotti, and Dr. Burney judges it impossible to enjoy singing and dancing at the same time, comparing the experience to the "drinking of two exquisite wines at once."[4] Mozart himself, having composed "those confounded dances" for *Idomeneo*, writes to his father, "Laus Deo — I have got rid of them at last."[5] But the truth of the matter is that in the Mozartian *"Gesamtkunstwerke" Le nozze di Figaro* and *Don Giovanni* dance had not disappeared; on the contrary, it had merely gone underground. No longer separated from the action and forced into affective autonomy, dance — or characteristic rhythmic gestures — had become an essential element of the dramatic harmony, providing for the dramatis personae choreographies for the motion of character. No longer were the measured gestures of dance the "illiberal" and "irrational" part of the spectacle; instead, if we take the word Classic in the sense often given it of imitating the ancient — Greek — models of perfection, then the integration of dance into Mozart's music drama made it most "classical," and was necessary, moreover, if the designation Classic were to be applied at all. It was not only possible, but desirable, to sing and dance at the same time. Indeed if such "dancing" (motions in accord with the particular kind of rhythm which animates each character in the drama) does not take place on our operatic stages, that is the fault not of the music, but of scholars, directors, and singers who fail to understand that all actors' motions on the stage are properly a part of the choraic art.

The welcoming of dance into the Classic equilibrium had to wait until the advent of *opera buffa*. For it was only when the possibility of developing an action was admitted to the formal music of arias and ensembles that rhythmic gesture could separate itself from the use of music for the mere expression of a passion *in vacuo*, and begin to depict the totality of a single human character. In the stilted noble leisure of the Metastasian libretto a character could only, in an aria, engage in solitary meditation on the passion which had him in its grip. Because the action could not lend its particular color to the formal music, an aria the affect of which was jealous rage could belong to any character in the same situation, it mattered not whom. Thus pasticcios were a frequent method of quick composition. In the celerity of *opera buffa* the gestures of the formal music, because they most frequently accompany moments of action, exhibit the will and intelligence of the particular human being who takes that action — the sardonic wit of Figaro planning revenge, the nobility of the servant girl Susanna confronting her ranting master — and it is hard to imagine those arias in their luminous particularity on the lips of any other character. When a character in *Figaro* or *Giovanni* who is drawn from *opera seria* retains the meditative convention of the old style, that in itself becomes a reflection on his nature — a complexity which would not be possible without the *buffa* frame.

Indeed, it seems that the remarkable energy of the popular theater was in many ways the motive force for these new creations of Mozart's. There is a striking anecdote about Baldassare Galuppi, an opera composer who worked both in the *seria* and *buffa* veins, that when in 1749 he set the Metastasian libretto *Artaserse*, he composed the last five scenes of act I as a single quartet like a *buffa* finale. But when the opera was given in Padua in 1751 he decomposed the finale back into separate arias, finding for whatever reason that the *seria* habit would not admit of such musical continuity.[6] And comedy not only brought to Mozart's operas the particular historical development of the *buffa* finale; the comic viewpoint in general also brings to a drama a greater range and power of comment than does the purely elevated, the "neoclassical" style. Without this mixing of modes there is not the same freedom to juxtapose disparate conventions, to reexamine stereotypes, to produce a startling identification (Susanna with the noble minuet, for example). In the case of *Le nozze di Figaro*, *buffa* style fused with the *aria d'affetto* gave rise to that rare creature, a true romantic comedy. The mixture of *buffa* and *seria* in *Don Giovanni* has darker implications, resulting in a work which has its abode in the netherworld beyond the tragic, and which tragedy by encompassing seems to deny its possibility.

The mixture of modes in Mozart's operas was not lightly received by his audiences, nor, once his operas had drawn their just measure of acclaim, did other composers find it an easily imitable path: *Fidelio* returns to a kind of affective purity, and Verdi had to struggle mightily to have his librettists agree to the possibility of mixing low and prosaic subject matters with the exalted.[7] It seems to be a balance which only the dramatists who are the most profound of human observers — Mozart and Shakespeare — found their way to. Shakespeare too took his energy from the popular theater, and the thorny combination of the abased with the elevated in his works has always drawn criticism from petty critics who would keep the genres pure. But in the famous phrase "negative capability" Keats praises Shakespeare for this enormous and encompassing vision — never in a series of works one particular stance frozen, never a polemic, an ax to grind. And as with Shakespeare, also Mozart — each opera is a facet, a momentary proportioning of musical styles, a particular way of taking the world, which is true and sufficient unto the day, but because of pressure from the other works in the corpus never pretends to inclusivity. Nothing could illustrate this more tellingly than the third of these great Italian *opera buffa*s of Mozart, the enigmatic *Così fan tutte* — an *opera seria* of an *opera buffa*, if such phenomenon is possible — for whose glassy and ironic remove little in its two predecessors prepares.

NOTES

INTRODUCTION

1. Violins and violas double the voice parts almost all the way through.

2. The type of the musette-gavotte is discussed on pp. 53–55.

3. For example, Edward Dent's notion of the collaboration between da Ponte and Mozart was that da Ponte endeavored to eliminate the "new social point of view" from Beaumarchais's text, but that Mozart put it back in his music (Edward Dent, *Mozart's Operas: A Critical Study*, 2nd ed. [London: Oxford University Press, 1947], p. 95).

4. From the Greek *topos*, "place," or in its technical use in rhetoric, "commonplace." Aristotle's *Topica* is a collection of general arguments which a rhetorician might consult for help in treating a particular theme. In music the term has been borrowed to designate "commonplace" musical styles or figures whose expressive connotations, derived from the circumstances in which they are habitually employed, are familiar to all.

5. A static scheme of symbolic key relations is one of the primary devices by which writers seek to uncover meaning in Mozart's operas. But while key relations are often important, they are more apt to lend confirmation to an insight than to suggest one; they offer no particularity of vision.

6. Theorists of the *Affektenlehre* include Johann Mattheson, *Der vollkommene Capellmeister* (Hamburg, 1739) and Johann Heinichen, *Der General-Bass in der Composition* (Dresden, 1728). See also Frederick Wessel, "The Affektenlehre in the Eighteenth Century" (Ph.D. diss., Indiana University, 1955); Brewster Rogerson, "The Art of Painting the Passions," *Journal of the History of Ideas* 14 (1953):81–87; George J. Buelow, "The *Loci Topici* and Affect in Late Baroque Music: Heinichen's Practical Demonstration," *Music Review* (1966):161–76.

7. See M. H. Abrams's illuminating discussion of nineteenth-century theories of poetry, *The Mirror and the Lamp: Romantic Theory and the Critical Tradition*

(London: Oxford University Press, 1953), pp. 1–69, for an account of the change.

8. Franz Liszt, "Berlioz and his 'Harold' Symphony," *Source Readings in Music History*, ed. and trans. Oliver Strunk (New York: Norton, 1950), p. 849.

9. Abrams, p. 48.

10. Aristotle, *Poetics*, 1448a.

11. "Indeed a slow movement is thought to be characteristic of the great-souled man, and a deep voice, and a steady way of speaking; for the man who pursues few things zealously is not likely to be hurried, nor is the man who thinks nothing great to be impetuous. But a shrill voice and swiftness of movement result from haste and impetuosity" (Aristotle, *Nichomachean Ethics*, 1125a12–16).

12. Aristotle, *Politics*, 1340a18–24.

13. Heinrich Christoph Koch, *Musikalisches Lexikon* (Frankfurt am Main: August Hermann, 1802), s.v. "Malerey."

14. Ibid., s.v. "Ausdruck."

15. Ibid., pp. 185–86.

16. This brief discussion of the doctrine of the affections is a paraphrase of Koch's article quoted above, itself partly a quotation from J. G. Sulzer's *Allgemeine Theorie der schönen Künste* (1771–74).

17. Today it is more commonly assumed that expression and action have mutually exclusive natures, a position which would be equivalent to stating that in the plays of Shakespeare the poetry of ethos and imagery is properly confined to reflective soliloquies, while speeches of individuals in act can convey only factual information. This thesis is untenable in both drama and music drama. On the contrary, the composers of *opera buffa*, and with them Mozart, had in admitting actions to their arias and ensembles succeeded in bringing the most revelatory part of the drama into music's domain, where it could contribute to the illumination of the whole. The modern difficulty lies, I suspect, with an artificial distinction between reflection and action. To Aristotle, the contemplative man, engaged in the highest activity men are capable of, was most in action when he was most reflective (*Nichomachean Ethics*, 1177a12–1178a8).

18. Michel Paul Gui de Chabanon, *De la musique considerée en elle-même et dans ses rapports avec la parole*, 2nd ed. rev. (Paris: Pissot et fils, 1785), p. 56.

19. I will use the word "motive" frequently, to designate the short figures with which Classic composers characteristically constructed melodic phrases. In using this word I wish to distinguish these figures from both "motifs," which are generally considered to be figures which have a significant recurrence in the course of a movement, and throughcomposed "tunes," which are a striking and rare occurrence in Classic music.

20. The type of bass which features broken figures such as the ones in the left hand in measures 1–4 (see ex. i–2) was given the sobriquet "Alberti," after the keyboard composer Domenico Alberti (1710–40?), who used them frequently.

21. C. J. von Feldtenstein, *Die Kunst nach der Choreographie zu tanzen und Tänze zu schreiben* (Braunschweig: Schröderschen Buchhandlung, 1767), pp.

21–22. He is quoting here from a letter written by the great-chancellor of France to his son.

22. Koch, *Lexikon*, s.v. "Acteur."

CHAPTER 1

1. *Musikalische Nachrichten und Anmerkungen die Musik betreffend*, ed. Johann Adam Hiller, 4 vols. (Leipzig, 1766–70), 4:20–21.

2. Johann George Sulzer, *Allgemeine Theorie der schönen Künste*, 2nd ed., 4 vols. (Leipzig, 1786–87), s.v. "Takt."

3. Johann Phillipp Kirnberger, *Die Kunst des reinen Satzes in der Musik*, 2 vols. (Berlin: Decker and Hartung, 1774–79), 2:134.

4. See for example Edward R. Reilly's discussion of the growing use of tempo markings in the latter half of the century in *Quantz and His "Versuch"* (New York: American Musicological Society, 1971), pp. 116–23.

5. For early eighteenth-century classifications of meter, see, for example, the catalogue of Michel de Saint-Lambert (Paris, 1702), paraphrased by Curt Sachs (*Rhythm and Tempo* [New York: W. W. Norton, 1953], p. 311), and that of Hotteterre (Paris, 1719), quoted by Reilly in *Quantz and His "Versuch"* (pp. 118–20).

6. A partial list of these classifications would include F. G. Drewis, *Freundschaftliche Briefe über die Theorie der Tonkunst und Composition* (1797), pp. 22–25; Francesco Galeazzi, *Elementi teorico-pratici di musica* (1791–96), 1:36–37; 2:295; Carlo Gervasoni, *La scuola della musica* (1800), 1:163–73; J. P. Kirnberger, *Die Kunst des reinen Satzes in der Musik* (1774–79), 2:113–36; H. C. Koch, *Musikalisches Lexikon* (1802), s.v. "Takt"; *Versuch einer Anleitung zur Komposition* (1782–93), 2:291–321; A. F. C. Kollmann, *An Essay on Musical Harmony* (1796), pp. 73–77; J. A. Scheibe, *Über die musikalische Composition*, vol. 1: *Die Theorie der Melodie und Harmonie* (1773), pp. 203–18; and J. G. Sulzer, *Allgemeine Theorie der schönen Künste* (1771–74), s.v. "Takt."

7. Kirnberger's method of cataloguing meters was somewhat eccentric, and he was, furthermore, aware that thirteen of the time signatures which he discussed were no longer in fashion, but he would have liked to see them revived in the interests of affective variety.

8. A modern discussion of meters of the "common-practice period" would probably feature only six: 2/2, 4/4, 2/4, 3/4, 3/8, and 6/8. To these Gervasoni adds 12/8, 6/4, 6/16, 12/16, 3/1, 3/2, 3/16, 9/4, 9/8, and 9/16 (six of these he characterizes as not in frequent use; see Carlo Gervasoni, *La Scuola della musica*, 3 vols. [Piacenza: N. Orcesi, 1800], 1:163–73).

9. Kirnberger, *Kunst*, 2:114.

10. *Tempo giusto* more commonly signifies the proper tempo for a given piece of music and not, as in this usage, a universal "mean tempo." But side by side with its usual meaning in the eighteenth century (see for example Koch, *Lexikon*, s.v. "Tempo giusto"), there existed the notion for which I have adopted the term. According to one French music encyclopedia, the words *a tempo giusto* indicate "that one must perform the piece with a moderate tempo, fairly close to andante, beating the notes distinctly" (*Encyclopédie méthodique*, vols. 1–2:

Musique, ed. Nicholas Etienne Framéry [Paris: Panckoucke, 1791], s.v. "A Tempo Giusto"). Thomas Busby uses for the same notion the phrase *tempo ordinario* (*A Musical Manual or Technical Directory* [London: Goulding and D'Almaine, 1828].

11. In duple meters 2/4 was often rendered as 2, although the sign did double duty as a symbol for *alla breve*.

12. Kirnberger, *Kunst*, 2:106.

13. Gervasoni, 1:165.

14. John Holden, *An Essay towards a Rational System of Music* (Glasgow: R. Urie, 1770), p. 35.

15. Sulzer, s.v. "Tanz."

16. Holden, p. 35.

17. Francesco Galeazzi, *Elementi teorico-pratici di musica*, 2 vols. (Rome: Stamperia Pilucchi Cracas, 1791–96), 2:295. See also Adolf Bernhard Marx, *Die Lehre von der musikalischen Komposition*, 2 vols. (Leipzig: Breitkopf and Härtel, 1837–38), 2:53–54; Sulzer, s.v. "Takt"; Gervasoni, 1:171.

18. Sulzer called the passepied the "natural movement of 3/8 meter" (s.v. "Takt"). Kirnberger used the same words to describe the minuet and 3/4 (*Kunst*, 2:129).

19. Johann Adolf Scheibe, *Über die musikalische Komposition*, vol. 1: *Die Theorie der Melodie und Harmonie* (Leipzig: Schwickert, 1773), p. 203; Gervasoni, 1:168; Kirnberger, *Kunst*, 2:118, 133; Sulzer, s.v. "Takt."

20. Fux's codification of Renaissance vocal counterpoint was as popular in the late eighteenth century as it had been earlier. Most later eighteenth-century theorists put their accounts of Renaissance polyphony in Fuxian terms, with *alla breve* examples (see for example Koch, *Lexikon*, s.v. "Contrapunkt").

21. *Weisse Note* ("white note") is a German term for the half note (Koch, *Lexikon*, s.v. "Weise Note").

22. A frequent characterization of the sarabande in the latter half of the century is a "slow minuet"; see for example Jean Leroud d'Alembert, *Elémens de musique théorique et pratique*, 3rd ed., rev. (Lyon: J.-M. Bruyset, 1766), p. 209; Holden, p. 40.

23. The key-area plan is discussed in n. 5, p. 340.

24. Yet underneath the blocks of sharply contrasted and punctuated materials and the unprepared dissonances which characterize the playful salon music, there can be discerned a tightly bound contrapuntal substructure, the sinew of the style. In deep structure the apparent antitheses merge.

25. Or one might substitute the last movement of the *Jupiter* Symphony and Donna Anna's "Fuggi, crudele, fuggi" (*Don Giovanni*, I, 2); there are many possible pairs.

26. See pp. 4 and 330 n. 11.

27. The ₵ often used as a sign for *alla breve* also betrays the old-fashioned origins of the style. As Koch reminds his readers, the sign is a slight alteration of the half-circle used by "our ancestors" to indicate *tempus imperfectum* (*Lexikon*, s.v. "Prolatio"; also "Takt"). Its ecclesiastical origins are reflected in its alias, *alla capella* (loosely, "as in church").

28. Leaving aside meters like 2/1, which some theorists only regretfully relinquished to the past.

29. F. G. Drewis, *Freundschaftliche Briefe über die Theorie der Tonkunst und Composition* (Halle: J. C. Hendel, 1797), p. 25.

30. Johann Philipp Kirnberger, *Anleitung zur Singcomposition* (Berlin: G. I. Decker, 1782), p. 12.

31. Scheibe, pp. 203–4.

32. Some of the confusion may have arisen from a simple misapprehension concerning the derivation of the term *alla breve*. One theorist translates it "with shortened notes," and moves from that translation to "every note as fast again as otherwise" (A. F. C. Kollmann, *An Essay on Musical Harmony* [London: J. Dale, 1796], p. 72). A better translation would be "beating the *breve*" (or double whole note) instead of the *semi breve* (or whole note), in other words taking a larger note value (in modern notation the half instead of the quarter note) as beat.

33. Kirnberger described the affect of 3/8 as "a gaiety with a wanton quality to it" (*Kunst*, 2:133).

34. See the discussions of the bourrée, the gavotte, and the 2/4 contredanse, pp. 48–59.

35. Kirnberger, *Kunst*, 2:120.

36. Leonard Ratner, in the preface to his recent book on the Classic style, makes the important point that the divergence between Baroque and Classic styles is far less than is usually assumed: they were "based upon the same criteria, a common set of premises, despite their obvious differences; they used one language, and their differences represented sublanguages of a universal 18th-century musical speech" (*Classic Music: Expression, Form, and Style* [New York: Schirmer Books, 1980], pp. xv–xvi). The assumption of a hiatus between the two styles, a necessary concomitant of the opinion that Classic music is abstract and nonreferential, constitutes a serious stumblingblock to any attempt to understand the Classic style.

37. Kirnberger, *Kunst*, 2:130 (9/16); 2:128 (9/4). Bach wrote many light gigues in such meters, for instance Fugue no. 4 of book 2 of *The Well-Tempered Clavier*.

38. See p. 20, Ex. 1–1.

39. Fugue 22 of book 1 of *The Well-Tempered Clavier*, for example, is set in 4/2 meter, or two whole notes per measure.

40. Dent, pp. 21–22.

41. See the discussions of the gigue and the bourrée on pp. 41–43 and 48–49 respectively.

42. See p. 340, n. 5.

43. Johann Adam Hiller, *Anweisung zum musikalisch-richtigen Gesange* (Leipzig: J. F. Junius, 1774), pp. 212–13. The kind of overparticular classification Hiller criticizes is exemplified in this paragraph of prescriptions by the *Affektenlehre* theorist Johann Mattheson: "Now it may be difficult to believe that even in simple little dance melodies the passions must be just as distinguishable as light and shade can always be. To give just a small example, in a *chaconne* the affect is more noble and proud than in a *passacaglia*; in a *courante* the feeling is

directed toward a tender hope (but I do not intend an Italian *corrente*); in a *sarabande* to a public, formal seriousness; in an *entrée* to pomp and vanity; in a *rigaudon* to pleasant joking; in a *bourrée* to contentment and a pleasing air; in a *rondeau* to cheerfulness; in a *passepied* to fickleness and inconstancy; in a *gigue* to passion and fervor; in a *minuet* to moderate gaiety, and so on" (Johann Mattheson, *Kern melodischer Wissenschaft* [Hamburg: Christian Herold, 1737], pp. 66–67).

44. "It must be confessed, that sometimes, while his [Handel's] carelessness neglected, his lax judgment even opposed the sentiment. . . . In *Alexander's Feast*, Thais is described *lighting another Troy*, by the slow and graceful movement of a minuet" (Thomas Busby, *A General History of Music*, 2 vol. [London: C. Whittaker, 1819], 2:386).

45. "Triple meter, above all that of the minuet, is only suitable to pleasant affections, to peaceful sentiments, at the most to plaintive notions; and I cannot keep from finding Jommelli ridiculous, when in his air *Già di nubbi*, etc., after having made the threat thunder in the mouth of an angry king, he finishes it off with a lovely little minuet on the words "If you want to find shelter from the storm, you, you indeed, know how to do it" (Laurent Garcin, *Traité du melodrama, ou réflexions sur la musique dramatique* [Paris: chez Vallat-la-Chapelle, 1772], p. 310).

46. J. J. Quantz, *Versuch einer Anweisung die Flöte traversière zu spielen*, trans. Edward R. Reilly (New York: Schirmer Books, 1966), p. 297.

47. Koch, *Lexikon*, s.v. "Charakter."

48. Kirnberger, *Kunst*, 1:202, n. 78. See also idem, 2:10; Newman Powell, "Kirnberger on Dance Rhythms, Fugues, and Characterization," *Festschrift Theodore Hoelty-Nichel*, ed. Newman Powell (Valparaiso: Valparaiso University, 1967), pp. 66–67; Sulzer, s.v. "Tanzstück"; Koch, *Lexikon*, s.v. "Tanzmusik"; A. F. C. Kollmann, *An Essay on Practical Musical Composition*, (London, 1799), p. 103.

49. Anton Bemetzrieder, *Music Made Easy to Every Capacity*, trans. Giffard Bernard (London: R. Ayre and G. Moore, 1778), pp. iii-iv.

CHAPTER 2

1. Von Feldtenstein, pp. 18–19. The dances he mentions are either French court dances or a particularly popular choreography of one of them which has been endowed with a descriptive title.

2. Michael Kelly, *Reminiscences of Michael Kelly*, 2 vols. (New York: Da Capo Press, 1969), 1:223.

3. Sulzer, s.v. "Menuet."

4. Von Feldtenstein, pp. 36–37 (italics mine).

5. The minuet quoted on p. 7 (ex. i–5), from the first movement of the Piano Sonata K. 332, is also an example of the quick version.

6. Sulzer, s.v. "Menuet."

7. A system of symbols capable of reflecting accurately the rhythm of any given measure or phrase is a necessary and helpful device, but one which is extremely difficult to fashion. Any abstraction from a rhythm will distort the

rhythm, yet abstraction is necessary for purposes of comparison. I have adopted the symbol (-) for a strong beat and (ᴗ) for a weak beat for purposes of calligraphic clarity, intending no suggestion of the relative duration or quality which these symbols take on in poetic notation, where (-) is usually twice (ᴗ). I intend both symbols to represent the quality of the beat, a factor influenced by quantity but not identical with it. For example, the paradigm 3/4 measure will be pictured / - ᴗᴗ/- ᴗᴗ/, the paradigm 2/4 measure /-ᴗ/-ᴗ/ In the schema for 4/4, /⸾ᴗ-ᴗ/⸾ᴗ-ᴗ/, the downstroke indicates that beat 1 is a "stronger strong beat" than beat 3. A weak beat can also receive a downstroke. For example, the minuet's two weak beats are stronger than the analogous weak beats in the waltz: /-ᵛᵛ/ as opposed to /⸾ᴗᴗ/ A comma will be used to indicate beat groupings which are not articulated by the barline, for example in the pattern of the bourrée: ᴗ/⸾ᴗᴗ,ᴗ/⸾ᴗᴗ

8. See M. E. Little, *The New Grove Dictionary of Music and Musicians*, ed. Stanley Sadie (London, 1980), s.v. "Minuet." Wendy Hilton refers to the "hypnotic cross-rhythm" which this counterpoint supplies (*Dance of Court and Theatre: The French Noble Style 1690–1725* [Princeton: Princeton Book Co., 1981], p. 294).

9. Anselm Bayley, *The Alliance of Musick, Poetry, and Oratory* (London: John Stockdale, 1789), p. 44.

10. A. Bacquoy-Guédon, *Méthode pour exercer l'oreille à la mesure dans l'art de la danse*, 2 vols. (Amsterdam: Valade, c. 1784), 1:9–10.

11. *A Collection of the Newest and Best Minuets* (Edinburgh: Neil Stewart, ca. 1770), pp. 1–2.

12. *The Letters of Mozart and His Family*, trans. and ed. Emily Anderson, 2nd ed., 3 vols. (New York: St. Martin's Press, 1966), 1:121.

13. These two clumsy minuets from the Edinburgh collection (pp. 28 and 12 respectively) are interesting because they imply a knowledge of the configurations of each topic, and therefore of the possibility of combining them, at the crudest level of musical skill.

14. See, for example, the sarabande "La Bourgogne", one of a suite of French court dance choreographies which Meredith Ellis Little analyzes in a recent article in *The Journal of the American Musicological Society*. She characterizes this sarabande as "dignified and serious but less complex than the courante . . . a bit more lively . . . and perhaps even playful" (M. E. Little, "The Contribution of Dance Steps to Musical Analysis and Performance: *La Bourgogne*," *Journal of the American Musicological Society* 28 [1975]:116).

15. Hilton, p. 36.

16. Mattheson, p. 119.

17. See pp. 17 and 332 n. 22.

18. The faster the tempo, the less a measure admits of rhythms which go against the grain of its usual pattern. In a rapid sarabande, the second beat of the measure would begin to sound like a downbeat.

19. Quantz, p. 291.

20. Beethoven uses the sarabande in his Piano Sonata opus 109, in the theme and variations *Andante molto espressivo ed cantabile*, and Schubert in the A-flat Major Impromptu, opus 142, #2, to name two later stylizations of the dance.

21. Koch, *Lexikon*, s.v. "Passepied."

22. See M. E. Little, *The New Grove Dictionary*, s.v. "Passepied."

23. See pp. 60–62 for a discussion of this development with regard to the contredanse.

24. a. William Crotch, *Specimens of Various Styles of Music* (London: R. Birchall, [1815]), p. 111 (no. 221).

  b. Michel Corrette, *Le parfait maitre à chanter* (Paris: chez l'auteur, [1782]), p. 28.

  c. J. P. Kirnberger, *Recueil d'airs de danse caractéristiques* (Berlin: J. J. Hummel, ca. 1783), pp. 9–10.

25. Corrette, p. 33, The practice is described by Quantz, p. 291.

26. See Hilton, p. 247.

27. Kollman's description of the affect of the gigue (*Practical Musical Composition*, p. 104).

28. Mattheson, p. 115.

29. Wendy Hilton quotes, for example, a gigue by Lully (from *Roland*, 1685) with a nine-measure opening strain (pp. 248–49).

30. Kirnberger, *Recueil*, p. 11.

31. See, for example, the gigues of the D Minor French Suite and the E Minor Partita.

32. Kirnberger, *Kunst*, 2:129.

33. Sébastien de Brossard, *A Musical Dictionary*, trans. under the supervision of Dr. Pepusch (London: J. Wilcox, 1740) s.v. "Saltarella"; Holden, p. 40. See, for example, Mozart's D Minor Quartet, K. 421, last movement.

34. Koch, *Lexikon*, s.v. "Pastorale."

35. Gervasoni, 1:477–78.

36. Kollmann, *Practical Musical Composition*, p. 105.

37. Ignaz Pleyel, *Méthode pour le piano forte* (Paris: Pleyel, [1799]), p. 16.

38. See pp. 52–55 for a discussion of the musette.

39. Koch, *Lexikon*, s.v. "Siciliano."

40. Quantz, p. 168.

41. Busby, *History*, 2:490–96. The text of the hymn as given by Busby is: "Again my mournful sighs/Prevent the rising morn;/Again my wishful eyes/Look out for His return./I weep and languish/And long my Lord to find,/But wake, alas! to all my grief/And load I left behind."

42. Koch tells an amusing anecdote about an expression, "Hurlebusch's Siciliano," which arose in Amsterdam to describe any expansive and overlengthy piece. Apparently a Mr. Hurlebusch, a skilled clavier player, in Amsterdam one day at a public concert played a siciliano so lengthy that one listener left the hall before it ended, and "the next morning, encountering Hurlebusch on the street, asked him whether his *siciliano* had already ended" (Koch, *Lexikon*, s.v. "Siciliano").

43. Mattheson, p. 113.

44. See pp. 48–52.

45. Sulzer, s.v. "Marsch." Rousseau's discussion (*Oeuvres complètes*, vols. 12 and 13: *Dictionnaire de musique*, ed. V. D. Musset-Pathay [Paris: P. Dupont, 1824], s.v. "Marche") is shorter, but the same in substance. Koch in his *Lexikon*

includes a version of the same discussion not under the rubric *Marsch*, but in the article on *Rhythmus*.

46. Gervasoni, 1:466–67.

47. Charles Burney, *Dr. Burney's Musical Tours in Europe*, vol. 2: *An Eighteenth-Century Musical Tour in Central Europe and the Netherlands*, ed. Percy Scholes (London: Oxford University Press, 1959), pp. 195–96.

48. Drewis, p. 67; Sulzer, s.v. "Marsch."

49. Johann L. Albrecht, *Gründliche Einleitung in die Anfangslehren der Tonkunst* (Langensalze: J. C. Martini, 1761), p. 117.

50. Daniel Gottlob Türk, *Klavierschule*, facsimile of the first edition, ed. Erwin R. Jacobi (Kassel: Bärenreiter, 1962), pp. 10–11.

51. See pp. 18–23.

52. See M. E. Little, "The Contribution of Dance Steps to Musical Analysis and Performance," pp. 114–17, for a description of the choreography of a French bourrée.

53. *Musikalische Nachrichten*, 1:400–401.

54. Mattheson (p. 112) characterizes the melody of the bourrée as "*flowing, smooth, gliding,* and *legato.*"

55. See pp. 68–69 for a discussion of Sulzer's classification of types of theatrical dance.

56. Sulzer, s.v. "Bourrée."

57. Sulzer, s.v. "Rigaudon."

58. Mattheson, p. 112.

59. The French court choreography of the gavotte provides even a further complication. The dance steps constitute a counterpoint to the rhythms of the music which is not resolved until the fourth measure of each phrase, when a *pas assemblé*, a "cadential" step which involves a leap to a position with both feet together, puts the period to the choreographic phrase coincidentally with the final thesis of the musical phrase (m. 4, beat 1). The complexity of the dance causes Wendy Hilton to characterize it as an experience which is at first "puzzling," but with greater familiarity "delectable" (p. 245).

60. Koch, *Lexikon*, s.v. "Gavotte"; Holden, p. 40.

61. Friedrich Wilhelm Marpurg, *Clavierstücke mit einem praktischen Unterricht für Anfänger und Geübtere*, 3 vols. (Berlin: Hande und Speuer, 1762), 2:23.

62. Charles Compan, *Dictionnaire de danse* (Paris, 1787), s.v. "Gavotte."

63. Joseph Barnabé Saint-Sévin, *Principes du violin*, facsimile, ed. Aristide Wirsta (Paris: Centre du Documentation Universitaire, 1961), pp. 37, 40.

64. M. E. Little, *The New Grove Dictionary*, s.v. "Gavotte."

65. Antonio Eximeno y Pujades, *Dell'origine e delle regole della musica* (Rome: M. A. Barbiellini, 1774), examples, p. 22.

66. Gavottes can be rendered in 4/4, *alla breve*, or 2/4. Mozart frequently uses 2/4. See for example the string quartets K. 169, movement 4, and K. 173, movement 2, or the Piano Sonata K. 547a, movement 3. Other examples of gavottes by Mozart are the third movements of the piano sonatas K. 281 and K. 284, and the second movement of the E-flat Major Quintet, K. 614, (all three in *alla breve*).

67. M. E. Little, *The New Grove Dictionary*, s.v. "Musette."

68. Compan, s.v. "Musette."

69. Sulzer, s.v. "Musette." See also Marpurg, 2:24; Türk, p. 401.

70. Sulzer, s.v. "Musette."

71. Louis Adam, *Méthode de forte piano* (no. 9 in a volume with binder's title: *Musique de piano* [18 —]), p. 94.

72. See p. 51.

73. *Musikalische Nachrichten*, 2:336.

74. Jean-Michel Guilcher, *La Contredanse et les renouvellements de la danse française* (Paris: Mouton, 1969), pp. 21–85.

75. Some writers specify a faster tempo and dotted rhythms for the angloise. The dancing master Bacquoy-Guédon couples it with the allemande, both "only composed of skippings and stampings suitable for making the body take up bad habits" (1:55–56), contrasting them with the française, in which, he claims, the expression is less vigorous and the movements better controlled.

76. The dancing master von Feldtenstein, considering the German dances to be an open invitation to uncivilized behavior, states that the only suitable companion for the minuet on the dance floor is the Englische Tanz (pp. 15, 18). Bacquoy-Guédon, despite his preference for things French, couples the françaises and angloises in tempo, time signature, and characteristic patterns; his allemandes are strikingly different (1:21, 23; 2:12–15).

77. Bacquoy-Guédon, 1:20.

78. Sulzer, s.v. "Englische Tänze."

79. Bacquoy-Guédon, 2:13.

80. Guilcher, p. 104.

81. Chabanon, pp. 93–94.

82. Two are in *alla breve* (K. 267, nos. 2 and 3), one in 3/8 (K. 609, no. 4), and one in 6/8 (K. 267, no. 1).

83. For example, the Haydn string-quartet finale quoted earlier as a bourrée (ex. 2–23, p. 49) can also be classed as a contredanse française in bourrée style. The tempo is *Allegro ma non troppo*, but the comically misplaced accents suggest a contredanse-style bourrée parody.

84. See ex. 2–34, a, b, c, and d.

85. See, for example, the dotted rhythms which characterize "La Résolue" ("The Resolute Lady"), ex. 2–34d, p. 58.

86. Marx, 2:57. Others who mention the special cadence include Kirnberger, *Kunst*, 2:131, and Sulzer, s.v. "Englische Tänze."

87. a-c. J. C. Joly, *Recueil de nouvelles contre-danses, waltzes, et anglaises* (Paris: Frère, [n. d.]), pp. 4–5, 8–9, 22–23. "La Chaumière" means "The Thatched Hut."

d and e. Auguste, *Troisième recueil de nouvelles contredanses et waltzers* (Paris: Sieber, [1799]), pp. 13, 26.

f. Adam, p. 93.

g. Mozart, K. 462, no. 5.

h. Haydn, Sonata in A-flat Major, movement 3 (Martienssen, 1, no. 8).

i. Mozart, Quartet in E-flat Major, K. 428, movement 4.

j. Mozart, Contretänze, K. 609, no. 1. The tune is of course "Non più andrai" from *Le nozze di Figaro.* After the enormous success of *Figaro* Mozart barred the 4/4 march as a contredanse, putting it into a form suitable for public consumption. Ex. 2–34k is the march tune which begins in m. 61 of the aria.

88. Sulzer, s.v. "Englische Tänze." This remark is also quoted by Koch in his *Versuch einer Anleitung zur Komposition*, 3 vols. (Leipzig: A. F. Böhme, 1782–93), 3:47.

89. Bacquoy-Guédon, 1:23, n. 20.

90. Ibid., 2:15.

91. K. 509, 536, 571, 586, 600, 602, 605, and 611.

92. One hallmark of its crudity, the awkward three-measure phrases, was necessary to fit the dance to the harmonic and rhythmic contours of the minuet and contredanse which are played simultaneously with it (see pp. 282–85).

93. Sulzer, s.v. "Englische Tänze." See also the remarks of the dancing master C. J. von Feldtenstein quoted on p. 31.

94. Gervasoni, 1:496.

95. Since each complete dance includes many figures, an entire tune may have to be played through as many as six to eight times before the dancing comes to an end.

96. Marx, 2:57 (italics mine).

97. See ex. 2–34, a–d, p. 58.

98. Guilcher, pp. 45–46, 138–39.

99. According to von Feldtenstein, the choice of figure for the second part of the contredanse was left up to the leader of the dance. In a dance involving so many people each participant could not be allowed to follow his fancy; license and carousing would result (C. J. von Feldtenstein, pp. 15–16).

100. Sulzer, s.v. "Allemande."

101. "CONTRE-DANSE. The tune of a kind of dance of the same name, which is performed by four, six, or eight people, and which is usually danced in balls after minuets, since it is gayer and occupies more dancers. *Contre-danse* melodies are usually in duple meter; they must be clearly punctuated, brilliant, and gay, and still be simple. For since they are repeated very often, they would be unbearable if they were complicated. In every style, the simplest things are those which one least tires of" (J. J. Rousseau, *Dictionnaire*, s.v. "Contre-danse"; quoted in the *Encyclopédie Méthodique*, s.v. "Contredanse").

102. *Encyclopédie Méthodique*, s.v. "Contredanse."

103. Koch, *Lexikon*, s.v. "Ländler," "Walzer"; Johann Gottlieb Kaye, *Kleine Klavier-Schule* (Sondershausen: B. F. Voigt, [1822]), s.v. "Walzer"; Sulzer, s.v. "Tanz," describing the *Schwäbische Tanz*; Peter Lichtenthal, *Dizionario e bibliografia della musica*, 2 vols. (Milan: A. Fontana, 1826), s.v. "Ländler."

104. Joly, pp. 44–45.

105. Marx, 2:55–56.

106. Ibid, 2:56 (italics mine).

107. Framéry uses almost the same phrase ("the sole pleasure of dancing") to describe what motivates the country people to dance their contredanses (see p. 62).

108. See p. 37.

109. The Teitsch is quoted as ex. 2–37, p. 285.

110. The role of the 2/4 contredanse in *Don Giovanni* is discussed further on pp. 220–23.

111. The English word "generous" traces its lineage to the Latin *generosus*, "highborn" or "noble-minded," and in turn to the Greek εὐγενής (εὖ — "well," γένος — "race" or "stock"), which also signifies either nobility of rank or nobility of character. "Generous" itself can mean "of noble birth," or "magnanimous," in the sense of "great-souled" rather than "openhanded," although these first and root meanings have little currency today.

112. I have adopted this spelling of the word "daemonic" rather than the more conventional "demonic" in order that its meaning not be restricted to a merely Christian context. For a further discussion of the word see p. 216.

113. Sulzer, s.v. "Tanz." Sulzer's comments are not restricted to the *ballet d'action*, the so-called pantomimic dance. "Each of the four forms of theatrical dance can be of two kinds. Either they portray only character and manners, or they perform a specific action with complications and resolution. In the first case . . . it is sufficient that the unity of affect be maintained throughout" (ibid., s.v. "Tanz"). The dances of the *ballet d'action* "suffer neither unity of character nor organization of phrases, and thus are like recitative" (ibid., s.v. "Tanzstück"); they are always at the service of a particular story. Only nonpantomimic dances depict the generalized passions of men, their "characters and manners," through the habitual union of a rhythm with a gesture.

114. Bacquoy-Guédon, p. 55. Bacquoy-Guédon was the first dancing master to open a public school of dance.

115. See p. 4. Training in music, and particularly in proper rhythms, was an important part of the moral education of the guardians in Plato's *Republic* (see, for example, 400a–402b) and of the citizens in Aristotle's *Politics* (8. 5–7).

CHAPTER 3

1. *The Crazy Day* was the alternate title of *Le mariage de Figaro*, and the sole title of the first German version (*Der närrische Tag*).

2. "No, Master Count, you will not have her . . . you will not have her. Because you are a great lord, you think you have a great nature! . . . Nobility, fortune, rank, position, all that makes you so proud! What have you done to gain so many advantages? You took the trouble to be born, and nothing else. Otherwise, a rather ordinary man" (*Le mariage de Figaro*, V, iii).

3. Pondering in a despondent moment the state to which the Count has reduced her, she sees as a symptom of her misery her need to conspire with a servant ("Fammi or cercar da una mia serva aita!" — "And now I am forced to seek aid from one of my servant-girls!" III, 19, 24–25). The Countess here is not rejecting Susanna, but merely evaluating her own situation in the light of her world's proper orders.

4. Brief accounts of all important dance patterns are given on pp. 33–60. The bourrée is discussed on pp. 48–49.

5. I have adopted certain terms used by Leonard Ratner to describe the entity so often called by the misnomer "sonata form." This so-called "form" is actually a

harmonic process, involving in essence a move from a well-established home key to its opposite pole, the dominant, and back again. The events of the motion out and of the return depend on many factors, among them the kinds of material employed, the relative stability of the opening tonic, and the nature of the move to the dominant; no hard and fast procedures can or should be enumerated. The harmonic skeleton has two parts. The first establishes the tonic and accomplishes the move to the dominant, confirming arrival in the new key with a series of strong cadences. The second part begins by undermining the dominant and building up expectations of the tonic: it then returns to the tonic, restating the motivic material of the opening and incorporating the material of the original dominant area into tonic harmony in some arrangement (it need not repeat the original sequence). The practice in opera with regard to motivic treatment is even more open-ended. Since the text already furnishes a dramatic continuity for the piece, the tonic may return cloaked in entirely new material.

The terms I will use in referring to the events of the harmonic process are as follows:

Key:	I	V	?	I I
Name:	Key Area I	Key Area II	X- Section	Return

Reprise I   Reprise II

I shall use the traditional terms exposition, development, and recapitulation occasionally, when in complicated situations they can provide a convenient shorthand for readers unfamiliar with the new terminology. (For a more detailed discussion of the process, see Leonard Ratner, "Harmonic Aspects of Classic Form," *Journal of the American Musicological Society* 2 (1949):159–68).

6. "Comic," of course, in its classic sense of distinguishing from "tragic" works stories which have happy endings.

7. Sulzer, s.v. "Tanz." Sulzer's classification of theater dance was previously quoted on pp. 68–69.

8. See pp. 127–31.

9. "If perchance Madame calls you at night, ding ding — in two steps you can be at her side" (mm. 5–20).

10. In shaping this movement Mozart seems to have had in mind an actual contredanse tune, in which a twenty-measure strain (never precisely realized) is repeated four times (with a long coda following, mm. 83 to the end). The first strain moves to V, the second cadences in B-flat again, the third begins in G minor and closes on V of B-flat, and the fourth is entirely in the tonic. Although not as taut as a regular key-area form, it allows the point of the duet to be made through the contrasts in the nearly similar strains.

11. "And look, in three leaps . . ." (mm. 66–68) — Susanna's description of Almaviva presenting himself at *her* door.

12. Figaro: "Have courage, my treasure." Susanna: "And you use your head" (I, i, 183–84).

13. "If you want to dance, my pretty little Count, I'll play the guitar for you."

14. In the manner of address also Figaro follows Susanna's lead. She first

used the insulting diminutive "Contino" (actually "il caro Contino," I, 2, 45–51), when describing the Count's subterfuge. In addition, Figaro sarcastically affects the most polite form of address, the third-person *Lei* (*lei suonerò*, for example); it is little used elsewhere in the opera.

15. "Se vuol ballare" is in key-area form, with a full cadence on the dominant in m. 42 and a brief X-section ending at m. 63. The return to the tonic is represented by a new dance (see below).

16. "If you want to come to my school, I'll teach you the capriole."

17. The dancer would rise in the air on a weak beat, perform "beats" with his feet in the air, and land on the first beat of the next measure — a virtuoso performance generally reserved for the ballet. I am grateful to M. E. Little for her help on this point.

18. "The extra-musical association of 'horn' in most languages (It. *corno*, Germ. *Horn*, Fr. *corne*) with 'cuckold' was close and obvious to everybody in an eighteenth-century audience" (Siegmund Levarie, *Mozart's Le Nozze de Figaro: A Critical Analysis* [Chicago: University of Chicago Press, 1952], p. 26).

19. "The art of fencing, the art of conniving, pricking from this side, tricking from that — I'll upset all your schemes."

20. A device frequently used in Baroque music whereby a single melodic line seems to imitate two voices at once in dialogue; the mordent figures in two different registers which constitute the opening motive of Bach's Brandenburg Concerto no. 3 are an example of a *Brechung* melody.

21. Mozart often orchestrated with choreographies in mind. Leopold Mozart, in a letter to his wife written from Rome in 1770, says: "Wolfgang is splendid and sends herewith a contredanse [K. 123]. He would like Herr Cirillus Hofmann [dancing master at the Salzburg court] to make up the steps for it; when the two violins play as leaders, only two persons should lead the dance; but whenever the orchestra comes in with all the instruments, the whole company should dance together. It would be by far the best arrangement if it were danced by five couples. The first couple should begin the first solo, the second dance the second, and so on, as there are five solos and five tutti passages" (Anderson, 1:127–28).

22. "Avrei pur gusto/Di dar in moglie la mia serva antica/A chi mi fece un dì rapir l'amica" ("It would give me great pleasure to marry off my aging servant to the man who once had my beloved snatched away from me" — I, iii, 149–52).

23. "La vendetta" is discussed further in connection with the Count's *alla breve* revenge aria "Vedrò, mentr'io," III, 17 (see pp. 144–45).

24. "The amour of all Spain" (mm. 28–29).

25. Before they close they repeat the glories of the second reprise, with added embellishments (mm. 38–55).

26. "Perbacco, precipito,/Se ancor resto qua!" ("By Bacchus I shall do something rash if I stay here any longer!" — mm. 33–36).

27. "You decrepit old Sibyl, you make me laugh" (mm. 36–38).

28. Marcellina "leaves in a rage."

29. "Go on, you old pedant, you stuck-up lady scholar; just because you once read two books, and annoyed Madame in her youth . . ." (I, v, 75–78).

30. "Leggila alla padrona,/Leggila tu medesma,/Leggila a Barbarina, a Marcellina,/Leggila ad ogni donna del palazzo!" ("Read it to my mistress, you read it yourself, read it to Barbarina, to Marcellina, read it to every woman in the palace!").

31. "Povero Cherubin, siete voi pazzo?" ("Poor Cherubino, are you mad?" — I, v, 115–116).

32. In the play the Countess explains that Cherubino is related to her family and is her godchild (I, x). Da Ponte omitted the scene in which these lines occur, but Cherubino refers to the Countess as his *comare* or godmother (I, v, 86 and II, 10, 165–66), and it was customary to take noble-born boys into noble households as pages.

33. "I don't know what I am, what I'm doing . . . Sometimes I'm on fire, sometimes I'm all ice . . . Every woman makes me blush, makes me tremble. At the mere names of love, of pleasure, I grow agitated, my heart skips a beat, and a desire which I cannot explain forces me to speak of love!"

34. See Putnam Aldrich, *Rhythm in Seventeenth-Century Italian Monody* (New York: Norton, 1966), pp. 103–14.

35. Lines three and four of the first stanza might seem to be an anomaly in an anapestic scheme because of the string of six eighth notes with which they begin:

But the first eighth note on the syllable *don* — is an appoggiatura which varies the line by embellishing the all-important word *donna*; it does not distract from the underlying rhythm.

36. M. 22, using for the first two lines the syncopation from the earlier cadence.

37. M. 27 — V^7 of F, the new dominant. Or the D-flat could be regarded as a chromatic appoggiatura to a V_5^6 of V; the effect is the same.

38. Ordinarily, in order to register "truest" passion in the middle of an operatic aria, the character moves from strictly measured music to the freer rhythms of recitative. For example, in the finale to the second act of *Figaro*, in the midst of a spirited 4/4 exchange between the Count and the Countess, he calls her suddenly by her Christian name and she, deeply stung, answers him in a phrase of recitative which brings the rhythmic action to an abrupt halt (II, 15, 229–33). In "Non so più," on the other hand, the regular rhythms of the strictly "poetic" setting are apprehended as the artifice, and the singer need not resort to declamation to register his natural voice.

39. "I speak of love when I'm awake, I speak of love when I'm dreaming: to the water, to the shadows, to the mountains, to the flowers, to the grass, to the fountains, to the echo, to the air, to the winds, which bear away with themselves the sound of the empty syllables" (mm. 54–91).

40. "E, se non ho chi m'oda,/Parlo d'amor con me" — the last two lines of "Non so più."

41. "Throw out the seducer!" (I, 7, 8–11).

42. "That's the way all beautiful women behave; it's no novelty." Da Ponte was as fond of self-quotation as Mozart (who himself includes a figure very like Basilio's in the overture to *Così fan tutte*, mm. 35–37 and *passim*).

43. "Ah, what I said about the page was just a suspicion of mine!" (mm. 85–92).

44. "Ah, better still" (mm. 145–46).

45. Although not as trim as it seems at first glance, for, divided three measures to the Count and one to Susanna and Basilio, it is actually a five-measure phrase truncated by an overlap with the Count's repetition of his proclamation (that the page must leave; m. 105). The scansion of a truncated five gives an implied length and weightiness to the Count's phrase in addition to the rhythmic briskness of the regular four-measure shape.

46. Basilio sets the subject each time, and the Count takes it up a measure later.

47. "My lord, how her heart is beating!"

48. Mm. 70–84. The substitution of the relative major for the relative minor via a deceptive cadence is a favorite device of Mozart's for surprise in X-sections; for example, he substitutes Leporello's F major for the implied D minor when Giovanni tries to put his valet forward as culprit after the Don's second attempt at seducing Zerlina (in the three-dance ballroom scene, I, 13, 499; see p. 285).

49. Basilio: "Siamo qui per aiutarvi,/E sicuro il vostro onor."
Count: "Siamo qui per aiutarti,/Non turbarti, o mio tesor." (Basilio: "We are here to help you; your honor is secure." Count: "We are here to help you; don't worry, my treasure.")

50. "Just Gods! what's going to happen!"

51. Her intent is to prevent the men, in their efforts to revive her, from carrying her to the chair where Cherubino is concealed.

52. The address "Oh, most virtuous Madam" (mm. 147–49, and five more times thereafter) picks up with heavy sarcasm Basilio's talk of Susanna's *onor*, and by the appellation *signora* implies an intended infidelity to her marriage bond. It is a more direct and vicious assault on her dignity than Basilio's airy epigram; once shored up, Almaviva's bitchery has a grim aptness which Basilio's does not attain.

53. "The divine innocence of an even lovelier flower" (than those which the chorus is scattering, mm. 21–28).

54. The next time the chorus appears, in act III, more is known about its individual members, particularly Barbarina and the blushing "maiden" beside her (Cherubino, dressed as a girl). A close-up glimpse robs the chorus of some of its anonymity, and also of some of its innocence; the madness of the day has spread to everyone. In the first act, however, the chorus remains a mass of undifferentiated young peasants, precisely the troop of celebrants for a confrontation with the Count.

55. "What is this comedy?" (I, 8, 41–42). "Devilish cleverness!" (I, 8, 58).

56. "No more, amorous butterfly, will you go flitting around night and day disturbing the beauties' beauty sleep, you little Narcissus, little Adonis of love.

No more will you have these fine little feathers, that light and sparkling air, that blushing, womanly color."

57. Some writers have seen the expanded form as revolutionary: vant expresses in the manner of a free individual what he thinks of a tionally rigid norm. The audience hears the subjective explosion of an eld form and it cheers. Not only an eighteenth-century form of music but whole eighteenth-century form of living suffers an insult by Figaro's rebellion (Levarie, p. 72). The identification of phrase extension as a metaphor for revolution would be enticing, were not expanded forms in fact the norm in the late eighteenth century. Spinning out the members of rondos and two-reprise forms was the rule, not the exception. Leporello's famous "Catalogue" aria (*Don Giovanni*, I, 4) is a prime example: the simple minuet beginning the second reprise (m. 85) swells to almost one hundred measures before it can achieve a final cadence. Leporello's expansion is clearly not at the service of a revolution, but of a list. Closer to home, Figaro's expansions of the minuet phrase structure in "Se vuol ballare" (I, 3) are entirely danceable, and not symbolic explosions of a rigid form (see pp. 79–82 and Levarie, p. 29). If anything bursts its bounds in "Non più andrai," it is Figaro's exuberant imagination.

"Sonata form" actually had its genesis in the expansion of the simple two-reprise or key-area plan. A chronicle of it would study the exercising of the imaginative powers against the fabric of a simply and clearly outlined harmonic structure — the two-part dance piece. The late eighteenth century had no rigid norms or forms; composition was a fluid process — an elaboration on a band of simple premises.

58. "All exit in military style."

59. This suggestion is made by Levarie (p. 72), and by Frits Noske ("Social Tensions in *Le nozze di Figaro*," *Music and Letters* [1969], p. 52). Because it is important ammunition for those who see the opera as a revolutionary comedy in the tradition of its original rather than as a pastoral romance about the nature of true attachment, this suggestion needs careful refutation. It depends partly on the assumption that Figaro, while he defers to Cherubino in public, addressing him in the second person plural at the beginning of this scene ("E *voi* non applaudite?"), is in private insolent (he addresses Cherubino thereafter exclusively as *tu*).

But since, as I shall explain in the ensuing discussion above, all Figaro's remarks but for one aside are made in the presence of the Count and Basilio, there is actually no distinction to be made in the scene between public and private. According to the original libretto, Figaro's final words to Cherubino before the aria ("Farewell, little Cherubino. How your [*tuo*] fate changes in a moment!") are said with *feigned* joy ("*finta* gioia"); Figaro is aware that he has an audience, and nevertheless addresses the boy familiarly. Although Cherubino is probably of gentle birth, he is nevertheless a child, not in his proper home, and in a position of service; ordinary protocol will probably not apply. The issue of Cherubino's aristocracy never seems to be a live one in his relationships with Susanna and Figaro, and so *tu* is no more necessarily insolent than *voi* defers. Susanna calls Cherubino *voi* perhaps for the same reasons as

: attractive and amorous boy at arm's length.
probably affectionate, his one public *voi* a per-
ms to his role as fond older brother, to conceal
r relationship as friends and — as I shall show
ɔrs.

efore you leave" (I, viii, 131–32).

ɘd" (I, viii, 129).

ɔn *my advice* hasn't left yet . . ." (II, ii, 122–24

face! Look at the little colt, see how beautiful he

12, 119).

65. See p. 104 ff. . . . g of some of their changes.

66. "And will destiny make me find this page everywhere!" (II, viii, 83–85).

67. "Little Narcissus, little Adonis of love . . . little feathers . . . sparkling air . . . scarlet, womanly color" (all from the first lines of "Non più andrai").

68. This metaphor will be encountered again in the discussions of "Porgi, amor" (II, 10), and of the finale to act III (see pp. 102 and 151–56).

CHAPTER 4

1. Postponing her entrance required a substantive alteration of Beaumarchais's scheme, for in *Le mariage* the Countess appeared in the first act to witness the chorus's petition to the Count (*Le mariage de Figaro*, I, x).

2. The adjective *amoroso* indicates music in the singing style for winds, often characterized by movement in parallel thirds and by the use of the flat keys. Mozart employs this designation, for example, in the second movement of the Piano Sonata in B-flat Major, K. 281, an imitation of the slow movement of a divertimento for winds and entitled *Andante amoroso*.

3. The Countess's song is a much expanded version of the orchestral introduction. Her mm. 18–21 correspond to mm. 3–6, and mm. 26–27 (orchestra only) to mm. 7–10, although they lack the topical contrast. Mm. 42–45, while corresponding in outline to mm. 12–15 (first chord), have a different topic. Halfway through m. 13 the martial enters in a dramatic shift, but in mm. 43–45 the winds continue instead the singing, *amoroso* topic, in order to harmonize with the close (mm. 15–17 correspond to mm. 49–51). The two most poignant touches of the cavatina are absent from the orchestral introduction — the sudden turn to the minor triad on 6 in m. 22, to begin the phrase *al mio duolo* ("Grant me, o love, some release *from my pain*") and the cadenzalike outburst before the return (mm. 34–37). The C-minor triad returns in mm. 40 and 43 as a deceptive cadence after the outburst, and an echo of that first haunting occurrence of the chord.

4. *Don Giovanni*, I, 1; see pp. 203–207.

5. Susanna: "And you have the nerve to joke about such a serious business?" Figaro: "Isn't it enough for you that I think while I joke?" (II, ii, 94–98).

6. In *Le mariage* Beaumarchais includes a short exchange between the Countess and Figaro just before Figaro's exit which explains his cockiness as

an attempt to inspirit the Countess: Countess: "Il a tant d'assurance qu'il finit par m'en inspirer." Figaro: "C'est mon dessein" (Countess: "He has such confidence that finally he gives it to me." Figaro: "That's my plan" — *Le mariage de Figaro*, II, iii). Da Ponte omitted the exchange and consequently an excuse for Figaro's tactlessness.

7. This scene makes it hard to credit statements that the servants resent Cherubino, or the reverse. Susanna teases Cherubino from affection, not resentment. When she addresses him as "Signor uffiziale" ("Mr. Officer"), Cherubino answers her joking reminder of his plight by railing not at her, but at the "nome sì fatale" ("that fatal title") in a mock-tragic vein over a C-minor chord, and bewailing his prospective exile from his patronness (II, 10, 161–66). The three never exchange a harsh word elsewhere in the opera.

8. "Ladies, you who know what love is, see if I have it in my heart."

9. "I shall repeat to you what I'm feeling; it's new for me, and I don't know how to understand it. I have a feeling full of desire; sometimes it's pleasure, sometimes torment. I'm cold, and then I feel my soul all ablaze, and in a moment I'm cold again. I'm looking for a good which is outside of me; I don't know who has it, or what it is. I sigh and moan without wanting to, I quiver and tremble without knowing it, I find no peace night or day, and yet it pleases me to languish this way."

10. The key and instrumentation of the aria (B-flat major; clarinets and bassoons with string accompaniment) attach it closely to "Porgi, amor."

11. Aldrich, pp. 105, 122–25.

12. "Ye women who comprehend love. . . ."

13. Which some writers criticize in Cherubino's version; see, for example, P. B. Moberly, *Three Mozart Operas* (London: Victor Gollancz, 1967), p. 81.

14. "Women who know what love is, who comprehend love" — the sentence is a conflation of the opening line of the aria and the opening line of Dante's poem.

15. "Little serpent" — an explicitly feminine view of Eros, stressing his masked power and craft. Susanna calls Cherubino "serpentello" in the dialogue after the present aria (II, 12, 121).

16. "Look at the little colt, see how beautiful he is!" and "What a crafty expression" (II, 12, 83–94).

17. "If women love him, they certainly have good reason" (II, 12, 94 to the end).

18. This procedure is not unlike the deployment of bourrée rhythms in Susanna's act I duet with Marcellina. One of its building blocks is a "bourrée measure," which is applied at will in groups of three to eight measures without producing expectations of periodic symmetry. "Se vuol ballare" is an example of the opposite procedure: the premise of the minuet shapes the limits of the aria's phrase structure from the beginning, never — except for a few moments in the X-section — abstracting the dance rhythm from its periodic context, as is the practice in the aria under discussion.

19. "Madame is not here."

20. "Let's see how you walk now when you're on your feet."

21. M. 73, although sharing the dotted rhythms of the beginning of bourrée

Example N4-1

C major

1, projects a martial posture — another example of the affective differences which can be wrought by slight changes in rhythmic scansion. The bourrée and the march, rhythmically much alike, often blend into one. The march affect tinges mm. 3 and 7 of bourrée 1 because they follow the flourish, and consist of dotted rhythms. The legato phrasing and syncopated patterns (♪♩ ♪) of the rest of the phrase shade away from hints of march to pure bourrée. A different treatment of harmony and texture and a position later in the key-area process make the dotted rhythms of m. 73 sound martial. After leisurely harmonic wandering reinforced by regular four-measure phrases, m. 73 closes the narrow end of the harmonic funnel back to G major (ex. N4–1). Its crisp dotted rhythms and punctuating bass are an abrupt contrast with the expansive phrase of bourrée 2 (which has a long-note introductory measure, a hypnotic harmonic rhythm, and a slow-moving bass). Furthermore, the orchestra has been engaged in a "terraced" crescendo since m. 61, adding a new wind instrument every four measures, and has just reached its height. All these elements combine to inflect the sudden and dominant march affect of m. 73.

22. "As long as she wears a skirt, you know what he'll do" (*Don Giovanni*, I, 4, 143–72).

23. Magic is indeed part of the armor of Eros, as Eros himself says in the bit of dialogue just after Susanna's aria where Cherubino blushingly tells the Countess of the strange healing powers possessed by an object belonging to one's beloved (in this case the ribbon he "borrowed" from the Countess herself). The Countess replies by teasing the *forestiero* ("outlandish one") affectionately about foolish superstitions (II, 12, 146–54).

24. "The situation is so ugly!" and "The situation is quite clear!" (m. 28).

25. Full-blown, that is, in exposition and recapitulation. Each section is a fully developed symphonic segment. The relation of the key areas — the first so brief, the second so expansive — is a little unusual, but this imbalance answers to the requirements of the situation, since the Count's curt formal challenge serves as a launching pad for the ladies' ensuing panic. The extensive development in the second key area curtails the X-section or development itself to ten measures of dominant pedal before the return.

26. "Oh heavens! this is surely the beginning of our downfall" (mm. 96–100).

27. Literal except for the repetition of the *disordine* section. An exclamatory recitative section bridges its two appearances (mm. 121–24), a brief passage which is itself a textual epitome of the A-flat major insertion: the Count and Countess cry one after another the fatal word *giudizio*, and Susanna recapitulates her own perception of the danger by finishing with the cry "O cielo."

28. In *Le mariage de Figaro* the Countess murmurs her excuses about Cherubino's dishabille abjectly, and falls to her knees in a suppliant's posture (II, xvi). Mozart animates the same words — "Per vestir femminee spoglie" ("To

put on ladies' clothes," mm. 34–36) with all the indignation of the exalted march.

29. The Eulenberg score has the Countess giving up the key in mm. 78–79, just before the next tonic period. But in both the 1786 libretto and the Neue Mozart-Ausgabe the Countess yields it up to the Count right here, at his first request.

30. "Indeed I read it in your face" (mm. 80–81).

31. "Die, die, and be no longer the guilty cause of my torment!" (mm. 83ff). Beaumarchais's Count talks of killing, but only Cherubino, in an anger which seems much more reasonable. Against the Countess he threatens merely possible confinement in her chamber.

32. "With astonishment" (mm. 124–25).

33. "They're all *confused*," or, more idiomatically, "Their heads are swimming" (mm. 149–50).

34. Von Feldtenstein, pp. 36–37 (quoted here on p. 33).

35. If there is any question that this was Mozart's intent in the scene, imagine how easily he could have set the pert irony of the servant girl's "Quel paggio malnato/Vedetelo qua" ("You see here that rascal page," mm. 137–45) to a quick triple dance or to *buffa* patter. Here, as with the Countess's indignation in the first piece of the finale, a surprising setting of a text reveals Mozart's high respect for these two extraordinary women.

36. ♪ equals ♫ .

37. B♭ F ‖ B♭ g E♭ (c) A♭ f E♭ c B♭ ‖

38. "He who will not give pardon to others does not deserve it himself." In mm. 191–95 their music, setting the only text not couched in aphoristic terms ("Le vostre follie/Non mertan pietà"—"Your extravagances don't deserve mercy"), provides the final cadence for the second key area (in F major). Susanna sings twice, to the same music, the pithy "Così si condanna/Chi può sospettar" ("So a suspicious man condemns himself"), making cadences for the second and third modulations in the X-section (G minor, mm. 207–11, and E-flat major, mm. 222–26). The Countess and Susanna together sing the passage quoted above for the central cadence of a second modulation to E-flat (mm. 267–71, part of a long subdominant area before the return to B-flat), and Susanna has the last word with "Girate, volgete,/Vedrete che ognora/Si cade poi là" ("Go around and look, you will see that [with men] it always happens this way"), an aphorism which cadences on the first B-flat chord of the return (m. 297).

39. "In an attitude of supplication" (m. 229).

40. "Cruel one! that I am no longer" (mm. 231–33).

41. The stage directions in these two passages last mentioned reinforce the impression of spontaneity, characterizing her speech first as *con forza e collera* ("with force and anger," m. 200) and *con risentimento* ("with resentment," mm. 211–12). The Countess is at this moment just recovering from the daze induced by her discovery that it was Susanna, not Cherubino, in the closet.

42. "Ah, Susanna, how soft-hearted I am!"

43. "I'm wrong" (mm. 302–4).

44. "Da questo momento/Quest'alma a conoscermi (-vi, -la)/Apprender potrà" — "From now on this soul will be able to learn to know me (you, her) better" (mm. 307 to the end).

45. "With the songs and dances of your peasants" (mm. 343–47).

46. "Slow down now, less haste" (mm. 355–58).

47. "You don't know?" (mm. 406–10).

48. "Your own mug already accuses you; it's clear you want to lie."

49. "My mug may lie, but I don't" (mm. 425–27).

50. "The farce is over" (mm. 439–41).

51. "A matrimonial tableau."

52. "Marcellina, Marcellina, how late you are in appearing!" (mm. 457–60).

53. "What a brain! what talent!" (mm. 549–52).

54. "Sono in trappola" (mm. 613–15).

55. "It's the custom . . ." (mm. 664–65).

56. Mm. 667 and 668: the A-natural turns the E-flat, the potential dominant pedal for the expected A-flat modulation, into the top of a B-flat tritone.

57. Lorenzo da Ponte, *Memoirs of Lorenzo da Ponte*, trans. Elizabeth Abbott, ed. Arthur Livingston (New York: Dover, 1967), p. 133.

58. Mm. 729–35, in the second key area; mm. 745–51, in the first key in the X-section (C minor); and mm. 761–67, in the second key in the X-section (A-flat major). The opening of this movement is often taken at such a brisk pace that the gavotte rhythm loses its distinctiveness. The designation of the movement is at first *Allegro assai*; to allow the accelerations which follow (*Più allegro* and *Prestissimo*) their effect, the opening ought not to begin at breakneck speed.

59. "Silence: I am here to judge" (mm. 738–45, 754–61, and 770–81, the last with a slightly different text).

60. Mm. 786–89, 792–95, 821–24, 826–30. In the last two phrases the bass drops out, emphasizing the motet style of the passage.

61. "Some Power which favors us has brought them (us) here."

62. Mm. 824–27, 830–33. The two groups perform this music as antiphonal choirs.

CHAPTER 5

1. Susanna has to persuade the suspicious Count that her only reason for previously refusing to make assignations with him was feminine whimsy.

2. "My lord, a woman can say yes any time" (mm. 10–14).

3. "You who understand love." Some writers make heavy weather of Susanna's obvious distraction in the second reprise of the duet, taking it for evidence of shallowness of character. The Count alternates two questions — "Verrai?" ("You'll come?") and "Non mancherai?" ("You'll not fail me?") — which demand opposite answers. Susanna's attention is clearly elsewhere; she manages once to give the wrong answer to each question, each time quickly catching herself two beats later (mm. 45 and 51). But her distraction argues for, not against, her noble fiber. Distaste for the lie and worry about Figaro's possible

misunderstanding and jealousy distract her, causing her repeatedly to give the truer answer to the Count's importunate questions. She instinctively feels the necessary lie to be a real betrayal — of Figaro, of love itself, even of the Count — and this instinct occasions her whispered apology to Eros.

4. Another ingenuity of the duet displays the flexibility of Mozart's rhythmic scansion. The return to the tonic consists of the Count's syncopated bourrée with Susanna's prayerful counterpoint, then a quicker-rhythmed section of alternating questions (mm. 36–53), and lastly the bourrée again for a final cadence. The middle section itself uses a bourrée scansion, in the orchestra, but in 2/4 instead of 4/4 (using half-measures as units):

mm. 29-32

mm. 36-40

After the Count's expansive bourrée period the orchestra's repeated bourrée fragments at twice the tempo provide a regular background of rhythmic action against which to measure the ardent accelerations of his questions. The phrase culminates in Susanna's confused negative response to the wrong one.

5. "'Io voglio/Di tal modo punirvi . . . A piacer mio/La sentenza sarà . . ."' ("I want to punish you in some way . . . The sentence will be up to me . . ."). Again the Count uses the metaphor of the tribunal.

6. "Shall I, while myself sighing, see a servant of mine happy? And is he to possess a good I desire in vain? Shall I see joined by the bond of love to a worthless object a woman who has aroused in me a feeling which she does not return?"

7. "You were not born, O bold one! to torment me and even perhaps to laugh at my unhappiness."

8. This cadence figure is itself an extension: maintaining duple measure-groups exclusively would have entailed an even more banal, and anticlimactic, final cadence, not ascending the octave to D but moving from the subdominant G of "ridere" directly to the dominant and then to the tonic (the third variant in ex. 5–3). The cliché of the extended cadence is already necessary even in the normalized version in order to balance the long-breathed eight measures of the rise.

9. It could be read as vii², if you will.

10. The exalted march makes clarion the gentle Countess's wistful contrary-to-fact supplication, "Ah! se almen la mia costanza/Nel languire amando ognor/Mi portasse una speranza/Di cangiar l'ingrato cor" ("Ah! if only my constancy for enduring in the pain of love would bear me some hope of changing his ungrateful heart"). But the *Andantino* which begins the aria is much closer in mood to "Porgi, amor." After the *recitativo accompagnato* makes a dramatic half-cadence on the dominant of A major, it takes a surprising turn to a cool C major and a slow march in 2/4. The atmosphere of the *Andantino* is elegiac: the Countess sings in alternation with a *concertante* band of *amoroso* winds. And reminiscences of "Porgi, amor" are scattered through the *Allegro* (which

serves, as does the *Allegro assai* of "Vedrò, mentr'io," as the second key area of the return; each phrase is an elaborate cadential formula in C major). Its exalted-march style gives way at times to pathetic accents (the C-minor inflection and rhythmic ritard on the words "Nel languire amando ognor," in mm. 80–81 and 99–100) or to passages of *amoroso* winds (mm. 89–90, 94–95); in mm. 106–9 the winds combine with horns for a military-windband sound, the same sound which made the merging of military and lyric topics possible in "Porgi, amor." The orchestral close of the aria serves as a recapitulation of its two contrasting affects, and of the musical iconography of the Countess's character. It consists of an eight-measure period, the first four measures taken by *amoroso* winds and the second cast as a noble military fanfare.

"Dove sono" is a stock-taking, an interior argument for the justification of action. The exalted march and elegiac winds are convoked in it to depict the Countess struggling against her nature to turn pain into anger—the point being the commingling of two modes, *mezzo carattere* and exalted, for a new musical vehicle and not, as it is in "Vedrò, mentr'io," the bare fact of the trope itself.

11. In *Figaro* trumpets and timpani are used in the overture, in the *finalissimi* of the second- and fourth-act finales, in the materializing of the marching bands in "Non più andrai" and the finale to act III, and in Bartolo's and the Count's vendetta arias. In *Don Giovanni* the two instruments are found in all analogous places except for the solo arias.

12. Heinrich Christoph Koch, ed., *Journal der Tonkunst*, 2 vols. (Erfurt, 1795), 2:102.

13. The opening gesture of the sextet following the recognition scene (III, 18)—Marcellina's *vecchia prepotente* gavotte—has already been described (see p. 135), as have the essential outlines of "Dove sono," the Countess's soliloquy which follows the sextet (see pp. 144 and 351 n. 10). The comic peg on which the sextet hangs is the marvelous dominant accumulation of question and answers in the reassurance of Susanna (mm. 80–85, 89–94), balanced by Figaro's solemn bourrée (mm. 86–89, 95–102). Bourrée rhythms characterize the opening of the return as Marcellina's gavotte did the beginning of the piece: she opens the return with a bourréelike melody double-time and on the edge of patter, as befits her tottering dignity, while over it the winds superimpose her original gavotte as a reminder of her "theme-rhythm":

The scene turns into a lovefeast for the newfound and unlikely family, made all the more satisfying by the discomfiture of the Count and Don Curzio.

14. "While the nocturnal torch does not yet shine in the heavens, while the air is still murky and the earth lies silent" (IV, 27).

15. "Tutto è tranquillo e placido:/Entrò la bella Venere./Col vago Marte prendere,/Nuovo Vulcan del secolo/In rete la potrò" ("All is tranquil and

peaceful: beautiful Venus has entered. The new Vulcan of the century will be able to trap her in his net with the charming Mars" — IV, 28, 111–21).

16. A review is in order for those who find the events of the fourth-act finale confusing. Cherubino mistakes the Countess for Susanna; the Count mistakes Cherubino for Figaro, the Countess for Susanna, and Susanna for the Countess; Figaro mistakes the Countess for Susanna and Susanna for the Countess; and Antonio, Basilio, and Bartolo are taken in by everyone.

17. "What a gentle little zephyr will sigh this evening beneath the pines of the grove."

18. "Now he will understand the rest."

19. Mm. 4–6 become mm. 39–41, mm. 9–10 mm. 42–43, and mm. 27–29 in substance mm. 43–45.

20. "Lovely moments of sweetness and pleasure."

21. "To demonstrate our love for you" (mm. 15–17).

22. Mm. 1–7, 9–13, 17–19, 29–31, and 33–35.

23. Mm. 5–7 (followed by staccato sixteenth-note runs), 15–16, 26–27, and 31–35.

24. "Signor . . . se trattenete/Tutte queste ragazze,/Addio festa . . . addio danza . . ." ("Sir . . . if you retain all these girls, good-bye festival . . . good-bye dancing . . ." — III, xiii, 82–85).

25. "To your places, fair ladies, to your places" (III, 22, 4–6).

26. "Such a wise master, yielding up an insulting and offensive privilege" (mm. 87–99).

27. This rhythmic shift resembles the change from contredanse to march in I, 2, where the march choreographs Figaro's proud swagger as the Count's valet.

28. "Hunters with guns on their shoulders; townspeople; country girls and boys; two young girls who carry the maiden's headdress with white plumes; two others with a white veil, two others [with] the gloves and the bouquet of flowers; two other young girls who carry a similar headdress for Susanna, etc."

29. "The extras dance" (m. 133).

CHAPTER 6

1. It might be objected here that Susanna too has a lapse of faith when, spying Figaro embracing Marcellina in the third-act sextet, she flies into a fury. But this moment provides a deliberate contrast to Figaro's kind of distrust. Circumstantial evidence has just delivered a crushing rebuff to a woman who is hastening to set her fiancé free from a terrible bargain, yet her rage lasts only a moment. Easily persuaded of the truth, she is excused for her anger on the spot; Figaro, Marcellina, and Bartolo all praise her: "È un effetto di buon core:/Tutto amore è quel che fa" ("That's the consequence of a good heart: love is the very cause of it" — III, 18, 54–72). The evidence which causes Figaro's lapse, on the other hand, issues from the end of an intrigue whose beginnings he himself had engineered. Had he been more patient and trusting, he would have soon recognized his own hand in the imbroglio. His anger is brooding and petulant — impervious even to the persuasions of his new-found mother.

2. Antonio, her own father, has accused her of taking the Count as her teacher (III, xii, 76–78), and Figaro here speaks of her rather cruelly as a go-between for the Count and Susanna ("E così tenerella . . ./Il mestiero già sai . . ./Di far tutto sì ben quel che tu fai?" ("At such a tender age . . . you already know . . . how to ply your trade so well?" — IV, ii, 41–44).

3. Mm. 2–4 are an example of one of those felicitous moments in Mozart when the alteration of a few notes turns a cliché into riches. The usual version would contain two measures of tonic harmony followed by the move to the di-minished-seventh chord (ex. N6–1a). Or if the composer wanted to touch on the subdominant in m. 3, he could change the treble line at the same time as the bass, rendering the second figure B-flat,D-flat, B-flat (ex. N6–1b). M. 3 of the first version is harmonically and rhythmically flat; the inflection of subdomi-nant harmony there is an improvement, since it provides the measure with some harmonic interest and makes a tighter, smoother skeleton (ex. N6–2). But Mozart combines both possibilities for a more subtle third version, making the first note in m. 3 a C held over from the tonic harmony of m. 2. The C is dissonant with the B-flat of the subdominant arpeggio, and the D-flat on beat 2 is the resolution of the dissonance (ex. N6–3). By moving the dissonance from beat 2 to beat 1, incidentally changing the pitch shape of the repeated figure, Mozart gives the measure new inflections and enlivens it harmonically, rhyth-mically, and melodically; it has no dead notes. The pathetic accent grows more

Example N6-1

Example N6-2

Example N6-3

Example N6-4

pronounced with each measure until the diminished seventh in m. 4 — in Barbarina's situation expressively excessive, a parody of lament.

4. "Ah, who knows where it is?" (mm. 14–15).

5. A frequent cliché when moving from a minor key to the relative major, usually employed at the seams of big sections (ex. N6–4).

6. She was played in the first production by Anna Gottlieb, a child of twelve. Barbarina is sometimes seen as an almost-adult who knows when and how to pretend herself a child. The device with which she traps the Count into giving Cherubino her hand — a public disclosure resembling Figaro's tricks — may seem preternaturally shrewd, but need not be so. In her cavatina and the ensuing dialogue with Figaro she appears to be a child mimicking habits of her elders which she doesn't understand. In that light her trap of the Count is not the arch and calculated cunning of a knowing adolescent but the innocent bargaining of a child, one who understands effects but not their causes.

7. "Treacherous woman! and in that form you would lie to me? I don't know whether I am waking or sleeping" (IV, xi, 75–77).

8. The "dark place" where Donna Elvira stands in *Don Giovanni*, II, 6.

9. Dent, p. 110.

10. For example, see Dent's remarks: "It is obvious that the arias for Basilio and Marcellina in Act IV are very much in the way and contribute nothing to the drama; and they come far too late to illustrate the characters of their singers — we were left in no doubt about those in Act I" (ibid., p. 110). Jahn judges that "Marcellina's air . . . does not assist the characterisation, and is the only piece in the whole opera which fails of its effect" (Otto Jahn, *The Life of Mozart*, trans. Pauline D. Townsend, 3 vols. [New York: Edwin F. Kalmus, n. d.], 3:84). For Jahn a mark of the aria's failure is its old-fashioned style, which is certainly on the contrary a stroke of clever characterization on Mozart's part.

11. "A spirited woman, who was born rather mettlesome, but whose faults and experience have reformed her character" (Beaumarchais, *Le mariage de Figaro*, "Caractères et Habillements de la Pièce").

12. "Seizing on *Marceline's* naive avowal at the moment of recognition, I showed this woman humiliated and *Bartholo* refusing her, and *Figaro*, their common son, directing public attention on those truly responsible for the confusion into which are mercilessly swept any lower-class girls who are endowed with good looks" (ibid., "Préface").

13. "Hommes plus qu'ingrats, qui flétrissez par le mépris les jouets de vos passions, vos victimes! c'est vous qu'il faut punir des erreurs de notre jeunesse; vous et vos magistrats, si vains du droit de nous juger, et qui nous laissent enlever, par leur coupable négligence, tout moyen honnête de subsister. . . . Dans les rangs même plus élevés, les femmes n'obtiennent de vous qu'une considération dérisoire; leurrées de respects apparents, dans une servitude réelle; traitées en mineures pour nos biens, punies en majeures pour nos fautes! ah, sous tous les aspects, votre conduite avec nous fait horreur, ou pitié!" ("Men more than ungrateful, who wither with scorn the playthings of your passion, your victims! You're the ones who should be punished for the errors of our youth; you and your magistrates, so proud of the right to judge us, who by their criminal negligence let every honest means of subsistence be taken from us. . . . Even women of more lofty rank obtain from you only a mocking respect. Seduced by a specious deference into a real servitude, treated as children for our assets, punished as adults for our faults! Ah, in all respects your conduct toward us causes horror, or pity" — ibid., III, xvi). In the latter half of her speech Marceline might be describing the very plight of the Countess.

14. The Count is enumerating the qualities of the ideal wife: "Je ne sais: moins d'uniformité peut-être, plus de piquant dans les manières, un je ne sais quoi qui fait le charme; quelquefois un refus, que sais-je? Nos femmes croient tout accomplir en nous aimant . . . et sont si complaisantes et si constamment obligeantes, et toujours, et sans relâche, qu'on est tout surpris, un beau soir, de trouver la satiété, où l'on recherchait le bonheur" ("I don't know — less monotony perhaps; more piquancy in their manner; a charming *je ne sais quoi*; sometimes a refusal; how do I know! Our wives think they fulfill everything by loving us . . . and are so civil and so constantly obliging, eternally, without intermission, that one is completely surprised one fine evening to find satiety where one was looking for happiness" — ibid., V, vii).

15. A "female impulse" (ibid,. IV, xiii).

16. "Respectfully kissing her hand" (ibid., IV, xv).

17. "This arrogant, this dreadful . . . and moreover this rather silly masculine sex" (ibid., IV, xvi).

18. Other changes were either cuts to shorten the more loquacious scenes which are proper for a play but not an opera, or additions of aria texts by means of the elaboration of a one-line sentiment in the Beaumarchais.

19. "Flemma, flemma, e poi flemma: il fatto è serio,/E pensarci convien. Ma guarda un poco/Che ancor non sai di chi si prenda gioco" ("Caution, caution, and yet again caution: the matter is serious, and requires thought. Just remember that you still have no idea whom the joke is on" — IV, iii, 70–74).

20. Marcellina: "Where are you going, my son?" Figaro: "To vindicate all husbands." Stage direction: "Leaves in a rage" (IV, iii, 83–85).

21. "Quick, let's warn Susanna . . . I believe her innocent: that expression

. . . that modest air . . . There's still a chance that she isn't . . ." (IV, iv, 86–90). Marcellina's speech concludes with Beaumarchais's words about defending one's sex, except for one alteration: her affectionate laugh about the foolishness of men is omitted and her last words are ringing ones about her poor sex "da questi uomini ingrati a torto oppresso" ("wrongfully oppressed by these ungrateful men" — IV, iv, 94–96).

22. "Bravo! Here's justice! With those modest eyes, with that pious air, and then . . ." (I, iv, 114–118).

23. "The sweet fruit of our old-time passion" (III, vi, 141–42).

24. "Sol noi, povere femmine,/Che tanto amiam questi uomini,/Trattate siam dai perfidi/Ognor con crudeltà" ("We alone, poor women, who love these men so much, are always treated cruelly by the deceivers").

25. See Dent, p. 110, n. 1.

26. "The he-goat and the little she-goat are always friendly; the lamb never makes war with his little ewe. The most ferocious beasts in the forests and in the fields leave their companions in peace and freedom."

27. Susanna's caricature of Marcellina in the recitative after their act I duet.

28. See K. M. Lea, *Italian Popular Comedy*, 2 vols. (New York: Russell and Russell, 1962), 2:110–74, for some examples of *commedia* scenarios. The tradition comes down to us most familiarly in *A Midsummer-Night's Dream*, where Nick Bottom is transformed into an ass and a lion comically threatens Pyramus and Thisbe. The notion of the ass's life as one of obscurity and thus security is as old as Aesop.

29. For Marcellina's use of the word *flemma* see p. 356 n. 19.

30. Or resembling in its suave legato the minuet section of Leporello's "Catalogue" aria (*Don Giovanni*, I, 4), another piece with its roots in the *commedia dell'arte* (see pp. 241–47). Mozart's servants are the many faces of Arlecchino: the respectable Figaro, the vulgar pander Basilio, Leporello the "common man," all at one time or another are described in *commedia* idioms.

31. "The thunder resounds [da Ponte is also amusing himself with onomatopoeia here]; mixed with hail, the rain pelts down."

32. "But the vile stench of my garment . . ." (m. 87).

33. The march is prototypical enough to puzzle Dent, who is sure it must be a well-known one but cannot identify it (see Dent, p. 110, n. 1).

34. "Thus fate taught me that disgraces, dangers, shame, and death can all be avoided with an ass's hide" (mm. 103 to the end).

35. The first phrase is the purport of Basilio's aria, the second Figaro's characterization of Susanna in the recitative preceding IV, 26, and the last three are from his list of paradoxical epithets for women in the aria itself: "Son streghe che incantano/Per farci penar,/ . . . Son rose spinose,/. . . Colombe maligne" ("They are witches who enchant in order to make one suffer, . . . they are thorny roses, . . . spiteful doves" — IV, 26, 49–61).

36. "The night is dark . . . and I am at last beginning to ply the sottish trade of a husband" (IV, 26, 5–9).

37. "La nuit est noire en diable, et me voilà faisant le sot métier de mari, quoique je ne le sois qu'à moitié!" (*Le mariage de Figaro*, V, iii).

38. "Susie, Susie, Susie! how you torment me!" (ibid., V, iii).

39. "With that candid face, with those innocent eyes. . . Who would have believed it! . . ." (IV, 26, 16–19).

40. "Ah, it's always madness to put your trust in a woman!" (IV, 26, 20–23). Mozart gives the phrase *a donna* special emphasis by having Figaro repeat it twice across his penultimate measure.

41. The trap which Figaro has set is testimony to the heartlessness with which he has turned on the people he cared for. If Susanna were really planning to meet the Count for the purpose proposed, the Countess's grief at her husband's infidelity would be compounded by the discovery that she has been betrayed by her trusted confidante. In his willful desire to hurt Susanna, Figaro ignores the sorrow he would bring on his protectress.

42. See p. 165. The interplay in the conceits about animals in these three arias — the contrast between Marcellina's pastoral beasts and Basilio's and Figaro's brutish ones — is more evidence that da Ponte conceived IV, 24–26, as a unified and significant sequence of texts.

43. The harmonic plot of the first section of the aria is a complete two-part form, with the usual Classic move to the dominant and return to the tonic:

I	V		(X)	I
E♭	B♭	B♭	V⁷/E♭	E♭
m. 24	37	49	54	58-70
(1)	(14)	(26)	(31)	(35-47)

The second half of the aria (mm. 71 to the end), although it looks to function as a repetition of the second part of the two-part plan (mm. 49–70, the list), turns instead into thirty-four measures of E-flat cadence — a broad coda tacked on by a short bridge on the dominant whose text is a truncated version of the introduction to the list. Mozart changes the list music, which originally rode on the dominant, into coda material by making it into a series of V⁷-I cadences, substituting for part of each metaphor Figaro's sardonic comment "Il resto nol dico" (see n. 44 below; ex. N6–5). The quickened harmonic rhythm of the oscillating V⁷-I cadences and the drumming repetition of the comment bring Figaro's restive anger to a climax.

44. "I won't say the rest; everyone already knows it" (mm. 94 to the end).

45. See p. 80. Figaro has already made explicit reference to cuckoldry in his recitative ("il scimunito mestiero di marito" — see p. 168). Like the Count's, his *amour-propre* has been punctured by the memory of a laugh, ironically the same laugh Almaviva feared — Figaro's own: "Nel momento/Della mia cerimonia/Ei godeva leggendo: e nel vederlo/Io rideva di me senza saperlo" ("In the middle of my ceremony he was reading with pleasure, and seeing that, I laughed at myself without knowing it" — IV, 26, 10–13).

Example N6-5

46. "A kind of pastorale" — Bernadin de Saint-Pierre, *Paul et Virginie*, ed. Maurice Souriau (Paris: Société de belles lettres, 1952), p. 2.

47. ". . . the bond between all beings, . . . the prime mover of our societies, and the originator of our lights and of our pleasures" (ibid., p. 161).

48. "Women have contributed more than philosophers to forming and re-forming nations. . . . It was in their arms that they made men taste the happi-ness of being by turns, in the circle of life, happy children, faithful lovers, con-stant husbands, virtuous fathers. They laid the first foundations of natural laws. The first founder of human society was the mother of a family.

. . . Men are born Asian, European, French, English; they are farmers, mer-chants, soldiers. But in every country women are born, live, and die women. They have other duties, other occupations, other destinies than men. They are scattered among men to remind them always that they are men, and to maintain, in spite of political laws, the fundamental laws of nature. . . . Thus women belong only to the human race. They call it back unceasingly to its humanity by their natural feelings, and even by their passions" (ibid., pp. 63–64).

49. "Our happiness consists in living according to nature and virtue" (ibid., pp. 1–2).

50. "The rascal's standing guard duty. . . . Let's pay him back for his suspi-cions" (IV, x, 128–31).

51. "Oh, how it seems that this pleasant place, the earth and sky, respond to the fires of love! how the night supports my secrets!" (IV, 27, 17–23). This phrase is from the accompanied recitative. The description of the pastoral twi-light in the aria text itself is quoted on p. 145.

52. "I want to crown your forehead with roses" (mm. 62 to the end).

53. The first two pairs of lines also form a larger iamb since the two domi-nant cadences have different weights: the first is only a half-cadence in F major while the second completes the modulation to C major.

54. As in the two middle cadences. The first one, in the orchestral introduc-tion, is shortened one half-measure by pairing oboe and bassoon in parallel thirds. In the last phrase the oboe comes first, adding a "descant" over the bas-soon's scale, an ornament which makes the final cadence of the piece a little more eloquent and also more secure.

55. "Come now; don't delay."

56. Since the *Larghetto*'s ♩ roughly equals the *Allegro molto*'s ♩. the first period of the first key area alone constitutes thirty-six of the first reprise's eighty-four measures. See fig. 4, p. 180.

57. Figaro: "Here I am at your feet. My heart is full of fire. Look about this place. . . . Think about the traitor!"
Susanna: "But what if there is no affection?"
Figaro: "Let respect replace it. Let's not waste time: give me your hand for a moment . . . [she slaps him] O gentlest slaps! O my happy love!"

58. Forty-four omitting the "false recapitulation" when Susanna interrupts Figaro with her slap. The minuet is a miniature two-reprise form without an X-section, but with clear and regular caesuras (see ex. 6–16, p. 182, where its eight-measure phrases are lined up one underneath the other). Line 4 is a four-

measure extension of the phrase in line 3 which cadences the second reprise, and line 5 is the false recapitulation.

59. Conductors often take this final pastoral duet at an alarming pace, like a quick gigue, despite its *Andante* marking (Levarie, p. 209, suggests a quick tempo for both this pastorale and "Deh, vieni"). A quick tempo is by no means a necessary concomitant of a dance in 6/8. Of the three 6/8 dances current in the late eighteenth century two are of slow to moderate pace — the siciliano and the pastorale. Internal evidence alone would require the duet to be taken at a moderate tempo: the transition from minuet to pastorale cannot be effected smoothly unless ♪ is taken roughly to equal ♩ in the E-flat duet. A quick tempo would hopelessly slur the leisurely strumming of "Deh, vieni" and render its end rhymes banal and superfluous.

60. Mm. 289–93, 309–13, 330 to the end.

61. "Peace, peace my sweet treasure! I recognized the voice that I adore and carry always engraved on my heart."

62. "Ah, let us hasten, my beloved, and let pleasure be the reward for our pains."

63. *Smorfiosa* ("flirtatious" or "mincing") is Cherubino's word for Susanna (the Countess) — quite unfairly, since he first introduces the mincing rhythm (gavotte 1).

64. Measures of gavotte pattern, not of the finale's actual 4/4.

65. It is a frequent practice in first movements of Classic symphonies to begin the X-section with the material opening the first key area, now on the dominant, and then to dissipate it into a strange harmonic and motivic place. Mozart imitates the habit in bringing back gavotte 1.

66. "Ah! he's given us a great advantage with his audacity (curiosity)."

67. An analogous masculine cadence closes the first reprise (mm. 16–21), but its motive is not nearly as distinctive.

68. "What dainty fingers! what delicate skin! I'm tingling, I'm titillated, I'm filled with a new passion."

69. See especially mm. 59–60 and 64–66. It has the same effect as his *alla breve* rhythms elsewhere in the opera.

70. "This day of torments, of caprice and folly" (mm. 449–56).

71. "Only love can finish in contentment and joy" (mm. 456–64).

72. "To the sound of a happy march let us hasten to celebrate." For some remarks on the use of the *topos* of music-making as it appears in the finales of Classic opera, see pp. 324–25.

73. With a quick tempo, the simplest of triadic and scale figurations, and an insistent drum tattoo.

CHAPTER 7

1. The minor is inflected in the *Figaro* overture not once but twice (mm. 76–80, 91–92), not before arrival on the dominant but between arrival and confirmation, and in passing, rather than as an independent gesture. But in both cases the turn to minor is a standard device of key-area procedure, used

to give the expected major dominant more conviction and brilliance when it finally arrives.

2. The word *ombra* (from the Latin *umbra*) means "shadow" or "shade," as of a tree, and thus "shade" as "specter" (the pun is available in Latin, Italian, and English). Scenes set in hell with oracular voices and choruses of infernal spirits were obligatory in the sixteenth-century *intermedios* (brief musical scenes inserted between the acts of a play), and were a popular feature of Italian — especially Venetian — opera of the seventeenth century. The tradition continued into the eighteenth century with works like Gluck's *Orfeo* and *Alceste*, and Mozart's *Idomeneo*. Choirs of trombones traditionally accompanied these scenes; here Mozart reserves them for the end of the opera, when the specter actually appears.

3. The introduction consists of two periods (mm. 1–15, 15–30), the second making an incomplete cadence near the beginning (mm. 22–23). The first period makes a long chromatic descent to the dominant with the chaconne bass. The dominant is preceded by an augmented sixth and gives rise to a quick and rhythmically weak cadence (the tonic occurs on unaccented measures). A move to the subdominant seems to be the start of a short coda to strengthen the cadence, but the expected G-sharp of the V of V becomes A-flat, the seventh of a dominant chord resolving to a Neapolitan sixth (G, B-flat, E-flat). It quickly clears to a cadential I⁶₄-V in D minor, but the harmonic imbalance has had its effect nonetheless. A tonic in first inversion and the obdurate minor scales begin a new line of action; the little coda has become a period in its own right. The scales elaborate a chain of parallel ascending first-inversion chords which move to the sixth degree (B-flat). There the rise is taken over by the upper voices, which extend the line past what is diatonically possible by means of a precariously balanced "Neapolitan six-four" (B-flat, E-flat, G), a companion piece to the earlier Neapolitan, but now the result not of an enharmonic depression but of a chromatic elevation. The "Neapolitan" stretches to another augmented sixth and the final cadence is thus finally rendered inevitable (for further discussion of this use of the lowered second degree, see pp. 305–6 and 367 n. 6). The reduction in example N7–1 reveals this underlying harmonic plan

Example N7-1

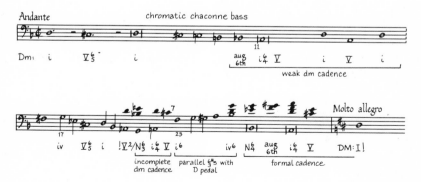

(barlines have been omitted in order to render the line more clearly; one mea-
sure equals one whole note, two measures a double whole note, or |o|). The
fantasy figures, although not connected by any formal motivic relationships,
are carefully ordered to reach a dynamic peak, moving from the least articulated and quietest of the figures to those at the other end of the spectrum.

4. Although the *Prague*'s introduction begins in D major, D minor enters
in m. 16, in a dramatic *Sturm und Drang* outburst. The *Sturm und Drang* style
prevails until the end of the introduction, moving in modulating sequences
through various keys, mostly minor, and settling into D minor for a long dominant pedal to close the section.

5. See, for example, the effusions of Kierkegaard's essayist A about the overture in *Either/Or*: "This overture is no interweaving of themes, it is not a laby-
rinth hodge-podge of associated ideas. . . . It is powerful as the thought of a
god, moving as a world's life, trembling in its earnestness, quivering in its passion, crushing in its terrible wrath, inspiring in its joy of life; it is faithful in its
judgement, strident in its lust, it is deliberately solemn in its imposing dignity,
it is stirring, flaming, dancing in its joy" (Sóren Kierkegaard, *Either/Or*, trans.
David F. and Lillian Marvin Swenson, 2 vols. (New York: Anchor Books,
1959), 1:126.

6. *Il dissoluto punito* (*The Profligate Punished*) is the alternate title of *Don
Giovanni*.

CHAPTER 8

1. *The Jester of Seville and the Stone Guest*, written by the Spanish playwright
Tirso de Molina in the early seventeenth century. For the texts of the principal
works of the Don Juan literature, see Oscar Mandel, *The Theatre of Don Juan:
A Collection of Plays and Views, 1660–1963* (Lincoln: University of Nebraska
Press, 1963). The plots of many of the plays and operas which preceded
Mozart's version have been ably summarized by Dent (pp. 120–35).

2. *Don Giovanni, or The Stone Guest*, a popular Don Juan opera which preceded Mozart's by less than a year (Venice, February, 1787; *Don Giovanni* was
performed first in October of the same year).

3. "To work night and day for someone whom nothing pleases; to put up
with rain and wind, to eat and sleep badly."

4. Some other examples of the musical gallop can be found in Cimarosa's *Il
Matrimonio Segreto* (II, v) and Schubert's *Der Erlkönig*.

5. Allowing for the repetition of the infantry march.

6. Leporello's words to the gavotte are "O che caro galant' uomo!/Voi star
dentro con la bella,/Ed io far la sentinella! . . . ("O what a precious gentleman! You stay inside with your pretty while I take guard duty! . . ."—
mm. 34–44).

7. "I want to be a gentleman" (mm. 20ff.).

8. "I don't want to serve any more" (mm. 23–32, 50–57); "I don't want anyone to hear me" (mm. 61–70).

9. The piece takes the shape of a short key-area plan with its "X-section" (an

accentuation of the dominant) and return repeated, and the repetition (mm. 112–34) itself extended by a reiteration of the four-measure cadence figure.

10. "Like a desperate fury" (mm. 101–3).

11. "If you don't kill me, don't hope that I will ever let you get away" (mm. 74–78).

12. "Constantly trying to conceal his identity" (mm. 79–81).

13. "Chi son'io tu non saprai" (mm. 81–83).

14. Tirso de Molina, *El Burlador de Sevilla y convidado di piedra*, act I, scene i.

15. *Odyssey* 9. 500–5.

16. "Questa furia disperata/Mi vuol far precipitar" ("This desperate fury wants to make trouble for me" — mm. 101ff) combines Donna Anna's epithet for herself with Leporello's predicate — "Sta a veder che il malandrino/Mi farà precipitar" ("It's clear that this rogue will make trouble for me").

17. Henry Fielding, *The History of Tom Jones, A Foundling*, book 12, chapter 12.

18. Published in 1782, just five years before *Don Giovanni* was produced in Prague.

19. Kierkegaard, p. 89. Kierkegaard's actual phrase is the "expression for the daemonic determined as the sensuous" (whereas Faust is the expression for the daemonic "determined as the intellectual or spiritual"). It is the power of this immediacy, the essay argues, which makes Don Juan "perhaps the only strictly musical subject, in the deeper sense, that life affords" (ibid., p. 46). It must be pointed out that Kierkegaard represents himself in the introduction to *Either/Or* as not having written this essay, or the writings bound with it which take up an opposing point of view. But whether we decide that all the opinions in the essay can be ultimately attributed to Kierkegaard or not, it has had, taken out of context, a considerable influence on modern thinking about *Don Giovanni*, and must be considered in this light.

20. The single stage direction returns Donna Anna to her house, and four measures later her father sings his first notes. Certainly, however, the intervening measures choreograph the Commendatore's formal confrontation with Don Giovanni: he appears on stage with the tremolo D's in the strings (m. 134), draws his sword with the *fortissimo* ascending scale passage (mm. 135–36), and advances in the succeeding measures to meet his daughter's attacker.

21. "Poor wretch! Just wait, if you want to die" (mm. 156–66).

22. I am indebted to Dr. Leonard Ratner for pointing out this symmetry of gesture to me. He uses a similar diagram in his analysis of *Don Giovanni* in *The Classic Style* (p. 401).

23. Free in the sense that it does not have to fulfill expectations of antecedent-consequent relations. As has already been pointed out, no fantasy is utterly "free," but is organized by some binding element — ascending and descending skeletal lines, sequences or small blocks of material repeated nonsequentially, or some combination of both devices.

24. In m. 154; all that the nearly parallel moment in m. 148 lacks to form the augmented sixth is a C-sharp against the E-flat in the bass.

25. "Ah, the poor devil falls already" (*sciagurato*, related to *sciagura*, "bad luck").

26. Because the exalted march gesture of the chase scene is projected so clearly, it is not necessary to alter the actual time signature to *alla breve*. Given the gestural indeterminateness of the fantasy, however, the *alla breve* sign must be written out, to forestall the stilted performance which would result from an accent on the first of each group of triplets. The triplets should float in even measure above the pizzicato bass which marks the *alla breve* beat, and a quarter-note pulse would thrust them all too firmly into the foreground. The *alla breve* sign is also appropriate *Augenmusik* for the motetlike quality of the death music.

27. Giovanni's words are a dispassionate report of the Commendatore's death throes: "Già dal seno palpitante/Veggo l'anima partir" ("Already I see his soul departing from his throbbing breast"). The Commendatore sings almost the same words.

28. A G-flat against the bass's F on the words "seno palpitante" (m. 182).

29. A dominant pedal weakens the tonic in mm. 177 and 179. Several times a new phrase or phrase member begins rhythmically just after a harmonic resolution (m. 181, over the tonic; m. 183, over iv, the resolution of the powerful V^7 of iv in the previous measure, its weight increased by Giovanni's minor-ninth appoggiatura). In m. 186 the expected A-flat in the F-minor tonic is raised to A-natural, as prelude to the V^7 of iv formed on the next beat. In all, the minor tonic is heard in root position for only five beats of the eighteen measures.

30. Mm. 184–85. The progression in its entirety is i-V^7_{iv}-iv-V-VI-ii⁶-V-i. In the VI-ii⁶ cliché (a variation on root movement by thirds) the bass and treble move up and down in contrary motion (ex. N8–1). The major triad on the sixth degree works as a ghostly intruder which renders the following minor triad all the darker.

31. "Leporello, where are you?" "I'm here, more's the pity. . . . Who's dead? You or the old man?" "What a stupid question! The old man." (I, ii, 194–98).

32. "And yonder musician, who used the greatest power which (in the art he knew) the Father of Spirits ever yet breathed into the clay of this world; who used it, I say, to follow and fit with perfect sound the words of the Zauberflöte and of Don Giovanni —foolishest and most monstrous of conceivable human words and subject of thought—for the future amusement of his race! No such spectacle of unconscious (and in that unconsciousness all the more fearful) moral degradation of the highest faculty to the lowest purpose can be found in history." (Quoted in G. B. Shaw, *Shaw on Shaw*, ed. Eric Bentley [New York: Anchor Books, 1955], pp. 50–51).

33. Ibid., pp. 51–52.

34. George Bernard Shaw, *Man and Superman*, act III.

35. Thomas Shadwell, *The Libertine*, act IV.

36. Kierkegaard, 1:106.

Example N8-1

37. Goethe, to whom the word "daemonic" is of great importance, defines it as "that which cannot be explained by Reason or Understanding," and which "manifests itself in the most varied way throughout all nature." He denies that it is an attribute of Mephistopheles (on the ground of his being too "negative" a creature), and when asked whether it enters into the "idea of the Divine," he responds, "My good friend, what do we know of the idea of the Divine? and what can our narrow ideas tell of the Highest Being?" (Johann Wolfgang von Goethe, *Conversations with Eckermann*, March 2–8, 1831).

38. Kierkegaard, 1:91.

39. Kierkegaard, 1:118.

40. Shaw, *Man and Superman*, act III.

41. "He wanted it — it's his loss" (I, ii, 201).

42. His most effective enemy, Madame de Volanges, says of the Vicomte: "Jamais, depuis sa plus grande jeunesse, il n'a fait pas un pas ou dit une parole sans avoir un projet, et jamais il n'eut un projet qui ne fût malhonnête ou criminel. . . . Sa conduite est le résultat de ses principes. Il sait calculer tous ce qu'un homme peut se permettre d'horreurs sans se compromettre; et pour être cruel et méchant sans danger, il a choisi les femmes pour victimes" ("He has never, since his youngest days, taken a step or said a word without having a project, and he has never had a project which wasn't dishonest and criminal. . . . His conduct is the result of his principles. He knows how to calculate all the evils a man can allow himself without being compromised; and so as to be cruel and wicked without danger, he has chosen women as his victims" — Choderlos de Laclos, *Les liaisons dangereuses*, lettre IX).

43. *Gio*: "Let the women alone! Madman! Let the women alone? You know they are more necessary to me than the bread I eat, than the air I breathe!"
Lep: "And yet you have the heart to deceive them all?"
Gio: "It's all love. Whoever is faithful to only one woman is cruel to all the others. Since I feel in myself such a generous sentiment, I love them all. Then the women, because they don't know how to reckon my good nature, call it deceit" (II, i, 82–95).

44. "I have never seen a nature more broad, or more kindly" (II, i, 95–97). The two then go on to plot the seduction of Donna Elvira's maid.

45. Frequently the Don describes the attractions of his new favorite with the imagery of food. Zerlina has a "viso inzuccherato" ("a sugared complexion") and fingers "like curds" (I, ix, 106, 115–16). Giovanni's *canzonetta* describes a beloved with "la bocca dolce più che il miele" ("a mouth sweeter than honey") who carries "zucchero . . . in mezzo al core" ("sugar . . . deep in her heart" — II, 3, 25–28, 29–32).

46. "And you tell me that with such indifference? . . . But what if she had been my wife?" (II, xi, 212–15). Giovanni answers "Meglio ancora!" ("Better still!").

47. "Quasi da piangere/Mi fa costei./Se non si muove/Del suo dolore,/Di sasso ha il core,/O cor non ha" ("She almost moves me to tears. If he isn't moved by her grief, he has a heart of stone, or no heart at all" — II, 11, 247–348).

48. In I, iv, Leporello tries to chide Giovanni for his wicked ways, but is immediately bullied out of it. In the *buffa* duet "Eh, via, buffone" at the opening of act II Leporello threatens to leave Giovanni, but easily changes his mind after a bribe of four gold pieces.

49. "Il padron con prepotenza/L'innocenza mi rubò" (II, 7, 22–33).

50. Tirso and Molière fill out the history of Don Juan by giving him a father (and Tirso an uncle) who appears in the play to chastise him for the dishonor his scurrilous acts are bringing on the family name. The libretti of Bertati and da Ponte drop the father from their cast of characters. One obvious motive for the omission is the necessity of streamlining the plot of a play which is to become a *dramma per musica*. As a result, however, Giovanni is freed from the impediment which a visible antecedent would pose to his chameleon nature; it strains credulity for No-Man to be at the same time a son.

51. "He can't be far from *here*" (m. 10).

52. "On his head he has a hat with white plumes; he has on his back a great cloak, and at his side a sword" (mm. 20–33).

53. I, 11. The traditional sobriquet "Champagne" aria is not actually appropriate to "Fin ch'han dal vino." Its music is inebriating, and its text speaks of intoxication, but on the part of others and not of the Don. The "champagne" of the aria's nickname apparently crept in from an early German mistranslation of the first line, which reads literally, "While their heads are hot with wine, have a grand *festa* prepared" ("Fin ch'han dal vino/Calda la testa,/Una gran festa/Fa' preparar"). To have Giovanni sing with champagne glass in hand is to obscure the important point that his galvanic energy arises from the spur of his obsession, and not from strong wine.

54. "Let the dancing be without any order: you'll make some dance the minuet, some the follia, some the allemande" (mm. 33–56, 105–19).

55. "Ah! by tomorrow morning you should increase my list by ten" (mm. 70–85, 97–104, 120–43).

56. The pure *buffa* duet between Leporello and Don Giovanni at the opening of act II, and the invitation to the Commendatore's statue, issued also by Leporello and Giovanni.

57. Even though *Don Giovanni* has only two more solo arias than does *Figaro* — sixteen instead of fourteen. It is interesting in this context that *Figaro* has many more soliloquies — eight, as opposed to three in *Don Giovanni* (by "soliloquies" I mean solo arias where the action stops while one character, alone on stage, sorts out his feelings aloud). One might expect to find the preponderance of soliloquies in *Don Giovanni*, both because the conventions of *opera seria* play a much greater part in the opera and because Mozart made concessions to singers in the writing of it. But in *Figaro* the secondary characters Marcellina, Bartolo, and Basilio are each allotted one meditative aria, the Count has an *opera seria scena* in which to vent his rage against Figaro, Figaro faces the audience to threaten once the Count and once Susanna, and the Countess, since she is a reflective figure, always sings alone. Many of *Don Giovanni's* numbers are neither duets nor soliloquies, but solo arias where the singer addresses another character or a crowd of silent auditors (Leporello to Donna Elvira in his "Catalogue" aria, for example, or Donna Anna to Don

Ottavio in both her grand *scenas*). Only Leporello, Don Ottavio, and Donna Elvira are allowed to sing a full-fledged solo aria from an empty stage.

58. Movements in *alla breve* style occur seventeen times in *Don Giovanni* and only six times in *Figaro*, although often in *Figaro* the Count's steely *alla breve* glints through the rhythms of another style.

CHAPTER 9

1. "Flee, cruel one, flee! Let me also die now that he is dead — oh God! — who gave me life."

2. Koch uses the words "grammatical," "oratorical," and "pathetic" to describe (1) the "almost unnoticeable accent" normally given the strong beat of a measure; (2) the attention given the notes of a melody to be performed "with a striking delivery, if the passion contained in them is to be expressed intelligibly"; (3) a stronger degree of the second, oratorical, accent. "The manner in which the emphasis of these [oratorical or pathetic] tones is to be produced . . . consists partly in a certain emphatic lingering, where it appears that [the performer] is stopping on a certain accented note a moment longer than its particular duration requires" (Koch, *Lexikon*, s.v. "Accent"). Mozart exaggerates this lingering by writing it out into a syncopation.

3. In the words quoted in example 9–1, p. 225, and n. 1 above. She later stammers an apology to Don Ottavio for the mistake (mm. 83–89).

4. "You have husband and father in me." In a nice touch, after Anna's stammered apology to Ottavio the orchestra has "delirium music" (mm. 89–96 — oscillating IV and I⁶ triads, arpeggiated) which first suggests Anna's confusion upon waking ("Il padre mio dov'è?") and then, darkening to a minor subdominant and a quick inflection of the minor tonic, sets Ottavio's inner struggle to tell her the awful truth. In the repeat Anna in her urgency takes over the minor subdominant from Ottavio (mm. 110–11).

5. In minor keys the triads on these altered notes (each with a root a half step from the note below) are major, and can prevail momentarily to create an independent harmonic cosmos at a crack's distance from the reigning tonality.

6. Anna and Ottavio have just exclaimed of the oath-taking "What a savage moment!" (mm. 140–42). The skeleton of the progression in question already contains a surprise harmonic move — to VI via its secondary dominant — on the way to a normal i⁶₄-V-i cadence (this skeleton could be considered an elaboration of a deceptive cadence — V moving to VI instead of to i; ex. N9–1). But the progression is further ornamented, and the new ornamentation becomes its substance (ex. N9–2). Mozart spells the G-flat of the dim. vii⁷ as F-sharp, turning it into an appoggiatura chord to an E-flat six-four. The six-four, its

Example N9-1

Example N9-2

root D minor's Neapolitan, is stressed until it begins to sound like a cadential six-four; it does indeed move properly to V in E-flat major (a B-flat triad, and the VI of the original deceptive cadence in D minor). Perched precariously atop D minor, the Neapolitan momentarily takes on a life of its own, until a G-sharp (until m. 153 it could be A-flat, making the B-flat triad the dominant of E-flat major) becomes an augmented sixth which must necessarily open out to i$^6_4$ in D minor. Thus with the cliff-hanging tertiary relation of the Neapolitan-turned-cadential-six-four — properly a deception worked on an expected deception (the feint of the secondary dominant vii[7] pointing to VI, but turning instead into an appoggiatura to a six-four) — Anna's G reaches an altitude no mere A or B-flat above it could have attained. The effect is qualitative rather than quantitative, because the pitch is outside the mode both in function and in color.

The *Andante* of the overture and the D-minor music in the second-act finale contain slightly less complicated versions of the same progression (Overture, mm. 26–31; II, 11, 465–70, 537–48) which clearly demonstrate the provenance of both the "Neapolitan six-four" and the augmented sixth as passing-tones ascending from iv[6] to i$^6_4$ or to V. See pp. 305–6 and 361 n. 3.

7. "Quegli accenti sì sommessi,/Quel cangiarsi di colore,/Son indizi troppo espressi/Che mi fan determinar" ("Those low tones, that change of color, are signs all too clear, which help me decide" — I, 9, 74 to the end). "Non dubitate più: gli ultimi accenti/Che l'empio proferì tutta la voce/Richiamar nel cor mio di quell' indegno/Che nel mio appartamento . . ." ("Doubt no longer: the last tones that wicked man uttered recalled to my heart the very voice of that scoundrel who in my chamber . . ." — I, 10, 16–20).

8. The first period ends with a strong cadence in D major (m. 86). The next phrase moves through D minor and F major to a dramatic half-cadence on A set up by two emphatic augmented sixths (mm. 97 and 99) — a typical cadence for the B-section of a *da capo* aria, and too unstable for the final cadence of an "exposition." These sixteen measures also offer a strong contrast to the D-major period in mode, rhythm (the accompaniment becomes syncopated), and affect (sorrow tinges her righteous anger), as is appropriate for a B-section. The return is a literal repetition of the closed first period rather than a "recapitulation."

9. E. T. A. Hoffmann, "A Tale of Don Juan," in *Pleasures of Music*, ed. Jacques Barzun (New York: Viking Press, 1960), pp. 32–33. For a more recent version of the same opinion, see Robert Moberly's vulgar analysis of the recitative (Moberly, pp. 167–69).

10. "Finally the pain, the horror of the unspeakable attempt so increased my strength that by wrenching away, twisting, and bending, I broke away from him" (mm. 45–51).

11. I have occasionally heard it said that the "deceptive" cadence punctuating Donna Anna's sentence is meant to imply that her tale is a deception. But this is musical cuteness of the sort that Mozart took pains to avoid. Clearly the surprise F-major chord is meant to portray the intensity of Ottavio's relief at Anna's narrow escape (some people find his earnestness here comic, but I think that those who do have a predisposition to finding him so). The juxtaposition of the A minor with the F major (Ottavio's key earlier in the opera) also continues the running contrast of the affects in the natures of the two lovers. Both of these effects are the audible results of the substitution of VI for i. The first interpretation is based on a too-literal understanding of the term "deceptive cadence." In the language of tonal harmony the point of the cadence is not the actual feint of the substitution itself, but the interruption it makes in the expected rhetoric of the harmonic "sentence"; the move does not imply "deceit," but denial of the expected closure.

12. "Sono/Assalitrice d'assalita" (mm. 61–62).

13. II, 10, a *scena* with the accompanied recitative "Crudele? Ah, no, mio bene!"

14. "But the world . . . oh God . . ." (II, 10, 9–10).

15. "Perhaps yet someday heaven will take pity on me" (II, 10, 64 to the end).

16. The Countess sings "Ah! se almen la mia costanza/Nel languir amando ognor/Mi portasse una speranza/Di cangiar l'ingrato cor" ("Ah! if only my constancy in a languishing love would bring me a hope of changing that ungrateful heart" — *Le nozze di Figaro*, III, 19, 77 to the end).

17. Again Moberly stands at the one extreme, calling Ottavio's music "nasty, insincere, complacent, self-congratulatory." He is prurient enough to suspect Ottavio of lustful thoughts for Elvira, on the evidence of his innocent concern for her plight (Moberly, pp. 150–51). E. T. A. Hoffman takes the middle ground, finding Ottavio merely frigid, unmanly, and commonplace (see p. 228 above). For an assessment at the other end of the spectrum, see Jean and Brigitte Massin, *Wolfgang Amadeus Mozart* (Paris: Librairie Arthème Fayard, 1970), p. 1067.

18. See Dent, p. 169.

19. "Quel che a lei piace/Vita mi rende,/Quel che le incresce/Morte mi dà" ("Whatever pleases her is life to me, whatever disturbs her is death").

20. Dent's objection to "Dalla sua pace" is in part that it is inseparable from an aria which would have ended "act I" in the hypothetical four-act scheme he suggests was originally the plan of *Don Giovanni* (see Dent, pp. 138, 141, 168–69). This scheme deserves examination, since it has gained some currency while its virtues are not altogether clear. If act I were to end with "Or sai chi l'onore" and "Dalla sua pace" were omitted, act II, consisting only of two arias and a finale, would be extremely short. The grand sextet of act II, Dent's candidate to end "act III" and the "anomaly" on which his thesis hinges, does resemble Mozart's usual finales in form and extent. But whereas finales habitually bring to resolution one wave of the action, the sextet leaves Leporello prisoner in a dark courtyard of Donna Anna's house; he must escape before one segment of the action can be said to have been fully concluded. Dent calls Leporello's "Ah, pietà" which follows the sextet "explanatory," but the piece is

really the escape aria which does conclude the action, with the explanations muttered to borrow time while he gropes for the door. It would be more of a dramatic awkwardness to break the action in the middle of the episode, returning to the same place and time at the beginning of the next act.

The length and complexity of the sextet need not in themselves make it a finale, especially since the main character of the opera is missing from it. Mozart and da Ponte probably saw the need for a larger ensemble halfway through the act to break up the succession of arias and duets, a function the Quartet no. 9 performs for act I. The sequence consisting of the sextet and "Ah, pietà" ends nicely with Ottavio's fervent (although perhaps somewhat inexplicable) decision to hand Giovanni over to secular justice, and, were the Viennese interpolation for Elvira, "Mi tradì," omitted, that scene would abut neatly on the graveyard scene, where the mechanisms of a higher justice are set into motion (not that Elvira's aria is a particular intrusion there, describing as it does her own foreboding vision of the jaws of hell). In the final analysis the most intrusive aria of the opera is Anna's "Non mi dir," which is not a later interpolation, yet can be justified merely in terms of dramatic *vraisemblance*: it gives Giovanni and Leporello time to get home from the cemetery and start their dinner.

21. "Or sai chi l'onore," "Dalla sua pace," and "Mi tradì" are the other three.

22. "Dalla sua pace" was added to the opera because Morella, Mozart's Viennese tenor, could not manage "Il mio tesoro" (see Dent, p. 143).

23. He refuses to believe Don Giovanni, a "cavaliere," capable of such a "nero delitto" ("black crime"—I, xiv, 142), and spends most of the opera "investigating" the matter. Near the end of act II something, it is not clear just what, convinces him of Giovanni's guilt (just preceding the scene where he declares his decision, the crimes have been Leporello's; since he has not seen Giovanni since the ball he must have on his mind the seduction of Zerlina and a vague sense that Giovanni is responsible for Leporello's mistreatment of Elvira), and he exits to call the police.

24. "That's what men are like! All equally scoundrels in their schemes, whatever weakness they bring to effecting them they call decency" (Laclos, *Les liaisons dangereuses*, p. 136).

CHAPTER 10

1. "Hush: I think I smell the scent of a woman! . . ." (I, iv, 254–55).

2. "Ah! who will ever tell me where to find that barbarian, whom I loved to my disgrace, who broke faith with me? Ah! if I find the beast, and he does not come back to me, I'll do him dreadful torture; I'll carve out his heart."

3. See Elvira's narration of her seduction, which she delivers just following this aria (I, v, 118–32). It is not clear whether Giovanni married Elvira in Burgos or not. When Elvira says "Mi dichiari tua sposa" ("You declared me your wife"), she seems to be referring to a lover's pledge and not a formal ceremony. In Molière's *Don Juan* Elvire is actually married to the Don, but Sganarelle warns her servant at the start of the play of the great ease with which the Don marries his victims: "You tell me he married your mistress; believe me he

would have done even more for his passion, and that along with her he would have married you, his dog, and his cat as well. A marriage costs him nothing to contract; he uses no other snares to catch beauties, and he's a marrier for all comers. Dame, demoiselle, bourgeoise, peasant girl, he finds nothing too hot or too cold for him; and if I told you the names of all the women he has married in various places, it would be a chapter which went on all evening" (*Don Juan*, I, i; note that the speech contains an embryonic version of Leporello's famous catalogue of conquests). It is in this spirit that Giovanni calls Elvira his wife, and promises Zerlina that "Là [al mio casinetto] . . . ci sposeremo" ("There [in my little cottage] . . . we'll get married" — I, ix, 130–31).

4. Achieved in m. 53; the aria lacks a fully developed X-section.

5. The italicized syllables in the quotation are the dotted top notes of octave leaps.

6. "Is she mad not to have changed her dress, and to come to this place in her country clothes?" (*Don Juan*, I, ii).

7. "In casa mia/Entri furtivamente" ("He entered my house furtively" — I, v, 119–20).

8. "I am no longer that Doña Elvire who was praying against you, and whose harassed soul hurled only threats and breathed only vengeance. Heaven has banished from my soul all that unworthy passion I felt for you, all those tumultuous transports of a criminal attachment, all those shameful outbursts of a coarse and earthly love" (*Don Juan*, IV, vi).

9. "Io men vado in un ritiro/A finir la vita mia" ("I at any rate shall enter a retreat for the rest of my life" — II, *scena ultima*, 740–42).

10. "A forza d'arte,/Di giuramenti e di lusinghe, arrivi/A sedurre il cor mio" ("By dint of art, of oaths, and of tricks, you managed to seduce my heart" — I, v, 121–23).

11. "Do you hear? Some beauty abandoned by an errant lover" (I, 3, 37–41).

12. "Poor little lady, poor little lady" (mm. 45–47).

13. In the first reprise they interrupt three times, the last a bridge to the return of E-flat. The second reprise is shortened by the omission of one of Elvira's cadences and of Giovanni's first interjection (the equivalent of mm. 31–41), in order to balance out Elvira's fiery cadenza at the close.

14. "I shall have this woman: I shall steal her away from the husband who profanes her; I shall dare to snatch her from the very God she adores. How delicious to be at once the object and the conqueror of her remorse! Far be it from me the idea of breaking down the prejudices which beset her! They will add to my happiness and to my glory" (*Les liaisons dangereuses*, p. 24).

15. "Do you know that I still had some little feeling for her, that I found a certain charm in this bizarre new style, and that her careless dress, her languishing manner, and her tears reawakened in me some small remains of an extinguished fire?" (Molière, *Don Juan*, IV, vii).

16. "Eh! lasciate che vada. Egli non merta/Che di lui ci pensiate . . ." ("Oh, let him go. He's not worth your thinking about him . . ." — I, v, 156–58).

17. In order to test the truth of this description, the reader is invited to imagine the dumbshow which a *commedia dell'arte* troupe might mount to choreograph the orchestra's "accompaniment." For a producer actually to use such a

troupe on stage, however, would be a breach of taste which I hope this gloss will not occasion; the suggestion of dumbshow loses its subtlety when it ceases to be subliminal.

18. "But in Spain there are 1003."

19. "Peasant women, maids, townswomen, . . . countesses, baronesses, marchesas, princesses" (mm. 38–45).

20. When Rossini made his famous remark about *Don Giovanni* ("All my music is in there"), he must have been referring to the "Catalogue" aria. So much of his music bypasses the subtle rhythmic vocabulary of social dance, reaching back to the unmediated mimesis, and the more stereotyped characters, of the *commedia dell'arte*. For Mozart, on the other hand, direct imitation of an action takes its place as one of several means of depicting character.

21. Jahn and Dent trace the name "Leporello," the invention of da Ponte, directly to Harlequin via the German *Lipperl*, the Austrian diminutive of *Phillip*, "a name sometimes given to that comic figure more generally known as *Kasperl* or *Käsperle*, the German Harlequin" (Dent, p. 156). Leporello and Harlequin share among other characteristics the gluttony which keeps them dependent on their masters: in the byplay opening the second-act finale Don Giovanni catches Leporello cadging morsels off the plates he is serving.

22. "The pale-complexioned woman" and her "sweetness" (mm. 97–100).

23. "The fat woman"; "the thin woman"; "the tall woman"; "the tiny woman" (mm. 101–23).

24. "But the young novice is his principal passion" (mm. 132–35).

25. Abraham mentions the thought only to reject it, but is at a loss for another explanation of the passage, suggesting that Mozart must have had some specific bit of stage business in mind here (see Gerald Abraham, "The Operas," in *The Mozart Companion*, ed. H. C. Robbins Landon and Donald Mitchell [New York: W. W. Norton, 1969], p. 299). If, as I think, Leporello's intended target is Donna Elvira (see above), then the necessary business is a portentous gesture in her direction.

26. "He's not offended if she's rich, if she's ugly, if she's beautiful."

27. For an account of the eighteenth-century use of permutation and combination in composition, see Leonard Ratner, "*Ars Combinatoria*: Chance and Choice in Eighteenth-Century Music," in *Studies in Eighteenth-Century Music*, ed. H. C. Robbins Landon (New York: Oxford University Press, 1970), pp. 343–63.

28. The two placements of the list music provide a striking example of the effect of rhythmic context on a particular gesture. When first the list music occurs (mm. 100ff.), it has been preceded only by the sixteen measures of symmetrical minuet, an opening gesture which ends properly on a half-cadence. The open-ended expansiveness of the list, contrasting sharply with the minuet's careful balances, marks it as X-section material. The repeated pendulum-swing of dominant-upbeat to tonic-downbeat, even in ratios of three beats of tonic to one of dominant, is too perfunctory for the tonic to signal return, so the tonic feels unstable, and enclosed in the X-section. Even the rising D-major scale of "È la grande maestosa" ("The tall girl is dignified") remains a suspenseful X-

like gesture, and the eventual half-cadence on "La piccina" (mm. 120–23) the narrowing of the funnel back toward the return.

But after the minuet return and the D-minor interruption, whose secondary dominant also moves to a half-cadence (mm. 135), the same list music manages to function as a convincing reestablishment of the tonic. Since another X-like phrase (the D minor) has already shattered the equilibrium of the minuet, the over-the-barline V-I can now sound like return rather than departure, playing the role which the minuet played just before the D-minor interruption (see fig. 7, p. 243).

Exploitation of the contrast between additive and symmetrical materials was an important resource for the clarity of the harmonic rhetoric of the key-area plan. The point is made forcefully here, where simple manipulations of two contrasting blocks of material — minuet and list — regulate the ebb and flow of musical energy.

29. "As long as she wears a skirt, you know what he'll do."

30. II, 2; the recitative which follows it; II, 3 (Giovanni's *canzonetta*); II, 6 (the elaborate sextet often called the "finale of act III" by those who cleave to the four-act theory of *Don Giovanni*'s original plan); and II, 7.

31. "Cieli, che aspetto nobile!/Che dolce maestà!/Il suo dolor, le lagrime,/ M'empiono di pietà" ("Heavens! what a noble countenance! What gentle dignity! Her grief and tears fill me with pity" — I, 9, 10–19).

32. The second time signature in ex. 10–12 is of course my own interpolation.

33. "Perhaps [if you leave her to me] she'll calm down."

34. "A little crazy" — Giovanni's description of Elvira in mm. 61–62.

35. "Scorn, fury, despair, fear" (mm. 37–38).

36. "I'm beginning to doubt" (mm. 66–68).

37. "Non sperarlo, o scellerato:/Ho perduto la prudenza" (mm. 70–71; her phrase begins the return to the tonic).

38. For a further discussion of this brief duo (II, 6, 28–61), see pp. 252–53.

39. "Ah, taci, ingiusto core,/Non palpitarmi in seno:/È un empio, è un traditore./È colpa aver pietà" ("Oh be silent, unjust heart, don't throb in my breast. He is a scoundrel, he is a traitor. It's a sin to feel compassion" — II, 2, 2–14). The music of the last line is quoted in ex. 10–15.

40. Perhaps Mozart had Giovanni repeat the vocative "O gioia bella" over two full measures to leave the impression that he is loosely improvising suitable words to his all-purpose serenade tune.

41. "Più fertile talento/Del mio, nò, non si dà" ("There is indeed no more fertile genius than mine" — mm. 62–67).

42. When Giovanni is at his most swoony, crying "Ah, credimi, o m'uccido!" ("Oh, believe me, or I'll kill myself!") over the lead-in to the return of the tonic (mm. 46–52), Leporello is convulsed with silent laughter and threatens, in a patter which accelerates to imitate laughter, "Se seguitate, io rido" ("If you go on, I'll laugh" — mm. 50–54).

43. "Deh! proteggete, o Dei,/La sua credulità" (mm. 62–67, 74 to the end). Again with Leporello the comedy of moral sloth — the implication is "the gods must protect her, for no one else will, certainly not I."

44. "Mi par che abbiate/Un'anima di bronzo" ("It seems to me you have a soul of bronze" — mm. 86–87).

45. "The rascal's heating up" (mm. 117–18).

46. "Alone, alone in a dark place, I feel my heart throb, and a kind of fear assails me, which seems to me to be of death."

47. "Vestiti a lutto" — stage direction, mm. 28–30.

48. "Only death, my treasure, can put an end to my lament" (mm. 50–61).

49. "Sentir già parmi/La fatale saetta/Che gli piomba sul capo! Aperto veggio/Il baratro mortal . . . Misera Elvira,/Che contrasto d'affetti in sen ti nasce" ("Already I seem to sense the fatal bolt falling on his head! I see the mortal abyss opening . . . Wretched Elvira, what contrasting feelings rise in your breast! — II, 8c, 17–29).

50. "Forse un giorno il cielo ancora/Sentirà pietà di me!" (II, 10, 64 to the end; see pp. 229 and 369 n. 15).

51. "Although betrayed and abandoned, I still feel compassion for him" (II, 8c, 54–74). The word "pietà" is on Elvira's lips frequently in the second act: see II, 2 ("Ah, taci"), 13–14, II, 6, 86–95 (the sextet, where her fervent cries for mercy are mocked by the revelation of the masquerade), and her eruption into the second-act finale, II, 11, 215–17. She is the figure of compassion in the opera, who because she feels it for others can rightfully demand it for herself. There is, of course, none granted.

52. The remainder of the second-act finale is discussed on pp. 287–325.

53.   *Elv*: "I still want to make the final test of my love with you. I no longer remember your deceptions; *I feel compassion.* . . . This battered soul does not ask from you any reward for its faithfulness. . . ."
    Gio: "What do you wish, my treasure?"
    Elv: "*That you change your life*" [mm. 201–66].

My italics are meant to point up the two lines which are set to the musical rhyme. Da Ponte too stresses the extreme passion of the cry "Pietade io sento," by making it the third line of a four-line strophe which remains incomplete.

54. "Il giusto cielo/Volle ch'io trovassi/Per far le sue, le mie vendette" ("Just Heaven willed that I find you, to take Its and my revenge" — I, v, 138–41).

55. "Let me eat" (mm. 280–86).

56. "And if you want to, you eat with me" (mm. 291–94).

57. "Long live women, long live good wine, *the mainstay and glory of mankind*!" (mm. 311–14, 333–36). My italics indicate the words of the toast which are set to this tune.

58. Giovanni's music has been identified variously as "a contemporary country waltz" (Pierre Jean Jouve, *Mozart's Don Juan* [London: Stuart, 1957], p. 87) and as a quotation from a Viennese popular song printed in a 1720 dance collection (Janos Liebner, *Mozart on the Stage* [New York: Praeger, 1961], p. 185).

Of the several rhythmic motifs from Mozart's operas which Bence Szabolcsi suggests are galliards (see "Mozart's Gagliarda," *Studies in Eighteenth-Century Music*, pp. 382–87), among them Figaro's minuet "Se vuol ballare" and a lovely slow sarabande from *Così fan tutte* (II, 23), Giovanni's toast music is the only example advanced which seems plausible. The Renaissance galliard was properly a leaping dance in which the performer left the ground on almost every beat. The rhythmic pattern of the dance consists of six beats, the fourth usually emphasized by a barline and a dot: ♩ ♩ ♩ | ♩ ♪♩ "Se vuol ballare" should be taken at a slightly slower tempo than would support the leaping in a galliard (the slower the tempo, the higher the leap must be), and furthermore a joyous and celebratory dance is a less potent conveyance for Figaro's sardonic broadside at the Count than the social irony of the minuet-contredanse sequence. Nor does it suit the *Andante grazioso* of the love duet between Guglielmo and Dorabella, not to mention that again the slow tempo of the piece makes the choreography of the galliard too awkward to negotiate. But the galliard is appropriate for the setting, rhythm, and tempo of Giovanni's toast: he delivers his amused rebuff to Elvira with the careless elegance of a noble host.

59. "Restati, barbaro,/Nel lezzo immondo:/Esempio orribile/D'iniquità" ("Rest in your filthy stench, you barbarian, dire example of wickedness"— mm. 295–302 and *passim*).

CHAPTER 11

1. By Leporello, perhaps involuntarily, in the "Catalogue" aria (see p. 245).

2. Gio: "Oh, caro il mio Masetto!/Cara la mia Zerlina! V'esibisco/La mia protezione. Leporello!/Cosa fai lì, birbone?" Lep: "Anch'io, caro padrone,/Esibisco la mia protezione" (Gio: "Oh my dear Masetto! My dear Zerlina! I offer you my protection. Leporello! What are you doing there, you rascal?" Lep: "I also, dear master, am offering my protection"—I, viii, 106–12).

3. "Zerlina is in the hands of a gentleman" (I, viii, 127–29).

4. "Nelle mani son'io d'un cavaliere" (I, viii, 131–32).

5. "Mostrandogli la spada" (stage direction, I, viii, 137).

6. "Have you got it?" "Yes, I've got it" (I, viii, 121–22).

7. "Ah, *I get it, I get it*, you little scoundrel. You're afraid I'll understand what happened between you" (I, 12, 111–15; italics mine).

8. "*I'll make out* if she is faithful to me, and how the business went" (I, 13, 35–50; italics mine).

9. "Your beautiful Zerlina can't, poor little thing, be without you any more" (I, 13, 128–36). Masetto's words were "La Zerlina/Senza me non può star" (I, viii, 124–25).

10. "Let our gentleman make you a gentlewoman!"

11. Jouve (pp. 31–32) describes the aria as having "a kind of sombre gaiety, a rhythm like the tramp of marching feet," and Moberly uses much the same imagery (p. 182). Even Dent sees in Masetto's indignation that "revolutionary feeling which appears in Figaro's arias, and is, of course, the social background of the whole opera." To Dent the "sole purpose" of Masetto and Zerlina in the opera is to dramatize the "social significance" of *Don Giovanni* (Dent, p. 162). See also Massin, p. 1055.

12. See the discussion of *Le nozze di Figaro* in part 2, especially p. 104 and 159–73.

13. "It's open to everybody; long live liberty!" (I, 13, 368–72 and *passim*).

14. See Massin, p. 1055.

15. II, x. "In questa casa/Per poche ore fermatevi: un ricorso/Vo' far a chi si deve, e in pochi istanti/Vendicarvi prometto" ("Stay in this house [Donna Anna's] for a few hours . . . I will have recourse to the proper authorities, and very soon I promise to avenge you"—mm. 114–18).

16. ♩ in the example equals ♪ in the actual duet.

17. Because the natural prose stress on "da-*rem*" and the melodic peak on C-sharp coincide, the first and fifth measures of the aria could be rebarred in gavotte fashion:

Là	ci da-	rem	la
3	4	1	2

but after that the resemblance to gavotte scansion disappears.

18. Alfred Einstein, *Mozart: His Character, His Work* (New York: Oxford University Press, 1962), p. 432. Kierkegaard's A carefully qualifies his comparison, saying "The Page is really the future Don Juan, though without this being understood in a ridiculous way, as if the Page by becoming older became Don Juan" (*Either/Or*, I, 99). Apparently Einstein, on the other hand, saw nothing ridiculous about the adolescent Cherubino actually growing into the manhood of Don Giovanni, and so gave credence to a more simplistic version of the conceit.

19. "I would like it, and I wouldn't . . . my heart shivers a little. . . . It's true, I'd be happy, but he can still be playing with me."

20. "I know that you gentlemen are seldom honest and sincere with women" (I, ix, 119–21).

21. "Soon I'll no longer be able to resist" (mm. 24–28), or, literally, "Soon I am no longer strong"; the Italian uses a vivid present instead of the future. Translations of the nature of "I'm weakening; let's hurry" are a coarse misrepresentation of the line.

22. When Elvira breaks in at the end of "Là ci darem" to announce the Don's perfidy, Zerlina's reaction is wide-eyed surprise: "Ma signor cavaliere,/È ver ch'ella dice?" ("But my lord, is what she says true?"—I, x, 93–95). One could conceive of Zerlina as a knowing strumpet and play this question for laughs. But da Ponte would surely have made the joke broader had he intended it; nothing else in the scene suggests that Zerlina is other than rudely startled when, in the person of Elvira, she is treated to a vision of the consequences in the real world of the act she is about to commit.

23. "Let us go, let us go, my treasure, to assuage the pangs of an innocent love!"

24. "Beds of grass," stage direction, I, xvi.

25. "Beat, oh beat, my fine Masetto, your poor Zerlina: I shall stand here like a little lamb awaiting your blows. I'll let you pull out my hair, I'll let you carve out my eyes; and then I'll be happy to kiss your dear little hands." Notice that the sixth line of the text is a playful version of Elvira's hysterical threat to Giovanni: "Gli vo' cavar il cor" (I, 3).

26. "Oh, I see, you don't have the heart" (mm. 53–60).

27. "Peace, peace, oh my life! We want to pass night and day in contentment and joy." Notice how evocatively the subdominant phrase just mentioned spins out the word "passar."

28. "See how well this witch knows to seduce me! We men are really weak in the head!" (I, 12, 100–102).

29. The aria which effects the division, "Metà di voi quà vadano" (II, 4), is discussed on p. 219.

30. "You promise me to be less jealous" (II, vi, 128–29).

31. "E un certo balsamo/Che porto addosso:/Dare tel posso,/Se il vuoi provar./Saper vorresti/Dove mi sta?/Sentilo battere,/Toccami qua" ("It is a certain balm which I carry myself. I can give it to you if you want to try it. Would you like to know where I have it? Feel it beat; touch me here").

32. In the move to the dominant and again just preceding the fermata, mm. 19–20, 23–24; 44–45, 48–50.

33. "You'll see, my dear little thing, if you're a good little man. . . ."

CHAPTER 12

1. "A little ironically" (stage direction, m. 136).

2. "Yes, let's take heart, and all three go off to dance with the others" (mm. 147–167).

3. "Backstage, from far off" (stage direction, mm. 139–41).

4. "My friend will also try out his love on these ladies" (mm. 247–51).

5. "Charming girls" (Giovanni's charge, mm. 284–85) and "fine young men" (in Leporello's words, mm. 286–87).

6. "That Masetto seems wild-eyed to me; this business will have an ugly outcome" (mm. 327–31).

7. As usual his gallantry is a little off-key: he calls the maskers "vezzose mascherette" ("charming little maskers," mm. 364–66), an affectedly genteel diminutive which is hardly commensurate with their dignity.

8. "It's open to everybody; long live liberty! (mm. 368–84).

9. "We are grateful for so many tokens of liberality" (mm. 372–78).

10. "Leading her away almost by force" (stage direction, mm. 456–57).

11. "Oh, heavens! I've been betrayed! . . ." (mm. 457–59).

12. "Good people! . . . Help! . . . Help, good people!" (mm. 467–70).

13. Dent (p. 163) includes a musical example which shows the three dances in combination, but he does not explain how the trick succeeds.

14. For example, in m. 450 of the minuet the contredanse remains on the tonic one quarter note longer than does the minuet, which has moved on to the subdominant. On that beat, however, the contredanse part is thinned out to a single G, the common tone between the triads on C and on G, thus avoiding sounding an actual dissonance.

15. "Everything's known already" (mm. 518ff.).

16. "È confusa la mia testa" ("My head is spinning" — mm. 541–43).

17. "But my courage doesn't fail me; I'm neither lost nor confounded. Even if the sky should fall, nothing ever frightens me!" (mm. 615–21).

18. I, 11. For a translation see p. 366 n. 54.

19. As it is called in the stage direction, mm. 437–40.

20. II, 11, 303–14. For a translation see p. 374 n. 57.

21. "As long as I'm spending my money, I want to enjoy myself" (mm. 25–29).

22. "Oh, how this great rejoicing delights and pleases. . . . We give thanks to Your Highness's generosity."

23. "Ah, what a barbarous appetite! What gigantic mouthfuls! I think I'm about to faint" (mm. 74ff).

24. "It suits your deserts" (mm. 63–67).

25. "Come un agnello/Che va al macello,/Belando andrai/Per la città./Io colla bella/Mia rondinella/Andrò rondando/Di quà di là./Io già m'aspetto/Sentir me dire:/'Guarda che amabile/Sposo perfetto!'/Di là ripetere/'Viva la sposa,/O impareggiabile/Coppia vezzosa,/Il Ciel concedavi/Felicità!'" ("Like a lamb to the slaughter you'll go bleating through the city. I'll go around here and there with my pretty little swallow. I already hear them saying, 'See how sweet — the perfect husband!' Over there they'll say, 'Here's to the wife! Oh, you incomparably charming couple, may Heaven grant you happiness!'").

26. Anderson, II, 903. The citizens of Prague had turned *Figaro* into music for "quadrilles and waltzes." Mozart himself took a hint from them and in 1791 arranged "Non più andrai" as a contredanse (K. 609; see ex. 2–34, p. 58).

27. "Now this one I know only too well" (mm. 164–66).

28. Leporello's remarks identifying the pieces are found only in the score of the opera, and not in the original libretto. Thus they must have been added during the rehearsals, at which the composer was present.

29. "Your cook is so excellent that I too wanted to try him out" (mm. 188ff). The cook referred to is an actual character in Bertati's libretto, named Lanterna; Bertati's libretto contains a like scene.

30. Luigi Bassi, the first Don Giovanni, is often quoted as having reported later that the *Tafelmusik* scene was indeed improvised in rehearsals (see for example William Mann, *The Operas of Mozart* [New York: Oxford University Press, 1977], p. 511).

31. This section has already been discussed on pp. 254–57.

32. Zerlina needs only the less dissonant V^7 (of E-flat major) to disturb the artificial tranquility of the ballroom scene.

33. "Whatever can that scream be!" (mm. 354–59; the augmented sixth occurs in m. 358).

34. "What a devilish scream! Leporello, what's going on?" (mm. 367–78).

35. To put it more precisely, Mozart used material from the penultimate scene of the opera in its overture, for the overture was composed last in order — just before the opera was first performed. But that does not alter the fact that Mozart thought it important to establish more than a vague and impressionistic connection of mood between the overture and the damnation of the Don.

36. Any designation for the traditional bass pattern in ex. 12–12 must be chosen advisedly. Is it a chaconne, a passacaglia, or should it be called merely by its descriptive title, descending-tetrachord bass? I have chosen the designa-

tion "chaconne bass" because it is a convenient shorthand label which underlines the traditional, formulaic nature of the pattern. Certain writers, Bukofzer among others, habitually call it so (see *Music in the Baroque Era* [New York: W. W. Norton, 1947], pp. 41–43), and recent research on the subject adduces little reason to prefer either historical title—chaconne or passacaglia—to the other (see Thomas Walker, "Ciaccona and Passacaglia: Remarks on their Origin and Early History," *Journal of the American Musicological Society* 21 [1968]: 300–20; and Richard Hudson, "Further Remarks on the Passacaglia and Ciaccona," *Journal of the American Musicological Society* 23 [1970]:302–14, especially p. 312, ex. 5).

37. Mozart uses the G-sharp both in the overture (m. 10) and in the recapitulation of the D-minor section of the finale. If it had been used in the opening of the scene (ex. 12–13, m. 442), it would have marred the grim diatonic line of the Commendatore.

38. "He who feeds on heavenly fare does not feed on earthly fare" (mm. 454–61).

39. "Solar" as opposed to "polar," because the tonic tended to be surrounded by a number of keys in planetary relation rather than being placed in strong opposition with a single one (the dominant). See Leonard Ratner, *Classic Music*, pp. 48–51.

40. "Altre cure più gravi di queste,/Altra brama quaggiù mi guidò" ("Other cares more weighty than these, another desire led me down here"—mm. 462–70).

41. In the introduction to the overture, where the progression is of course a double of this one, but transposed up a fourth in order to remain in D minor, and in the recapitulation of the D minor duet between Donna Anna and Don Ottavio (I, 2). See nn. 7–3 and 9–6.

42. "La terzana d'avere mi sembra,/E le membra fermar più non so" ("I think I have tertian fever, and I can't move my limbs any more"— mm. 470–74).

43. See for example m. 443, where the syncopated motive in the first violins overlaps with the Commendatore's last and thetic measure, or m. 470, where Leporello's line keeps up the ongoing motion after the first A-minor cadence.

44. "I am speaking, listen; I have no more time" (mm. 474–77).

45. "Speak, speak; I'm right here listening to you" (mm. 477–79).

46. "Tu m'invitasti a cena:/Il tuo dover or sai./Rispondimi: verrai/Tu a cenar meco?" ("You invited me to dinner; now you know your duty. Answer me: will you come to dinner with me?"—mm. 487–501).

47. "I shall never be accused of the crime of cowardice!" (mm. 504–7).

48. "I am not afraid. I will come!" (mm. 514–16).

49. "Give me your hand in token" (mm. 517–20)—a chilling reminiscence of "Là ci darem la mano."

50. "Oh no! Whatever can this chill be?" (mm. 521–23), words uttered just after the bass has made its disjunct leap up a sixth to E-natural to start the chromatic drop.

51. "Ah, there is no more time" (mm. 549–54).

52. An "unaccustomed tremor" and "terrible whirlpools of fire."

53. "All is as little to your crimes. Come; there is a worse pain."

54. It was a Renaissance habit always to end a composition with a perfect consonance, as being closest to perfection in the order of nature. When the third was admitted to the roster of possible cadential intervals, it was characteristically major, even in a work in which the third of the mode was minor. The practice was continued in Baroque music.

55. Abram Loft, "The Comic Servant in Mozart's Operas," *Musical Quarterly* 32 (1946):383. Jahn (III, 213–14) after a catalogue of the appalling liberties producers took in the nineteenth century in their efforts to invent a (to them) suitable final scene, recommends that there be none, and that the opera end with the Don's descent into hell. See also Paul Henry Lang, *Music in Western Civilization* (New York: W. W. Norton, 1941), p. 644.

56. As Mozart certainly did not. He entered the opera in his private catalogue as an *opera buffa*, and *dramma giocoso* was merely an alternate designation for *opera buffa*.

57. The gavotte is misbarred: the beat is the eighth note, and there are two gavotte measures for every actual 2/2 measure.

58. "Ah, that must have been the shade that ran into her (me)!" (mm. 681–711).

59. "Then let that rascal rest with Proserpina and Pluto. And let all of us, good people, happily repeat that most ancient song. This is the end of the evil man; and the death of wicked men is always equal to their lives!"

60. Again "misbarred," with an eighth-note beat.

AFTERWORD

1. Which term one adopts to describe the style — "Classic" or "Classical" — is clearly a matter of the lesser of two evils. "Classic" is probably an improper usage — consider the phrase "classic car" for example — but with "Classical" one is continually forced up against the expression "classical music," an identification which is obviously unfortunate. It is because of this offense to the ear and to the discriminating faculty that I have chosen the term "Classic" to designate the style. Scholars are evenly divided on the issue, as a glance at the titles in n. A–2 will suggest.

2. A quick résumé of those authors surveyed gives one a sense of the difficulties involved. Charles Rosen in his book on Classic music does not attempt an extensive definition of the word, being content to call "classical" any style "that is exemplary and normative" (*The Classical Style*, [New York: Viking Press, 1971], p. 8). Leonard Ratner gives the most sensible description of the limits of the term when applied to Classic music; for instance, he points out the absence in music of the late eighteenth century of many qualities usually associated with the classic such as "objectivity, austerity, noble simplicity, purity of style, lack of disturbing irregularities or mixtures" (*Classic Music*, p. xv). (This is an important point, especially given the attempts of some writers thoroughly to purify the style; see the definition of Classic by Friedrich Blume given below.) Daniel Heartz, in his article entitled "The Viennese 'Classical' Idiom" in *The New Grove*, has the most interesting things to say; he centers a large part of

his discussion around a perhaps debatable but thought-provoking point made by the French aesthetician Henri Peyre, that a "classical" artist rarely struggles against convention, and is not reluctant to heed the tastes of his audience. Gerald Abraham, in his recent one-volume history of music (*The Concise Oxford History of Music*, London: Oxford University Press, 1979), eschews any reference either in his index or in his chapter headings to the terms "Classic" or "Classical" (or, for that matter, "Baroque") — a path which, given the reductive nature of these labels, is perhaps the truest one. With only one definition is there reason to take issue — that of Friedrich Blume in his *Classic and Romantic Music* (trans. M. D. Herter Norton [New York: W. W. Norton, 1970]), a translation of an article which originally appeared in *Die Musik in Geschichte und Gegenwart*. Describing Classic music as a kind of contentless form, he concludes, "Thus from the 'classic' is excluded every sort of music that undertakes to lead the listener's feeling in too definite, too individual a manner, to give his fantasy and collaboration too definite a direction, and to infringe upon his autonomy as co-creator" (p. 10). Blume's formulations are close to those of Eduard Hanslick, the nineteenth-century theorist who pitted his concept of musical *Immanenz* (autonomy) against Wagner's notion of the *Gesamtkunstwerk*, and spoke of Classic music as "tonally animated form." It is hoped that after the foregoing discussions of the expressive implications of various rhythms little credence will be given to those who have spoken in defense of the "autonomy" or "purity" of the Classic style.

3. Francesco Algarotti, *An Essay on the Opera* (London: 1767), p. 66. This volume is a translation of the author's well-known *Saggio sopra l'opera in musica* (1750).

4. Charles Burney, *Dr. Burney's Musical Tours in Europe. Vol. I: An Eighteenth-Century Musical Tour in France and Italy*, ed. Percy Scholes (London: Oxford University Press, 1959), p. 20.

5. Anderson, 2:708.

6. Daniel Heartz, *The New Grove Dictionary*, s.v. "Opera."

7. See the interesting article on this subject by Piero Weiss, "Verdi and the Fusion of Genres," *Journal of the American Musicological Society* 35 (1982): 138–56.

INDEX

Arias and Ensembles in Le nozze di Figaro and Don Giovanni

General Index

Nativity music, siciliano in, 44
Nature, imitation of, 3–6, 243. *See also* Madrigalism
Neapolitan, 186, 198, 214, 240, 252; "six-four chord," 227, 305–6, 314, 361 n.3, 367 n.6. *See also* Key relations
Notation: rhythmic, less precise in Classic style, 23–25, 66; symbolic, for dance rhythms, 334 n.7
Nozze di Figaro, Le: *alla breve* movements in, 367 n.58; act IV, construction of, 159–60, 170–71; characters in, 223–24; compared to *Don Giovanni*, 82, 97, 100, 102–3, 197–99, 206–7, 216, 223–24, 229–30, 232, 243, 257, 261, 273–74, 275–77, 327–28; compared to *Paul et Virginie*, 172–73; libretto of, classical references in, 96–97, 136, 146; libretto of 1786, 95, 349 n.29; soliloquies in, 366 n.57; subjects of, 73–75, 136, 157–58, 160, 162, 167, 170–73, 194, 207, 224, 257, 261. *See also* index of individual arias

Obbligato, 'cello, in *Don Giovanni* (I. 12), 269–70
Ombra style: defined, 361 n.2; in overture, *Don Giovanni*, 197–98, 210–11; in act II finale, *Don Giovanni*, 288, 292–319, 322–23
Opera buffa: action in the arias of, 5, 25–27, 140, 327, 330 n.17; conventions of, 119–20, 133–36, 145, 275; *Don Giovanni* termed an, 380 n.56; opening scenes in, 201. *See also* Buffa style; Patter
Opera seria: characters from, in Mozart's operas, 19, 100, 102–3, 230, 327; clichés from, in Mozart's operas, 158, 164–65; conventions of, 5, 231; moral epigrams of, 19, 112; reformers of, 235; repetition of text in arias of, 235. *See also* Exalted style; *Scena, opera seria*; Seria style
Orchestra: used as dance band, 80–82, 127, 149, 278–79, 280–85; mimetic role of, in "Catalogue" aria, 241–42,

244, 246, 371 n.17; postlude, prominent, 221–22, 272, 351 n.10; role of, in Elvira's music, 233–34, 237; "terrace" effects in, 150–51, 347 n.21; as *topos* in *galant* style, 18. *See also* Horn calls; *Musica da tavola*
Ottavio, Don: a *mezzo carattere* hero, 224, 226–29, 230–32, 369 n.11, 370 n. 23; mocked by *buffa* perspective of opera, 231–32, 240

Pas assemblé, 337 n.59
Pas de bourrée, 48
Pas de menuet, 34, 39, 80
Passacaglia, 333 n.43, 378 n.36
Passepied, 28, 31, 32, 48; qualities of, 15, 39–40; in *Figaro*, 127
Passions: meter as expressing, 13–16, 22–23; as movements of the soul, 8–9; painting of, in music, 4–5, 46. *See also* Affect; Character
Pastoral: dances associated with, 44, 50–51, 53, 54; farces of *commedia dell'arte*, 165; in minuets, 36; pathetic fallacy in, 174; *Paul et Virginie* as, 171–73; in Cherubino's music, 87–88, 94, 96–97, 109; in *Figaro*, 1–2, 137, 145–46, 148–49, 159, 267; and musette-gavotte in act II finale of *Figaro*, 1–2, 127–31, 136; poetry, in *Figaro*, 88, 163, 175, 358 n.42; as private place in *Figaro*, 131, 145–48, 172–74, 185, 191; in Susanna's music, 174–77; in Epilogue to *Don Giovanni*, 320, 323; stock vision of, in *Don Giovanni*, 245; in Zerlina's music, 262, 266–67, 270–71, 272–74. *See also* Drone bass; Key-area plan; Musette-gavotte; Pastorale
Pastorale, 32, 41; characteristics and affect of, 17, 43–44, 53, 63, 66, 128, 147, 360 n.59; in *Figaro*, 92, 146–48, 158–59, 178, 184–85, 191, 274; in *Don Giovanni* 250, 252, 266–67, 268, 270–71, 274
Pathetic style, 201, 223. *See also* Fantasy style; Tragic style